EPUB 3 Best Practices

Matt Garrish and Markus Gylling

O'REILLY®

Beijing · Cambridge · Farnham · Köln · Sebastopol · Tokyo

EPUB 3 Best Practices

by Matt Garrish and Markus Gylling

Published by O'Reilly Media, Inc., 1005 Gravenstein Highway North, Sebastopol, CA 95472.

O'Reilly books may be purchased for educational, business, or sales promotional use. Online editions are also available for most titles (*http://my.safaribooksonline.com*). For more information, contact our corporate/institutional sales department: 800-998-9938 or *corporate@oreilly.com*.

Editor: Brian Sawyer	**Proofreader:** Kiel Van Horn
Production Editor: Kristen Borg	**Indexer:** Jill Edwards
	Cover Designer: Karen Montgomery
	Interior Designer: David Futato
	Illustrator: Robert Romano

February 2013:   First Edition

Revision History for the First Edition:

2013-01-23   First release

See *http://oreilly.com/catalog/errata.csp?isbn=9781449329143* for release details.

ISBN: 978-1-449-32914-3

[LSI]

Table of Contents

Preface. . . . . **ix**

Introduction. . . . . **xix**

1. Package Document and Metadata. **1**

Vocabularies 2
    The Default Vocabulary 3
    The Reserved Vocabularies 3
    Using Other Vocabularies 4
    The All-Powerful meta Element 5
Publication Metadata 7
    The Package Document Structure 8
    The metadata Element 9
Identifiers 11
Types of Titles 14
The Manifest and Spine 15
    The manifest and Fallbacks 16
    The spine 17
Document Metadata 19
Links and Bindings 20
Metadata for Fixed Layout Publications 22
The Container 22

2. Navigation. **25**

The EPUB Navigation Document 26
Building a Navigation Document 29
    Repeated Patterns 31
    Table of Contents 35
    Landmarks 41
    Page List 44
    Extensibility 45

Adding the Navigation Document   46
    Embedding as Content   47
    Hiding Lists   48
    Styling Lists   49
The NCX   50

3. Content Documents. **53**
Terminology Refresher   53
XHTML   55
    New in HTML5   56
    EPUB Support Gotchas   62
    DTDs Are Dead   63
    Linking and Referencing   64
    Content Chunking   67
epub:type and Structural Semantics   68
    Adding Semantics   70
    Multiple Semantics   72
MathML   72
SVG   78
Fixed Layouts   80
Covers   85
Styling   87
    EPUB CSS Profile   88
    CSS 2.1   88
    CSS3   91
    Ruby   96
    Headers and Footers   97
    Alt Style Tags   99
    CSS Resets   102
Fallback Content   102
    Manifest Fallbacks   103
    Content Fallbacks   105
    The epub:switch element   107
    Bindings   112

4. Font Embedding and Licensing. **117**
Why Embed Fonts?   118
    Maybe You Shouldn't   118
    Maybe You Should   122
Font Embedding in EPUB 3   130
How to Embed Fonts   131
    Add the Font to Your EPUB Package   132

Include the File in the EPUB Manifest   132
Reference the Font in the EPUB CSS   133
Obfuscating Fonts   134
Subsetting a Font   137
Licensing Fonts for Embedding in EPUB   138
Use an Open Font   139
Contact the Foundry Directly   139

5. Multimedia. **141**
The Codec Issue   142
The Media Elements   144
Sources   145
Control   153
Posters   155
Dimensions   156
The Rest   157
Timed Tracks   157
Fallbacks   162
Alternate Content   163
Triggers   165

6. Media Overlays. **173**
The EPUB Spectrum   174
Overlays in a Nutshell   176
Synchronization Granularity   177
Constructing an Overlay   178
Sequences   180
Parallel Playback   181
Adding to the Container   184
Styling the Active Element   185
Structural Considerations   186
Advanced Synchronization   187
Audio Considerations   188

7. Interactivity. **191**
First Principles: Interaction Scope and Design   192
Progressive Enhancement   192
Procedural Interaction: JavaScript   193
JavaScript in EPUB 2   193
The EPUB 3 epubReadingSystem Object   193
Inclusion Models   197
Ebook State and Storage   199

    Identifying Scripted Content Documents   199
   Animation and Graphics: Canvas   200
    Best Practices in Canvas Usage   201
    Canvas in a Nonscripted Reading System   202
   Object   203
   Other Graphical Interaction Models   204
   Accessibility and Scripting Summary   204

8. Global Language Support. **205**
   Characters and Encodings   206
    Unicode   206
    Declaring Encodings   207
    Private Characters   208
    Names   209
   Specifying the Natural Language   211
   Vertical Writing   212
    Writing Modes   213
   Page Progression Direction   215
    Global Direction   220
    Content Direction   221
   Ruby and Emphasis Dots   222
    Ruby   222
    Emphasis Dots   224
   Line Breaks, Word Breaks, and Hyphenation   226
   Itemized Lists   227

9. Accessibility. **229**
   Accessibility and Usability   230
   Fundamentals of Accessibility   232
    Structure and Semantics   233
    Data Integrity   235
    Separation of Style   237
    Semantic Inflection   238
    Language   239
    Logical Reading Order   239
    Sections and Headings   241
    Context Changes   244
    Lists   245
    Tables   246
    Figures   249
    Images   250
    SVG   253

MathML	254
Footnotes	255
Page Numbering	256
Styling	258
Avoiding Conflicts	258
Color	258
Hiding Content	260
Emphasis	260
Fixed Layouts	261
Image Layouts	262
Mixed Layouts	265
Text Layouts	266
Interactive Layouts	266
Scripted Interactivity	267
Progressive Enhancement	267
WAI-ARIA	269
Canvas	280
Metadata	281

10. Text-to-Speech (TTS)... **285**
PLS Lexicons	287
SSML	292
CSS3 Speech	297

11. Validation.. **303**
epubcheck	304
Installing	304
Running	305
Options	308
Reading Errors	313
Beyond the Command Line	314
Web Validation	314
Graphical Interface	316
Commercial Options	316
Understanding Errors	317
Common XML Errors	318
Container Errors	321
Package Validation	323
Content Validation	326
Style	329
Scripting	329

Accessibility   330

Index. 333

Preface

When I first wrote *What Is EPUB 3?* (*http://oreil.ly/what_is_epub3*) in the summer of 2011, it was envisioned as both a brief standalone piece that would orient people to the new EPUB 3.0 revision the International Digital Publishing Forum (IDPF) was about to release and also as an introduction to what we hoped would evolve into a larger best practices guide—the one you're reading now.

You'll find that book distilled down to its bare essentials in this book's introduction, but if you are new to EPUB, there is much information put into that original guide that is helpful to know before tackling this one, so if I can recommend some advance reading, it would be to grab a copy of that ebook and give it a skim. If you're not familiar with EPUBs generally, or what's changed from 2 to 3, it'll help give you a general view of the big picture before launching into the details that we'll be covering here. It's only a small-chapter-length in size, too (and free!), so it won't take you long to get through, and it will give you a condensed perspective on what an EPUB is.

This guide instead delves right into the EPUB container and walks you through best practices as they relate to production of your publications; you'll find a bit of a mixture of practices and guidance on how to use EPUB technologies. You don't necessarily have to know the technology of publishing EPUBs inside and out to find value here, nor do you have to be a programmer or tech geek, but this book *is* for the ebook practitioner.

In planning out this guide, one of the challenges was trying to keep straight where the boundaries are between EPUB 3 and the technologies it combines under its format umbrella. Can a single book about EPUB 3 best practices try to detail every nuance of HTML5, CSS3, JavaScript, MathML and SVG, just to pick out some of the prime content document technologies? The answer should be obvious, considering the volume of material that's already been written on those subjects.

What we've tried to do in this guide is find the key areas of overlap between those technologies as they relate to publishing. You're going to find a lot of discussion about all of the features just listed, and more, but if you're just getting started with the technologies used in EPUBs this book will be more of a starting point on your journey. You will learn about potential issues when scripting in the reading system environment, for example, but you won't find a tutorial on the JavaScript language.

Each of the chapters in this book deals with a unique aspect of the creation and distribution process. There is no assumption that you're familiar with the entire format, because the production of EPUBs often involves expertise from a number of different functional areas. The people responsible for ensuring the technology of your ebooks probably aren't going to be the same people who are responsible for the metadata. The authors and editors creating the content are likewise not going to be the people bundling and distributing the ebook. So although the book will move over EPUB 3 in a linear fashion, and can be read from cover to cover to learn about production as a whole, each chapter is also intended to be readable in isolation, with pointers forward and back as necessary.

And although we hope you'll implement all the best practices you can, the book is not designed to be a checklist to content conformity, and is not written as such. Everyone produces using different methods, and everyone has to work within the constraints of their production workflows, so we've tried hard not to target specific processes or reading systems but stick to the ultimate outcome. If you can't implement every accessibility practice, for example, the hope is that at least you'll understand where, and how, you can improve later on down the road.

This guide also isn't intended to be the final word on EPUB, as EPUB is always evolving. It's about preparing you for producing EPUB 3 content using all the features it makes available, helping you avoid known pitfalls, and giving you a heads up on the issues you'll face. If successful, it will also hopefully enlighten you to why the specification is defined the way that it is. A specification is just an artifact of agreement on how to implement a technology, after all. It tells you what the creators decided you must and should and may do—and not do—but specifications don't spend time retelling you the story of why.

It doesn't mean you'll agree with all the decisions that were made, but specifications by nature portray a myth of homogeneity. It's the discussions and debate that continue around EPUB that keep it at the forefront of ebook technologies.

If we've done our job writing this book, you should not have new ideas for your own production, but be well equipped to join in the discussions on the future.

The Future

By the time this book comes out, the EPUB 3 specification will be more than a year old. It's hard to believe how fast time flies, but it's not surprising that technology is only just catching up to the standard. That was a goal of the revision after all: to position the specification so that features and best practices could be defined ahead of the pack instead of trying to constantly play the catch-up game.

The modular nature of the specification has also proven its worth. Since the specification was published in October 2011, IDPF subgroups have published two new documents: fixed layouts and advanced adaptive layouts. Work on grammars for marking up indexes and dictionaries has been ongoing since the beginning of 2012, and a new group dealing with hybrid layouts is also in the process of being chartered. The IDPF is continuing to work with its members to evolve the standard to meet their needs; it's not sitting on its laurels or creating a format by fiat.

Another major revision of the standard is not on the horizon at this point, but minor revisions are anticipated to add new CSS functionality, fix bugs, and see if consensus can be found on open issues like codecs and metadata. A new minor revision is expected to begin as this book gets readied for print, which will effect the information in this guide, but it's anticipated only for the positive.

You may have RDFa and microdata for content documents by the time you read this, for example, or at least a firm promise of them. Fixed layout support could be stronger if the information document it's currently defined in gets rolled into the main specification. The HTML5 landscape should be clearer, too, as the W3C pushes to finalize the standard by 2014. EPUB 3 itself also is hoped to become an ISO Technical Specification during the process.

But don't worry that this means you're going to be fed lots of point-in-time ideas. The areas of instability are not that numerous, and the practices that exist solely to deal with them are clearly marked. The point of this book is to look at the core of the standard, so the information should stand for as long as EPUB 3s are being produced.

And even as we began wrapping up this book, a new project to create a conformance test suite for reading systems was announced, which will help standardize rendering across reading systems, more and more of which are appearing that support EPUB 3 content. In natural step, publishers are also announcing their plans to start releasing content (the Hachette Book Group, for example).

EPUB 3 is here, now, in other words.

But we're not here for long-winded introductions. Let's get on with the show!

How to Use This Book

Although you can read this book cover to cover, each chapter contains information about a unique aspect of the EPUB 3 format allowing them to also be read in isolation. To simplify jumping through the content, here's a quick summary of the information in each:

Introduction

> The introduction provides a brief, high-level overview of the EPUB format and specifications. If you're coming to this book with no background in EPUB production, this chapter will get you grounded before you head into the details.

Chapter 1: Package Document and Metadata

> The first chapter introduces the package document at the heart of every EPUB and walks you through the process of adding publication metadata. The structure of the package document is reviewed, as is the required publication metadata. The new, flexible model for adding metadata to publications via `meta` elements is also introduced.

Chapter 2: Navigation

> This chapter details the new EPUB navigation document, including how to construct the required table of contents and optional landmarks and page list navigation aids. It also shows how the document can now double as content in your publication, removing the need to have two documents for the same basic function.

Chapter 3: Content Documents

> This chapter is more wide-ranging in scope, as it provides a general overview of content documents. It reviews the new features and requirements of XHTML5, from the new additions to the core HTML grammar to the inclusion of MathML and SVG. It also reviews the new `epub:type` attribute for semantic inflection. EPUB style sheets, alt style tags and other styling issues are also covered. The chapter concludes by looking at the various fallback mechanisms at your disposal when using nonstandard content types.

Chapter 4: Font Embedding and Licensing

> The ability to embed fonts allows rich typography in EPUBs. This chapter looks at the technical details involved in embedding WOFF and OTF fonts, and it also reviews the licensing issues to be aware of when you do.

Chapter 5: Multimedia

> This chapter looks at the new `audio` and `video` elements in HTML5 for embedding multimedia content in your publications. It covers how to include resources, poster images, and timed tracks, as well as the issues surrounding the lack of a universal codec for video. The chapter concludes by looking at `epub:trigger` elements for building scriptless user interfaces.

Chapter 6: Media Overlays

Media overlays is the new technology that enables synchronized text and audio playback in reading systems, and this chapter reviews the process of creating these documents. The issues involved in creating overlays for different levels of playback granularity gets explored, as does the impact on production.

Chapter 7: Interactivity

The addition of scripting in EPUB 3 opens up a whole new dimension in ebooks. This chapter explores the scripting capabilities supported by the format, the new `epubReadingSystem` JavaScript property for querying reading system capabilities, and also reviews the issues you'll need to consider when choosing to make your content dynamic. It also covers the new HTML5 `canvas` element.

Chapter 8: Global Language Support

To become a truly global standard for ebooks, EPUB 3 was augmented to enable more than just left-to-right page progressions and horizontal writing styles. This chapter looks at the mechanics and mechanisms for handling both right-to-left page progressions and vertical writing styles. It also reviews the new CSS additions that give greater control over such features as line and word breaking, as well as the use of ruby annotations.

Chapter 9: Accessibility

Although this book tries to keep a focus on accessibility throughout each chapter, this one delves into unique accessibility requirements for markup, styling, fixed layouts, and scripting. WAI-ARIA roles, states and properties are introduced for dynamic content, as numerous best practices for markup, many drawn from WCAG 2.0.

Chapter 10: Text-to-Speech (TTS)

One of the shortcomings of ebooks for aural readers has been the inability to control the quality of text-to-speech playback. EPUB 3 introduces three new technologies to fill this void: PLS lexicon files enable producers to create reusable phonetic pronunciation libraries, SSML markup allows specific pronunciation overrides to be embedded in the markup of a document, and the CSS3 Speech properties provide a variety of playback controls. This chapter reviews how to include all these technologies to improve the rendering on compliant reading systems.

Chapter 11: Validation

Before distributing your finished EPUB files, you want to make sure that they conform to the specifications, otherwise you run the risk of them not being usable by readers. The final chapter looks at the epubcheck validation program, including how to run it and how to understand the errors it emits.

Conventions Used in This Book

The following typographical conventions are used in this book:

Italic

> Indicates new terms, URLs, email addresses, filenames, and file extensions.

`Constant width`

> Used for program listings, as well as within paragraphs to refer to program elements such as variable or function names, databases, data types, environment variables, statements, and keywords.

`Constant width bold`

> Shows commands or other text that should be typed literally by the user.

`Constant width italic`

> Shows text that should be replaced with user-supplied values or by values determined by context.

 This icon signifies a tip, suggestion, or general note.

 This icon indicates a warning or caution.

Using Code Examples

This book is here to help you get your job done. In general, if this book includes code examples, you may use the code in this book in your programs and documentation. You do not need to contact us for permission unless you're reproducing a significant portion of the code. For example, writing a program that uses several chunks of code from this book does not require permission. Selling or distributing a CD-ROM of examples from O'Reilly books does require permission. Answering a question by citing this book and quoting example code does not require permission. Incorporating a significant amount of example code from this book into your product's documentation does require permission.

We appreciate, but do not require, attribution. An attribution usually includes the title, author, publisher, and ISBN. For example: "*EPUB 3 Best Practices* by Matt Garrish and Markus Gylling (O'Reilly). Copyright 2013 Matt Garrish and Markus Gylling, 9781449329143."

If you feel your use of code examples falls outside fair use or the permission given above, feel free to contact us at *permissions@oreilly.com*.

Credits

Matt Garrish has been working in both mainstream and accessible publishing for more than 15 years. He was the chief editor of the EPUB 3 suite of specifications and has authored a number of works on EPUB 3 and accessibility, including the O'Reilly books *What Is EPUB 3?* (*http://shop.oreilly.com/product/0636920022442.do*) and *Accessible EPUB 3* (*http://shop.oreilly.com/product/0636920025283.do*). He currently resides in Toronto, where he continues to work on EPUB and accessibility initiatives for the DAISY Consortium and others.

Markus Gylling has worked in the field of information accessibility since the late 90s. As CTO of the DAISY Consortium, he has been engaged in the development of specifications, tools, and educational efforts for inclusive publishing on a global scale. Markus is the chair of the EPUB 3 Working Group, and during 2011 he led the development of the EPUB 3 specification. Since October 2011, he has served as CTO of the IDPF alongside his job with the DAISY Consortium. Markus lives and works in Stockholm, Sweden.

Liza Daly is the Vice President of Engineering at Safari Books Online and an experienced developer of digital publishing and web technologies. She served on the Board of Directors of the IDPF and has published a number of articles and seminars on EPUB 2, EPUB 3, and best practices in digital publishing. Liza developed several web-based reading systems including the first HTML5 EPUB reader, and was an active participant in the OPDS ebook distribution standard. As a consultant, Liza has worked with technical, trade, academic, and educational publishers, including O'Reilly Media, Wiley, Penguin, Oxford University Press, A Book Apart, and Harvard Business School Publishing. Liza founded Threepress Consulting in 2008, which was later acquired by Safari Books Online.

Bill Kasdorf, General Editor of *The Columbia Guide to Digital Publishing*, is Vice President and principal consultant of Apex Content Solutions, a leading supplier of data conversion, editorial, production, and content enhancement services to publishers and other organizations worldwide. Active in many standards initiatives, Bill serves on the IDPF Working Group developing the EPUB 3 standard (he was coordinator of its Metadata Subgroup and is now active in the Indexing Working Group); the IDEAlliance working group developing the nextPub PSV source format for magazines and other design- and feature-rich publications (chairing its Packaging PSV as EPUB Committee); he is Chair of the BISG Content Structure Committee; and he is a member of the Publishing Business STM/Scholarly Advisory Board and the NISO eBook SIG. Past President of the Society for Scholarly Publishing (SSP) and recipient of SSP's Distinguished Service Award, Bill has led seminars, written articles, and spoken widely for publishing industry organizations such as SSP, O'Reilly TOC, NISO, BISG, IDPF, DBW, AAP, AAUP,

ALPSP, STM, Seybold Seminars, and the Library of Congress. In his consulting practice, Bill has served clients globally, including large international publishers such as Pearson, Cengage, Wolters Kluwer, and Sage; scholarly presses and societies such as Harvard, MIT, Toronto, ASME, and IEEE; aggregators such as CourseSmart and netLibrary; and global publishing organizations such as the World Bank, the British Library, and the European Union.

Murata Makoto (Murata is his family name) has been involved in XML for 15 years, since he joined the W3C XML WG, which created XML 1.0. As the lead of the Enhanced Global Language Support subgroup of the EPUB 3 working group, he contributed to internationalization of EPUB 3. He is a co-chair of the Advanced/Hybrid Layouts WG of IDPF and a committee (ISO/IEC JTC1/SC34/AHG4) for the planning of EPUB standardization at ISO/IEC JTC1. He has contributed to other XML activities such as RELAX NG (a schema language used for EPUB) and OOXML. He graduated from Kyoto University, and holds a Doctor of Engineering from Tsukuba University. He is the CTO of Japan Electronic Publishing Association. Makoto lives in Fuisawa-shi, Japan.

Adam Witwer has worked in publishing for twelve years, the last eight at O'Reilly Media. At O'Reilly, he created and ran the Publishing Services division, managing print, ebook/digital development, video production, and manufacturing. Along the way, Adam led O'Reilly through process and technical transitions to position the company for a digital-first world. In his current role as Director of Publishing Technology, he creates products that explore new ways to write, develop, manage, distribute, and present digital and print books. His team is currently beta testing a next-generation authoring platform.

Acknowledgments

Matt Garrish would like to thank the following people for their invaluable input while writing the accessibility chapters: Markus Gylling, George Kerscher, Daniel Weck, Romain Deltour and Marisa DeMeglio from the DAISY Consortium, Graham Bell from EDItEUR, Dave Gunn from RNIB, Ping Mei Law, Richard Wilson, Joan McGouran and Sean Brooks from CNIB, and Dave Cramer from Hachette Book Group. He'd also like to give a wide-ranging thank you to Bill McCoy and all the members of the EPUB 3 working group he's had the opportunity to work with, and from whom he learned much of the information in this book, especially the other coauthors. He'd also like to thank John Quinlan, who foolishly acceded to his endless entreaties to join his electronic publishing department those many years ago, and dedicate his chapters to the memory of Paul Seaton, who passed away far too young during the writing. And a very special thanks goes out to the DAISY Consortium for their work fostering digital equality, and without whose sponsorship he never would have been able to undertake this project.

Markus Gylling would especially like to thank Matt Garrish for his flair for making technical concepts readable by mortals; George Kerscher for his never-ending perseverance. Also, special thanks goes to Mike Smith (W3C) and Fantasai (now with Mozilla) for invaluable help and advice during the EPUB 3 specification development.

Bill Kasdorf would especially like to acknowledge the expert leadership Markus Gylling and Bill McCoy provided and provide to the EPUB 3 working group and the IDPF, as well as the invaluable guidance they have given both to himself personally and to the many other industry groups they have graciously let him pull them into. The same goes for the technical and editorial consultation Matt Garrish has so generously contributed to some of those same groups as well as to this book and, most importantly, to the EPUB 3 spec. Finally, he is particularly grateful to the excellent team who comprised the EPUB 3 Metadata Subgroup, with particular thanks to the dedicated work and invaluable contributions of Daniel Hughes and Graham Bell.

Makoto Murata is grateful to the members of the Enhanced Global Language Support subgroup of the EPUB 3 WG as well as the editors of W3C CSS Writing Modes and CSS Text. Internationalization of EPUB 3 would not have been achieved without their significant contributions. He would like to thank the members of W3C Japanese Layout Taskforce for creating Requirements for Japanese Text Layout (W3C Group Note) and allowing the use of figures from it.

Liza Daly acknowledges the work of The Open University for continuing to push the boundaries of accessible, interactive publications, all created using an open-source toolchain. She continues to be inspired by the interactive fiction community, who have been collectively demonstrating the narrative power of nonlinear storytelling long before the EPUB format was conceived.

Adam Witwer would like to thank Ron Bilodeau at O'Reilly for consulting and running tests on font obfuscation and subsetting. Ron knows more about those topics than the entire Internet. Thanks, also, to Deirdre Silver from Wiley for speaking openly from the perspective of a large publisher. And thanks to Alin Jardin and Vladimir Levantovsky from Monotype Imaging for providing information (and great conversation) around all things font related, but especially licensing.

And a final thank you from all the authors goes to Brian Sawyer and all the people at O'Reilly for their work putting this book together!

Safari® Books Online

 *Safari Books Online* is an on-demand digital library that delivers expert content in both book and video form from the world's leading authors in technology and business.

Technology professionals, software developers, web designers, and business and creative professionals use Safari Books Online as their primary resource for research, problem solving, learning, and certification training.

Safari Books Online offers a range of product mixes and pricing programs for organizations, government agencies, and individuals. Subscribers have access to thousands of books, training videos, and prepublication manuscripts in one fully searchable database from publishers like O'Reilly Media, Prentice Hall Professional, Addison-Wesley Professional, Microsoft Press, Sams, Que, Peachpit Press, Focal Press, Cisco Press, John Wiley & Sons, Syngress, Morgan Kaufmann, IBM Redbooks, Packt, Adobe Press, FT Press, Apress, Manning, New Riders, McGraw-Hill, Jones & Bartlett, Course Technology, and dozens more. For more information about Safari Books Online, please visit us online.

How to Contact Us

Please address comments and questions concerning this book to the publisher:

O'Reilly Media, Inc.
1005 Gravenstein Highway North
Sebastopol, CA 95472
800-998-9938 (in the United States or Canada)
707-829-0515 (international or local)
707-829-0104 (fax)

We have a web page for this book, where we list errata, examples, and any additional information. You can access this page at *http://oreil.ly/epub3-best-practices*.

To comment or ask technical questions about this book, send email to *bookquestions@oreilly.com*.

For more information about our books, courses, conferences, and news, see our website at *http://www.oreilly.com*.

Find us on Facebook: *http://facebook.com/oreilly*

Follow us on Twitter: *http://twitter.com/oreillymedia*

Watch us on YouTube: *http://www.youtube.com/oreillymedia*

Introduction

Before jumping right into the best practices, let's take a brief moment to answer the question: what exactly is an EPUB?

If you're already familiar with the inner workings of the format, whether from creating EPUB 2 content or experimenting with EPUB 3, you can safely skip ahead to Chapter 1, but this introduction will take everyone else through a quick tour of the format (at the macro level, instead of the micro level to come) to see how the pieces fit together.

Since you're reading a book about EPUB, you must already be familiar with the term, but you may have seen or heard it incorrectly being used as a synonym for *ebook* (as a shorthand for talking about *electronic books*). Although the two terms share a common relation in electronic book production, they aren't interchangeable. EPUB is a *format* for representing documents in electronic form. *Ebook*, on the other hand, is just an abstract term used to encompass any electronic representation of a book, including formats such as PDF, HTML, ASCII text, Word, and a host of others, in addition to EPUB.

EPUB is designed to be a general-purpose document format, and it can be used to represent many kinds of publications other than just books: from magazines to newspapers to journals, and on through office documents and policies and beyond. Just about any document type you want to distribute electronically can be represented as an EPUB. Likewise, this book is not just about how to create books in electronic form, but how to optimally use the EPUB format for any content production. A natural bias to book production will be evident at times, but recommendations should be read as publication-agnostic.

On a practical level, EPUB defines both the format for your content and how reading systems go about discovering it and rendering it to readers (we'll avoid the word *display* for what a reading system does with content, because EPUBs aren't only for the sighted and don't contain only visual content).

But perhaps the best way to understand what goes into an EPUB is to quickly break down the creation process:

1. The first step in making an EPUB is to create your *content document(s)*. These must be either XHTML5 documents, SVG images, or a mixture of the two. Chapter 3 begins looking at the issues involved in creating these documents.

2. Once you've crafted your content, the next step is to create the *package document*, a special document used by reading systems to glean information about your publication (for ordering in your bookshelf, to render the content, and the like). The first step in creating this file is to list all of the resources you assembled in the content creation step in the *manifest section* of the package document. Reading systems need this list to determine whether a publication is complete and to discover which remote files will have to be retrieved. All your publication metadata (title, author, etc.) also goes in this file, consolidating it in a single, common location so that it can be easily extracted and used in distribution channels and by reading systems. You also have to include the default reading order in the *spine section* (a sequential list of your content files, from the first one to display to the last). Understanding metadata and packaging is key to understanding the EPUB format, as you might imagine, and that's why this book begins by exploring these issues in "Metadata" (page 281).

3. The last step is to zip up your content documents, associated resources, and the package document into a single file for distribution. This process isn't quite as simple as a standard zipping, however: a special mimetype file has to be added first to indicate that your ZIP file contains an EPUB and not something else, and a file called *container.xml* has to go in a directory named *META-INF* to tell reading systems where to find your package document.

This manual process is not one you will typically carry out in full, because there are programs that allow you to focus on creating your content while taking care of the export and packaging for you. It's invaluable to get clear in your head, though, because content and the package document are interrelated in many ways that will be explored throughout this book.

 If you read the previous numbered list in reverse, you'll also understand how reading systems work: they examine your ZIP container, determine it's an EPUB, find the package document, and from there discover how to render the resources to readers.

The other aspect of EPUB to understand before getting started is that it draws many of its capabilities and its versatility from web technologies, but the Web alone doesn't tell the whole story of EPUB. Without the complementary technologies the EPUB format brings under its common umbrella, the ability to create distributable publications would be much more complex.

Some of the technologies used in EPUBs have been specially developed by the International Digital Publishing Forum (IDPF), but most of the standards that have been leveraged are internationally recognized. The key ones you'll find in EPUB 3 publications include:

XHTML5
> For representing text and multimedia content, which now includes native support for MathML equations, ruby pronunciation markup, and embedded SVG images

SVG 1.1
> For representing graphical works (for example, manga and comics)

CSS 2.1 and 3
> To facilitate visual display and rendering of content

JavaScript
> For interactivity and automation

TrueType and WOFF
> To provide font support beyond the minimal base set that reading systems typically have available

SSML/PLS/CSS3 Speech
> For improved text-to-speech rendering

SMIL3
> For synchronizing text and audio playback

RDF vocabularies
> For embedding semantic information about the publication and content

XML
> A number of specialized grammars facilitate the discovery and processing aspects of EPUBs

ZIP
> To wrap all the resources up into a single file

You'll learn more about how to use all of these technologies as you progress through the chapters.

The EPUB format is specifically designed to be free and open for anyone to use without having to sift through a litany of patent encumbrances and restrictions. EPUB's widespread adoption has been due in no small part to the fact that basic text editing tools can be used to create publications, and the EPUB 3 revision of the specification has not deviated from this core tenet.

But that's really all there is to an EPUB file under the hood. If you feel comfortable with the concept of an EPUB as a predictable, discoverable container of your content, you're ready to begin tackling the best practices.

The EPUB 3.0 Specifications

Although EPUB 3 aggregates a number of technologies, an EPUB is not just a loose collection of these technologies. The term *EPUB 3* actually encompasses four separate specification documents, each of which details an aspect of how the employed technologies interact. This allows anyone to author an EPUB without struggling through all the related specifications, and allows the development of reading systems that can predictably process them. Another way to think of EPUB 3 is as the glue that binds these technologies into a usable reading experience.

The number and size of the specification documents can be intimidating the first time you go looking in them for guidance, but once you understand which aspect of the content creation and rendering process each handles, they're not very difficult reads. Pointers to the specifications are provided throughout this book where relevant, but we'll quickly break the documents down here so you can also explore them on your own as you go:

EPUB Publications 3.0 (http://idpf.org/epub/30/spec/epub30-publications.html)
> The Publications specification defines the XML format used in the package document to store information about a publication. As noted earlier, the package document contains metadata about the publication (such as the title, author, and language), lists all the resources used, defines the default reading order, and indicates where to find the navigation document. The Publications specification also defines general content requirements that all EPUBs must adhere to, such as required content types and when and how to provide fallbacks for content that isn't guaranteed to render on all devices.

EPUB Content Documents 3.0 (http://idpf.org/epub/30/spec/epub30-contentdocs.html)
> The Content Documents specification defines profiles of XHTML5, SVG 1.1, and CSS 2.1 and 3 for use in authoring content. A *profile* can perhaps best be described as a snapshot of the specific functionality that you are allowed to use (that is, you may not get to use everything defined in those specifications just because it exists). If you skip or skim this specification, not only might you wind up using illegal elements, styles, and features, but you also might miss the additions that EPUB

makes to improve the reading experience. The Content Documents specification also defines the format of the special navigation document. This document contains the table of contents for a publication, but it may also include other navigational aids, from tables of figures and illustrations to specialized tours of content.

EPUB Media Overlays 3.0 (http://idpf.org/epub/30/spec/epub30-mediaoverlays.html)
For those already familiar with EPUB 2, the Media Overlays specification is the new kid on the specification block. The ability to include audio content in EPUB 3 does not limit you just to embedding audio clips in your documents. Media Overlays take advantage of the SMIL specification to enable the text content rendered in the reading system's display area to be synchronized with audio narration, so that, for example, words can be highlighted as they are narrated.

EPUB Open Container Format (OCF) 3.0 (http://idpf.org/epub/30/spec/epub30-ocf.html)
And, finally, the Container specification defines how you bundle all your resources together into a single file. As noted previously, creating an EPUB file is more complex than just a simple instruction to zip up content, and this specification defines the discovery aspects discussed previously.

CHAPTER 1

Package Document and Metadata

Bill Kasdorf

Vice President, Apex CoVantage

One of the most common misconceptions about EPUB is that it is a "flavor" of XML. ("Should I use EPUB or DocBook?" or, even worse, "Should I use EPUB or HTML5?" *Hint:* EPUB (pretty much) = HTML5.) Due partly to the convenient single-file format provided as *.epub*, people sometimes fail to realize that EPUB is not just, and not mainly, a specification for the markup of content documents. It is a *publication format*, and as such it specifies and documents a host of things that publications need to include— content documents, style sheets, images, media, scripts, fonts, and more, as discussed in detail in the other chapters of this book. In fact, EPUB is sometimes thought of as "a website in a box," though it is actually much more than that.

What is arguably the most important thing about it is this: it *organizes* all the stuff in the box. It's designed to enable reading systems to easily and reliably know, up front, what's contained in a given publication, where to find each thing, what to do with it, how the parts relate to each other. And it enables publishers to provide that information in one clear, consistent form that all reading systems should understand, rather than in different, proprietary ways for each recipient system.

This, of course, is what metadata is for: it's not the content, it's information about the content. EPUB 3 accommodates much richer metadata than EPUB 2 did, and it enables that metadata to be associated not just with the publication as a whole, but also with individual components of the publication and even with elements within the content documents themselves. While it doesn't *require* much more than EPUB 2 did (in the interest of backward compatibility), it *accommodates* the much richer metadata that makes publications so much more discoverable and dynamic, so much more usable and useful.

The place where all this information is organized is the *package document*, an XML file that is one of the fundamental components of an EPUB, the *.opf* file. (The extension *.opf* stands for Open Package Format, which was the precursor to the new Publications specification.) In addition to containing most of the EPUB's metadata, the package document serves as a hub that associates that metadata with the other resources comprising the EPUB. All of this is then literally "zipped up" in a single-file container, the *.epub* file. *Voilá*, the "website in a box"—but one with a complete packing list and indispensable assembly instructions that ensure that an EPUB 3–compliant reading system will deliver the publication properly to the end user.

Before we take the lid off the box, let's look at the basic building blocks of EPUB 3 metadata.

Vocabularies

In order to make EPUBs easy to create, very little metadata is actually required, and the requirements are almost identical to those in EPUB 2. Like EPUB 2, EPUB 3 uses the Dublin Core Metadata Element Set (DCMES) for much of its required and optional metadata. Commonly referred to as "Dublin Core," DCMES is widely used as a basic framework for metadata of all sorts, from publication metadata to metadata for media like movies, audio, and images. You'll see examples throughout the balance of this chapter.

But EPUBs need to handle richer metadata as well, both to provide important information to the reading system and the end user, and to enable the more sophisticated functionality EPUB 3 offers. This simplicity-plus-complexity dilemma is addressed by providing:

- A basic *default vocabulary* that all EPUB 3 reading systems are required to understand;

- A short list of *reserved vocabularies* that can be used with their standard prefixes without declaration; and

- A mechanism by which any other vocabulary and its prefix can be declared, along with a pointer to where the authoritative definition of that vocabulary (in either human-readable or machine-readable form) can be found.

It's important to realize that this is not just designed to make it easy to create EPUBs; equally important is that it is designed to make it easy for reading systems to process EPUBs. While EPUB 3 enables full-blown metadata records like ONIX files for distribution and MARC records for cataloguing to be provided, such records are rich, complex, and can be used quite differently by different publishers.

ONIX is a good example of that: it provides for literally hundreds of different features and codes by which book supply chain metadata can be described; no publisher uses all of it, and different publishers make different choices as to what to use. This is very useful to the publisher who needs to convey that metadata to a recipient who knows how to handle it, but it is too much to ask all EPUB 3 reading systems to be able to handle. Plus, that standard changes frequently as more terms and features are added. And EPUB 3 is not just for books; many publishers who create EPUBs don't use ONIX at all.

EPUB 3 metadata, by contrast, is designed to provide a clear, consistent foundation, describing metadata that all EPUB 3 reading systems can be expected to handle, for all types of content, and clearly specifying which things are optional. So while you can include an ONIX file or MARC record if you want to, for the EPUB 3 metadata itself, you need to follow EPUB 3's rules. That's what this chapter is all about.

The Default Vocabulary

The basic vocabulary on which EPUB 3 metadata depends is simple but powerful. It provides specific, clearly defined terms that are used to describe fundamental properties of key elements:

meta
> The workhorse of EPUB 3 metadata

link
> Enabling the inclusion of external resources

item
> Providing metadata about each item in the manifest

itemref
> For metadata associated with items in the spine

These default vocabulary terms are specific to each of those elements and provide reading systems with a reliable, consistent way to understand how to handle each of them. For example, some of the default vocabulary terms for item in the manifest provide a means to alert the reading system to which files include MathML or SVG, and to identify which file is the cover image. One of the default vocabulary terms for link identifies that the resource being linked to is an ONIX record. The default vocabulary terms for each of these components are discussed in more detail below.

The Reserved Vocabularies

The reserved vocabularies provide commonly used sets of terms that can be used, with the proper prefix, without requiring those prefixes to be declared in the EPUB. In other words, the reading system is supposed to know where to find authoritative documentation of these vocabularies.

The four vocabularies reserved in EPUB 3.0 are:

dcterms
> A richer but more restrictive counterpart to DCMES in Dublin Core, designed to enable "linked data"

marc
> A vocabulary commonly used by libraries for bibliographic metadata

media
> The vocabulary on which EPUB 3's Media Overlays specification depends

onix
> The vocabulary used for book supply chain metadata

 The prefix *xsd* is also reserved for defining W3C XML Schema data types.

Using Other Vocabularies

Of course, there are many more vocabularies that are useful to publishers, and new ones are being created all the time. Ideally, these are public standards for which authoritative documentation can be referenced. But in order to be as flexible as possible, EPUB 3 even permits proprietary vocabularies to be used.

To use any of these other vocabularies, their terms must include a *prefix* (similar to how namespaces work), and each such prefix used in an EPUB must be declared in the prefix attribute of the package element, which is the root container of the package document (more on that below). This is done by "mapping" each prefix to a URI (Uniform Resource Identifier) that tells where its vocabulary is documented. Examples commonly used by publishers include:

xmp
> The Extensible Metadata Platform, widely used for metadata about images and other media:
>
> ```
> prefix="xmp: http://ns.adobe.com/xap/1.0/"
> ```

prism
> The very rich vocabulary used for magazine and other publication metadata:
>
> ```
> prefix="prism: http://prismstandard.org/namespaces/basic/3.0/"
> ```

custom
> A proprietary metadata scheme used by a publisher:
>
> ```
> prefix="TimeInc: http://www.timeinc.com/PRISM/2.1/"
> ```

And what about EPUB 3's default vocabulary? That is both the simplest and, potentially, the most complicated of all.

The All-Powerful meta Element

The workhorse of EPUB 3 metadata is the meta element, which provides a simple, generic, and yet surprisingly flexible and powerful mechanism for associating metadata of virtually unlimited richness with the EPUB package and its contents. An EPUB can have any number of meta elements. They're contained in the metadata element, the first child of the package element, and from that central location they serve as a hub for metadata about the EPUB, its resources, its content documents, and even locations within the content documents.

Here's how it works.

The meta element uses the refines attribute to specify what it applies to, using an ID in the form of a relative IRI. So, for example, a meta element can tell you something about chapter 5:

```
<meta refines="#[ID of chapter 5]">...</meta>
```

or about the author's name:

```
<meta refines="#creator">...</meta>
```

or about a video:

```
<meta refines="#video3">...</meta>
```

When the refines attribute is not provided, it is assumed that the meta element applies to the package as a whole; this is referred to as a *primary expression*. When the meta element does have a refines attribute, it is called a *subexpression*.

Each meta has a property attribute that defines what kind of statement is being made in the text of the meta element. The values of property can be the default vocabulary, a term from one of the reserved vocabularies, or a term from one of the vocabularies defined via the prefix mechanism. For example, you can provide the author Haruki Murakami's name in Japanese like this:

```
<meta refines="#creator"
property="alternate-script"
xml:lang="ja">
    村上 春樹
</meta>
```

The default vocabulary for meta consists of the following property values:

alternate-script
> Typically used to provide versions of titles and the names of authors or contributors in a language and script identified by the xml:lang attribute, as shown in the previous example.

display-seq
> Used to specify the sequence in which multiple versions of the same thing—for example, multiple forms of the title—should be displayed:
>
> ```
> <meta refines="#title2" property="display-seq">1</meta>
> ```

file-as
> Provides an alternate version—again, typically of a title or the name of an author or other contributor—in a form that will alphabetize properly, e.g., last-name-first for an author's name or putting "The" at the end of a title that begins with it:
>
> ```
> <meta refines="#creator" property="file-as">Murakami, Haruki</meta>
> ```

group-position
> Specifies the position of the referenced item in relation to others that it is grouped with. This is useful, for example, so that all the titles in a series are displayed in proper order in a reader's bookshelf:
>
> ```
> <meta refines="#title3" property="group-position">2</meta>
> ```

identifier-type
> Provides a way to distinguish between different types of identifiers (e.g., ISBN versus DOI). Its values can be drawn from an authority like the ONIX Code List 5, which is specified with the scheme attribute:
>
> ```
> <meta refines="#src-id"
> property="identifier-type"
> scheme="onix:codelist5">
>    15
> </meta>
> ```

meta-auth
> Documents the "metadata authority" responsible for a given instance of metadata:
>
> ```
> <meta refines="isbn-id" property="meta-auth">isbn-international.org</meta>
> ```

role
> Most often used to specify the exact role performed by a contributor—for example, a translator or illustrator:
>
> ```
> <meta refines="#creator" property="role" scheme="marc:relators">ill</meta>
> ```

title-type
> Distinguishes six specific forms of titles (see "Types of Titles" (page 14)):
>
> ```
> <meta refines="#title" property="title-type">subtitle</meta>
> ```

A meta element may also have an ID of its own, as the value of the id attribute:

```
<meta refines="isbn-id"
property="meta-auth"
id="meta-auth">
  isbn-international.org
</meta>
```

This ID can be used to make metadata chains, where one `meta` refines another. The element may also have a formal identifier of the scheme used for the value of the property (using the `scheme` attribute).

You can also use property values, which must include the proper prefix, from any of the reserved vocabularies or any vocabulary for which you've declared the prefix:

```
<meta property="dcterms:dateCopyrighted">2012</meta>
```

You'll notice that the previous example did not include a `refines` attribute. This was intentional, as the other use for the `meta` element is to define metadata for the publication as a whole. We'll look at the Dublin Core elements for publication metadata shortly, but you are not limited to using them. If another vocabulary provides richer metadata, you can use the `meta` element to express it.

You will see examples of the `meta` element throughout this chapter. While it is a bit abstract and thus can be hard to grasp at first, once you get the hang of it you'll find it to be easy to use, and indispensable, for enriching and empowering your EPUB with metadata.

Publication Metadata

Most of the metadata in a typical EPUB is associated with the publication as a whole. (An exception is an EPUB of an issue of a magazine, where most of the metadata is at the article, or content document, level; see "Types of Titles" (page 14).) This is intended to tell a reading system, when it opens up the EPUB, everything it needs to know about what's inside. Which EPUB is this (*identifiers*)? What names is it known by (*titles*)? Does it use any vocabularies I don't necessarily understand (*prefixes*)? What language does it use? What are all the things in the box (*manifest*)? Which one is the cover image, and do any of them contain MathML or SVG or scripting (*spine itemref properties*)? In what order should I present the content (*spine*), and how can a user navigate this EPUB (*the nav document*)? Are there resources I need to link to (*link*)? Are there any media objects I'm not designed by default to handle (*bindings*)?

Having all of this information up-front in the EPUB makes things much easier for a reading system, rather than requiring it to simply discover that unrecognized vocabulary, or that MathML buried deep in a content document, only when it comes across it, as a browser does with a normal website.

We'll take a look at each of these, followed by a deeper dive into some of the more interesting ones.

The Package Document Structure

An EPUB provides almost all of this fundamental information in an XML file called the package document. This contains that invaluable packing list and those indispensable assembly instructions that enable a reading system to know what it has and what to do with it.

The root element of the package document is the package element. This, in turn, contains the metadata and resource information in its child elements, in this order:

- metadata (required)
- manifest (required)
- spine (required)
- guide (optional and deprecated; a carryover from EPUB 2)
- bindings (optional)

The following markup shows the typical structure you'll find:

```
<package ... version="3.0" xmlns="http://www.idpf.org/2007/opf">
    <metadata xmlns:dc="http://purl.org/dc/elements/1.1/">
        ...
    </metadata>
    <manifest>
        ...
    </manifest>
    <spine>
        ...
    </spine>
</package>
```

In addition to declaring the namespace on the root package element, you must also declare the version (EPUB 3s must declare 3.0). The following attributes are also recommended:

xml:lang
> The language of the package document (not necessarily the same as the publication!)

dir
> The text directionality of the package document: left-to-right (ltr) or right-to-left (rtl)

The metadata Element

The `metadata` element contains the same three required elements as it did in EPUB 2, one new required element, and a number of optional elements, including that all-powerful `meta` element described previously.

As mentioned earlier, EPUB continues to use the Dublin Core Metadata Element Set (DCMES) for most of its required and optional metadata.

XML rules require that you declare the Dublin Core namespace in order to use the elements. This declaration is typically added to the `metadata` element, but can also be added to the root `package` element. For example:

```
<metadata xmlns:dc="http://purl.org/dc/elements/1.1/">
```

The required elements, which can occur in any order, are the following:

`dc:identifier`
> Contains an identifier for the publication. An EPUB can have any number of these (for example, an ISBN, a DOI, and even a proprietary identifier), but it must have at least one. And one must be designated as the *unique identifier* for the publication by the `unique-identifier` attribute on the root `package` element. (In a departure from EPUB 2, this is not, however, a unique *package* identifier; see "Identifiers" (page 11) for more on this.) A `dc:identifier` in `metadata` may or may not have an `id` attribute; the `id` is only required for the one designated as the publication's unique identifier.

`dc:title`
> Contains a title for the publication. Like `dc:identifier`, there can be more than one of these, but there must be at least one. While an `id` is not required on `dc:title`, it is a good idea to provide one, in order to associate metadata with it; you'll see why this is useful in "Types of Titles" (page 14). In addition, the optional `xml:lang` attribute enables the language of a title to be specified, and the optional `dir` attribute specifies its reading direction, with values of `ltr` (left-to-right) and `rtl` (right-to-left).

`dc:language`
> Specifies the language of the publication's content. (You can specify the language of many *metadata* elements with the `xml:lang` attribute; this `dc:language` element on `metadata` is about the *content* of the EPUB.) There can be more than one—for example, an EPUB might mainly be in English but have sections in French—but there must be at least one. And languages must be specified with the scheme provided in RFC5646, "Tags for Identifying Languages"; you can't just say "French."

Here is how you would express the required metadata for this book:

```
<dc:identifier id="pub-identifier">urn:isbn:9781449325299</dc:identifier>
<dc:title id="pub-title">EPUB 3 Best Practices</dc:title>
<dc:language id="pub-language">en</dc:language>
```

All of the other elements in the Dublin Core Metadata Elements Set (DCMES) are optional, but many of them are quite useful. These are dc:contributor, dc:coverage, dc:creator, dc:date, dc:description, dc:format, dc:publisher, dc:relation, dc:rights, dc:source, dc:subject, and dc:type. You'll see these in many of the examples in this chapter. They may all have optional id, xml:lang, and dir attributes. The ones most publishers will be likely to use are these:

dc:creator

> Contains the name of a person or organization with primary responsibility for creating the content, such as an author; dc:contributor is used in the same way, but indicates a secondary level of involvement (for example, a translator or an illustrator). The EPUB default vocabulary for properties can be used to provide further information, using that workhorse meta mechanism described above. For example, property="role" can be used to specify that a contributor was the translator, and property="file-as" can be used to provide her name in last-name-first form so it will sort properly alphabetically:
>
> ```
> <dc:creator id="author">Bill Kasdorf</dc:creator>
> <meta refines="#author" property="role" scheme="marc:relators">aut</meta>
> ```

dc:date

> Used to provide *the date of the EPUB publication*, not the publication date of a source publication, such as the print book from which the EPUB has been derived. Only one dc:date is allowed. Its content should be provided in the standard W3C date and time format, for example:
>
> ```
> <dc:date>2000-01-01T00:00:00Z</dc:date>
> ```

dc:source

> Contains the identifier of the source publication from which the EPUB was derived, such as the print version. Only one dc:source is allowed:
>
> ```
> <dc:source id="src-id">urn:isbn:9780375704024</dc:source>
> ```

dc:type

> Presents a bit of a curveball at the moment, because the IDPF has not yet defined values for it. It is intended to distinguish specialized types of EPUBs like dictionaries or indexes. Since it's optional, it may be best not to use it until there is a standard set of values available.

The metadata element can also contain any number of those useful meta elements described in "The All-Powerful meta Element" (page 5). An EPUB with rich metadata is likely to include lots of them, each one with its refines attribute identifying what its property attribute applies to, its optional id enabling *itself* to subsequently be refined by another `meta`, and its optional `scheme` documenting a formal definition of the property it describes. This is deliberately generic and abstract: in order to enable you to use virtually any kind of metadata in an EPUB, it specifies nothing but this bare-bones mechanism. Users often look in vain for more specifics at first; it is only after you begin to use `meta` that you come to realize its flexibility and power.

There is one very specific use of the `meta` element that is quite important; in fact, it is a requirement for EPUB 3. The `meta` element is used to provide a *timestamp* that records the *modification date* on which the EPUB was created. It uses the `dcterms:modified` property and requires a value conforming to the W3C dateTime form, like this:

```
<meta property="dcterms:modified">2011-01-01T12:00:00Z</meta>
```

When used with the *unique identifier* that identifies the publication, this further identifies the package.

 More on this later in "Identifiers" (page 11).

Mention should be made here of the `meta` element as defined in the previous EPUB specification, OPF2. That OPF2 version of `meta` has been replaced by the new definition in EPUB 3. However, despite the fact that it is obsolete, it is still permitted in an EPUB so that EPUB 3 reading systems don't reject older EPUB 2s—but they're required to ignore those obsolete OPF2-style `meta`s. We'll see a use for this element when we look at covers in "Covers" (page 85) in Chapter 3.

Finally, the `metadata` element can also include `link` elements. These are designed to associate resources with the publication that are not a part of its direct rendering. Unlike most publication resources, linked resources can be provided either within the container or outside it. The element is primarily designed to enable metadata records of different types to be included in an EPUB.

 The `link` element, along with the `bindings` element that is a sibling, rather than a child, of `metadata`, is discussed in more detail later in "Links and Bindings" (page 20).

Identifiers

Andy Tanenbaum's joke about standards, "The nice thing about standards is that there are so many of them to choose from," applies just as well to identifiers. The ironic implication of the joke (shouldn't one standard, one identifier, be sufficient?) turns out to be far from the truth. Identifiers have different purposes: the ISBN is a product identifier, the ISTC identifies textual works, the DOI provides an "actionable" and persistent identifier, the ISSN identifies a serial publication; and publishers typically have proprietary identifiers for their publications as well. Many of these can apply to a given EPUB.

Providing these identifiers—and, ideally, documenting them properly—uses a combination of the Dublin Core `dc:identifier` and EPUB 3's `meta` element. Here's an example from the EPUB 3 specs:

```
<metadata xmlns:dc="http://purl.org/dc/elements/1.1/">
    <dc:identifier id="pub-id">
      urn:doi:10.1016/j.iheduc.2008.03.001
    </dc:identifier>
    <meta refines="#pub-id"
    property="identifier-type"
    scheme="onix:codelist5">
      06
    </meta>
    ...
  </metadata>
```

Since we can have any number of these, we need to give this one an ID; we've named it `pub-id`. Then the content of `dc:identifier` is the identifier itself, which in this case is a *digital object identifier* (DOI).

While it might seem obvious that that identifier is a DOI (it does begin with `doi:`, after all), that is not true of every possible identifier we might want to use. In the interest of making things as clear and explicit as possible (for either human or machine interpretation), we need to identify what kind of identifier that is and where its authoritative definition can be found. That's what the `meta` element is doing. It says, "I'm refining the element I designated as `pub-id`; what I'm telling you about it is what type of identifier it is; and the type of identifier is the one described as item 06 in ONIX Codelist 5." While a reading system is not, of course, required to go and consult ONIX Codelist 5, there is a clear, unambiguous record in the EPUB metadata of exactly what kind of identifier this one is. ONIX Codelist 5 provides a convenient, authoritative reference to types of identifiers; but if this were a publisher's own proprietary identifier (a common type of identifier a publisher might want to include), then it could simply say `scheme="propri etary"`.

As mentioned previously, an EPUB 3 can have any number of `dc:identifier` elements in its `metadata`. And one of them must be designated, via the `unique-identifier` attribute on the root `package` element, as the unique identifier of the publication. Isn't this the same as saying it's the unique identifier of the EPUB, just as EPUB 2 specified?

It turns out that the meaning of *unique* is not "unique." When technologists—or reading systems—say an identifier uniquely identifies an EPUB, they mean it quite literally: if one EPUB is not bit-for-bit identical to another EPUB, it needs a different unique identifier, because it's not the same thing; systems need to tell them apart. Publishers, on the other hand, want the identifier to be persistent. To them, a new EPUB that corrects some typographical errors or adds some metadata is still "the same EPUB"; giving it a different identifier creates ambiguity and potentially makes it difficult for a user to realize that the corrected EPUB and the uncorrected EPUB are really "the same book."

After quite a bit of struggle, the EPUB 3 Working Group came up with an elegant solution to this dilemma by doing two simple things: changing the definition of *unique identifier* and adding the *timestamp* mentioned earlier.

The specifications for EPUB 3 say that the *unique identifier*—the value of the unique-identifier attribute on the package—should be persistent in terms of the *publication*. It's a *publication identifier*. It should not change when the only differences between the old and new versions of the EPUB are minor changes like additions to metadata or fixing errata. (New editions, on the other hand, or derivative versions of various sorts, like a translation or even an illustrated version of a previously nonillustrated text, obviously must get a new "unique identifier.")

But the EPUB 3 specs also require the package to contain a meta element that records the date and time, via the timestamp, when that EPUB file was created. It is the combination of these two things, the publication identifier and the timestamp, that serves as the package identifier that tells the reading system exactly which EPUB file it is dealing with.

So although the exact meaning of "unique" is still fuzzy—two EPUBs with the same "unique identifier" don't have to be identical, and of course there can be many copies of an EPUB file with a given timestamp—we have neatly addressed the needs of the publishers and the technologists, and in a way that is easy for anybody to do.

Here's an example of how the metadata looks in an EPUB:

```
<metadata xmlns:dc="http://purl.org/dc/elements/1.1/">
   <dc:identifier id="pub-id">
      urn:uuid:A1B0D67E-2E81-4DF5-9E67-A64CBE366809
   </dc:identifier>
   <meta property="dcterms:modified">2011-01-01T12:00:00Z</meta>
   ...
</metadata>
```

This results in the Package ID that only a computer could love:

```
urn:uuid:A1B0D67E-2E81-4DF5-9E67-A64CBE366809@2011-01-01T12:00:00Z
```

Although there is an id provided for the dc:identifier element, it isn't referenced by the meta element with the dcterms:modified attribute. That's because this meta does not "refine" the dc:identifier; rather, it applies to the package and is thus a *primary expression*.

Types of Titles

It might also be assumed that one title for an EPUB should be sufficient, and usually, this is in fact the case. However, the EPUB 3 Working Group realized that there are actually quite a few different types of titles that publishers might want to provide in an EPUB's metadata, and that some titles are actually quite complex, with different components serving different purposes. Moreover, different types of publications use different types of titles. ONIX, for example, provides an extensive list of title types used in books; PRISM, the standard for magazine metadata, uses a different scheme.

In keeping with its desire to be both comprehensive, accommodating whatever vocabularies a given publisher might need, as well as being simple to implement and practical as a requirement for reading systems, the EPUB 3.0 specification provides a simple set of six built-in types that reading systems are required to recognize as values of the title-type property, but also permits other values with the use of the scheme attribute in order to specify where they are documented (e.g., the ONIX Code List 15).

The six basic values of the title-type property specified by EPUB 3 are:

main
> The title that reading systems should normally display, for example in a user's library or bookshelf. If no values for the title-type property are provided, it is assumed that the first or only dc:title should be considered the "main title."

subtitle
> A secondary title that augments the main title but is separate from it.

short
> A shortened version of the main title, often used when referring to a book with a long title (for example, "Huck Finn" for *The Adventures of Huckleberry Finn*) or a brief expression by which a book is known (for example, "Strunk and White" for *The Elements of Style* or "Fowler" for *A Dictionary of Modern English Usage*).

collection
> A title given to a set (either finite or ongoing) to which the given publication is a member. This can be a "series title," when the publications are in a specific sequence (e.g., *The Lord of the Rings*), or one in which the members are not necessarily in a particular order (e.g., "Columbia Studies in South Asian Art").

edition

A designation that indicates substantive changes from one to the next.

extended

A fully expressed title that may be a combination of some of the other title types, for example: *The Great Cookbooks of the World: Mon premier guide de caisson, un Mémoire. The New French Cuisine Masters, Volume Two. Special Anniversary Edition.*

The use of these title types provides a good example of how the id attribute and the all-powerful meta element with its refines and property attributes are used in EPUB metadata. This is one of many examples provided in the formal EPUB Publications 3.0 specification:

```
<metadata xmlns:dc="http://purl.org/dc/elements/1.1/">
    ...
    <dc:title id="t1">A Dictionary of Modern English Usage</dc:title>
    <meta refines="#t1" property="title-type">main</meta>
    <dc:title id="t2">First Edition</dc:title>
    <meta refines="#t2" property="title-type">edition</meta>
    <dc:title id="t3">Fowler's</dc:title>
    <meta refines="#t3" property="title-type">short</meta>
    ...
</metadata>
```

Note that the other *default vocabulary* values for property on meta, besides title-type, can also be used. Two that publishers may find particularly useful in the context of titles are:

display-seq

Indicates the sequence in which the given dc:title should be displayed in relation to the other dc:titles

file-as

Provides a version of a title that will alphabetize properly, for example "Canterbury Tales, The."

The Manifest and Spine

The next elements in the EPUB package following metadata are the manifest and spine; both of them are required. They constitute the "packing list" and a key aspect of the "assembly instructions" that make an EPUB so much more than just a "website in a box." The manifest documents all of the individual resources that together constitute the EPUB, and the spine provides a default reading order by which those resources may be presented to a user.

The manifest and Fallbacks

Each and every resource that is part of the EPUB—every content document, every image, every video and audio file, every font, every style sheet: *every* individual resource —is documented by an `item` element in the `manifest`. The purpose is to alert a reading system, up front, about everything it must find in the publication, what kind of media each thing is, and where it can find it. They can be in any order, but they all have to be in the `manifest`.

Each `item` contains these three required attributes:

id

> This is essential, so that each constituent part of the EPUB can be uniquely identified. It is what enables that versatile `meta` element to provide metadata associated with specific `items`, via its `refines` attribute.

href

> An internationalized resource identifier (IRI) specifying the location of the resource. Resource names should be restricted to the ASCII character set.

media-type

> The MIME media type that specifies the type and format of the resource.

Here's a typical entry for an XHTML content document:

```
<item id="chapter01"
      href="xhtml/c01.xhtml"
      media-type="application/xhtml+xml"/>
```

The EPUB 3 specification designates 14 Core Media Types that all EPUB 3 reading systems are required to recognize. For example, XHTML and SVG are the Core Media Types for content documents; GIF, JPEG, PNG, and SVG are the Core Media Types for images.

 Core Media Types are discussed in detail in the other chapters in this book to which they apply.

If a resource in an EPUB is of any *other* media type (which are referred to as *Foreign Resources*), a *fallback* must be provided that *is* a Core Media Type. This is done via the `fallback` attribute on the `item`. Note that an EPUB can have a *fallback chain* in which one non-Core Media Type `item` falls back to another, which eventually resolves to an `item` that is a Core Media Type. We'll look at fallbacks in more detail in "Fallback Content" (page 102) in Chapter 3.

An `item` may also have a `properties` attribute with one or more space-separated property values that alert the reading system to some useful information about the `item`. The values for manifest property values in EPUB 3 are:

`cover-image`
> Clearly documenting which `item` should be displayed as the cover.

`mathml`, `scripted`, `svg`, `remote-resources`, *and* `switch`
> Alerting the reading system to where it will have to deal with MathML, JavaScript, SVG, remote resources, or non-EPUB XML fragments (see the other chapters for more detail on these).

`nav`
> The XHTML5 document that is the required Navigation Document (see Chapter 2).

And finally, an `item` may have a `media-overlay` attribute, the value of which is an IDREF of the Media Overlay Document for the `item`. Media Overlays are the EPUB 3 mechanism for synchronizing text and recorded audio; they are discussed in detail in Chapter 6.

The spine

Whereas the `manifest` documents each and every `item` in the EPUB, in no particular order, the `spine` provides a default reading order, and it is required to list only those components that are not referenced by other components (*primary* content). The point is to provide at least one path by which everything in the EPUB will be presented to the reader, in at least one logical order. So, for example, the `spine` will list the content document for chapter 5 in a book (presumably between those for chapters 4 and 6), but it will not necessarily list images or media or scripts that are contained in chapter 5 (*auxiliary* content), because they will be presented in the context of chapter 5 being presented, and may not necessarily be presented in linear order (e.g., perhaps as a pop up):

```
<spine>
  ...
  <itemref idref="chapter04"/>
  <itemref idref="chapter05"/>
  <itemref idref="chapter06"/>
  ...
</spine>
```

Note that the `spine` is also not the same as the Navigation Document. That document can provide much richer information about the internal structure of content documents (see Chapter 2). The spine ensures that a reading system can recognize the first primary content document in the EPUB and then render the successive primary content documents. It does not, however, mandate that a user must access the content in this order; it just provides a *default reading order* that the user is free to depart from.

Instead of the item element used in the manifest, each element in the spine is an itemref element. Each of these elements contains an idref attribute identifying the appropriate item in the manifest, as well as an optional linear attribute that specifies whether the item is *primary* (yes, the default) or *auxiliary* (no), and an optional properties attribute that can specify whether the given content document starts on the left or right side of a spread:

```
<spine>
    <itemref idref="cover" linear="no"/>
    <itemref idref="chapter01"/>
    ...
</spine>
```

The spine may also contain a toc attribute that identifies an NCX file. The NCX is how EPUB 2 specified navigation; it is superseded in EPUB 3 by the Navigation Document (nav, an XHTML document, as described in Chapter 2). In order to enable an EPUB 3 to be rendered by an EPUB 2 reading system, it has to include an NCX even though it *also* has to have a nav to conform to EPUB 3. Until EPUB 2 reading systems have become obsolete (no sign of that in the near future), publishers generally need to include both. The collision is prevented by the fact that the nav is pointed to by the manifest's nav property and the NCX is pointed to by the spine's toc attribute:

```
<package ...>
    ...
    <manifest>
        ...
        <item id="nav"
              href="nav.xhtml"
              media-type="application/xhtml+xml"
              properties="nav"/>
        <item href="toc.ncx"
              id="ncx"
              media-type="application/x-dtbncx+xml"/>
        ...
    </manifest>
    <spine toc="ncx">
        ...
    </spine>
</package>
```

Document Metadata

While the metadata for most EPUBs is typically associated with the publication as a whole, EPUB 3 also enables metadata to be associated with content documents and even with elements within content documents. This is particularly useful for publications that are article-based, like magazines and journals, as well as for *contributed volumes*, books in which each chapter is by a different author. In these cases, much metadata is at the article or chapter level. But you don't need to stop there; you can even associate metadata with elements within the XHTML content documents, down to the phrase level with the span element.

It will be no surprise, if you've been paying attention, that this is done with our all-purpose meta element. And it depends on each document or element that you want to reference having an id attribute that is unique within the EPUB. (Because EPUBs are designed to be self-contained, the IDs are not required to be unique between EPUBs, although for publishers of potentially related EPUBs it is a good practice to do that, to better enable linking and referencing between EPUBs, though most reading systems don't yet enable that.)

Again, the mechanism is a simple and generic one: each meta element has a refines attribute, the value of which is the ID of what it's referencing, and a property attribute that provides either a property value from the default vocabulary (see "The All-Powerful meta Element" (page 5) earlier in this chapter) or a value that uses a prefix and term from one of the reserved vocabularies or from one for which you've declared the prefix.

 These meta elements are in the metadata within the package; they are not in the content documents themselves. They reference the content documents (or elements within them) via the relative URI, which means they begin with a # symbol.

Here's an example of some metadata for a hypothetical article from *Sports Illustrated* contained in an EPUB along with other articles, ads, and other resources:

```
<meta refines="#ID12345" property="prism:contentType">article</meta>
<meta property="dc:title" id="t4main">
   Meet The Rejuvenated, Revitalized LeBron
</meta>
<meta refines="#t4main" property="title-type">main</meta>
<meta property="dc:title" id="t4sub">
   After a tumultuous first year in Miami, LeBron James locked himself
   in his house, rued disappointing his teammates—then worked hard to
   hone his game. The result: one of the best seasons in NBA history
</meta>
<meta refines="#t4sub" property="title-type">subtitle</meta>
```

```
<meta refines="#ID12345" property="dc:creator">LEE JENKINS</meta>
<meta refines="#ID12345" property="prism:genre">coverStory</meta>
<meta refines="#ID12345" property="prism:genre">profile</meta>
<meta refines="#ID12345" property="TimeInc:enhancer">Digitization Co.</meta>
<meta refines="#ID12345" property="TimeInc:checker">Michael Smith</meta>
```

This metadata all applies to the article that has an ID in the form `id="ID12345"` (note that as a *type ID*, XML rules require this ID to begin with an alpha character). Because the `refines` attribute for `meta` is a relative URI, it begins with a # and then the ID of the article.

This example shows that Time, Inc., chose to provide the `contentType` (`article`) and genre categorizations (`coverStory` and `profile`) from the PRISM vocabulary. And they've recorded the firm that created the EPUB and the person who checked it using their own proprietary vocabulary. The `PRISM` and `TimeInc` prefixes would be declared using the `prefix` attribute on the root-level `package` element.

This example also shows the use of the EPUB 3 `title-type` properties for the main title and the subtitle.

 Think of how cumbersome it would be if the title and subtitle were combined into one long title!

Links and Bindings

While its main purpose is to provide a specification for consistent, predictable content in EPUBs, the EPUB 3 spec recognizes that it is sometimes necessary to provide things that are not covered by that specification. One way this is done is via the `epub:switch` element, which applies to XML fragments in content documents; it is discussed in detail in Chapter 3. But two other mechanisms are part of the package metadata: the `link` and `bindings` elements.

The OPF meta elements are only intended to be used for identity and version information, and metadata that reading systems might want to expose to users or use to organize and manage the bookshelf. Publishers have much richer "real" bibliographical records, which can be incorporated into an EPUB using a link. Using the `link` element, a child of `metadata` within `package`, is not the same as simply linking to an external location with a link in a content document. The things linked to on the Web from the content documents are not considered part of the publication; and these links do not work if the EPUB is offline. In contrast, the `link` element in an EPUB's `metadata` provides access to a resource that is considered more integral to the publication, although it is not formally part of the EPUB itself. The resource may be provided in the container, so it is available when the EPUB is offline, but a reading system is not required to process or use the resource.

The `link` element requires an `href` attribute to provide either an absolute or relative IRI to a resource, and a `rel` attribute to provide the property value—i.e., what kind of resource is being linked to. The values defined for the `rel` attribute in EPUB 3.0 are:

`marc21xml-record`
> For a MARC21 record providing bibliographic metadata for the publication

`mods-record`
> For a MODS record of the publication conforming to the Library of Congress's Metadata Object Description Schema

`onix-record`
> For an ONIX record providing book supply chain metadata for the publication conforming to EDItEUR's ONIX for Books specification

`xml-signature`
> For an XML Signature applying to the publication or an associated property conforming to the W3C's XML Signature specification

`xmp-record`
> For an XMP record conforming to the ISO Extensible Metadata Platform that applies to the *publication* (not just a component, like an image, for which the prefix mechanism and `meta` element should be used to provide metadata using the `xmp:` prefix)

Here is how you might reference an external ONIX record:

```
<link rel="onix-record" href="http://example.org/meta/records/onix/121099"/>
```

The `bindings` element is a child of the root `package` element. Its chief purpose is to enable an EPUB to contain fallbacks that are more sophisticated than those provided by the HTML5 `object` element's fallback mechanisms. The `bindings` element documents the presence of handlers for such *foreign media* via its `media-type` attribute. When a reading system encounters such an unsupported media type, it looks in the `bindings` element to see if a handler is provided for it, and if so, it is supposed to use that handler instead of the usual fallback. Bindings are discussed in more detail in "Bindings" (page 112) in Chapter 3.

Metadata for Fixed Layout Publications

After the original EPUB 3.0 specification was published in September 2011, it was recognized that despite the importance of EPUB as a reflowable format, many publishers need to use it in a "fixed layout" form in which pagination is fixed, typically via fixed-layout XHTML, SVG, or bitmap images. While there is nothing in that EPUB 3.0 specification to prevent this, it became clear that some metadata should be added to aid in the publication of fixed layout EPUBs. So in March 2012, the IDPF published an informational document to do that.

This provides a number of useful properties. These require the `rendition` prefix to be declared as `prefix="rendition: http://www.idpf.org/vocab/rendition#"` on the `package` element. With one exception as noted below, these properties may be used on the `meta` element to apply to the publication as a whole or on an `itemref` element in the spine. The available properties are:

`rendition:layout`
    With the values `reflowable` or `pre-paginated`.

`rendition:orientation`
    With the values `landscape`, `portrait`, or `auto`.

`rendition:spread`
    Specifies how reading systems should render spreads, with the values `none`, `landscape`, `portrait`, `both`, or `auto`.

`rendition:page-spread-center`
    Complements the already existing `page-spread-left` and `page-spread-right` properties to force a specific placement on a spread. It is used only on the `itemref` element in the `spine`.

We'll return to look at how to use these properties to create fixed layouts in more detail in "Fixed Layouts" (page 80) in Chapter 3.

The Container

Now for the easiest part of all: zipping everything up to make it an *.epub*. The specification for this is the Open Container Format (OCF) 3.0, and it is literally a *.zip* file, though it uses the *.epub* extension. It contains all the content documents and other resources, including all the metadata that has been described in this chapter.

All of this is contained in a directory called *META-INF*. This *META-INF* directory contains the following files:

A required container.xml file

Contains a `rootfiles` element with one or more `rootfile` elements, each of which references a publication's package document, the *.opf* file. Reading systems must use the `manifest` in this `package` (see "The manifest and Fallbacks" (page 16)) to process the EPUB.

There is an optional *manifest.xml* file that may provide a manifest for the container; this is not used in rendering the EPUB that the container contains.

An optional encryption.xml file

Holds all the encryption information (if any). Its root element is `encryption`, which contains child elements `EncryptedKey` and `EncryptedData` that describe how the files are encrypted and provide the key to access them. OCF uses the XML Encryption Syntax and Processing Version 1.1 specification. Note, however, that the *META-INF* files themselves as listed here, along with the `package` document that is the root file of the EPUB, must not be encrypted.

An optional manifest.xml file

Simply provides a manifest for the container (not to be confused with the `mani fest` in the EPUB `package`).

An optional metadata.xml file

May provide metadata for the container (not to be confused with the `metadata` in the EPUB `package`).

An optional rights.xml file

Contains rights or DRM (Digital Rights Management) information about the EPUB. No DRM scheme is specified; EPUB is deliberately agnostic as to the issue of DRM.

An optional signatures.xml file

Can hold digital signatures of the container and its contents. Its root element is `signatures`, which contains child `Signature` elements that conform to the XML Signature Syntax and Processing Version 1.1 specification.

The EPUB Open Container Format 3.0 specification provides detailed instructions regarding the creation of the OCF. But for most publishers, this is the simplest part of the process, and is usually quite automated. The result is a single-file EPUB with the extension *.epub* that contains a publication with all the rich content and functionality that EPUB 3 provides—and for which the *.opf* document that is the subject of this chapter provides such an invaluable guide.

One requirement that often trips people up when manually creating an EPUB is that the *mimetype* file has to be the first file added to the ZIP container. The default zipping of an EPUB directory typically results in the *META-INF* directory being packaged first, leading to validation errors. See "Validating unpacked EPUBs" (page 309) in Chapter 11 for information on how to use epubcheck to automate the packaging process and avoid this problem. Free Mac scripts to zip and unzip archives are also available at *http://code.google.com/p/epub-applescripts/*.

CHAPTER 2

Navigation

Although you may not often think of them this way, the navigation aids provided in a publication (such as the table of contents) represent another form of metadata. Tables of contents, lists of tables and illustrations, guides to major structures and even page numbers themselves all provide information about the publication that allow you to quickly move about it, whether in print or digital form.

One of the clear advantages that electronic documents have over print publications is that they provide a faster, easier and all-around better experience for navigating content. Even diehard print fans have to admit that the print table of contents, and its requisite page-flipping approach to finding where you want to go, hardly measures up to hyperlinked entries that immediately reveal the content. And there's nothing like a table of contents that is instantly available at the push of a button.

It's not surprising then that pretty much every electronic format facilitates navigation by the document structure, as shown in Figure 2-1. Microsoft Word has the document map, for example, which allows for accessible navigation of all the heading-styled sections of a Word document. Adobe Reader provides similar functionality for PDFs with text headings through the bookmarks panel, and DAISY digital talking books and EPUB 2 both use the Navigation Control file for XML applications (NCX), as does Amazon's Mobi format.

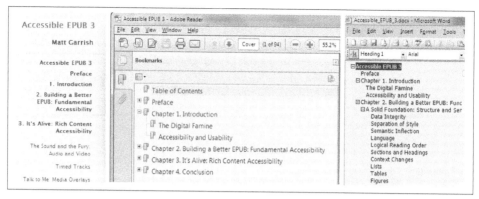

Figure 2-1. Examples of document navigation for EPUB 2, Word, and PDF

Although this might sound like a case for why navigation is just required functionality—and it is—the EPUB 3 revision took a number of much-needed changes in direction to beef up support. The biggest of these was dropping the NCX in favor of a new format: the *EPUB navigation document*.

The EPUB Navigation Document

If you're familiar with the NCX format used in EPUB 2, and know how complex it could be to create for the functionality it provided, you can breathe a sigh of relief at this point, because the new navigation document markup is based on a subset of HTML5—part of bringing EPUB more in line with web standards. You get the same functionality, but with less work and no need for new knowledge acquisition.

 There is still a use for the NCX if you plan to target your content to both EPUB 2 and 3 reading systems, but we'll return to this topic at the end of the chapter, because its necessity diminishes as time goes by.

The easy way to tackle the navigation document would be to state the obvious, that it's for navigation, and run through a few code snippets to give a feel for the markup. But because our goal is to look deeper into the format and lay out best practices, let's instead delve first into the nature of the document to get grounded in why it exists and for what purposes.

If you want to amaze your friends and colleagues with your knowledge of EPUB (and who doesn't?), you need to grasp two key concepts in relation to the changeover to the navigation document. The first is that the markup it contains now serves a dual purpose.

Like the NCX, it is still designed to enable reading systems to provide the reader with a specialized table of contents view, but it also has a new presentational role as content in the publication. Disambiguating these roles can be a bit confusing, though, because it's not the case with the navigation document that XHTML is always XHTML.

Anyone who has used any EPUB reading system should already be familiar with the options they provide to quickly bring up the table of contents and move around. Dedicated devices sometimes integrate buttons right into the hardware, while software players typically build an option into the chrome to allow quick access and activation at any point while reading (a little swipe here or there and a button bar appears, for example), as shown in Figure 2-2. Opening the table of contents via these mechanisms might result in a table of links appearing in a new sidebar, or a floating view being overlaid on the current page.

Figure 2-2. Table of contents activation button in Readium

But knowing the implementation particulars are not as important as understanding that this specialized view is not a part of the EPUB content itself; the navigation menu is a feature that the reading system provides using the navigation document markup. The rendering is completely up to the developers who built that particular system. The generation of this *specialized table of contents view* is the primary reason for the existence of the navigation document.

While these specialized views are effective tools, embedding a table of contents in the publication body is a common practice that has survived the digital transition, because not every reader wants to leave the book to orient themselves to the content when they first start reading. Usually, after passing over a cover and title page, the reader will encounter this more traditional text table of contents. This *embedded table of contents* has no special behaviors associated with it by the reading system, and it renders in the content viewport just like any other document in the publication.

Figure 2-3 shows these two uses for the navigation document as rendered in Readium.

Some people might assume the foreign-looking XML grammar used to construct the NCX file required some special magic in the reading system in order to turn the tagging into an ordered set of links in the specialized view. Not so with the new navigation document. By choosing to reformulate the NCX as HTML5 lists of hyperlinks, when you see the markup for the new navigation file, your first thought is more likely going to be: "Oh, reading systems must just render the navigation document as web content."

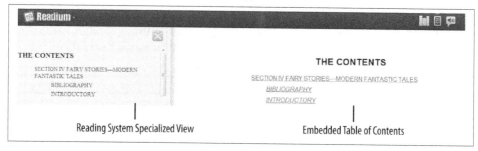

THE CONTENTS

SECTION IV FAIRY STORIES—MODERN
FANTASTIC TALES
BIBLIOGRAPHY
INTRODUCTORY

THE CONTENTS

SECTION IV FAIRY STORIES—MODERN FANTASTIC TALES
BIBLIOGRAPHY
INTRODUCTORY

Reading System Specialized View   Embedded Table of Contents

Figure 2-3. Readium's specialized table of contents (in a separate pane on the left, with no styling and grey background) and a styled embedded table of contents (on the right)

The actual rendering of the document is not so straightforward, however. The EPUB 3 specification gives a lot of leeway in terms of how the document can be presented by a reading system, so it's actually quite hard to make definitive statements about how it will get rendered.

The current crop of EPUB 3 reading systems (such as Readium, iBooks, Google Play, Adobe Digital Editions, and others) continue to use the markup as a feed into their specialized rendering (part of the reason is undoubtedly to ensure a consistent reading experience between EPUB 2 and EPUB 3 publications, despite the different markup grammars). But this behavior is not required by the specification. A reading system could possibly appear one day that simply leverages XHTML processing to present the document and its links within the content pane (not to be confused with embedding the navigation document in the spine as content).

> To render the navigation document as XHTML, a reading system has to perform some tweaking of the content to make it compatible, which is also why this is not a common practice. Some features of the specialized view deviate from the HTML5 specification, such as the way the hidden attribute has been appropriated for hiding content, as discussed later.

This point might seem belabored, but it is important to understand if you want to avoid fruitless time trying to style the navigation document for rendering in a reading system's specialized view. As a content creator, you just have to accept that you will have little control over these specialized renderings beyond the text of your links. A reading system will typically ignore all CSS you include in the navigation document when building its own view, likewise all scripting, and even in an extreme case could ignore all inline markup within the links (although that would be taking the minimalism of presentation to a new level). As of this writing, no known reading systems honor styling or scripting added by the content creator in the specialized view, for example.

Of course, the flip side of all this warning about what a reading system won't do with your content in the specialized view is that it will usually make up for it by providing its own rich experience for readers (expanding/collapsing sections, accessible keyboard shortcuts and navigation, etc.), without forcing content creators to double as developers.

The second concept to understand is that the navigation document is, first and foremost, a kind of *container* file. It is not just a table of contents, as it is often equated with, but encapsulates a set of discrete navigational aids of which the table of contents is just one. These unique lists are the inputs reading systems use to define their specialized navigation views. That you can use the document as content without modification does not alter this fact, nor that you can intersperse the lists with other HTML content for rendering in the spine. Reading systems will typically extract just these lists to create their specialized views.

The EPUB 3 specification defines three types of these navigation lists, and each serves a unique role: the table of contents typically gets the most attention, but the specification also defines a *landmarks list* and a *page list*. The format is also extensible, so you can create your own new types. The key is simply to think of each list as a self-contained unit. Although they share a common structure, each has its own differences, designed to meet its unique role in facilitating navigation.

But that's as much theory as you need to know, and probably more than you wanted, but grasping the distinction really is vital to understanding which table of contents is which (when they come from the same source file) and why you have more control in one rendering and not the other.

Now, onward and upward into actually making one these documents.

Building a Navigation Document

The first question you might reasonably ask yourself is why you would ever want to handcraft any of the lists in the navigation document, and the answer is no one ever *wants* to build them all up from scratch! Programs that can create EPUBs have no problem autogenerating the lists from the publication's markup, and you'd be wise to get a leg up on the creation process that way than going through the often laborious task of marking the navigation document up by hand.

But even if you don't manually create one from the ground up, there are a few reasons why you'll inevitably find yourself in your navigation document markup more often than you might think. One is that not all the navigation lists lend themselves perfectly to autogeneration. The table of contents and page list are perfect candidates for machine output (they just parallel information already coded in the publication markup), but landmarks are often included on a case-by-case basis only. You're also going to come across situations where the document structure is so deeply nested (more than four or five levels deep) that you'll want to control the rendering appearance. And, perhaps more than any other reason, when you embed the document in the content, you'll to want to add post-production styling and any additional content that cannot be auto-generated from the document structure.

But let's start at the beginning. As mentioned earlier, the navigation document is marked up like any other XHTML content document in EPUB, but with some notable rules and restrictions.

First, you need to declare the EPUB namespace on your navigation document's root element:

```
<html xmlns="http://www.w3.org/1999/xhtml"
      xmlns:epub="http://www.idpf.org/2007/ops" ... >
```

Each navigation list is identified by the epub:type attribute it carries, so this declaration is required in order for the document to validate.

> The epub:type attribute (described in "epub:type and Structural Se-mantics" (page 68)) is a new mechanism added in EPUB 3 for annotating your markup and is covered in Chapter 3. But you don't need to jump ahead and learn its inner workings in order to understand its use for navigation.

Because the navigation document is effectively a list of navigation aids, you typically aren't going to find a lot in the body of the document. If you choose to start your navigation document with a heading, you need to ensure that it makes sense as a superordinate heading to the table of contents, lists of table and illustrations, and any other navigation lists, especially when embedded as content.

A heading like this might prove to be both misleading and redundant, depending on how the document gets presented:

```
<body>
   <section>
      <h1>Table of Contents</h1>
      ...
   </section>
<body>
```

The headings for lists of tables and illustrations are often the same level as the table of contents, but this heading would place them as child sections of the table of contents.

A better option is to use the title of work as the primary heading, especially if this is the first content document you present to the reader. For example, a navigation document for Charles Madison Curry's *Children's Literature* could start like this:

```
<body>
    <section>
        <h1>Children's Literature</h1>
        ...
    </section>
</body>
```

The rest of the process of creating a navigation document is simply creating the nav lists. This chapter won't discuss how you might decorate your navigation document with content between these lists, because that will differ from publication to publication. Suffice it to say, any legal XHTML content can be included within the body of the document, just not within the nav elements.

 Because you cannot control how a reading system will present the navigation document, be wary about adding too much additional information. It's entirely possible that the entire document will get rendered in a customized view, potentially cluttering the display and making navigation problematic for some readers. Minimal is often better, even if it means having to create a second table of contents to embed as content (it's not required that you use the navigation document as content; it's just a convenience).

Repeated Patterns

Constructing a navigation list is an almost embarrassingly simple process. Each nav element must include an epub:type attribute to identify its purpose, may contain an optional heading, and must include a single ordered list (ol), as shown in the following mock markup:

```
<nav epub:type="list-type">
    <h1>List Title</h1>
    <ol>
        ...
    </ol>
</nav>
```

That's all there is at the core of each navigation list. We'll see some of the real values you can use in the epub:type attribute as we build the various list types, but the rules for creating the ordered list provide the only small measure of complexity, and even they just follow a simple repeating pattern.

It's useful to think of the ordered list within the nav as the primary branch of a tree, where each list item it contains either represents a leaf or a new branch. Leaves are terminal points, as nothing else grows out from them, while branches may continue to sprout new leaves and additional offshoots.

In practical markup terms, a leaf is an entry that contains a link (a) into the content:

```
<ol>
   <li>
      <a href="c01.xhtml">Chapter 1</a>
   </li>
</ol>
```

Every list eventually peters out into leaves; otherwise, it would grow on forever and you'd have developed the first infinite ebook! But if we only had leaves, we wouldn't be able to recreate the actual document hierarchy, because everything would get flattened out like this:

```
<!-- Bad: -->
<ol>
   <li>
      <a href="p01.xhtml">Part 1</a>
   </li>
   <li>
      <a href="c01.xhtml">Chapter 1</a>
   </li>
   ...
   <li>
      <a href="p02.xhtml">Part 2</a>
   </li>
   <li>
      <a href="c08.xhtml">Chapter 8</a>
   </li>
   ...
</ol>
```

Trying to read a table of contents without any indenting is hard enough, but try using an assistive technology to traverse this kind of mash up, especially when you have numerous entries to wade through. Moving one item at a time, with no structural context to what is primary or subsidiary to what, does not facilitate the reading experience. Even if you could use CSS to set an indent visually, it wouldn't improve the situation for users of assistive technologies, as you'll see again for lists in Chapter 9.

Of course, this is branches form, by allowing another ordered list to follow the link. The chapters from the previous example can now be logically grouped under their respective parts, as follows:

```
<ol>
   <li>
      <a href="p01.xhtml">Part 1</a>
      <ol>
```

```
        <li>
            <a href="c01.xhtml">Chapter 1</a>
        </li>
        ...
    </ol>
</li>
<li>
    <a href="p02.xhtml">Part 2</a>
    <ol>
        <li>
            <a href="c08.xhtml">Chapter 8</a>
        </li>
        ...
    </ol>
</li>
</ol>
```

As you might expect, the rules for creating these sublists are the same as the rules for creating the top-most ordered list; each list item is again either a leaf or a branch that follows the same rules.

There's only one more case left to review: headings. Not every branch header links to a location in the document, as you'll see soon with a real table of contents. In this case, you can substitute a span tag for the a:

```
<li>
    <span>Part 1</span>
    <ol>
        <li>
            <a href="c01.xhtml">Chapter 1</a>
        </li>
        <li>
            <a href="c02.xhtml">Chapter 2</a>
        </li>
        ...
    </ol>
</li>
```

Note that you can use a span only when it's followed by an ordered list. This means you can't accommodate one pattern at this time: inactive links. For example, if you wanted to provide a preview of your ebook with a complete table of contents but only a section or two of available content, you wouldn't be able to create a navigation document like this:

```
<!-- Bad: -->
<ol>
    <li>
        <a href="foreword.xhtml">Foreword</a>
    </li>
    <li>
        <a href="c01.xhtml">Chapter 1: The Great Beyond</a>
    </li>
```

```
<li>
    <span>Chapter 2: A Fool's Egress</span>
</li>
...
<li>
    <span>Glossary</span>
</li>
</ol>
```

Hacking at the a elements isn't going to work, either. The href attribute has to contain a URI pointing to the location in the document to load, and the disabled attribute is ignored in the specialized view. JavaScript and DOM events are likewise ignored, as discussed earlier, so using an onclick event to trap reader activation won't work:

```
<li><a href="#c1" id="c1" onclick="return false;">Chapter 1</a></li>
```

If someone were to click on this link, the reading system would load the navigation document as content and scroll the link into view; the JavaScript override would work only in the embedded version.

In either case, the links would be misleading to readers and could cause some frustration, because they might assume the table of contents must be broken. A future revision to the specification may allow a method for including inactive labels, but for now you would have to create a separate embedded table of contents to show the complete structure.

As a final note, there is no flexibility in these patterns. Each entry must include only an a element or a span or an a element followed by an ordered list. Mixing plain text and hyperlinked text, like in the following example, is *not* legal:

```
<ol>
    <li>
        Chapter 1: <a href="c01.xhtml">Story of the Door</a>
    </li>
</ol>
```

Navigation Labels

Although the structure of your navigation document must always follow the same basic pattern, another of the significant improvements that the navigation document brings over the NCX is the allowance for markup inside the link and heading labels. Where the NCX allowed only plain text labels, the a and span elements accept any HTML5 phrasing content (*http://dev.w3.org/html5/spec/single-page.html#phrasing-content*), so you can include such elements as em, strong, sup, sub, and even math and svg:

```
<li><a href="...">Chapter 11: H<sub>2</sub>0, <em>Too</em>?</a></li>
```

Although CSS and JavaScript are generally ignored, this tagging should be rendered as shown in Figure 2-4.

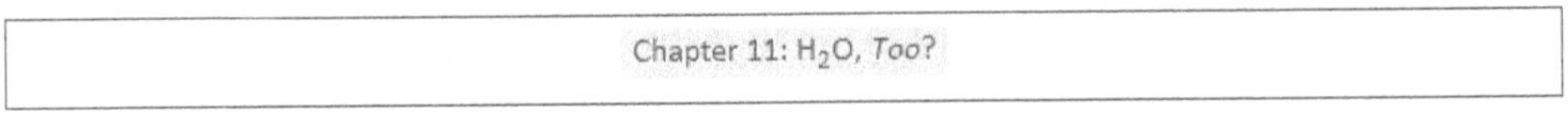

> Chapter 11: H₂O, *Too?*

Figure 2-4. Phrasing elements in table of contents rendering

The ability to embed `ruby` is a notable gain for global language support. For example, this tagging is rendered as shown in Figure 2-5:

```
<li>
   <a href="c01.xhtml">第一巻　<ruby>甦<rp>（</rp><rt>よみがえ</rt><rp>）</rp></
ruby>る</a>
</li>
```

> 第一巻　甦る

Figure 2-5. Ruby elements in table of contents rendering

But with this additional flexibility comes a requirement to ensure you're making accessible content. Since the `a` and `span` labels allow nontext elements, MathML, and Unicode characters that may not pronounce properly when rendered by text-to-speech engines, you need to make sure you don't fall into the trap of assuming that the content will be rendered only visually.

If the content of the label will present a challenge for voice playback, you should include a `title` attribute with an equivalent text rendition to use instead. For example:

```
<li><a href="pi.xhtml" title="The life of pi">The Life of π</a></li>
```

Some assistive technologies might voice the pi character in this example as the letter p (i.e., "The Life of P"), which might make sense in a biology book but would be an awkwardly confusing title to announce in a math book.

Hopefully now, as we turn to the specific types of navigation lists you can create, the process will feel like second nature. Although we've run through the construction requirements, there are still many aspects to review unique to each list type, beginning with the table of contents.

Table of Contents

Every publication is required to include a table of contents. You may come across specification geeks who refer to this a `toc` `nav`, which is a combination of the `epub:type` attribute value and the `nav` element that contains the list (each list has one of these abbreviated names), which is the term we'll use here when talking about the markup.

The key point to note with the toc nav is that it should include links to *every* section of the document, regardless of whether you want all the links visually rendered either in the specialized table of contents or as embedded content. The table of contents is a navigation aid to the entire publication for all readers, not just sighted ones.

If you remove heading levels from it, you end up forcing readers using assistive technologies to move through the document manually to find the subsection they're looking for—a, tedious, time-consuming, and completely unnecessary process. You can visually unclutter the rendering of the table of contents without taking the entries away from readers using assistive technologies.

To see the patterns in action, let's start by looking at a real table of contents: section four of Charles Madison Curry's *Children's Literature*, which exhibits a bit of everything, as shown in Figure 2-6.

THE CONTENTS

SECTION IV

FAIRY STORIES—MODERN FANTASTIC TALES

Bibliography
Introductory
ABRAM S. ISAACS
  190. A Four-Leaved Clover
    I. The Rabbi and the Diadem
    II. Friendship
    III. True Charity
    IV. An Eastern Garden
SAMUEL TAYLOR COLERIDGE
  191. The Lord Helpeth Man and
    Beast
HANS CHRISTIAN ANDERSEN
  192. The Real Princess
  193. The Emperor's New Clothes
  194. The Nightingale
  195. The Fir Tree

  196. The Tinder Box
  197. The Hardy Tin Soldier
  198. The Ugly Duckling
FRANCES BROWNE
  199. The Story of Fairyfoot
OSCAR WILDE
  200. The Happy Prince
RAYMOND MACDONALD ALDEN
  201. The Knights of the Silver
    Shield
JEAN INGELOW
  202. The Prince's Dream
FRANK R. STOCKTON
  203. Old Pipes and the Dryad
JOHN RUSKIN
  204. The King of the Golden River

Figure 2-6. Section Four of the table of contents from Children's Literature by Charles Madison Curry

 The finished EPUB source, including content, is available from the EPUB 3 Sample Documents Project (*http://code.google.com/p/epub-samples/downloads/list*). The source can be found at Project Gutenberg.

First, indicate to the reading system that the nav element contains a table of contents by adding an epub:type attribute with the value toc, and also include the human-readable heading:

```
<nav epub:type="toc">
   <h1>The Contents<h1>
   ...
</nav>
```

Section four conveniently exhibits each of the link types previously discussed. The entry for the section contains the linked heading followed by an ordered list containing all the subsections (a branch). The first two entries for the bibliography and introductory prose are simple links, as is each short story link (leaves).

And although it's not apparent from the table of contents, the author headings exist only in the table of contents; the body moves directly from short story to short story with the author name only appearing in a byline. These entries will also be marked up as branches, but using span tags for the author names.

Putting all the pieces together results in the following markup:

```
<nav epub:type="toc">
   <h1>The Contents</h1>
   <ol>
      <li>
         <a href="s04.xhtml">SECTION IV
            FAIRY STORIES—MODERN FANTASTIC TALES</a>
         <ol>
            <li>
               <a href="s04.xhtml#s4-biblio">
                  Bibliography
               </a>
            </li>
            <li>
               <a href="s04.xhtml#s4-intro">
                  Introductory
               </a>
            </li>
            <li>
               <span>Abram S. Isaacs</span>
               <ol>
                  <li>
                     <a href="s04.xhtml#s190">
                        190. A Four-Leaved Clover
                     </a>
                     <ol>
                        <li>
                           <a href="s04.xhtml#s190-1">
                              I. The Rabbi and the Diadem
                           </a>
                        </li>
```

```
                <li>
                    <a href="s04.xhtml#s190-2">
                        II. Friendship
                    </a>
                </li>
                ...
            </ol>
        </li>
    </ol>
    ...
        </li>
    </ol>
    </li>
    </ol>
</nav>
```

For brevity, the repetitive parts have been removed, because you've already seen how these lists follow an unchanging pattern. The result in Readium's specialized view is shown in Figure 2-7.

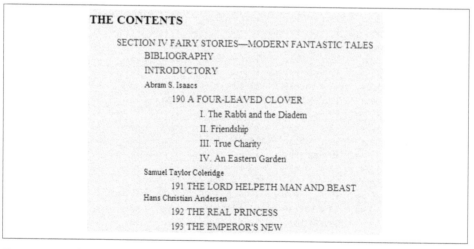

THE CONTENTS

SECTION IV FAIRY STORIES—MODERN FANTASTIC TALES
BIBLIOGRAPHY
INTRODUCTORY
Abram S. Isaacs
190 A FOUR-LEAVED CLOVER
I. The Rabbi and the Diadem
II. Friendship
III. True Charity
IV. An Eastern Garden
Samuel Taylor Coleridge
191 THE LORD HELPETH MAN AND BEAST
Hans Christian Andersen
192 THE REAL PRINCESS
193 THE EMPEROR'S NEW

Figure 2-7. Indented document hierarchy

Note that Readium was still in development at the time of this writing, so appearances should change and improve over time. Regardless, the headings can be distinguished from the links, although they've come out in a smaller font.

To make things look prettier, the previous image is doctored to give the illusion of expanding space to fit the table of contents entries, which is not the reality you'll find out in the wild.

More typically, each reading system has allotted a set amount of space for its specialized view, whether fixed or relative to the viewing area. The result, shown in Figure 2-8, is that line wrapping will become a factor the less real estate there is in the viewport, such as on tables, smartphones, and the like.

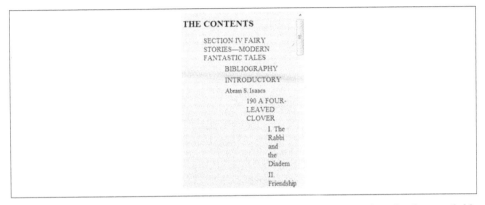

Figure 2-8. Table of contents display with entries forced downward to fit the available space

This is the point where aesthetics would often win out in the old NCX format and the last level that only handles the divisions within the short story would be dropped, since it carries the least structurally important information. But you'd have also just sacrificed completeness for visual clarity, an accessibility no-no. It might not seem like a big issue here, but consider the many levels of depth typical textbooks contain (numbered and unnumbered) and how difficult it makes navigating when the structure outline is gone.

Hiding Content

At this point, the HTML5 hidden attribute arrives to save the day. This attribute is the promised solution to indicate where visual display should end without the requirement to remove entries. Since we've decided we only want to visually render down to the level of the tales each author wrote, we can attach the attribute to the ordered list containing the part links. Removing a couple of levels for readability, our previous example would now be tagged as follows:

```
<li>
    <a href="s04.xhtml#s190">190. A Four-Leaved Clover</a>
    <ol hidden="hidden">
       <li>
          <a href="s04.xhtml#s190-1">I. The Rabbi and the Diadem</a>
       </li>
       <li>
          <a href="s04.xhtml#s190-2">II. Friendship</a>
```

```
        </li>
          ...
      </ol>
    </li>
```

By adding the `hidden` attribute to the ordered list on the third line of the example, all a sighted reader will see is the linkable name of the tale. Someone using an assistive technology will still be able to descend to the part level to move around, however. Opening the table of contents again in Readium we see that the headings have now been removed from visual rendering, as shown in Figure 2-9.

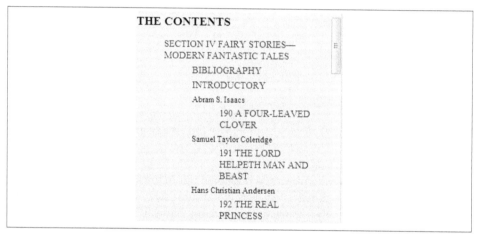

Figure 2-9. Table of contents with only three visible heading levels

As you can see, the links are still wrapped, because the text length exceeds the visible space, but removing the fourth heading level provides a higher degree of visual clarity.

 This use of the `hidden` attribute is unique to the navigation document specialized rendering and is a deviation from HTML5. You must *not* use the attribute to hide content in XHTML content documents on the assumption that it will be made available to assistive technologies.

Another advantage of this attribute is that it allows you to selectively decide how to hide rendering. For example, if your leveling changes from section to section, you aren't locked into a single "nothing below level 3" approach to tailoring your content. Only the ordered lists you attach the attribute to are hidden from view.

The hidden branches could also be removed dynamically when the document is embedded as content, so you aren't confined to what works for the specialized view. You could add a recursive JavaScript function like the following to run through all the list items in the toc nav and remove any hidden attributes when the document is rendered as content:

```
var navs = document.getElementsByTagName('nav');

for (var i = 0; i < navs.length; i++) {
    // find the toc nav by the epub:type attribute on it
    if (navs[i].getAttributeNS('http://www.idpf.org/2007/ops','type')=='toc') {
      removeHiddenAttributes(navs[i]);
      break;
    }
}

function removeHiddenAttributes(tocList) {
    var liNodes = tocList.getElementsByTagName('li');
    for (var i = 0; i < liNodes.length; i++) {
        for (var j = 0; j < liNodes[i].childNodes.length; j++) {
            // check if the entry contains an ordered list
            if (liNodes[i].childNodes[j].nodeName == 'ol') {
                // remove hidden attribute from it
                liNodes[i].childNodes[j].removeAttribute('hidden');
                // call the function again to also check this list's items
                removeHiddenAttributes(liNodes[i].childNodes[j]);
            }
        }
    }
}
```

An observant JavaScript developer will probably realize this could be shortened to using the getElementsByTagName function to grab all the ol elements in the document, but this more verbose version gives some ideas on how to selectively operate on the nav lists.

Unfortunately, there is a downside to the use of the hidden attribute, and that's that content can't be hidden based on screen size, at least in the specialized view. Once you pick heading levels to remove, you have to live with that decision on all devices.

So far, we have very plain, but effective, table of contents markup that can be used by any reading system to create a specialized view. Of course, it's not going to look very pretty if it's embedded as content, but let's continue on to take a look at the other lists before moving into styling.

Landmarks

Just as the name suggests, the *landmarks navigation list* (landmarks nav) provides links to key sections of interest in your publication. While visiting New York City, you can't immediately jump from the Statue of Liberty to the Empire State Building to the

Manhattan Bridge in the physics-bound world of reality, but there's nothing stopping you from taking a quick virtual tour of an ebook about the city, from the table of contents to the first chapter to the index. Except the absence of a landmarks list, that is. (Granted, quick access to an ebook's index isn't quite as awe-inspiring as the view from the 82nd floor observatory.)

This list actually serves two purposes, beyond the rendering dichotomy for the navigation document. The first, obviously, is to provide the reader with a list of points they can quickly reach without having to traverse the full table of contents (and that may not be clearly recognizable in it, such as the first page of the body), but the list also facilitates reading system behaviors.

If the reading system includes a dedicated link to open an index, for example, it would use the landmarks navigation list to look up whether the book includes one and identify what document to load when the reader activates the link.

Without the information in the landmarks nav, the reading system wouldn't be able to provide this kind of built-in functionality, because discoverability is key when it comes to data (i.e., the link would not be made available to the reader, or would appear disabled, because as far as the reading system would be able to tell, you didn't include one). These kinds of connections between the markup and the functionality it enables aren't always readily apparent but are another reason to strive to create the richest data you can. You never know when someone will take advantage of it.

The landmarks nav starts off just like any other list, with the landmarks value in the epub:type attribute identifying the purpose:

```
<nav epub:type="landmarks">
   <h1>Guide</h1>
   ...
</nav>
```

This example could have used the title Landmarks, but Guide is equally appropriate and sets up a little aside. If you recall the guide element from the EPUB 2 package file, you're probably already thinking that the landmarks nav sounds like a direct replacement for it, and you're right. The guide element is now deprecated and won't be used by EPUB 3 reading systems, but it can still be included in the package for compatibility purposes to provide lookups in EPUB 2 reading systems.

 If you're not familiar with guide, the concept is the same, but the markup is different. You can find more information, including sample markup, in Section 2.6 (*http://bit.ly/105zhiF*) of the OPF 2.0.1 specification.

The landmarks nav improves on the guide element by providing the ability to use rich markup instead of plain-text labels and also standardizes the semantic inflection mechanism, which is how reading systems determine which entry contains what information. If a reading system had to work by labels alone, developers would have to account for changes not only in name but also in language. Adding semantics to each entry in the landmarks is consequently a requirement, one that the other two list types don't have:

```
<nav epub:type="landmarks">
   <h1>Guide</h1>
   <ol>
      <li>
         <a epub:type="cover" href="cover.xhtml">
            Cover
         </a>
      </li>
      <li>
         <a epub:type="toc" href="#toc">
            Table of Contents
         </a>
      </li>
      <li>
         <a epub:type="bodymatter" href="chapter001.xhtml#bodymatter">
            Begin Reading
         </a>
      </li>
      <li>
         <a epub:type="index" href="index.xhtml#idx">
            Index
         </a>
      </li>
   </ol>
</nav>
```

You can see that each a element in this example has an epub:type attribute attached to it carrying a property that has the equivalent meaning of the text label. These properties are all taken from the EPUB 3 Structural Semantics vocabulary, which also defines the following properties for other common landmarks:

lot
   A list of tables

loi
   A list of figures

preface
   A preface

bibliography
   A bibliography

```
glossary
```
The primary glossary

But you're free to add links to any major points of interest in your publication, as long as a semantic label exists.

In almost all cases, the `landmarks nav` will be a simple one-dimensional listing of points of interest, but if a section contained multiple subsections that were imperative to include, you could construct a sublist under any of the links. Just be wary of conflating the landmarks into a table of contents. It's designed to provide quick access.

And, conversely, don't concern yourself over an apparent lack of landmarks in the list. Many publications, such as novels, will have only a single landmark or two—to show the cover and jump to the start of the body to begin reading, for example. If you take the stance that adding a `landmarks nav` isn't worth the bother because you only have one link to the body, consider that reading systems that do provide the reader the option won't be able to do so.

A final interesting feature on display here is that the a elements can directly reference the lists in the navigation document. If you look at the link to the table of contents, you'll see the fragment identifier `#toc` in the `href` attribute. In XHTML rendering, this would scroll the document up to the start of that list, but when activated in a specialized view a reading system will first load the navigation document in the content frame and then jump it to the correct spot.

But if it makes life simpler, and because it's more intuitive, you can qualify the fragment identifier with the navigation document filename (e.g., `nav.xhtml#toc`).

Page List

The last of the predefined lists to review is the *page list* (`page-list nav`), and it's also the simplest. The question that invariably rises with the page list is why you'd keep such an conspicuous artifact of the print world. But despite the trends, we're still living in a print-driven world, and production processes that see books laid out for print and then exported to EPUB format are still common. Including the print page markers in the export is a useful aid, but on its own it doesn't facilitate navigation by readers working in mixed print/digital environments, like schools. To enable navigation to print page locations, a `page-list nav` also needs to be included.

Similar to the `landmarks nav`, reading systems that provide page navigation will use this list to look up the requested page location. The alternative would be content scanning to find the page breaks, which is why those markers on their own are ineffective for jumping around.

The reading system may present the entire page list in the specialized view, but leaving the reader to scroll through hundreds of hyperlinked numbers is not the most effective navigation aid. If a reading system provides page jump functionality, it's more likely, and useful, to provide a means of inputting the page number to jump to.

Readium, for example, has a sophisticated little drop-down box that allows you to scroll the page numbers and also narrows down the list of available pages as you type, as shown in Figure 2-10.

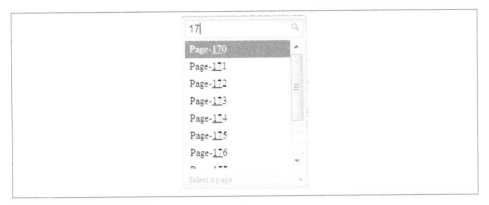

Figure 2-10. Drop-down page list selection box

There's nothing exciting or special about the markup for this particular list to go into; it really is just one long list of page numbers. You've seen enough of these lists now that the following markup should speak for itself:

```
<nav epub:type="page-list">
   <h1>Pages</h1>
   <ol>
      <li><a href="preface.xhtml#pagei">i</a></li>
      <li><a href="preface.xhtml#pageii">ii</a></li>
      ...
      <li><a href="s04.xhtml#page176">176</a></li>
      <li><a href="s04.xhtml#page177">177</a></li>
      ...
   </ol>
</nav>
```

See "Page Numbering" (page 256) in Chapter 9 for more information about including print page markers. You're also required to tie the pagination to the print source.

Extensibility

Although the EPUB specification defines only the preceding three navigation list types, it also makes the navigation document extensible so that new types can be created as needed, which is one of the document's really powerful features. The NCX was also extensible, to a degree, but it allowed only unstructured lists that had weak semantics for identifying their purpose, often relying on a text title. New nav elements can now be added that can be as structured as a table of contents or as unstructured as the page list.

The use of epub:type to define semantics is the real step up, though. A reading system might, for example, support a list of illustrations using the loi property defined in the Structural Semantics Vocabulary as follows:

```
<nav epub:type="loi">
    <h1>List of Figures</h1>
    <ol>
        <li><a href="c01.xhtml#fig001">Figure 1-1: Lanthanides</a></li>
        <li><a href="c01.xhtml#fig002">Figure 1-2: Actinides</a></li>
        ...
    </ol>
</nav>
```

The same could be done for lists of tables (and hopefully semantics for lists of audio and video clips will be included in a future update of the semantic vocabulary). You're free to create any new navigation list types you want, with the only limitation being that reading systems might not recognize or render them. If you embed your navigation document in the content body, the list will always be available to readers that way, regardless of whether the reading system renders it or not. And if you're going to create a navigation list for the body, you might as well define it in the navigation document on the chance that it will be supported in some fashion either now or in the future.

Also, don't limit yourself to resource thinking. The navigation document allows any useful navigation lists you can devise. Maybe you want to give readers a quick reference to major scenes in your story, for example. There are innumerable ways you could expand on this functionality.

The last topics left to tackle are adding the navigation document to an EPUB and then embedding it as content.

Adding the Navigation Document

Adding the document to the publication is a rote task. You simply have to add an entry for it in the package document manifest:

```
<manifest>
    ...
    <item id="navdoc"
          href="nav.xhtml"
          media-type="application/xhtml+xml"
          properties="nav"/>
    ...
</manifest>
```

The specification does not require you to give your navigation document any particular name, because the reading systems don't discover its purpose through the name. The nav value in the `properties` attribute carries the needed semantic for reading system discovery. And only one entry in the `manifest` can specify the nav property. It's not possible to split the individual lists into separate files.

The `properties` attribute for the navigation document is just like any other content document; it can include additional properties like `script`, `mathml` or `svg`, depending on what markup and functionality you've included in the content.

Embedding as Content

Including the navigation document in the manifest only ensures that your EPUB validates and that reading systems can find it. To include it as content, you still need to add entry in the `spine`. You could add the navigation document after the cover as follows:

```
<spine>
    <itemref idref="cover"/>
    <itemref idref="navdoc/>
    ...
</spine>
```

If you were to now open the rudimentary navigation document built in the previous section, you'd see it rendered in the content pane as shown in Figure 2-11.

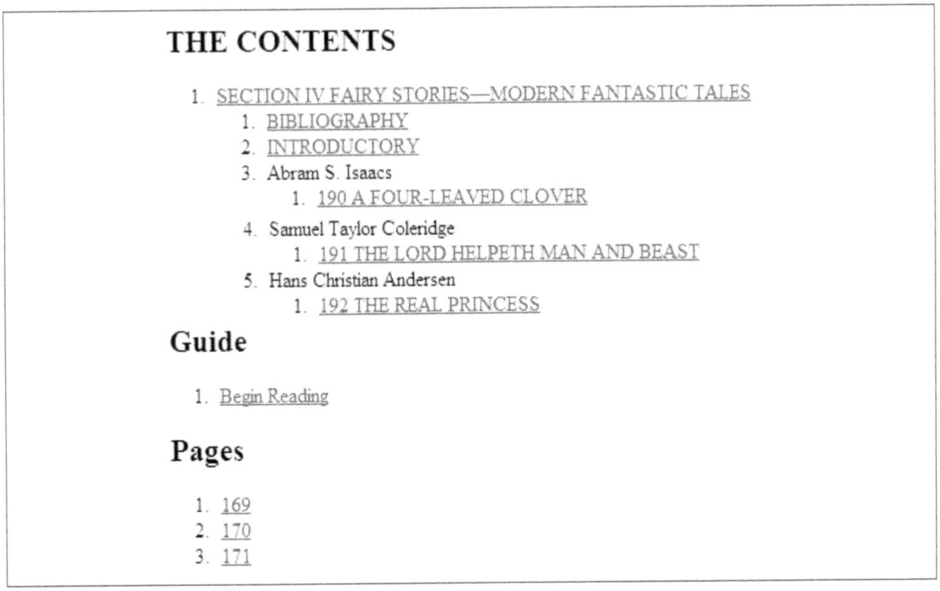

THE CONTENTS

1. SECTION IV FAIRY STORIES—MODERN FANTASTIC TALES
   1. BIBLIOGRAPHY
   2. INTRODUCTORY
   3. Abram S. Isaacs
      1. 190 A FOUR-LEAVED CLOVER
   4. Samuel Taylor Coleridge
      1. 191 THE LORD HELPETH MAN AND BEAST
   5. Hans Christian Andersen
      1. 192 THE REAL PRINCESS

Guide

1. Begin Reading

Pages

1. 169
2. 170
3. 171

Figure 2-11. Embedded navigation document sections rendered as plain HTML

You definitely wouldn't want to unleash this content on your reading public. Aside from the plain old HTML styling, each list item is prefixed by a number and both the landmarks and page list are being rendered. The first step to improve this is to remove these unwanted lists.

Hiding Lists

You've already seen how to hide individual branches of the table of contents, but when embedding the navigation document as content, you'd likely also want to hide the landmarks and page list from view. Although useful for specialized navigation, no reader is going to want to be presented with a list of hundreds of linkable page numbers. The EPUB specification defines a convenient way to accomplish this using the `hidden` attribute:

```
<nav epub:type="landmarks" hidden="hidden">
```

When it comes to specialized renderings, the attribute has no meaning outside of hiding branches in the `toc nav`. Adding it to the `nav` element does not remove the navigation list from use by the reading system, in other words, but *will* hide the list when the navigation document is embedded as content and the attribute is used in its natural XHTML context.

Checking the ebook again, the unwanted lists are now gone, as expected, as shown in Figure 2-12.

THE CONTENTS

1. SECTION IV FAIRY STORIES—MODERN FANTASTIC TALES
    1. BIBLIOGRAPHY
    2. INTRODUCTORY
    3. Abram S. Isaacs
        1. 190 A FOUR-LEAVED CLOVER
    4. Samuel Taylor Coleridge
        1. 191 THE LORD HELPETH MAN AND BEAST
    5. Hans Christian Andersen
        1. 192 THE REAL PRINCESS

Figure 2-12. Embedded navigation document with only the table of contents rendered

The great thing about this approach to hiding is that it doesn't rely on CSS, so there's no issue of the lists appearing if the reader doesn't have a CSS-aware reading system, or disables or modifies the default styling (e.g., for accessibility purposes).

If, however, you're also targeting readers using EPUB 2 reading systems, you'll need a fallback CSS solution, because the `hidden` attribute won't be recognized. Now that EPUB 3 supports CSS namespaces, the following rules might seem to fit the case:

```
@namespace epub "http://www.idpf.org/2007/ops";

nav[epub|type~='landmarks'], nav[epub|type~='page-list'] {
    display: none;
    visibility: hidden;
}
```

But EPUB 2 reading systems typically lack support for the new CSS3 modules. The only good option in this case is to escape the colons in the attribute name:

```
nav[epub\:type~='landmarks'], nav[epub\:type~='page-list'] {
    display: none;
    visibility: hidden;
}
```

EPUB 2 reading systems should now hide the unwanted lists, as well, although there's nothing you can do for ones that lack CSS support. This is one of the inevitable sticking points when you try to coerce content to work in older systems.

Styling Lists

Now that we've started drifting into CSS territory, it's time to take a quick look at some styling considerations when embedding the navigation document as content. The CSS specifications of setting fonts, link styles, colors, and so on are beyond the scope of this section, but there are two practices worth noting.

The first is to remember to remove list numbering when embedding the document as content. Reading systems are required to remove numbers when rendering the lists in their specialized view (even when rendering the document as XHTML). When the document is embedded as content, it is treated just like any other content document in the spine, which means the ordered lists will be prefixed without some CSS intervention.

The other is to consider changing the viewable levels of links based on the available screen space, either by reducing the indentation or hiding branches. You've seen how to use JavaScript to remove the hidden attributes to show all the branches in the embedded view, which then frees you up to use CSS media queries to tailor the view based on the screen size. Essentially, you're re-hiding the content again, but now in a more flexible manner for the content view.

Although trying to target specific devices is unreliable, responsive designs should account for the size of the content and the available viewing area. With list indenting, you don't want ugly links running down the side of the screen, because they get pressed into a shrinking display area, as in the specialized view. If your table of contents ran six levels deep on a mobile screen with a maximum width of 480px, you'd probably want to use CSS to hide all but the first couple of levels:

```
@media only screen and (max-device-width:480px) {
    nav[epub|type~='toc'] > ol > li > ol > li ol {
```

```
        display: none;
        visibility: hidden;
    }
}
```

Set up a few more display rules like this to progressively show more of the table of contents as more space is available and you'll give readers on different devices a much better experience. Someone with a large screen will see the full table of contents and someone with a small screen a reduced one. Shrinking the indentation is an equally good option, but compress too much and it can become hard to discern the document hierarchy.

The only thing to be mindful of is that your table of contents still makes sense if you hide entries. If you applied the above CSS rule to the earlier table of contents, the un-linked author headings would be visible but all of the links to the short stories would be hidden! As this is only the embedded version, it won't be the end of the world, but it will seem odd to someone reading your ebook. (This visual trickery won't impact on the overall accessibility, because readers will still have the full structure available in the specialized view.)

The NCX

This chapter will wind down with a final quick stroll down memory lane to take a very brief look at the NCX. As mentioned at the outset, it's no longer a part of EPUB 3, but if your goal is to facilitate the rendering of EPUB 3 content in EPUB 2 reading systems, you'll want to include one in your publication.

Although HTML rendering rules reasonably ensure that your content will render on an old EPUB 2 reading system (at least what is recognized as XHTML 1.1), there's no guarantee what an EPUB 2 reading system will do when encountering a publication without an NCX. It could open the publication and provide no table of contents, as Adobe Digital Editions does, or it could throw an error and not render the publication at all. The only way to know is to try them all.

For this reason, the EPUB 3 working group chose to perpetuate the mechanism for including the NCX. There is no change to the way that you declare the NCX in the package document manifest, nor in the way it gets identified on the spine:

```
<manifest>
    ...
    <item id="ncx" href="toc.ncx" media-type="application/x-dtbncx+xml"/>
    ...
</manifest>

<spine toc="ncx">
    ...
</spine>
```

Building an NCX is beyond the scope of this book, but if you're interested in learning more, see section 2.4.1 in the Open Packaging Format 2.0.1 specification (*http://idpf.org/epub/20/spec/OPF_2.0.1_draft.htm#Section2.4.1*). XSLT style sheets that can transform an EPUB navigation document back to an NCX are freely available with a little searching of the Web.

But, again, don't worry too much about the NCX. It's good if you can include one if you're planning to be out on the bleeding edge of EPUB 3 adoption, but it's not a content imperative. Most readers are sensible enough to know that content designed for a new platform isn't necessarily going to work on an older one.

CHAPTER 3

Content Documents

The most recognizable part of an EPUB to readers is the content itself, so it's not surprising that many of the integral components that make up an EPUB are often overlooked and the conclusion drawn that the format is simply what gets rendered. EPUB is not just a website in a box, though, as you've seen in the last couple chapters. Content is one piece of a much larger puzzle.

The journey through EPUB content is actually going to be spread out across a number of chapters. This one aims to provide a general overview of content documents, covering the major features and additions in EPUB 3, as well as the CSS profile.

The following chapters will then build on this foundation by looking in more detail at how to embed fonts, use the new `audio` and `video` multimedia elements, create media overlays for synchronizing audio with text, add scripted interactivity, include global language support, and finally wrap up content by covering accessibility concerns, which is where many of the best practices for marking up your content will be laid out. In other words, by the time you've worked your way through the heart of this book, you should be well versed in the features and functionality at your disposal.

Terminology Refresher

Before plunging too far into content, a good grounding in the language of EPUB resources will be helpful to the coming discussions. EPUB has a rich lexicon when it comes to content, and each term has a specific meaning. When reading over the specification, it sometimes seems to have an unlimited number of these definitions: publication resources, core media type resources, foreign resources, EPUB content documents, XHTML content documents, SVG content documents, scripted content documents, and top-level content documents.

There is a method to the seeming madness, though. A *publication resource*, for example, is any resource that contributes to the rendering of an EPUB, whether a content document, a style sheet, audio and video clips, fonts, etc. Publication resources are divided into two types: core media type resources and foreign resources. A *core media type* is one that is required to be supported by EPUB 3 reading systems, and a *foreign resource* is one that is not. MP3 and AAC-LC (MP4) audio files are core media types, for example, because a compliant reading system must be able to play them back for you. Ogg Vorbis and Speex audio files are foreign resources, because the same is not true of them.

There's nothing stopping you from including Ogg Vorbis audio files in your EPUB, but because support cannot be guaranteed, foreign resources require a core media type fallback to be included as well (e.g., an equivalent MP3-encoded file). That's the key to EPUB that you'll continue to see throughout this book: there always must be a way to render the content according to the conventions.

The EPUB specification also distinguishes between publication resources and content documents. *Content documents* are unique in EPUB, because they are the only core media type resources allowed to be referenced in the spine without needing a fallback. All reading systems must support two types of content document, XHTML and SVG, which will be discussed later in this chapter.

But to repeat the pattern of publication resources, you are *not* required to use only XHTML and SVG content documents in the spine; they're just the only ones that are guaranteed to render. You could include a DocBook file, a DTBook file, a PDF, or any other document format, but you'd also have to include a fallback XHTML or SVG equivalent. You can even reference other core media types from the spine, like JPEG or PNG images, but you still need an XHTML or SVG fallback for them. You'll learn how to create fallbacks later in "Fallback Content" (page 102).

And finally, the specification subcategorizes certain important types of content documents. A *scripted content document*, as its name suggests, is any SVG or XHTML content document that contains JavaScript (whether directly or embedded via an `iframe`). A scripted content document also includes HTML5 form elements, but this use sometimes causes confusion, because form elements can appear in a document without any scripting in it (e.g., the `details` element). The use of a single identifier simplifies the metadata process, as the goal is to identify a document with potentially unsupported interactive features.

The other subcategory is *top-level documents*, which are referenced in the spine, as opposed to being included in another document via an `iframe` element, for example. Later in the book, when we get to scripting in Chapter 7, you'll see why this designation exists, because it's tied to what you are allowed and not allowed to do with script.

XHTML

Easily the biggest change in EPUB 3 is the addition of XHTML5, but its inclusion over-shadows the fact that it is now the sole text markup grammar natively supported (gone is DTBook as an option). DTBook's removal should not be missed, though, because the additional markup richness that it supported for accessible ebooks is now accommo-dated without the need for a separate grammar. If you take full advantage of the new elements added to HTML5, and combine them with the new accessibility and semantic markup features (like the epub:type attribute, shown in "epub:type and Structural Se-mantics" (page 68)), you can make publications even richer and more accessible than you could using DTBook in EPUB 2.

The branching of HTML that resulted in HTML4 and XHTML 1.1 coexisting as separate specifications has also been undone in HTML5, with a single specification now defining both the XML and non-XML versions. EPUB 3 adopts the elements and attributes de-fined in this specification, but it retains the XML tagging conventions (called the XML serialization of HTML5, or XHTML5 for short). In other words, don't go looking for a separate document that defines XHTML5, because the definitions all come from the same specification. What you can use in HTML5 you can use in XHTML5, but we'll cover a few restrictions to what EPUB supports as we go.

What this means to you as a content creator is that all the old familiar XML requirements remain in place, even if they aren't all spelled out in the HTML5 element and attribute definitions:

- There are no optional end tags; every element must have an opening and closing tag (e.g., it is common in HTML to omit closing `</p>` tags, but this practice is not allowed in XHTML).
- Empty tags such as `<br>` in HTML must be self-closing (include a trailing slash before the closing bracket) in XHTML: `<br/>`
- Element and attribute names are case-sensitive and always lowercase.
- Namespaces must be declared (e.g., for embedded MathML, SVG, EPUB elements and attributes, etc.).
- Ampersands (&) must be escaped as `&amp;`.

But unlike XML, you aren't bound to the old id attribute naming convention anymore. In XHTML 1.1, your IDs had to begin with a letter. But short of not using spaces, any-thing goes in HTML5 IDs (except each one still has to be unique). That said, for com-patibility with EPUB 2 reading systems, the best practice is to keep using the XML naming convention.

And always remember, if your content does not adhere to the XML rules, your readers are likely to see either an ugly parsing-error message displayed when they load the document or nothing at all (i.e., a blank page). As long as you run the epubcheck validator on your content (covered in Chapter 11), none of these problems will slip through and ruin your readers' days.

Why XML?

Although the migration to HTML5 presented an opportunity to move the content markup grammar away from XML, there were a number of reasons the working group didn't make that change.

First, the working group wanted to keep EPUB 3 content compatible with EPUB 2 reading systems. If they had opted to change to HTML, EPUB 2 reading systems would have rejected the markup as malformed and/or rendered incorrectly features in EPUB 3 that are compatible with EPUB 2 (e.g., the switch element).

But perhaps more importantly, even if the namespaced-extensions developed for EPUB 3 had been implemented using native HTML5 mechanisms, the need to accommodate different content serializations between EPUB 2 and 3 would be shifted not just onto reading systems developers but anyone in the entire chain from production to distribution to consumption. EPUB already has an ecosystem developed around XML, and without a compelling reason to change, the cost was seen as too high.

New in HTML5

Key among the additions to HTML5 for document publishing are the new structural elements. Where previous versions only had the generic div element to group content, you can now properly identify the major structural sections of your document using these tags:

section

> The section element is used to group primary sections of your document, such as prologues, forewords, parts, chapters, indexes, and bibliographies. This tag finally gives structure to the sea of loosely grouped content that had been HTML. In the past, the only way to indicate a new section in HTML was through a numbered heading, and even then the abuse of headings for styling instead of structure made them confusing. Content that constituted a section might be wrapped in a div tag, but div tags were largely meaningless and overused containers that could mean just about anything.

> Using the section element, you can explicitly define the hierarchical structure of your document, where each section typically corresponds to an entry you would

place in your table of contents (although in the case of traditional front matter, this correlation to the table of contents can't always be made). Even if you've split your publication up so that each document contains only a single section of content, it is still advisable to wrap it in a `section` tag:

```
<body>
    <section epub:type="chapter">
        ...
    </section>
</body>
```

Being overt in your tagging leaves no ambiguity about why the content exists in your publication. The `epub:type` attribute allows you to be even more specific about the nature of the section, as you'll see in more depth later in the chapter.

article

If you're tagging a magazine, newspaper, journal, or similar article-based publication, the `article` tag is the more semantically correct alternative to a `section`. Both play a similar content structuring role, but `article` is designed for self-contained publications within your publication:

```
<article>
    <h1>A brief history of time</h1>
    <p class="byline">By Prof. Farnsworth</p>
    ...
</article>
```

If the article has a hierarchical structure of its own, you can use `section` tags within the `article` to delineate each part:

```
<article>
    <h1>A brief history of time</h1>
    <section>
        <h2>In the beginning...</h2>
        ...
    </section>
    ...
</article>
```

Articles can also be embedded within a `section`.

aside

The `aside` element is a particularly useful addition, because it provides a meaningful way to differentiate primary content from secondary. If you're tagging all your chapters using `section` tags, you don't also want to tag all your sidebars the same way, as you lose the structure of your document and obscure the narrative from users of assistive technologies:

```
<aside epub:type="sidebar">
  <h1>Roman Empire Timeline</h1>
  ...
</aside>
```

And similar to the `article` element, an `aside` can have a structure all its own:

```
<aside epub:type="sidebar">
  <h1>The Seasons</h1>
  <section>
    <h2>Winter</h2>
    ...
  </section>
  ...
</aside>
```

The `aside` element can also be used for annotations and footnotes:

```
<aside id="c01-en01" epub:type="endnote">
  <p>1. This argument was first presented in ...</p>
</aside>

<aside id="c01-en02" epub:type="endnote">
  <p>2. The Holy Roman Emperor ...</p>
</aside>
```

nav

The nav element isn't quite as sexy as the previous elements, because its primary use is to group lists of navigation links. Its role on the Web is to reduce the clutter of navigation aids that adorn websites, but it also can play a role in publishing in tidying markup. Although the nav element's primary use in EPUB is in the navigation document (as discussed in Chapter 2), it can also be used to embed tables of contents at the beginning of each section:

```
<nav>
  <h2>Quick Guide</h2>
  <ol>
    <li>
      <a href="#intro">Introduction</a>
    </li>
    <li>
      <a href="#pt">Particle Theory</a>
    </li>
    ...
  </ol>
</nav>
```

You can also use it to tag supplementary lists of links within your content:

```
<nav>
  <h2>See Also</h2>
  <ul>
    <li>
```

```
        <a href="http://idpf.org/epub/30/">EPUB 3</a>
      </li>
      ...
    </ul>
  </nav>
```

The structure elements are not the only way that HTML5 improves the ability to distinguish areas of content in your document. You can also use the `header` and `footer` elements to define the corresponding regions within sections. Although typically associated with web page headers and footers, the semantics of prefatory and supplementary material for a page applies equally to documents.

header

Any `section` can have a block of header material. The `header` element is not usually needed when a page contains only a single heading, but it could be used to group prefatory content before the body of the section, such as an epigraph or an author bio:

```
<header>
  <h1>Chapter 1</h1>
  <blockquote>
    <p>&amp; that no man remember me.</p>
    <cite>The Mayor of Casterbridge</cite>
  </blockquote>
</header>
```

footer

Like headers, the `footer` element can group information that is ancillary to the section. You could add all your endnotes to this element, for example:

```
<footer>
  <aside epub:type="rearnote" id="c01-en01">
    <p>1. ...</p>
  </aside>
  <aside epub:type="rearnote" id="c01-en02">
    <p>2. ...</p>
  </aside>
</footer>
```

HTML5 also includes another new element for distinguishing supplementary content, the `figure` element:

```
<figure id="fig01">
  <figcaption>Table 1: Facts and Figures</figcaption>
  <table>
    ...
  </table>
</figure>
```

Chapter 9 covers this element in more detail, but in short, it allows figures, whose placement is not central to the primary narrative, to be included wherever they need to appear in the markup for visual rendering, while still distinguishing that they are not part of the logical reading order. The `figcaption` element is another useful addition that allows the caption to be determined programmatically, regardless of its position in the content (HTML5 requires that it must be either the first or last element in the `figure`).

HTML5 includes a number of other new elements, including these that will be covered in more detail in the coming chapters:

`audio` *and* `video`
> For native support of rich content

`ruby` *and* `rt`
> For over- and under-line annotations

`bdo`
> To override the directionality of text (e.g., embedding right-to-left prose in an left-to-right document)

`wbr`
> To indicate possible word break locations

`mark`
> To distinguish author emphasis and highlighting that has been added to a quote or passage (as opposed to emphasis that was in the original source)

`time`
> To mark dates and times and adding machine-processable equivalents

And a number of new form elements and `input` types have been added to show progress bars and output, create data lists, etc.

HTML5 also more clearly defines the semantics of a number of other elements:

`em`
> For vocal stress

`strong`
> For importance

`i`
> Allows semantics without stress, such as to signify changes in voice or mood

`b`
> Also provides for semantic markup, but without any voice or mood change

`hr`
> Now defined for thematic breaks, not just random separator lines

small

> For small-print statements like copyrights (big has been dropped from the grammar)

Covering every element in the specification is beyond the scope of this book, because there are many more that haven't changed between versions. If you want more information, the W3C maintains an HTML5 change document (*http://www.w3.org/TR/html5-diff/*) that is worth the time to skim through.

But before moving on, some special cases are also worth noting. First, there are a couple of elements that regularly cause confusion:

cite

> For the title of a work mentioned. Although this element is often equated with the citation line that accompanies a quote or epigraph, it is only used to reference the title of works, at least as defined by the specification. If the citation line contains only an author's name, there would be no specific tag for it beyond a paragraph.

address

> Defined as contact information for the nearest article or body element. By this definition, the only realistic use in a book would be to tag the publisher's location.

Whether these element definitions will stand the test of time remains to be seen. To strictly adhere to the specification, this is how they should be used, but misuse of either for their more general meanings is also unlikely to cause any issues in ebooks, or for accessibility.

And second, there are some elements you may want to avoid, or use sparingly:

embed

> For non-HTML applications, like plug-ins, but reading systems are not required to support plug-ins or external applications. The EPUB specification also actively discourages the use of this element because of the lack of fallbacks for accessibility. The object tag should be used instead.

rp

> Because ruby annotations are supported in EPUB 3, the EPUB specification also discourages the use of the rp element for adding fallback parentheses.

hgroup

> Will be split into a separate sub-specification to get HTML5 to recommendation, so should be treated as unstable at least as of this writing.

The W3C has put the HTML5 specification on a fast track to recommendation by 2014, but until it is finalized, there's always going to be some possibility of change, both in terms of additions and deletions. Part of the plan the W3C has established to publish the standard has been to take the most contentious issues and evolve them as separate sub-specifications, as is being done with hgroup. As a result, some feature that appeared to be out of HTML5 could resurface, such as the longdesc attribute, as groups define specification documents for them. The choice could then be made by the EPUB 3 working group in future revisions of the specification whether to support these additions as add-on modules and/or to pursue other options.

EPUB Support Gotchas

In addition to the remaining support issues as HTML5 matures, you also need to be aware that there isn't a single universal concept of what constitutes a reading system. A number of features that can be used in, and with, content documents are optional, meaning that you shouldn't take for granted that everything you can do in EPUB 3 will work in every reading system.

Most notably, support for all of the following is optional:

JavaScript
  A reading system may provide no support, and even if it does, there is no requirement that it provide all the power that scripting can provide. Network connectivity may be restricted, for example.

HTML5 forms elements and/or processing
  Before using buttons, sliders, input fields, or any other form element, you need to consider that there is a possibility that they may not be rendered. Likewise, any forms you embed in your content may not be submittable to remote servers for processing, regardless of whether the form elements are rendered.

HTML Document Object Model (DOM)
  Even if you have scripting support, if no DOM is exposed, you will not be able to dynamically manipulate or access any part of the document. The ability to read your content must not depend on DOM manipulations.

The EPUB CSS profile
  Although reading systems should support the styles in the profile, they might support only some, or none at all. Your content should be designed to degrade gracefully in the absence of styling.

Media Overlays
  More of an issue for the reader, but just because you create an overlay does not mean it will be possible to play it back.

Text-to-speech enhancements
  Again, a reading system may not support some or all of PLS lexicons, SSML attributes, and CSS3 speech properties, with the obvious inconvenience being for the reader.

The scripting abilities you'll find in any given reading system may prove to be the most perplexing from a content creation perspective, certainly when trying to achieve consistency of rendering across devices. Using progressive enhancement techniques is strongly recommended to ensure a baseline for rendering, but Chapter 7 and Chapter 9 will cover these issues in more detail.

Also, because HTML5 is liberal in terms of where and how you can use form elements, it's easy to forget that EPUB 3 reading systems may not support them. The `details` element, for example, is useful for collapsing a description that accompanies an image. But, if you use this method, there is a chance it won't work on those reading systems that choose not to support form elements.

Inevitably, you're going to have to decide if the functionality provided is more important than potential rendering issues on some segment of reading systems. So far, most of these features have been supported, with some bugs and quirks considering the stage of development to this point. Only support for the text-to-speech enhancements hasn't appeared, so there is a small risk to including that functionality.

DTDs Are Dead

In addition to changes to the elements, HTML5 has also made a more fundamental change to the way that HTML documents are recognized and validated in abandoning DTDs for defining the markup structure. The doctype statement, which used to point to the DTD your document conformed to, has been retained for identification purposes, but it has been stripped down to just identifying the root element:

```
<!DOCTYPE html>
```

This doctype is recommended for regular HTML5 pages but is optional in XHTML5. You may still want to include the new doctype, however, because without it there is no way to distinguish individual content files from XHTML 1.1. If you use XML tools to work on your files, for example, they may report erroneous errors without the doctype.

Including a doctype is recommended in the WhatWG HTML/XHTML comparison (*http://wiki.whatwg.org/wiki/HTML_vs._XHTML*) page to avoid quirks mode in browsers, but that's guidance for creating HTML pages that can render optimally as either HTML or XHTML. Unless you're expecting your content to be consumed as HTML (outside of a reading system), it should not be required.

 That is, it *should not* because the EPUB 3 specification requires that compliant reading systems render the content as `application/xhtml +xml`. Developers often disregard specifications, and since there's no harm in including the doctype, it's worth getting in the habit of always inserting it.

The other notable technical change that comes with dropping DTDs is that the HTML named entities are no longer supported. If you're used to adding — to your XHTML content instead of the actual Unicode character or the numeric entity —, you're not going to enjoy the new world order that now requires you to choose one of those two options.

For the data architects out there, before thinking you can revive them as an external library pulled in through the doctype, note that EPUB 3 forbids external identifiers. Short of creating an entity definition for every needed named entity in every file that uses them, resuscitation is a lost cause.

Linking and Referencing

Linking and referencing are easy to mix up, but there is a key distinction to be made in EPUB. *Linking* is the activity of providing the reader with the ability to traverse to some new content, whether a location in the current publication or an address on the Web. Links are created using the HTML a element, with the href attribute pointing to the destination. You're free to link to anything you want. If you link to a content document in the container, the reading system will open it in the application. If you link to external resources, a new browser window will typically be launched.

Referencing is more complex, because it involves bringing the referenced resource into the current document, whether an image to display, an audio clip to listen to, a CSS style sheet to visually render the content, etc. You can reference content from a variety of different tags (audio, video, iframe, link, object, and script), but referenced resources *must* be included in the container. In other words, you cannot pull content into your document that lives on the Web.

The exception is audio and video, but those are covered in detail in Chapter 5.

Linking and referencing in EPUB content documents is done almost exactly as it is on the Web, except you always use relative paths for content in your publication and full paths for resources outside it.

Relative paths are created in relation to where the referencing document is in the container, not to the root of the container. For example, if you had the file *chapter01.xhtml* in the directory *EPUB/xhtml* and your style sheets in the directory *EPUB/css*, all style sheet link elements in the document would reference up one level and then down into the *css* directory:

```
<link rel="stylesheet" type="text/css" href="../css/epub3.css"/>
```

You cannot use absolute path references, such as */EPUB/css/*, because the concept of a web root does not exist in EPUB, so there is no guarantee how they will be resolved. Using a leading slash is not the equivalent of starting at the container root, and doing so will typically result in an invalid reference when running epubcheck.

Also be aware that there is nothing special about the directory where you house your content. Although you will typically store an entire rendition in a single directory, you're free to locate and reference resources outside this default folder. If you have a publication that contains both an SVG and XHTML rendition, for example, instead of picking one or the other directory for housing common resources and then setting up relative linking across renditions, you can create shared folders off the root (for example, a common fonts folder). This scenario is where absolute path references would be really helpful, but you have to use the parent directory operator (..) to step back to the root. Granted, this is a bit of future knowledge, because rendition mapping is still in the early stages of development.

EPUB Canonical Fragment Identifiers

Canonical Fragment Identifiers (*epubcfis* for short) is a new kind of linking in EPUB. You don't have to know how these work in order to link to content in your documents (you'll typically be using URIs), but some understanding of them doesn't hurt, either. Reading systems must support them now, and the more you delve into the guts of EPUBs, the more you're likely to bump into them or hear people talking about them.

One of the prime limitations of EPUBs, as far as referencing them goes, has been the lack of a universal way to locate any arbitrary point within one, especially from outside one (e.g., to link from a web page into a specific point). With URIs, you can specify a resource and also point to an element within it (via its id), but that works only when you're in the EPUB and can find the other resources relative to the current one. If all you have is a zipped-up EPUB, how do you get from the outside in?

If you're a reading system developer trying to implement random reader highlighting of passages, or synchronize audio to random text strings, or show a range in an index that doesn't begin and end nicely with markup, you need more than just simple anchor points to work with.

And this is where epubcfis come in. Reading systems can already find your publication by going through a lookup process that starts in the *container.xml* file, because it's required to be in the *META-INF* directory. Epubcfis use a similar method, but reformulated from a load and lookup process into one that can be represented as a simple string.

The string is *simple* only in the sense that it is text data. Here's what a relatively simple one looks like:

```
mybooks.epub#epubcfi(/6/4[chap01ref]!/4[body01]/10[para05]/2:5)
```

And they only get more complex!

Without trying to fill in all the details, which are technically complex, each / in the epubcfi represents a step on the path to the location you want to reach in *mybooks.epub* and #epubcfi() is the special fragment identifier syntax developed for expressing epubcfis. Even numbers indicate an element and odd numbers are all non-element content that can come before, between, or after any element (text content, whitespace and CDATA blocks).

For example, consider this spine:

```
<spine>
    <itemref idref="c01"/>
    <itemref idref="c02"/>
</spine>
```

Although there is nothing but whitespace between the opening spine tag and the first itemref, this is the first instance of non-element content. In an epubcfi, it's referenced as /1. The itemref tag is the first element, but because it's the second significant point it is /2. Then there's another non-element instance of whitespace (/3), then the second element (/4), and finally an ending non-element (/5) between the end of the second itemref and the closing spine tag.

The following example shows the sequence locations by linearizing the markup:

```
     /1           /2            /3          /4           /5
  <spine>  <itemref idref="c01"/>  <itemref idref="c02"/>  </spine>
```

There are never gaps in the sequencing, even if there is no text or space between the elements (e.g., /1 would still exist as a reference point, even if the markup was <spine><itemref idref="c01"/>). This ensures a consistent odd/even sequencing, regardless of the text and elements used, which ensures you can determine from the path whether an element or text is referenced.

Even as mere humans, we can use this syntax to make out the basic structure of the EPUB to the point referenced by the epubcfi, without ever opening the EPUB. Look again at the earlier example:

```
mybooks.epub#epubcfi(/6/4[chap01ref]!/4/10[para05]/2:5)
```

Starting from the package document, this epubcfi first references the third element in it, which must be the spine (/6). It then indicates to go to the second element within it (/4). The square brackets after it indicate the id of the element (additional verification the reading system can use to ensure the document has not been changed). The exclamation point after the closing square bracket is a special operator that says the current document is done, now open the referenced document and continue from there. In this case, you can guess from the ID that the referenced document is Chapter 1. After opening Chapter 1, you move to the second element in it (/4, which is the body in XHTML documents), go five elements down (/10, which appears to be the fifth paragraph from the ID), find the first child element (/2), and go five characters into it.

An incredibly precise place to go, no doubt, but this is the power of epubcfis. Reading system developers no longer have to work around the limitations of the markup quality, and that opens up many exciting possibilities for the future. Unfortunately, there is no support for this fragment identifier scheme outside of EPUB reading systems, so you can't yet point people into a book hosted on the Web.

You can get much fancier epubcfis than this example, and they aren't just for text content. It's possible to link to a point in a bitmap image and even to find an offset into an audio or video clip. You can indicate text you expect to find before and after the referenced point, to ensure that the link still points to the right place and potentially to allow autocorrection by the reading system if it finds it has shifted.

But sitting and counting elements and text offsets to create these kinds of links manually is not something you're going to want to do on any kind of regular basis. Reading systems are expected to use this functionality for highlighting, bookmarking, and similar tasks, but for the scheme to gain authoring traction, it will take tools that can generate the path from the location you pick.

Epubcfis aren't just for reading systems, either. Using epubcfis to indicate the full range of text that corresponds to an index entry is another possible use that has been discussed. Creating media overlays to the word level without having to tag every word in your file is another.

But again, tools will undoubtedly do the heavy lifting for you, if and when epubcfis do work their way into the mainstream, but for now, your knowledge of linking is now a little more complete.

Content Chunking

Getting back to XHTML data, a common technique used to improve rendering, and force new page breaks before headings, is to break up an EPUB so that each content document contains only a single section. Each new document referenced in the spine forces the content to load in a new page, which has historically been more reliable than relying on support for the CSS `page-break-*` properties. Data chunking also speeds up rendering, because even though devices have become more powerful since EPUB 2 first arrived, it's still the case that the less that must be rendered at a time the faster the document will load.

As support for the CSS pagination properties has not yet appeared in current EPUB 3 reading systems, breaking up content at major structural points remains a best practice. But there's one common problem that gets highlighted with HTML5 `section` tagging: what to do when you have to pull child sections out of a parent. For example, if a part has ten chapters, do you remove all ten and leave the part heading alone in a file, or leave the heading with the first chapter and remove the other nine?

Neither option is particularly great, but to keep the part heading on its own page and to not give the illusion at the markup level that the part is only one chapter long, separating the heading is the best option:

```
<section epub:type="part">
    <h1>Part One</h1>
</section>
```

epub:type and Structural Semantics

You've probably noticed that the epub:type attribute has appeared on numerous examples in this chapter, and hopefully you're already getting a sense for what it does just from seeing its use. There's always a chicken-and-egg problem when deciding whether to talk about markup or semantics first. Now that we have the new HTML5 tagging under our belts, though, it's time to delve a little deeper into how you layer semantics on them.

The addition of the epub:type attribute allows more precise statements to be made about your markup in your markup, a practice commonly referred to as *semantic inflection*. It's like metadata for your tags, as the somewhat limited element set that HTML5 makes available inevitably leads to the same tags being used in your content documents for many different purposes. Is an aside a sidebar, a footnote, a warning, or something else entirely? Does your section contain a prologue, epilogue, index, glossary, part, or chapter? These are the questions you can't answer at the markup level with only the default HTML5 element semantics to go by.

Using semantic inflection, however, you can differentiate what the structural elements in your document represent. To indicate a section is a chapter, for example, you would attach the attribute like this:

```
<section epub:type="chapter">
    <h2>Chapter One</h2>
    ...
</section>
```

We'll look more at why generic tagging is a bad thing later in "Structure and Semantics" (page 233), but you don't have to be solely interested in accessibility in order to find value in this kind of rich data. Rich data allows reading systems to do wild and wonderful things with your data. It makes your content better for archiving and later reuse. And it allows content to be combined and repurposed into new publications. Hopefully, those are enough reasons!

In order to use this attribute, you only need to declare the EPUB prefix (xmlns:epub) on the root HTML element:

```
<html xmlns="http://www.w3.org/1999/xhtml"
      xmlns:epub="http://www.idpf.org/2007/ops" ... >
```

You're now free to add the attribute to any element in the document, provided it adds structural information. The following examples show a few of the more common uses beyond annotating sections.

Footnotes and annotations:

```
<a href="#c01fn01" epub:type="noteref">1</a>
<aside id="c01fn01" epub:type="footnote">
   <p>1. ...</p>
</aside>
```

A glossary:

```
<dl epub:type="glossary">
   <dt><dfn>Brimstone</dfn></dt>
   <dd>Sulphur; See <a href="#def-sulphur">Sulphur</a>.</dd>
</dl>
```

A Table of Contents:

```
<nav epub:type="toc">
   <h2>Table of Contents</h2>
   <ol>
       <li><a href="c01.xhtml#c01">Chapter 1</a></li>
       ...
   </ol>
</nav>
```

If you're wondering why the word *structural* keeps coming up, it's because the epub:type attribute is not intended for semantic *enrichment* of your content. Semantic enrichment is the ability to make statements and connections within your content. In a biography about Henry the VIII, for example, you might tag information such as when he was born and died, how long he reigned, who his various wives were, when they were born and died, etc. It would then be possible for someone to query all this information without having to sift through the book to find it. Very powerful stuff when you think of the possibilities, and it's also the basis of the semantic web.

Creating linked metadata like this was the idea behind RDFa, and later microdata. At the time of the EPUB 3 revision, however, the metadata landscape was considered too unstable to try and pick a method for enriching data over the long term. As the W3C has since endorsed both RDFa and microdata, semantic enrichment should find its way into the specification at the next revision. For now, what you absolutely must not do is abuse the epub:type attribute to create metadata-like tags for your content:

```
<!-- Invalid: -->
<span epub:type="foaf:name">Henry VII</span>
<span epub:type="ex:landmark">The Tower of London</span>
```

There is little practical value to this tagging, because it cannot be linked and gives only a general idea of what the tag contains, at best. And that's overlooking that it's non-conformant and a reading system programmed to make use of known structural information would just ignore it.

One question with semantic inflection, or enrichment, is why do it unless you can prove specific value? But that's a narrow-sighted way of looking at your data. Even if a reading system isn't taking advantage of the semantics now, tagging your documents richly means you won't be left out as new advances are made. If all you add for notes is an a tag linking to an `aside` somewhere, you're ensuring that developers will never be able to do anything with that data. If you mark the link as a `noteref` and the `aside` as a `footnote`, you may get pop-up footnotes instead of plain old text, as Apple was first to take advantage of.

You should still lay out your content as though nothing special will be done with it, though. Plan for the least functionality and anticipate the best.

Adding Semantics

The one key question that hasn't been answered yet is what values can be used with the `epub:type` attribute.

By default, the attribute only accepts properties defined in the EPUB 3 Structural Semantics Vocabulary (*http://idpf.org/epub/vocab/structure/*), as shown in Figure 3-1. This vocabulary not only defines the terms you can use, but also provides hints as to what elements they are appropriate to use on. You wouldn't normally define a `section` to be a sidebar, for example; nor would you define anything but an `a` element to be a note reference.

You are not limited to using only this vocabulary. If you want to use another standardized set of properties, or even if you want to make up your own, the framework on which this attribute is based is flexible. In order to use a value that isn't defined in the Structural Semantics Vocabulary, you prefix it, similar to how you add namespace prefixes to MathML and SVG elements. The process is identical to adding additional prefixes for use in refining package metadata, as discussed in "Using Other Vocabularies" (page 4).

What you don't do is declare a prefix using the XML `xmlns` pseudoattribute, as you do for XML grammars. XML namespace prefixes are for XML elements and attributes only. Instead, you define a prefix in an `epub:prefix` attribute on the root `html` element.

To use terms from the ANSI/NISO Z39.98 Structural Semantics Vocabulary, for example, you could first define the prefix `z3998` like this:

```
<html ...
      xmlns:epub="http://www.idpf.org/2007/ops"
      epub:prefix="z3998: http://www.daisy.org/z3998/2012/vocab/structure/#">
```

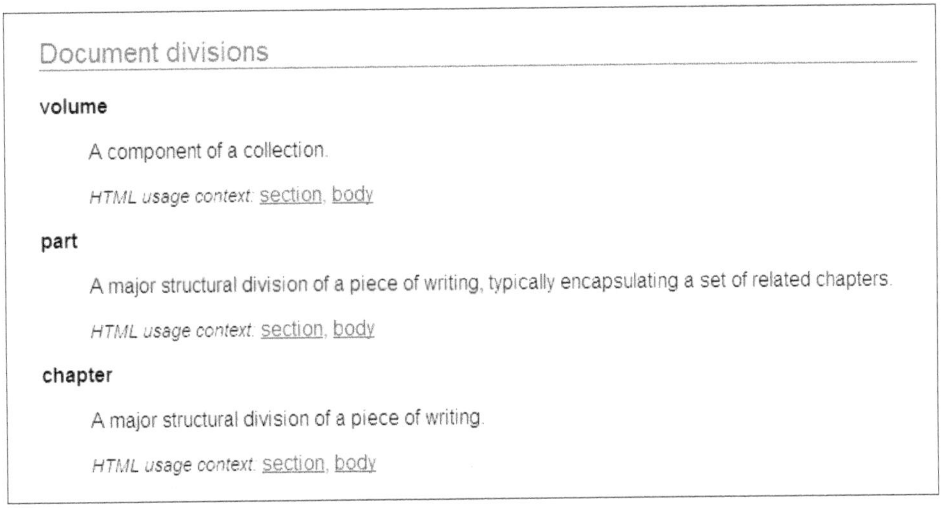

Document divisions

volume

> A component of a collection.
>
> *HTML usage context:* section, body

part

> A major structural division of a piece of writing, typically encapsulating a set of related chapters.
>
> *HTML usage context:* section, body

chapter

> A major structural division of a piece of writing.
>
> *HTML usage context:* section, body

Figure 3-1. Property definitions found in the Structural Semantics Vocabulary

You could now use properties from that vocabulary as follows:

```
<section epub:type="z3998:published-works">
  <h2>Also By The Author</h2>
   ...
<ol>
```

Although helpful in terms of anyone knowing what your semantics mean, the URI you map your prefix to does not have to resolve to a vocabulary document. If you can't find the semantics you need defined in a publicly available vocabulary, you can create your own by defining your own prefix:

```
<html ...
       epub:prefix="mine: http://www.example.org/mystructure/">
```

You're now free to define any property you want, as long as it begins with the prefix mine:. Bear in mind when using any prefixed vocabulary properties, or when creating your own custom ones, reading systems will ignore all semantics they don't understand and don't have built-in processing for. (This includes properties in the Structural Semantics Vocabulary.)

Note also that even if the prefix URI does map to a vocabulary you use for internal production purposes, it doesn't have to be resolvable when you distribute your publication. If you want to keep your vocabulary document private, but don't want to strip all your production semantics or just aren't concerned with them being in the distributed EPUB, it's perfectly fine to leave the prefix definition in. It will be treated just like any other unresolvable reference.

Multiple Semantics

Before moving on, one last note on the `epub:type` attribute. It is not limited to defining a single semantic, but takes a space-separated list of all the applicable semantics.

A `section`, for example, may have more than one semantic associated with it:

```
<section epub:type="toc backmatter">
    ...
</section>
```

The order in which you add semantics to the attribute does not infer importance, or affect accessibility, so the previous example could have just as meaningfully been reversed (`epub:type="backmatter toc"`).

The `frontmatter`, `bodymatter`, and `backmatter` properties are somewhat unique, too, in that they relate a kind of positional structural information. Rather than adding to the top-most structural elements in each document, you could split these designators and add them to the body tag instead:

```
<body epub:type="backmatter">
    <section epub:type="toc">
        ...
    </section>
</body>
```

As long as the semantics are in scope, a reading system can build the general relationship between them. In most cases, it is preferable to add front/body/back matter to the body, because it represents a more general relationship. Although not wrong to add to the `section`, the more precise semantic is that the section represents a table of contents.

MathML

A key new addition to HTML5 is MathML. Where EPUB 2 required you to write basic equations using XHTML, or insert pictures for complex equations, with MathML support you can create accurate, and accessible, math content. Not only does this allow for clearer, scalable equations for everyone, but it also has the potential to greatly improve access to the information by readers using assistive technologies.

EPUB 3 provides support for Presentational MathML (*http://www.w3.org/TR/MathML2/chapter3.html*), which is a way of writing MathML for visual rendering. You can include Content MathML (*http://www.w3.org/TR/MathML3/chapter4.html*), which is a way of encoding the meaning of equations (e.g., for machine use), with your Presentational MathML, but it will typically be ignored by reading systems, because there is no requirement in the specification to do anything with it. (As a result, this book doesn't cover how to add Content MathML.)

Each instance of MathML is contained within math tags and contains a complete presentational rendering:

```
<math xmlns="http://www.w3.org/1998/Math/MathML">
    <mrow>
        <mi>x</mi>
        <mo>=</mo>
        <mfrac>
            <mrow>
                <mn>2</mn>
                <mi>c</mi>
            </mrow>
            <mrow>
                <mo>-</mo>
                <mi>b</mi>
                <mo>±</mo>
                <msqrt>
                    <mrow>
                        <msup>
                            <mi>b</mi>
                            <mn>2</mn>
                        </msup>
                        <mo>-</mo>
                        <mn>4</mn>
                        <mi>a</mi>
                        <mi>c</mi>
                    </mrow>
                </msqrt>
            </mrow>
        </mfrac>
    </mrow>
</math>
```

This equation renders in Readium as shown in Figure 3-2.

$$x = \frac{2c}{-b \mp \sqrt{b^2 - 4ac}}$$

Figure 3-2. MathML rendering of the inverse quadratic equation

When adding MathML, be aware that support is still developing. Gecko-based reading systems should be able to provide some measure of native support for MathML, but it's still a work in progress. Others typically rely on MathJax (*http://www.mathjax.org/*) for rendering (e.g., Readium). This discrepancy may lead to inconsistencies across reading systems, especially as browser cores evolve native support and further muddy the waters.

At least for a while, non-Gecko-based reading systems without scripting may not provide any MathML rendering at all. Including an image fallback using the `altimg` tag is recommended for these systems, because they may still be able to display the image until support develops. "The epub:switch element" (page 107) covers another method EPUB 3 includes to degrade gracefully.

You may have noticed in Figure 3-2 that the square root symbol is poorly formatted where the overline bar begins (the runover lines). This is just one type of inconsistency that can occur depending on the method of rendering you happen to encounter. Figure 3-3 shows what the equivalent equation looks like in Firefox.

$$x = \frac{2c}{-b \mp \sqrt{b^2 - 4ac}}$$

Figure 3-3. Crisper Firefox rendering of the square root symbol with no overlapping lines

Part of the difference is that Readium uses the SVG rendering provided by MathJax, so it is drawing an image of the equation. Picking at minor inconsistencies shouldn't be used to justify including only images instead of MathML. For a small amount of visual inconsistency (and that should improve in time), you are potentially obstructing access to a segment of your readers. Both equations are readable, which is ultimately what you want.

Although styling of math via CSS is possible when done natively in the browser, it's not yet clear which, if any, of the reading systems that depend on MathJax will enable similar functionality. Although MathJax content can be styled through a programmatic interface, the reading system itself calls the MathJax engine, ignoring local attempts to override the styling.

Since styling support appears like it will be inconsistent for a while, one good habit to get into is to set the `display` attribute on the root `math` element when it's used as a block element:

```
<p>As seen in the following equation:</p>

<math display="block">
  ...
</math>
```

The context in which the math gets rendered effects the typography used, and inline rendering is the default when the attribute is not specified.

Fonts also play an important role in the quality of your final form MathML. With the SVG MathJax rendering, you don't currently have an option to change the default font used; it uses its own Tex font. But that doesn't mean you shouldn't consider embedding your own fonts, because native rendering is dependent on what is installed in the underlying operating system. To avoid potential random font selection based on what's available, STIX Fonts Project (*http://www.stixfonts.org*) provides royalty-free fonts that cover the range of math symbols and operators.

Chapter 4 discusses how to embed fonts, so you can jump ahead if you want more information now, but here's a sample of the CSS that you'd add to use a STIX font:

```
@namespace m "http://www.w3.org/1998/Math/MathML";

@font-face {
    font-family: 'Stix';
    font-weight: normal;
    font-style: normal;
    src:url(../fonts/STIXGeneral.otf);
}

m|math {
    font-family: Stix;
}
```

Though it sometimes seems like a nuisance, it is vitally important to always add the MathML namespace to your equations. It doesn't matter if you use the xmlns pseudoattribute to declare the namespace for all math elements like in the example at the start of the section, or whether you declare a prefix and use it on every MathML element:

```
<m:math xmlns:m="http://www.w3.org/1998/Math/MathML">
    <m:mrow>
        ...
    </m:mrow>
</m:math>
```

Omitting the namespace causes two nasty consequences beyond just the epubcheck validator complaining at you. The first is that the document containing the MathML won't load, which is what would happen if you didn't declare the m: prefix in the previous example. The second is that your equation will render as plain text. If the xmlns pseudoattribute were left off from the first example, and we ignored epubcheck's validation complaints about an unknown math element, the equation would render as shown in Figure 3-4.

$$x = 2c - b \mp b2 - 4ac$$

Figure 3-4. Quadratic equation rendered as linear text

Not only is this the wrong equation, but there is nothing (except for, possibly, the context of the nearby prose) to alert the reader that something has gone wrong. The reading system doesn't recognize the math element as part of the XHTML element set without its namespace, so it does what it's designed to do and renders the text content it finds instead, ignoring the tags.

Namespaces also play a role in the styling of your MathML content. To avoid information overload, the earlier fonts example intentionally didn't mention the namespace, but EPUB 3 supports CSS @namespace declarations and you need to use them to properly match namespaced elements. Here's the earlier line again that shows how to define a prefix for MathML elements:

```
@namespace m "http://www.w3.org/1998/Math/MathML";
```

You need to add this declaration only once to the top of your style sheet.

The other oddity to be aware of is that CSS replaces the colon in the prefixed element name with a pipe character (|). Here, then, is how to define a blue border for all the block m:math equations in the file:

```
m|math[display='block'] {
    border: 1px solid rgb(0,0,190);
}
```

Note also that you need to set the namespace prefix in your CSS, regardless of whether you've used a prefix on the element in the document (the prefix you use in the CSS and in the content also don't have to match, but that's one for the XML geeks). For example, the following CSS shows how to add a border to the math element, even though there is no prefix on the element:

```
<style>
@namespace m "http://www.w3.org/1998/Math/MathML";

m|math {
    border: 1px solid rgb(0,0,190);
}
</style>

<math xmlns="http://www.w3.org/1998/Math/MathML">
    ...
</math>
```

This is true of all namespaced content you add.

A common mistake when using a global xmlns declaration on the math element is to forget that all embedded XHTML tagging has to be redeclared in the XHTML namespace. The following embedded description in the annotation-xml element would trigger an error to be reported on the p tag, since MathML does not define one:

```
<math xmlns="http://www.w3.org/1998/Math/MathML">
  <semantics>
    <mrow>
      ...
    </mrow>
    <annotation-xml
               encoding="application/xhtml+xml"
               name="alternate-representation">
       <p>a squared plus b squared equals c squared</p>
    </annotation-xml>
  </semantics>
</math>
```

To fix the problem, you simply redeclare the p element back in its proper namespace:

```
<p  xmlns="http://www.w3.org/1999/xhtml">a  squared  plus  b  squared  equals  c
squared</p>
```

But this is why it's better to use prefixes on MathML elements, because then there'd be no need to redeclare child content. Plus, it's clearer which tags belong to which grammar:

```
<m:math xmlns:m="http://www.w3.org/1998/Math/MathML">
   ...
     <m:annotation-xml>
        <p>a squared plus b squared equals c squared</p>
     </m:annotation-xml>
   ...
</m:math>
```

It's worth nothing here, too, that the description inside the `annotation-xml` element is the only place where HTML fragments can appear inside of MathML markup. Although HTML5 technically allows HTML markup to be included inside of `mtext` elements, EPUB 3 restricts that usage.

Whenever you embed MathML in a content document, you also need to mark as much in the manifest. Each document that includes MathML must include the `math` property in its `properties` attribute:

```
<item href="chapter01.xhtml" ... properties="mathml"/>
```

And finally, remember that named entities (including named math entities) are not allowed in XHTML5 documents. If you cannot insert the proper Unicode characters, you can always use their decimal or hex entity equivalents. For example, to insert a minus character (which is not the same as the hyphen character on your keyboard), you could encode it like this:

```
<mo>&#8722;</mo>
```

As long as you are using a MathML editor that can export the equations, the namespace and entity issues shouldn't arise.

SVG

Unlike MathML, support for SVG is not new to EPUB 3. That is, you could embed SVG images within XHTML content documents in EPUB 2, but now the images can stand alone as content documents in the spine. It's a great choice if you want your images to be able to scale to the size of the viewing area, but it's not a format that you're going to be using to include photos and other image types that aren't easily composed of vector shapes. JPEGs, PNGs, and GIFs are going to be around for the long haul.

EPUB 3 maintains compatibility with EPUB 2 through its continued use of SVG 1.1, with the same three restrictions:

- SVG animation elements and event attributes cannot be used.
- The `svg:foreignObject` element can be used to embed XHTML content, but only XHTML content. It cannot be used to embed other XML grammars.
- The `svg:title` element must contain only valid XHTML phrasing content.

In addition to the power of scalability that SVG images provide, they are extremely useful where text content is needed to accompany the image. Text can be written directly into the image rendering, but also remain visible in the underlying markup for searching and for exposing to assistive technologies, unlike text drawn into a raster image, which becomes nothing more than colored pixels. This makes SVG a prime choice for drawing graphs, pie charts, and similar text/data representations, in addition to text/image formats like comics and cartoons.

The only equivalent that raster images provide is to layer text content on top of the image using absolute CSS positioning, which typically requires a fixed-layout document. The `canvas` tag has similar failings.

An additional benefit of an SVG image is scalability: the text will scale in proportion, so you don't end up with the pixelation that occurs when zooming raster images, or the potential for text and image to be different sizes or out of alignment when enlarged.

That SVGs can be styled using CSS also aids the reader experience. Assuming the reading system includes the ability for readers to change style sheets, the appearance can be tailored to their preferences. Chapter 9 discusses more of the accessibility benefits.

The primary knocks against using SVG have traditionally been in support and rendering. Although SVG support in browser cores is evolving now that it has a special place in the HTML5 specification, and most newer browsers and browser cores support most of the basic drawing functionality, none has complete support. Using SVG in dedicated EPUB 3 reading systems should be relatively safe, but SVG gets problematic (as with any new HTML5 features) when you factor in cloud reading experiences. When you can't be sure what browser a reader might be using, you can't be sure what SVG support it will have. Despite improvements in support, rendering of SVG can still be slow and/or CPU intensive.

Although SVGs can stand alone in the spine, there are two ways to embed them inside of XHTML content documents. The first is to include the SVG markup directly in the XHTML:

```
<body>
  <svg xmlns="http://www.w3.org/2000/svg">
      ...
  </svg>
</body>
```

And the second is to reference an SVG file from an object element:

```
<object data="image01.svg" type="image/svg+xml" width="640" height="480">
    <img src="image01.png" alt="..." />
</object>
```

The second method is the more common, and the more legible, way to embed SVG images. Although some SVG markup is small in size, complex images can run into the hundreds and thousands of lines. Including this markup directly in your content file has the potential to inflate your XHTML file and slow its rendering, not to mention making any further manual editing and correction of your content difficult.

Using an object tag also allows you to embed a fallback image for those reading systems that don't support SVG (but is not required). Although object should be preferred, there are a number of other ways to embed SVGs:

- By reference from an img tag, but you can't include a fallback and the SVG cannot be scripted
- By reference from an embed element, but no fallback method is available
- Via the CSS background-image property

The iframe element can also be used to include an SVG file.

Similar to MathML and the epub:switch, when embedding SVG images in XHTML content documents, you need to include an svg identifier in the document's manifest entry:

```
<item href="chapter01.xhtml" ... properties="svg"/>
```

When using SVGs as standalone documents in the spine, the property is assumed and does not need to be added.

Fixed Layouts

Although EPUB excels at reflowing text to fit the available screen, for many publishers the reflowing nature of EPUBs is a hindrance to the kind of pixel-precise layouts that are essential to their craft. Children's books, coffee table and photography books, comics, manga, cookbooks, magazines, and many other specialty formats do not reflow well, or at least an ideal way to flow them hasn't yet evolved. Purely image-based formats are typically unreadable when scaled too small or too large.

Although reading systems have always given the illusion of pagination to reflowable EPUBs, the content rendered in any reading system's viewport on any given "page" changes depending variously on the size of the viewable area, the type of font being used, and the font size. With fixed layouts, the reading system is instead told via the metadata what size area to allocate, which then allows precise sizing and/or positioning of the content in the virtual canvas.

The need for fixed layouts led to the invention of a number of proprietary solutions to enable their creation in various reading systems. As mentioned in "Metadata for Fixed Layout Publications" (page 22), the IDPF now has defined metadata to standardize the creation of fixed layout publications, and as of this writing it is supported in both Apple iBooks and Google Play. This section will show how to create fixed layout publications and documents in more detail.

As you might imagine, fixed layouts are often equated with a final form format like PDF, where the page size dimensions are fixed by the author and content is positioned precisely on the page. EPUB has a number of significant differences in how it implements fixed layouts from PDF, of course. One key difference is that EPUB doesn't require an all-or-nothing choice when creating a fixed layout publication; EPUBs can mix reflowable and fixed documents in the same publication.

Fixed layouts are a bit of a step backward from the strengths of the EPUB format, which you'll also need to consider before using them. Foremost among the drawbacks is that trying to maintain a page size makes your content less adaptive and usable for readers. If the viewport does not exactly match the size you specified for your page, the nuisance for the reader is not just being forced to pan and zoom to get around, but they may find your content only occupies some smaller area than is available with no way to enlarge.

To understand these issues, you need to understand how fixed-layout documents are defined, which begins with a return to the package document metadata. There is one property to indicate a fixed layout publication/document, plus two additional properties that control its rendering:

rendition:layout

This property defines whether the publication is reflowable or fixed, using one of the values `reflowable` or `pre-paginated`. For example, for a fixed layout publication, you would add this `meta` tag:

```
<meta property="rendition:layout">pre-paginated</meta>
```

If you are defining a reflowable document with only some fixed layout pages, you use the `reflowable` value, which is also the default value when the property isn't specified, to be consistent with all the reflowable EPUBs that exist and have never implemented this metadata. Likewise, if you have created a predominantly fixed format, you would use `pre-paginated` for your global setting even if you have some reflowable documents.

Having set the global option, the property can then be used to override the rendering of individual spine items, but in a slightly different form. For example, if your publication is reflowable, you would mark individual fixed documents by adding a `properties` attribute to the corresponding spine `itemref` tag like this:

```
<itemref idref="plate01" properties="rendition:layout-pre-paginated"/>
```

As you can see in the example, the `pre-paginated` value has been appended to the property name `rendition:layout` to make the new property `rendition:layout-pre-paginated` (for reflowable, you would use `rendition:layout-reflowable`). This naming convention is how all the local overrides for the `rendition:` properties are created, as you'll see.

rendition:orientation

The `orientation` property indicates whether the publication should be rendered in portrait or landscape mode, regardless of how the reader is holding their device. There are three values you can use: `portrait`, `landscape`, and `auto`. The auto value is the default, indicating that the content can be adapted to the current orientation, however the reading system does that by default.

To indicate that the publication must render in landscape mode, add the following tag:

```
<meta property="rendition:orientation">landscape</meta>
```

To override the global orientation on single documents, you again add the `properties` attribute to their spine `itemref`:

```
<itemref idref="plate01" properties="rendition:orientation-portrait"/>
```

The override properties are a combination of property and value, as already noted (that is, `rendition:orientation-portrait`, `rendition:orientation-portrait`, and `rendition:orientation-auto`).

`rendition:spread`

> This property defines that a reading system should create a synthetic spread for rendering the content in a specific orientation (a *synthetic* spread is when the reading system creates two adjacent pages simultaneously on the device screen). The value can be any of the following:

`none`

> The content must never be rendered using a synthetic spread.

`landscape`

> The content must be rendered in a synthetic spread in landscape mode.

`portrait`

> The content must be rendered in a synthetic spread in portrait mode.

`both`

> The content must be rendered in a synthetic spread, but the reading system can determine the orientation.

`auto`

> The reading system can choose whether or not to render the content in a synthetic spread, in either orientation.

> A magazine might set the following `meta` tag to indicate that a landscape two-page spread should be used:

```
<meta property="rendition:spread">landscape</meta>
```

> To override for individual documents, you once again combine the property and value:

```
<itemref idref="plate01" properties="rendition:spread-portrait"/>
```

The fixed layout information document also makes an addition to the `page-spread-right` and `page-spread-left` properties, defined in EPUB 3, to indicate which side of a two-page spread a document is supposed to begin on: `rendition:page-spread-center`. This new property indicates that the reading system must create a one-page, centered spread for rendering the content. There is no global version of this property, just as the `page-spread-*` properties cannot be defined globally. It must be set on the `itemref` for each content document you want to position. For example, you could position a plate on each side of a two-page spread followed by a centered plate like this:

```
<itemref
        idref="plate01"
        properties="page-spread-right"/>
<itemref
        idref="plate02"
```

```
        properties="page-spread-left"/>
<itemref
        idref="plate03"
        properties="rendition:page-spread-center"/>
```

 You must use the rendition prefix on the centering property, because it is not standard to the EPUB specification and not recognized.

In order to use any of these properties in the package document, you must declare the rendition prefix on the package element:

```
<package ...   prefix="rendition: http://www.idpf.org/vocab/rendition/#">
    ...
</package>
```

Each of the three global rendition properties can be used as overrides on any given itemref, as well. A typical EPUB is designed as reflowable and orientation- and spread-agnostic. But if you want your cover rendered as a single pre-paginated document always in portrait orientation and never in a spread, you simply set each of those properties:

```
<itemref
        idref="cover"
        properties="rendition:layout-pre-paginated
        rendition:orientation-portrait
        rendition:spread-none"/>
```

If you accidentally specify more than one of the page-spread-* properties on an item ref element, you should get an error from epubcheck, because the same content can't start in different pages of a spread.

But that's a quick overview of the package-level metadata you can specify. What remains is how to specify the dimensions of your content document. This information is not contained in the package, but in the content documents themselves. It is defined differently depending on the type of fixed-layout document you've created:

- For XHTML content documents, you add a meta tag to the head that specifies the width and height of the page in pixels: `<meta name="viewport" con tent="width=640, height=480"/>`.

- For SVG content documents, you must include a viewBox attribute on the root svg element defining the coordinates of the top-right and bottom-left corners: `<svg ... viewBox="0 0 640 480">`.

- For other bitmap image types like JPEG and PNG, the dimensions are determined automatically from the image metadata.

If the last bullet seems a little confusing, fixed layouts support raster image types being used in the spine. This usage is not conformant with EPUB 3, so at this time you have to provide a fallback to an XHTML content document, which would typically just be a wrapper for the same image (the same way that cover images have to be embedded in an XHTML wrapper to be added to the spine).

There is an open issue to allow greater image format flexibility in the spine, but one reason images have historically been discouraged in the spine has been a lack of support for accessibility. By wrapping in XHTML, it is at least possible to provide text alternatives and long descriptions. While rendition mapping (being able to switch back and forth from text and image representations of the same publication) is currently being discussed, it might be possible in the future to see images used in the spine without compromising accessibility.

And that's all there is to creating fixed-layout documents, at least from the perspective of how you define them in an EPUB. Chapter 9 will return to the topic, to look at some best practices for making content accessible.

That you can create fixed layouts doesn't necessarily mean that you should, however. As mentioned at the outset, the variability of screen sizes makes their choice suboptimal in most cases. Devices change over the years both in size and shape, directly impacting the viewing area. Creating a perfect layout for a screen resolution today may date your content in a couple of years when it suddenly becomes too big or too small for the latest generation of devices. And that doesn't account for the wide variety of devices that content may be rendered on, from phones to tablets, and from laptops to desktops. The menu bars, buttons, and other chrome visible in reading systems may also change and alter the viewing area.

In other words, what might start out as a beautifully designed book for a particular device may rapidly become a nuisance to read. Are readers going to enjoy having to scroll each page because part of content doesn't fit their device's screen? Does it make sense to restrict any scaling of your cover image only to have it not expand to fully fit the screen on devices with higher resolutions? These are some of the reasons why EPUB did not begin life as a fixed format.

In other words, you need to assess the benefits and drawbacks of this kind of document before adding to your workflow. The search will continue to find more flexible methods for incorporating this kind of layout-specific content, but for now you do have at least one option.

 For additional information on fixed layouts, BISG will be releasing a Field Guide to Fixed Layouts possibly as this book goes to print, written by a number of the EPUB working group members.

Covers

One thing that hasn't changed in the shift from print to digital is the need for a compelling cover for your publication. Your cover is important not just for selling in an electronic bookstore, but it's also what readers will see on their bookshelf and, depending on your preference, will greet them when they first load your ebook.

With EPUB 3, you can use either an SVG or raster image format for your cover. From a format perspective, SVG offers better scaling, but it also comes with the rendering considerations noted earlier. Raster formats like JPEG and PNG, on the other hand, don't generally scale well, and must be embedded inside an XHTML content document in order to be referenced from the spine, but there are no rendering worries with them.

Assuming you have a stunning cover image for your book in hand, this section will show how to add it to your EPUB. Including it in the EPUB container is only the most basic work you have to do, after all; you still have to tell a reading system how to find it.

Chapter 1 touched briefly on the metadata to do this, but not how to use it. The cover, as mentioned earlier, is defined by adding a cover-image property to the item that defines it in the package document manifest:

```
<item
      id="cover-img"
      href="cover.jpg"
      media-type="image/jpeg"
      properties="cover-image"/>
```

That's all there is to identifying the image. Any reading system wanting to use the image for a specialized purpose, like display on a bookshelf, can now easily pick it out from the manifest entries for all the other images you might have in your publication (it can also be picked out in a distribution channel for display in an ebookstore).

Figure 3-5 shows how Readium uses the cover in its bookshelf, for example, as compared to the drab default image the reader is presented when you don't include one.

Figure 3-5. The O'Reilly cover for the Accessible EPUB 3 (left) and a Readium placeholder icon (right)

Only one image in your publication can be marked as the cover image; it's not possible to create multiple covers for different devices or uses at this time.

A common question at this point is what size image to create for your cover. The EPUB specification does not provide any guidance, as cover display is reading system- and bookstore-dependent. A standard print book cover is 1.5 times taller than it is wide, so ensuring your digital image has dimensions roughly equivalent is a good practice to strive for to ensure that your image can be rendered as thumbnail without distortion. A good discussion of the various image sizes vendors require, and how to size your cover to meet them, can be found on the SmashWords blog (*http://blog.smashwords.com/ 2012/06/new-ebook-cover-image-requirements.html*).

Although including and marking the image facilitates external usage of your cover, to be able to reference a non-SVG cover in the spine (i.e., to render in your ebook), you have to wrap the image in an XHTML content document. This wrapper document often contains just a single img tag:

```
<html >
   <head>
      <title>Cover</title>
      <style type="text/css">
         body {
            margin: 0em;
            padding: 0em;
         }
         img{
            max-width:100%;
            max-height:100%;
         }
      </style>
   </head>
   <body>
      <img src="images/cover.jpg" alt="cover image"/>
   </body>
</head>
```

Note the use of the CSS max-width property for the image in this example. Not all reading systems will scale your image properly, so setting the image size to be no wider than the maximum available width can help prevent some really ugly chunking behavior. Your image may spill across more than one page vertically, but it should be relatively more legible. The max-height property is not as well supported, but can be used on some systems (such as Readium) to correct this problem.

The next step is to add a manifest entry for the XHTML content document (or SVG image):

```
<item
    id="cover"
    href="cover.xhtml"
    media-type="application/xhtml+xml"/>
```

And, finally, add a reference to the `spine`:

```
<spine>
    <itemref idref="cover"/>
    ...
</spine>
```

Whether or not to mark the cover as nonlinear is an oft-debated topic. General practice in EPUB 2 was to add `linear="no"` to the `itemref`, which indicates to the reading system that the cover page is auxiliary content. Doing so then requires that the reading system present the image in some specialized fashion (e.g., as a splash screen), because that will be the only way the reader can reach it from inside the book.

From a usability and accessibility perspective, allowing the reader to choose whether to view the page might seem like the better option, but if you add the cover to your books landmarks, they can reach it that way. To attempt a sliding-scale best practice, if you absolutely want the cover to be shown, set the cover as linear content, if you don't care if the reading system wants to display it in some specialized fashion, set it to nonlinear, and if you don't want it shown at all don't include it in the spine.

If you're expecting that people might read your EPUB using EPUB 2 reading systems, you also need to include an EPUB 2 `meta` element in the package document metadata section. EPUB 2 reading systems do not recognize the `properties` attribute defined earlier, but they will recognize a `meta` element with its `name` attribute set to `cover`. The `content` attribute is then interpreted as pointing to the ID of the manifest entry for the cover image:

```
<meta name="cover" content="cover-img"/>
```

Although this allows a reading system to find the image, you may run into problems if you're using an SVG image and reference it directly from the spine instead of creating an XHTML wrapper document, as shown in previously. EPUB 2 files were not allowed to reference SVG images in the spine, so an EPUB 2 reading system might not load the document as invalid or might skip using the SVG within the publication. For safety, you may want to add a wrapper XHTML document regardless of the image type.

Styling

Although the new markup features in EPUB 3 generally garner all the attention, and again got first billing here, equally impressive is the new styling power that is evolving within the specification. With roots bound up in the limitations of eInk devices, a constant knock on current ebooks has been the lack of typographical beauty when compared to their print peers. Centuries of accumulated knowledge about book design was going to waste for want of support. The lack of rich styling support has also been a hindrance for global adoption, because many of the features needed to make high-quality publications outside of Romance languages simply weren't available.

EPUB CSS Profile

EPUB 3 makes a significant effort to knock down these support barriers by embracing the power of CSS3. Add in the ability to embed fonts (covered in Chapter 4), and suddenly rich digital layouts and typography are no longer just theory. The EPUB 3 specification is also not rigid about support, meaning that reading system developers are encouraged to include more than just the basic profile. As CSS3 matures, in other words, even more complex EPUB 3 layouts will be possible.

But before getting too far ahead of ourselves, it's also prudent to note that you will find variations in support across devices and reading systems, even in the base profile discussed in this section. eInk devices, for example, will still typically provide a more limited set of CSS functionality than tablets, by nature of their display capabilities. Even across similar devices, there is often varying support within the actual reading systems. Sometimes, the variation stems from the state of the underlying rendering engine, but other times a lack of control may be a deliberate decision of the developer. The goal of content creators to lay out their content the way they want and the goal of reading system developers to create a unique reading experience sometimes clash.

There is no perfect solution to this collision of interests, and developers and content creators will undoubtedly always be bickering about who has the ultimate right of way. To help document where the discrepancies lie, and to help standardize support across reading systems, there is a significant effort underway in the recently announced EPUB Reading System Conformance Test Suite project (*https://github.com/mgylling/epub-testsuite*) to create a comprehensive set of tests for supported properties. This project aims to provide a greatly simplified method for anyone to conduct a review of any reading system's capabilities and be able to discover where holes exist. It won't address whether the omissions are intentional or not, but the feedback it allows will help bridge the support gaps that do exist because of a lack of a common testing suite.

As you might imagine, the best practical advice at this time is to test your content on as many devices as you can. And remember that it's better to ensure that your content degrades gracefully in the absence of styling than hack at your markup to work around any limitations you might find, but Chapter 9 will return to this topic.

CSS 2.1

All reading systems with a viewport are expected to provide baseline support for CSS 2.1, with the following exceptions:

- The fixed property cannot be used with position property. (Content cannot remain fixed in a paginated view, and the oeb-page-head and oeb-page-foot extensions are designed for running headers and footers.)
- The direction and unicode-bidi properties must not be used. (HTML5 provides elements for internationalization.)

In addition, the following properties from CSS 2 are also included for use with the list-style-type property to improve global support for list styling:

- cjk-ideographic
- hebrew
- hiragana
- hiragana-iroha
- katakana
- katakana-iroha

A comprehensive guide to CSS 2.1 is beyond the scope of this chapter, but it includes the most widely known and used CSS properties, such as:

- background
- border
- color
- display
- font
- float
- height
- line-height
- margin
- outline
- text-align
- text-indent
- visibility
- width

These properties are usually well supported, but with some caveats. Background images have not been widely supported, for example, because of the reflowable nature of EPUBs (but that changes with fixed layout EPUBs). Lack of support for page breaking we touched on earlier in the chapter, and control over margins are the other notable exceptions.

CSS 2.1 also includes the following pseudoclasses:

- `:active`
- `:first-child`
- `:focus`
- `:hover`
- `:lang`
- `:link`
- `:visited`

 Use of the `:hover` pseudoclass is typically not recommended for ebooks, because mobile devices often lack this functionality.

It also includes the following pseudoelements:

- `:after`
- `:before`
- `:first-letter`
- `:first-line`

The pseudoclasses and pseudoelements can also be combined to create interesting new styling possibilities. For example, to change the appearance of the first letter in the first paragraph in a section, you could combine `:first-child` with `:first-letter`:

```
section > p:first-child:first-letter {
    font-size: 200%;
    margin: 0em 0.2em 0em 0em;
    float: left;
}
```

Just beware that the :first-child has to be the *first* child, not just the first of its kind. The previous rule to create a drop cap would work only if a paragraph element is the first child of the section. If the section includes a heading, for example, the selector will no longer match. CSS3 Selectors greatly improves on this functionality, but because it is not in the baseline, you should use only the new pseudoclasses and elements defined in it with care (i.e., when it doesn't matter if the formatting isn't rendered).

CSS3

EPUB 3 introduces support for a number of the newly minted CSS3 modules. This section provides a quick tour of the new functionality, and later sections of the book will return to a number of the features in more detail.

Media Queries

On the more technical side of the new additions, support for the enhanced @media and @import rules defined in Media Queries is now included.

The @import rule is used to import one style sheet into another, allowing you to modularize your style sheets by functionality or purpose. Instead of one giant style sheet containing all your rules, you can break them down and then simply import them into your main style sheet with a series of @import rules like these:

```
@import 'tables.css';
@import 'sidebars.css';
```

This technology is not new, but the CSS3 module adds the ability to use its more expressive media queries with imports:

```
@import url(color.css) screen and (color);
@import url(grayscale.css) screen and (not color);
```

In this example, only the color CSS style sheet will be imported when the device rendering the ebook has a color screen (tablets); otherwise, only the grayscale CSS styles are imported (traditional eInk). In other words, you don't have to worry about conflicts, because only one or the other set of styles will be applied. The functionality of media queries in CSS 2.1 was limited to just a few basic media types. The ability to define specific features of the medium to match on top of those was not possible.

The @media rule has similarly been enhanced, allowing you to define the applicable medium for your style definitions from within the style sheet. For example, you could make rules for different screen sizes and differentiate them like this:

```
@media screen and (max-width: 720px) {
    .alert {
        width: 200px;
    }
}
```

```
@media screen and (max-width: 1024px) {
    .alert {
        width: 200px;
    }
}
```

As with imports, the rules defined within these @media sections are not applied to the content unless the specified parameters match.

Namespaces

Support for the @namespace rule from CSS Namespaces is now included, as you've seen a few times already in this chapter.

You need to use namespaces, for example, to define the EPUB namespace for styling elements that carry the epub:type attribute:

```
@namespace epub "http://www.idpf.org/2007/ops";

section[epub|type='dedication'] {
    background-color: rgb(210,210,210);
}
```

The one aspect of the CSS implementation that tends to trip people up is that the colon between the prefix and the element or attribute name is replaced by a pipe character (|) when creating a selector (e.g., epub|type in the previous example instead of epub:type). Although escaping the colon by placing a backslash (\) in front of it is sometimes offered up as a solution, you're no longer using namespaces when you do this. If you escape the colon, the prefix in your CSS *must* exactly match the one in the content file.

But for more detail on how to use namespaces to style content, see the discussion in the earlier section "MathML" (page 72).

Fonts

The EPUB profile also includes the @font-face rules and descriptors as defined in CSS Fonts Level 3, with minimum required support for:

- font-family
- font-style
- font-weight
- src
- unicode-range

This rule is used to define the fonts you've embedded in your publication for referencing in your style sheets. For example, the following declaration would allow you to reference the font `Baskerville` anywhere in your style sheet:

```
@font-face {
    font-family: 'Baskerville';
    font-weight: normal;
    font-style: normal;
    src:url(../fonts/Baskerville-Regular.otf);
}
```

Chapter 4 will address the details of how this is done.

Multicolumn Layout

The CSS Multicolumn Layout Module is also supported in the EPUB 3 profile, with the one exception of the `column-span` property. This module allows you to define more than one column of text within a document, which will be useful for rendering newspaper, magazine, journal, and similar multicolumn layouts.

The `column-count` property is used to set the number of columns to render the text in. For example, you could set all articles to render in two columns with the following rule:

```
article {
    column-count: 2;
}
```

The reading system will automatically fit the columns to the available space in this case, as shown in Figure 3-6.

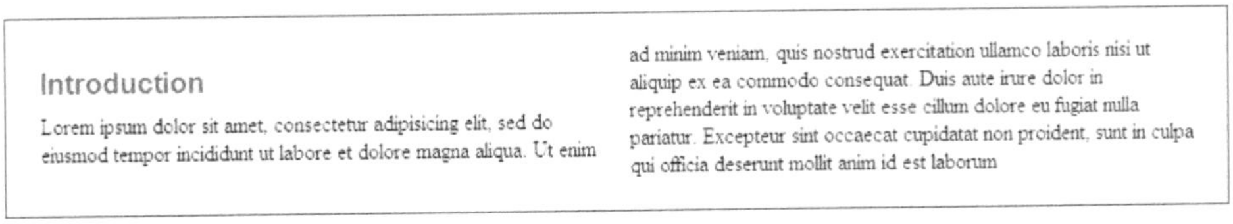

Figure 3-6. Two-column text

Alternatively, you can specify a desired width using the `column-width` property. For example, the previous example could change to create a set of 10em wide columns as follows:

```
article {
    column-width: 10em;
}
```

This would appear in the reading system as shown in Figure 3-7.

Introduction

Lorem ipsum dolor sit amet, consectetur adipisicing elit, sed do eiusmod tempor incididunt ut labore et dolore

magna aliqua. Ut enim ad minim veniam, quis nostrud exercitation ullamco laboris nisi ut aliquip ex ea commodo consequat. Duis aute irure dolor in reprehenderit in

voluptate velit esse cillum dolore eu fugiat nulla pariatur. Excepteur sint occaecat cupidatat non proident, sunt in culpa qui officia deserunt mollit anim id est laborum

Figure 3-7. Three columns of text

If you set both properties, the reading system will create columns of the width you've specified to a maximum of the count you've specified (i.e., if there is not enough space, only as many as can fit by width will be created).

The module also defines the following properties for controlling various rendering aspects of the columns:

- `column-gap` specifies the spacing between columns

  ```
  column-gap: 1em;
  ```

- `column-rule`, `column-rule-color`, `column-rule-style`, and `column-rule-width` allow you to control the styling of rules between columns

  ```
  column-rule: rgb(0,0,0) dashed 1px;
  ```

- `break-before`, `break-after`, and `break-inside` control page breaking

  ```
  break-before: always;
  ```

- `column-fill` controls whether or not to balance the length of text in each column

  ```
  column-fill: balanced;
  ```

 As of this writing, proprietary prefix extensions are still required to get this feature to work (e.g., the `-webkit-` extension was used in Readium in the previous examples).

Writing Modes, Text, and Speech

The EPUB working group also chose to include support for three CSS3 modules that were not yet recommendations at the time that EPUB 3 was formalized: Writing Modes, Text, and Speech.

As a result, you must prefix any properties you use from these modules with `-epub-`:

- CSS Writing Modes Level 3:
  — `-epub-writing-mode`
  — `-epub-direction`
  — `-epub-text-orientation`
- CSS Text Level 3:
  — `-epub-hyphens`
  — `-epub-line-break`
  — `-epub-text-align-last`
  — `-epub-text-emphasis`
  — `-epub-text-emphasis-color`
  — `-epub-text-emphasis-style`
  — `-epub-word-break`
- CSS 3 Speech:
  — `-epub-cue`
  — `-epub-pause`
  — `-epub-rest`
  — `-epub-speak`
  — `-epub-speak-as`
  — `-epub-voice-family`

This required prefixing ensures that if the properties change or are removed before the specifications they are defined in become recommendations, you can still count on the reading system providing the expected layout behavior defined by EPUB 3 (i.e., the EPUB 3 specification essentially took a snapshot in time of the CSS3 specifications and referenced those for required support).

 CSS3 Speech became a formal recommendation in early 2012, so you should be able to drop the prefixes whenever the next minor revision to the specification occurs.

Chapter 8 covers the Writing Modes and Text module properties in more detail, and Chapter 10 covers the Speech properties in "CSS3 Speech" (page 297).

Additional Support

As noted at the beginning of the section, you aren't limited to using only the CSS3 modules defined in the specification. The further afield you go, however, the less likely you are to find support across a broad range of reading systems.

The first consideration you should make when venturing into the unknown of CSS3 support is what impact a lack of support will have on the reading experience. If you're just defining manual line breaks and the like, the reader probably won't even notice if support is lacking. If you add copious CSS animations to drive the primary narrative forward, however, readers without support won't be able to follow. Use progressive enhancement techniques whenever there is any question of support. Readers may not have any CSS support, after all, so ensuring that the information you're conveying with CSS is always available should be a paramount concern.

A common practice on the Web is to use a script-based solution like Modernizr (*http://modernizr.com/*) to provide graceful fallbacks for properties that aren't supported by the reading system. If a reading system supports scripting, all you need to do is include the library file in your EPUB and reference it from each content document:

```
<html ... class="no-js">
   <head>
      ...
      <script src="js/modernizr.js"></script>
   </head>
   ...
</html>
```

The script will test for support and either use your primary style definition or a fallback depending on whether support is found. Your mileage will vary, though, as fallbacks are only realistic for a small subset of properties. More information is available from the project website.

Ruby

EPUB 3 also introduces a new property to handle ruby annotation positioning called -epub-ruby-position. It accepts any of the following values, as defined in the specification:

over
> Ruby text is positioned on the over side of the ruby base.

under
> Ruby text is positioned on the under side of the ruby base.

inter-character
> Ruby text is positioned on the right side of the base text.

For example, to indicate that all rt annotations should be placed over the base text they annotate, you would create a rule like this:

```
ruby {
    -epub-ruby-position: over;
}
```

Use of this property will be covered in more detail in Chapter 8.

Headers and Footers

Finally, EPUB 3 includes the custom oeb-page-head and oeb-page-foot values for the display property, as originally defined in EPUB 2. These values set custom running headers and footers in your ebooks. Support for these properties is not required in reading systems, and, by and large, has not materialized. They are the only option available to generate headers and footers, however, because there is no reliable mechanism for determining when a page has turned, and no method for inserting content above and below the existing flow.

 Although some reading systems will automatically display the book or chapter title at the top/bottom of the screen, such behavior is not defined by the EPUB specification and no control is typically provided over what gets displayed.

To implement headers and footers, you simply need to define the display property on the element containing the header or footer text. A div element is typically used to contain this information:

```
<div class="header">
    Chapter I: Loomings
</div>

<div class="footer">
    Moby Dick
</div>
```

You could then define the CSS styles for these divs as follows:

```
div.header {
    display: none;
    display: oeb-page-head;
}

div.footer {
    display: none;
    display: oeb-page-foot;
}
```

Note that each declaration includes the display value none. If a reading system does not support headers or footers, you typically won't want the text to be rendered or announced at the point where it has been inserted in the markup. Setting the display initially to none ensures that reading systems that do not support custom headers or footers will not render the elements if the override in the second display declaration is not supported.

You also need to be aware of scoping when using headers or footers. If you have a section of multiple short stories contained in a single content document, for example, you may want to change the running header each time a new story begins. To accommodate this behavior, EPUB 3 headers and footers are defined to begin and end with the element they are contained in.

For example, if you had a single content file containing all of chapter one of *Moby Dick*, you'd simply add our previous example to the markup as follows:

```
<section id="c01">
    <h1>Chapter I: Loomings</h1>
    <div class="header">Chapter I: Loomings</div>
    <div class="footer">Moby Dick</div>
    ...
</section>
```

The header and footer begin and end with this single document, because it contains only a single section. To reset the header each time a new short story begins within a file, you instead define a new div for each as you go:

```
<section id="p04">
    <h1>SECTION IV FAIRY STORIES—MODERN FANTASTIC TALES</h1>
    <div class="footer">SECTION IV</div>

    <section>
        <h2>A FOUR-LEAVED CLOVER</h2>
        <div class="header">A Four-Leaved Clover</div>
        ...
    </section>
    <section>
        <h4>THE LORD HELPETH MAN AND BEAST</h4>
        <div class="header">The Lord Helpeth Man and Beast</div>
        ...
    </section>
    ...
</section>
```

The first running header ("A Four-Leaved Clover") will be displayed until the first full page containing no more content from that story is displayed, at which point the next running header will take its place.

When setting headers and footers, you need to be aware of where you place their definitions because of this scoping. If you were to define the header inside of a `header` element like this:

```
<section>
  <header>
    <h2>A FOUR-LEAVED CLOVER</h2>
    <div class="header">A Four-Leaved Clover</div>
  </header>
  ...
</section>
```

As soon as the reader flipped past the first page, the running head would fall out of scope and no header would be rendered on the next page. The elements should always be the children of a `section`.

Alt Style Tags

The Alt Style Tags specification (*http://idpf.org/epub/altss-tags/*) is another new technology introduced during the EPUB 3 revision. This specification defines a method for including alternative style sheets for use by the reading system when the reader wants to switch text direction or contrast, or a combination of both.

The ability to provide alternative style sheets with your content isn't new; it's been available for use since HTML4 introduced the `alternate` property for the `link` element's `rel` attribute. The distinction of an alternative style sheet is not widely known, though, because support has never fully materialized in browsers.

The style sheets that most people are familiar with are called *persistent style sheets*:

```
<link
     rel="stylesheet"
     type="text/css"
     href="epub.css"/>
```

The `rel` attribute value `stylesheet` indicates to the reading system that the `link` references a style sheet that is to be imported and applied to your content as part of its normal rendering process.

But you can also use the element to define an alternative style sheet (one that isn't to be applied by default) by adding the additional `alternate` keyword to the `rel` attribute and adding a `title` attribute with a human-readable label:

```
<link
     rel="alternate stylesheet"
     type="text/css"
     href="epub-night.css"
     title="Night Reading"/>
```

Browsers that support alternative style sheets typically expose the option to use these style sheets somewhere in their menus, using the label you've supplied. Figure 3-8 shows an example of how Firefox handles this option.

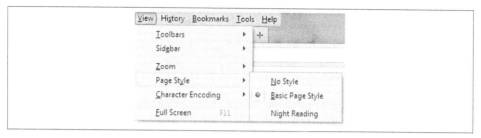

Figure 3-8. Night Reading option in Firefox

If the user selects the alternative style sheet, its styles are applied to the current document. The persistent styles are not removed, so all that changes is what you specify in your alternative style sheet.

 There is a third kind of style sheet called *preferred*. These have a `ti tle` but omit the `alternate` keyword. They are loaded with the persistent styles, but are removed when an alternative is selected, so are a bit like a default alternative style sheet.

As currently deployed, alternative style sheets have another deficiency beyond just the general lack of support: the lack of any standardization about what to write in the `title` makes it impossible for machines to use them intelligently. And that's where the Alt Style Tags specification steps in. It builds on top of the existing functionality without changing it, adding the unused `class` attribute to define its tags.

The specification currently includes four tags you can use in the `class` attribute:

`day`
    Indicates the style sheet optimizes the display for daytime reading.

`night`
    Indicates the style sheet optimizes the display for nighttime reading.

`vertical`
    Indicates the style sheet optimizes the display for reading vertical text.

`horizontal`
    Indicates the style sheet optimizes the display for reading horizontal text.

Here's an equivalent `link` element for a night reading style sheet using an alt style tag:

```
<link
      rel="alternate stylesheet"
      type="text/css"
      href="epub-night.css"
      title="Night Reading"
      class="night"/>
```

Although the ability to switch contrasts based on lighting is useful, the specification does not provide guidance on what daytime or nighttime reading means in practical styling terms. As a result, you'll have to do some tinkering to determine what works best for your content in well-lit versus low-light settings.

As most reading systems provide an option to switch the contrast from black text on white background to white text on black background, if you add a night reading style sheet you might opt for some less stark contrast. White text on black can be very difficult to read, except when there is no other source of light. Finding a bright scheme, but one that fits more naturally with soft lighting might be one option.

You could also use this mechanism to make a white-on-black night reading option more readable. Instead of washing out all background colors, which could make distinguishing secondary content like figures and sidebars difficult to perceive from the primary narrative, you might want to find another shading for them, or provide more noticeable borders to highlight their boundaries. Distinguishing headings in another color, such as yellow, might be another option to help readers perceive changes in the text.

Being able to tailor vertical and horizontal text modes is particularly useful for global language support; Chapter 8 will cover those CSS options.

Note that you aren't limited to setting only one option for a reader. If you use the same title on multiple alternative style sheets, it indicates that they constitute a group and should be applied together. For example, here's how you would define daytime and nighttime vertical reading styles:

```
<link
      rel="alternate stylesheet"
      type="text/css"
      href="epub-vertical.css"
      title="Vertical Day"
      class="vertical"/>
<link
      rel="alternate stylesheet"
      type="text/css"
      href="epub-day.css"
      title="Vertical Day"
      class="day"/>

<link
      rel="alternate stylesheet"
      type="text/css"
      href="epub-vertical.css"
```

```
            title="Vertical Night"
            class="vertical"/>
      <link
            rel="alternate stylesheet"
            type="text/css"
            href="epub-night.css"
            title="Vertical Night"
            class="night"/>
```

You'll notice that the vertical style sheet has to be referenced twice, once for daytime and once for nighttime, because of the requirement for the `titles` to match.

Unfortunately, at the time of this writing, no known reading systems support alternate style sheets, but ignoring alternate style sheets is the default behavior defined in HTML, so there's no harm in adding them, either.

CSS Resets

A common practice in web design is to include an initial style sheet that resets basic browser-defined properties like the margins, padding, line heights, and font sizes. The rationale is that browser default styles can cause small permutations in the rendering that can mar the appearance of the site in certain browsers. A reset style sheet is the first one added to your document and sets the potentially offending properties back to their default state (e.g., margins and padding to `0em`). You then include your own style sheets, knowing that the reading system's defaults will not impact them.

That you can reset styles doesn't mean you should, however. If you haven't ever used a style sheet reset, there's no reason to rush out and start using them now. Although enormously useful to some designers, there are also a number of reasons why they are bad, from causing accessibility issues when resetting properties that shouldn't be reset to not realizing how the resets will cascade and forgetting to check for, or missing in quality assurance, styling bugs that actually make your content worse.

The best advice to give for EPUBs is to consider CSS resets only if you're creating fixed layout publications. If you need pixel-perfect layouts, a reset may help ensure consistency in how your content gets laid out in the predefined area. For reflowable EPUBs, the value diminishes quickly. You're better off setting the properties you need to set than worrying about the problems that can arise from globalling out styles.

Fallback Content

The last topic to address before winding down this chapter is how to provide fallbacks, as the need for reliable rendering has been mentioned a few times without a lot of detail about how you go about accounting for foreign resources.

Fallbacks in EPUB have two principal uses. One is to ensure that content documents can be rendered, and the other is to provide content alternatives for potentially unsupported features and markup. This section examines how to provide each of these through the various mechanisms EPUB 3 makes available.

Manifest Fallbacks

Chapter 1 touched on manifest fallbacks as a means of providing a core media type fallback for foreign resources, so this section won't recap all of that information. There are two keys uses for them: providing document-level fallback for spine content and resource replacements at the content level.

To reference a nonstandard document type in the spine, you must include a `fallback` attribute on the `item` tag for the corresponding document in the manifest. This attribute points to the `id` of the next document to try if the first cannot be rendered, effectively creating a fallback chain.

For example, to reference a JPEG from the spine, you could define it as having an XHTML fallback as follows:

```
<item id="p1"
      href="panel01.jpeg"
      media-type="image/jpeg"
      fallback="p1-fallback"/>

<item id="p1-fallback"
      href="panel01.xhtml"
      media-type="application/xhtml+xml"/>
```

If a reading system cannot render the JPEG, or does not accept it being referenced directly in the spine, it will automatically follow the fallback chain until it reaches the required core media type. In this case, there is only a single fallback, but there is no limit to the number of alternate formats you can provide in the chain (beyond what is reasonable to create, of course).

For example, you could define a fallback chain from a DocBook file to a DTBook file to a default XHTML file as follows:

```
<item id="c1"
      href="chapter1_docbook.xml"
      media-type="application/docbook+xml"
      fallback="c1-fallback1"/>

<item id="c1-fallback1"
      href="chapter1_dtbook.xml"
      media-type="application/x-dtbook+xml"
      fallback="c1-fallback2"/>
```

```
<item id="c1-fallback2"
      href="chapter1.xhtml"
      media-type="application/xhtml+xml"/>
```

But there's no value in putting noncore media types into your publication unless you know that some reading system somewhere can render the content. It's not incumbent upon the reading system to find a way to render the foreign document types you include (e.g., do not expect the reading system to render a PDF, or launch a viewer, just because you referenced a PDF directly from the spine). A format chain that simply runs through a variety of XML files isn't hugely helpful, either, because the other formats would not give you many additional benefits over the core XHTML media type.

When creating chains of three or more items, you do need to be conscious that you don't create an infinite loop by referencing an earlier link in the chain. If you forgot that our DocBook file was falling back to the DTBook file in the previous example, and made the DTBook file fall back to the DocBook, the XHTML document would never be reachable:

```
<item id="c1db"
      href="chapter1_docbook.xml"
      media-type="application/docbook+xml"
      fallback="c1dtb"/>

<item id="c1dtb"
      href="chapter1_dtbook.xml"
      media-type="application/x-dtbook+xml"
      fallback="c1db"/>    <-- circular reference created here

<item id="c1xhtm"
      href="chapter1.xhtml"
      media-type="application/xhtml+xml"/>
```

Fortunately, cases like this should be rare, and a validator like epubcheck will flag the lack of a core media type fallback as an error for you.

When creating fallback chains, you must also never add an entry for each possible resource to the spine, because it results in duplication. For example, take the earlier JPEG example:

```
<!-- Bad: -->
<spine>
  <itemref idref="p1"/>
  <itemref idref="p1-fallback"/>
</spine>
```

A reader opening this book would be presented the document two times in a row, since the reading system will render the JPEG or the fallback for the first itemref and then the XHTML version again for the second.

Sometimes, though, you may find yourself in a situation where you have no choice but to present content in a nonstandard format. For example, you may have supplementary information that you can distribute but don't have rights to modify, or modifying would invalidate it or alter it in unusable ways. Although the fallback should be a content equivalent, it does not have to be.

For example, if you had a PDF of a government tax form you wanted to include for any reading system that might be able to render it, you could include it in the spine with a fallback to an XHTML content document that provides a link to the online location of the form. As long as the reader is able to obtain equivalent information, you haven't broken the spirit of the format (but your readers will not be very happy if large portions of your book are made natively unreadable like this).

Manifest fallbacks aren't just limited to replacing content documents in the spine, either. One of the really cool features this fallback mechanism provides is to allow any foreign resource to be replaced by a core media type, regardless of how it is called.

Suppose, for example, you wanted to include a TIFF image file in one of your content documents:

```
<img src="sunset.tif" alt="Sunset over tranquil lake"/>
```

All you'd need to do to make this use valid is supply a JPEG fallback in the manifest:

```
<item id="img01"
      href="sunset.tif"
      media-type="image/tiff"
      fallback="img02"/>

<item id="img02"
      href="sunset.jpeg"
      media-type="image/jpeg"/>
```

If the reading system cannot render the TIFF file, it will automatically replace it with the JPEG while rendering the content document.

Manifest fallbacks are required for elements that have no other fallback mechanism (img, embed, and iframe), because it is the only way that foreign resources can be referenced by them and still remain valid to the specification. It's not the only way to handle foreign content fallbacks, though, as you'll now see.

Content Fallbacks

A few HTML5 elements have their own intrinsic fallback mechanisms, or the ability to provide core media type fallbacks directly in their markup.

For example, you can embed XHTML content directly inside an object element:

```
<object width="400" height="300" data="video/croc.swf">
  <param name="movie" value="video/v001.swf"/>
  <img src="img/vid01-fallback.png" alt="Crocodiles feeding at Mara river"/>
</object>
```

If a reading system does not support the referenced Flash video, it will instead display the image embedded inside the `object`.

You can also nest `object` elements to create a fallback chain similar to the ones we just saw in the manifest:

```
<object data="stats.xls" type="application/vnd.ms-excel">
  <object data="stats.ods"
  type="application/vnd.oasis.opendocument.spreadsheet">
    <table>
      ...
    </table>
  </object>
</object>
```

As the chain ends in an XHTML `table`, the reader will have access to the data regardless of whether the reading system supports Excel or Open Office spreadsheets. You could have used this nesting fallback method for the TIFF example in the previous section, too:

```
<object data="sunset.tif" type="image/tiff">
  <object data="sunset.jpeg" type="image/jpeg">
    Sunset over tranquil lake
  </object>
</object>
```

The `canvas` element provides a similar fallback mechanism, although without the nesting capabilities:

```
<canvas id="tictactoe">
  <img src="ttt_board.jpg" alt="an empty tic-tac-toe board"/>
</canvas>
```

The XHTML content you embed inside the element gets displayed if the `canvas` element is not supported, if there is no visual viewport, or if scripting is disabled. Chapter 7 provides more detail on this element.

And as you'll see in more detail later in the book, the `audio` and `video` elements allow the use of multiple `source` child elements for fallbacks, each of which defines a possible format the reading system might be able to render:

```
<audio controls="controls">
  <source src="clip01.ogg"/>
  <source src="clip01.mp3"/>
</audio>
```

Unlike the preceding elements, any HTML content inside the `audio` and `video` tags is only a fallback when the element itself is unsupported (e.g., in EPUB 2 reading systems).

Those are the only elements that allow foreign resources using intrinsic fallback methods instead of manifest fallbacks, but between manifest fallbacks and intrinsic fallbacks, there is always a way to experiment with foreign resources without losing the renderability of your publications.

So far, you've seen only how to handle resources. Now it's time to explore what to do with unsupported new HTML markup and XML extension grammars.

The epub:switch element

The intrinsic fallback mechanisms that HTML5 elements provide are not the only ones available to you at the content document level. EPUB also adds its own content-level fallback mechanism in the `epub:switch` element.

This element is another example of declarative markup in EPUB 3, or using markup to define what should happen but leaving it to the reading system to make it happen. Although HTML5 natively supports SVG and MathML, as does EPUB 3 by extension, XHTML5 content documents actually allow any XML grammar to be embedded in them. When embedding an unsupported XML grammar like ChemML, however, you quickly run into the problem of how to alternate what gets rendered when the format is not supported.

Content switching takes the programming hassle out of this need and allows content creators to experiment with unsupported new markup grammars and elements without having to worry that a segment of their readership may not be able to view the content, or view it in a comprehensible way.

The `switch` element is not new to EPUB 3, but it has been modified from the version in EPUB 2 to better reflect where the specification and HTML are going. Gone is the `required-modules` attribute for indicating which XHTML 1.1 module the markup employs features from, leaving only the `required-namespace` attribute.

But before getting ahead of ourselves, let's slow down and take a look at how this element works. Even if you haven't done any programming in your life, you're undoubtedly familiar with the concept of choose cases: depending on some specified criteria, you want the first of two or more possible matches to be used (similar to "if/else if/else" conditionals).

If you are a programmer, the `epub:switch` element strays slightly in its inner working from a true programming `switch` case, but the idea is similar. Instead of matching a value, each case identifies the markup grammar it contains, allowing the reading system to pick the first match. If none are supported, a required XHTML default must be included to fall back on.

The process can be abstracted like this:

```
<switch>
  <case 1 is supported?>
    show specialized markup1
  <case 2 is supported?>
    show specialized markup2
  <default>
    show XHTML content
```

Not coincidentally, the three pseudotags in the previous example are also the three elements used to build a switch case. The first is the root epub:switch element, which
must contain one or more epub:case elements followed by exactly one epub:default.

To evaluate the switch, each case must have a required-namespace attribute attached
to it, containing the namespace or unique URI that identifies the content it contains.
For example, you would add the MathML namespace to this attribute to indicate that
the case contains math content:

```
<epub:switch>
  <epub:case required-namespace="http://www.w3.org/1998/Math/MathML">
    <math xmlns="http://www.w3.org/1998/Math/MathML">
      <mrow>
        <msup>
          <mi>a</mi>
          <mn>2</mn>
        </msup>
        <mo>+</mo>
        <msup>
          <mi>b</mi>
          <mn>2</mn>
        </msup>
        <mo>=</mo>
        <msup>
          <mi>c</mi>
          <mn>2</mn>
        </msup>
      </mrow>
    </math>
  </epub:case>
  <epub:default>
    a<sup>2</sup> + b<sup>2</sup> = c<sup>2</sup>
  </epub:default>
</epub:switch>
```

When a reading system steps through this switch, if it recognizes http://www.w3.org/
1998/Math/MathML as a grammar it supports, it will render the MathML for the reader.
If not, the XHTML default equivalent gets displayed. Readium, for example, displays
the MathML as shown in Figure 3-9.

$$a^2 + b^2 = c^2$$

Figure 3-9. MathML font rendering of the equation

But Adobe Digital Editions 1.7, an EPUB 2 reading system, renders the fallback shown in Figure 3-10.

$$a^2 + b^2 = c^2$$

Figure 3-10. XHTML rendering of the equation

 You can use image fallbacks for complex equations, but make sure to provide an adequate description for readers who cannot see the image.

When using switches, you need to ensure that your fallback content does not invalidate your document. If you intend to use the specialized markup in an inline context, for example, make sure that your `default` element contains equivalent inline XHTML markup. The following `switch` would incorrectly embed one p tag inside another if MathML is not supported:

```
<p>
   <epub:switch>
      <epub:case required-namespace="http://www.w3.org/1998/Math/MathML">
         <math ...>
            ...
         </math>
      </epub:case>
      <epub:default>
         <p>...</p>        <-- p tag inside p tag
      </epub:default>
   </epub:switch>
</p>
```

Invalid markup post-evaluation can lead to your document not rendering, or rendering in awkward and unsightly ways.

Using the `epub:switch` markup to provide alternatives for MathML, ChemML, and any other XML grammar is just a matter of putting their namespace in the `required-namespace` attribute. All EPUB 2 reading systems will recognize this usage (if perhaps not the grammars), because it remains unchanged from the original design. The only thing to be careful about when using the element to make content backward compatible is to be careful not to overuse new HTML5 elements in the default fallback, as they may not render as expected.

As mentioned earlier, the old `required-modules` attribute has been dropped. No XHTML 1.1 means no more modules. The other, more interesting change that goes in step with this removal is that the `required-namespace` attribute now allows any URI, not just the namespace of the XML markup its `case` contains.

Because namespaces are a form of URI, the change is perfectly backward compatible, but there was some discussion during the revision that this change no longer made `required-namespace` an ideal name for the attribute, since namespaces were only going to be one use moving forward. To retain compatibility without creating yet another attribute, a little misnomer was deemed not a worthy sacrifice for the greater good.

Let's step back from theory and look at why changing to allow any URI matters in more practical terms. It wasn't done just to confuse anyone who isn't already confused at this point about the relationship between namespaces and URIs. It was done to provide an extension point for experimenting with new HTML elements before they become part of the standard (or part of EPUB). As any experimental markup cannot be distinguished from support markup until a reading system tries to render it, a new way to allow switching was needed that didn't rely on namespaces alone.

HTML5 may be winding down, for example, but many ideas evolved during its development that have been pushed forward to *HTML.next* (*http://www.w3.org/wiki/HTML/next*). As browser engines are updated faster than specifications, reading systems will eventually appear with the ability to display new nonstandard markup, even though the markup won't render on reading systems that more strictly adhere to the specification. To ensure compatibility, while providing the freedom to experiment, `epub:switch` is envisioned as the means of allowing the new markup to be included, while providing a fallback for the general reading population.

How this will work in practice remains to be seen, as we haven't reached the point where any new functionality can be incorporated. The IDPF may provide an extension URI for including new markup, for example. A new fancy HTML input type called `pin wheel` that spins its label round and round aimlessly while you wait for your form information to submit might then be includable like this:

```
<epub:switch>
    <epub:case required-namespace="http://idpf.org/epub/30/ext/xhtml/pinwheel">
        <pinwheel
                spin="clockwise"
                colors="randomize"
                onclick="submit()">Submit</pinwheel>
    </epub:case>
```

```
<epub:default>
    <button onclick="submit()">Submit</button>
</epub:default>
</epub:switch>
```

To help standardize the usage of the `required-namespace` attribute so reading system developers and content creators have a common base of reference, the IDPF maintains a document called "Extension identifiers for EPUB switch" (*http://idpf.org/epub/switch/*). This page contains an informative list of identifiers, and may be updated at any time independent of EPUB itself (i.e., check back periodically). Currently, only the MathML namespace URI is listed, but as identities are developed for new cases they will appear here.

This chapter won't get into the actual technical details of how `switch` elements are evaluated, partly because they are reading system dependent and will change from system to system, but also because it should not impact the final rendering. A reading system may choose to hide the unwanted branches via CSS or may preprocess and strip the unwanted content before rendering. The only reason to mention it at all is because you must not rely on any branch in your switch being available or being referenceable from outside the `case` it belongs to after evaluation.

No two elements in the `epub:switch` can have the same `id`, either, even though only one of them will survive through to rendering. The following switch is invalid because both the `math` element and the fallback `p` have the same `id` value, `eq01`:

```
<!-- Bad: -->
<epub:switch>
    <epub:case required-namespace="...">
        <math id="eq01" xmlns="...">
            ...
        </math>
    </epub:case>
    <epub:default>
        <p id="eq01">...</p>
    </epub:default>
</epub:switch>
```

This may seem like a major headache at first, because now there's no way to link to the content in the `switch` (because you can't be sure which branch will render). The root `epub:switch` element may also be stripped, so it's unreliable to link to it. The simple solution to avoid the linking problem is to wrap your `switch` in a `div` or `span`, depending on the context in which it's used, and link to that element instead:

```
<!-- Good: -->
<div id="eq01">
    <epub:switch>
        <epub:case required-namespace="...">
            <math xmlns="...">
                ...
```

```
          </math>
       </epub:case>
       <epub:default>
          <p>...</p>
       </epub:default>
    </epub:switch>
  </div>
```

On what will become a familiar final note as this book moves on, when using the `epub:switch` element, you need to indicate as much in the manifest by adding the `switch` term to the `properties` attribute for the containing document:

```
<item href="chapter01.xhtml" ... properties="switch"/>
```

Bindings

The `bindings` element is another that was briefly mentioned in Chapter 1, but that needs further explanation when discussing content. This element represents another instance of declarative markup, but it offers a kind of cross in functionality between markup-level fallbacks and manifest-level fallbacks.

The first thing to know about bindings is that they work only with `object` tags, and they're only for providing scripted XHTML content alternatives for unsupported content types (foreign resources). If you set up a binding, and the reading system supports scripting but not the media type you're trying to display in the `object`, it will instead attempt to insert the content referenced by the binding. The fallback in the `object` will be used only if the reading system doesn't support scripting.

But to approach this by way of example, suppose that a reading system appears that can support embedded Excel spreadsheets. You'd typically set up the `object` with a static HTML table fallback like this:

```
<object data="data01.xlsx" type="application/vnd.ms-excel">
   <table>
      ...
   </table>
</object>
```

But what if you also discovered a fancy HTML-based interface that could take the Excel markup and render it in a more attractive and dynamic way? (Or that could take a CSV equivalent.) Your first thought might be to embed this viewing interface inside the `object` as a fallback, but there are two problems with this approach. First, what if you have other data sets you want to display? Duplicating the interface inside every object is wasteful if it only requires the name of the file to load. Second, what if the reading system doesn't support scripting? Now you have an interface that doesn't work and no way to display the data to the reader.

When trying to work within the functionality that HTML exposes, your next thought might be to embed an `object` within an `object`, as discussed earlier in content fallbacks:

```
<object data="data01.xlsx" type="application/vnd.ms-excel">
   <object data="excelViewer.xhtml?data=data01.xslx"
   type="application/xhtml+xml"/>
</object>
```

This approach might appear to work, but it's also flawed. When scripting isn't supported, the referenced interface will render, as much as it can, without any data. Because there is no scripting to make it work, you just get whatever shell appears by default.

If you were only embedding the interface once, you might think to take a progressive enhancement approach. Show your fallback table in the *excelViewer.xhtml* file by default, and when scripting is enabled hide it and render the specialized interface instead. While an appropriate technique, it doesn't work where you want to reuse the same interface over and over. Without scripting, there is no way to know which `object` tag is calling the interface or control which fallback data set to show.

And that's what makes bindings so powerful. You set up your `object` exactly like you would for normal rendering, and then let the binding decide when to invoke the scripted interface.

Knowing that nothing changes in the way you tag the `object`, let's look at how the reading system intercedes.

The `binding` element is one of the five elements allowed as children of the `package` element in the package document (see "The Package Document Structure" (page 8)). It is actually nothing more than a container element for a series of one or more `medi aType` elements, which are what establish the bindings to make. Each of these elements defines a media type to watch for and the scripted content document to invoke.

For example, if you had this manifest entry for the scripted Excel viewer:

```
<item id="xlViewer"
      href="excelViewer.xhtml"
      media-type="application/xhtml+xml"
      properties="scripted"/>
```

you would set up a handler for it in the `bindings` section like this:

```
<bindings>
   <mediaType handler="xlViewer"
              media-type="application/vnd.ms-excel"/>
</bindings>
```

And that's all there is to creating a binding. Now, each time the reading system encounters an `object` tag in a content document, it will apply the following logic to determine what to do:

1. If the media type is supported, render the document referenced in the object.

2. If the media type is not supported, but scripting is, invoke the content document referenced in the handler attribute.

3. If the media type is not supported, and neither is scripting, use the fallback content supplied in the object.

One of the limitations of bindings is that you cannot specify different bindings for the same media type, but you could handle different rendering scenarios within the same handler file if the need were to arise. Of course, this sets up the remaining question of how information gets to the scripted content document.

Another piece of magic the binding performs for you is to automatically parameterize all the relevant information about the object and pass that in the calling URL. The data and type attributes are both sent to the handler page, as are any param children of the object.

In other words, the reading system is not just invoking the Excel viewer page, but is actually calling it like this:

```
excelViewer.xhtml?data=data01.xslx&type=application/vnd.ms-excel
```

You can now use some simple JavaScript to process the arguments out of the query string:

```
<script>
<![CDATA[
    var param = new Array();
    var args = location.href.split("?")[1].split("&");
    for(var i = 0; i < args.length; i++)
    {
        var p = args[i].split('=');
        param[p[0]] = p[1];
    }
]]>
</script>
```

After processing this code, the variable param["data"] will hold the original file that was called from the object, which you could then feed into your custom viewer to determine what to render.

Each param element within the object is also added to the query string in much the same way, where the name attribute becomes the parameter name in the query string and the value attribute becomes the corresponding value.

For example, if you included a slideshow viewer that enabled custom display options like this:

```
<object data="slides01.xml" type="application/x-slideshow">
    <param name="orientation" value="landscape"/>
    <param name="borderColor" value="blue"/>
    <param name="borderType" value="inset"/>
    ...
</object>
```

each of the param elements would get encoded like this:

```
slideshow.xhtml?data=slides01.xml&type=application/x-slideshow
&orientation=landscape&borderColor=blue&borderType=inset
```

If your scripted interface can also make use of this information, it is automatically available.

Although the need for bindings probably won't come up repeatedly in most people's day-to-day production lives, it's another of the useful options that EPUB makes available to not only ensure the rendering of content, but to enhance it based on the capabilities of the reading system. You may find script libraries that can take your fallback data and enhance it without the need to create a separate fallback document and invoke a binding, but the element is not intended to replace these use cases. Bindings are a complement to that kind of enhancement, when a separate viewer file is the only viable solution.

CHAPTER 4

Font Embedding and Licensing

Adam Witwer

Director of Publishing Technology, O'Reilly Media

When you "embed" a font within an EPUB file, you include single or multiple font files in the EPUB package. You must then include references to that font within the CSS and the OPF manifest of the EPUB so that the font is rendered across reading systems. Sounds simple enough, right? From a technical perspective, embedding fonts *is* simple, and the EPUB 3 specification (*http://bit.ly/U6csMH*) leaves little room for ambiguity on this topic. It is a straightforward enough process that a technical overview can be summarized succinctly in a single (*http://bit.ly/XilwL8*) blog post (*http://bit.ly/10ElZja*).[1]

While embedding fonts in an EPUB file is simple enough, how reading systems support embedding has been and remains spotty and inconsistent, often frustratingly so. Also, while embedding fonts is trivial, adding the required obfuscation (*http://bit.ly/XipbJ0*) —required by most commercial font foundries—is much less so. Also, licensing for embedding in general can be an administrative and technical nightmare.

This chapter does not argue for or against embedding fonts, or perhaps more accurately, it argues for both. In doing so, the chapter aims to give you the information that you need to decide for yourself what the "best practice" is around font embedding, which will be influenced by a number of factors, including—perhaps most importantly—the kind of content that you publish. There is not one reason why you might want to embed a font in an EPUB—your reasons may range from capturing a particular aesthetic to fit the content, to creating a consistent brand across your product lines, to addressing more pragmatic concerns such as embedding for unusual or specialized glyphs that are unlikely to be found in a standard system font.

---

1. Posted in 2009 and 2011, respectively, both Liz's and Liza's overviews are written in the context of EPUB 2.0.1, but the information is still largely applicable to EPUB 3. You'll read more about this topic in "Font Embedding in EPUB 3" (page 130).

Because of these potential complexities, this chapter—instead of diving immediately into the technical specifications—starts by asking you to consider your reasons for embedding. From there, you'll see how font embedding has changed in the EPUB 3 specification from 2.0.1, and you'll learn how to embed, obfuscate, and style fonts. Finally, you'll gain an understanding of the various font licensing options and how those options are evolving as digital book reading systems mature.

Why Embed Fonts?

Embedding fonts in EPUB is optional. This section looks at the pros and cons of embedding.

Maybe You Shouldn't

When you decide to embed fonts in your EPUB files, you are effectively signing yourself up for added technical and administrative overhead. Before you take on that extra work, it makes sense to ask yourself whether embedding fonts is a good idea at all. This chapter is part of a larger collection of EPUB 3 best practices, and the "best practice" in this case may be to not embed fonts and rely on reading system fonts exclusively. Let's look at the reasons you might want to *not* embed fonts in your EPUB.

Historically, reading system support for font embedding has been poor and inconsistent

Reading system support of embedded fonts in EPUB 2.0.1 has been all over the place. Systems that support it have done so poorly, oddly, and inconsistently. These idiosyncrasies have been well documented on Liz Castro's blog, *Pigs, Gourds, and Wikis* (*http://www.pigsgourdsandwikis.com/*). For example, here (*http://bit.ly/XJkMl0*) is a post in which Liz describes working around the inability of iBooks to render correctly a simple bold variant by adding `-webkit-text-stroke` to the CSS. If you're an ebook developer, read the details of that post at your own risk: you won't know if you should laugh or cry.

This history of buggy, inconsistent, or sometimes non-existent support in reading systems has persisted perhaps in part because of the squishiness of the 2.0.1 specification (*http://bit.ly/TepdTg*):

> It is advisable for a Reading System to support the OpenType font format, but this is not a conformance requirement; a reading system **may** support no embedded font formats at all.

And while it's encouraging that the EPUB 3 specification takes a much clearer stance on the issue of reading system support for font embedding—requiring support (*http://bit.ly/UdJcAX*) for OpenType and WOFF fonts—the precedence for poor support has been established. There's been little indication that reading system vendors are likely to get their acts together anytime soon.

Even more discouraging, perhaps, is that even if a reading system supports font embedding correctly and consistently, the user may never see those fonts because many reading systems default to system fonts. The embedded fonts must be toggled on, and that toggle can be buried in a menu option that a user may never think to access. If a reading system does default to the embedded fonts, the user can override those fonts at any time, which can sometimes lead to unexpected and undesirable results.

Figure 4-1 and Figure 4-2 show an example of a reading system behaving oddly. In Figure 4-1, the Google Play Books iOS app defaults to the embedded font, which in this case is UbuntuMono (*http://font.ubuntu.com/#charset-mono-regular*). Great!

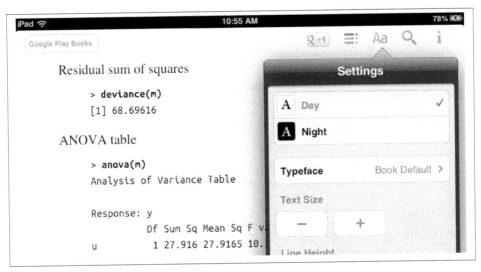

Figure 4-1. The Google Play Reader defaults to the embedded font

Figure 4-2 shows what happens when a user selects another font. Note that the user's choice of Georgia overrides UbuntuMono, but strangely, the bold variant of Ubuntu-Mono remains.

Ideally, in this case, we'd want Google Play Books to override the *body* font but leave the `<pre>` block as is, which is exactly what iBooks version 3.0.2 does. While it's great that iBooks does the right thing in this case (but see Liz Castro's post above for an example of iBooks exhibiting its own quirks), the fact that you, as an ebook developer, can expect such varying behavior across reading systems should really make you question your motives for embedding and ask if your time might be better spent on other tasks (see Chapter 9, for example).

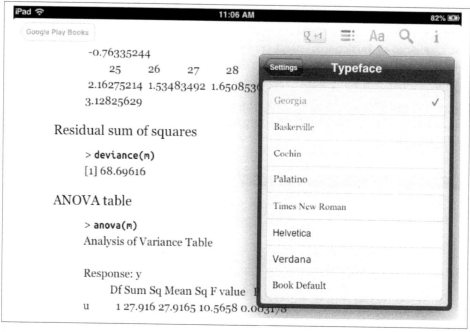

Figure 4-2. The same reading system behaves oddly when a user selects a font override

Embedding adds complexity

If you're in the business of creating EPUB files, one reason to be wary of embedding fonts is that it makes your job harder. Embedding creates potentially unnecessary complexity in the following ways:

- Figuring out the licensing can be daunting. If you decide to embed commercial fonts, your font foundry may or may not grant you a license to do so. Many foundries are still figuring out realistic licensing models that both the publisher and foundry can live with. See "Licensing Fonts for Embedding in EPUB" (page 138) for more details around how font licensing is evolving with the EPUB 3 specification.

- Assuming you've sorted out the licensing, you will probably need to obfuscate the fonts, which means finding a tool to add the obfuscation algorithm. Then, you will need to test the reader support of that obfuscation. While it's great that the IDPF includes a standardized obfuscation algorithm (*http://bit.ly/UduxFD*) in the EPUB 3 specification, the ebook ecosystem is still catching up on implementing the tools to add obfuscation and the reading systems to decrypt it. See "Obfuscating Fonts" (page 134) for more details on this topic.

- Font embedding is a feature of EPUB, and if you're adding features, you're going to need to test and QA those features. When the embedding doesn't work as expected, you're in for more iteration and testing until you generate acceptable results. As described in "Historically, reading system support for font embedding has been poor and inconsistent" (page 118), this process can be frustrating since you're subject to the whims of the various reading platforms.

For much published content, system reader fonts function well and, let's face it, look perfectly fine for most of your readers. Keeping things simple and not embedding may make the most sense in many cases.

Device makers have already done the work for you

Any best practice consideration around EPUB font embedding should take into account that reading device makers routinely work with font foundries and typography experts to identify and then customize and optimize fonts for the screens of those devices.

Publishers and content creators can take advantage of these optimized fonts by foregoing embedding and relying instead strictly on device system fonts. Potentially, you could even target particular system fonts in the EPUB of your CSS (see "How to Embed Fonts" (page 131) to learn how), although that strategy means you will probably end up optimizing for a single or small handful of devices that include those particular fonts.

Still, given that the clearest and best typefaces for that particular reading system already reside on the device, why would you want to override those typefaces by embedding your own? Arguably, the best experience for your readers can be found via the system fonts. See "Embedding to be forward-thinking" (page 122) for the counterargument to this line of thinking.

Embedding inflates file size

When you embed a font, you are making the EPUB file larger—an obvious point, but one that shouldn't be readily dismissed. If you publish and sell your ebook into digital retail markets, your customers may attempt to purchase it over a slower network connection, such as a cellular phone network. Embedded fonts can make a significant impact on file size, which could potentially lead to a customer passing on an ebook purchase or becoming frustrated when the download takes too long.

On digital reading forums such as MobileRead (*http://www.mobileread.com/*), it is not uncommon to read complaints of ebook "bloat" in the context of embedded fonts, and posters on the forum share tips on the quickest way to remove embedded fonts.

One way you can minimize the impact font embedding has on file size is to use subsetting, the details of which are described in "Subsetting a Font" (page 137).

Maybe You Should

There are plenty of very good reasons why you may want to embed fonts in your EPUB files. This section examines when the best practice suggests to embed.

Embedding to be forward-thinking

As described in "Historically, reading system support for font embedding has been poor and inconsistent" (page 118), EPUB reading system support for font embedding through the end of 2012 has been something of a mess. Given these circumstances, no one would blame you if you decided to throw up your hands and forget the whole thing. However, by giving up now, you may be consigning yourself to future work if and when reading systems finally provide proper support. By working through the technical and administrative complexities of font embedding today, your EPUB file will be ready to take advantage of support when it comes. As the reading systems improve their rendering platforms, the typography in your ebooks will improve, too.

Furthermore, embedding now sends a message to device makers that you value good typography and creative control. It lets them know that you are not ready to cede a lifetime of hard-won typographical knowledge and expertise to device and reading system developers who lack that expertise and have little idea how it affects your content, brand, and readership. The publishers and content creators that go the extra mile to license and embed fonts, knowing that they probably won't be supported today, let these developers know that support for font embedding is important and reading system support should be a priority.

"Device makers have already done the work for you" (page 121) argues against font embedding because device makers normally include system fonts that are optimized for that device. However, this argument is potentially flawed for two reasons:

- Reading system device makers may not have the expertise that publishers have around long-form typography and design. You may not want to (and probably shouldn't) *assume* due diligence or competence on the part of the device maker. The typefaces that device makers choose are not above scrutiny.[2]

---

2. As one example, Amazon has been particularly remiss and wrong-headed in its font and typographical choices across the Kindle platform. To say nothing of the font faces themselves, Amazon's insistence on fully justified text reveals a lack of even a rudimentary understanding of presenting text in a clear and distraction-free manner. John Gruber's eloquent rant (*http://daringfireball.net/2012/10/kindle_paperwhite*) on the topic summarizes it nicely, ending with this assertion: "Amazon should hire a world-class book designer to serve as product manager for the Kindle."

- Even if you assume that device makers know what they're doing, there's no reason you can't work with your own typeface designers to create or modify an existing typeface so that it is optimized for the reading system device screens. Whether you are presenting type in print or on screen, the same basic typographical principles apply. The best practices around these principles are perhaps best understood by traditional print publishers who bring a tradition of craft that is centuries old.

Considered in light of the above, taking the time to craft, optimize for digital, and embed a font is the responsible thing to do because it contributes to, improves, and influences the emerging digital reading ecosystems. On all digital platforms (be they ereading systems or the Web in general), typography has a long way to go before it catches up to print. One way that traditional publishers can help move it forward is to embed chosen fonts skillfully and carefully, regardless of whether device makers know how to treat those fonts or not.

Embedding to create a consistent look and feel across "platforms"

Another reason you might consider embedding fonts is to create a consistent look and feel across the digital and print versions of your product. By taking this approach, you are effectively creating a kind of "brand" for your publication or series of publications. Or to use Craig Mod's term, you are "platforming books (*http://craigmod.com/journal/platforming_books/*)," part of which is to create a "unified design" across digital and print.

Craig's description of a unified design is judicious, smart, and practical. He doesn't suggest slavishly and mindlessly trying to re-create the print product in digital and in fact warns against "forced representations." Rather, he suggests letting each medium do what it does best while taking steps to unify the design across platforms, part of which includes typography.

Craig (with help from O'Reilly's own Ron Bilodeau (*http://www.oreillynet.com/pub/au/3771*)) goes all out in his *Art Space Tokyo* project and embeds fonts for both body and headings, but you could achieve a similar effect by scaling back and including a font for the headings only. Effective examples of using an embedded font for headings can be found across the Web. Figure 4-3 shows one example from the *New Yorker* website, which serves up via Typekit (*http://blog.typekit.com/2010/11/30/bring-your-own-fonts-to-typekit/*) the magazine's iconographic and immediately recognizable NY Irvin font (*http://www.myfonts.com/fonts/wiescherdesign/new-yorker-type/*) for the headings.

The *New Yorker's* use of its trademark font on its website is a simple but effective way of creating a "unified design" across the print and digital products. Employing a similar strategy around font embedding in your EPUB files can help you create a consistent look and feel across the various mediums in which your publications are sold.

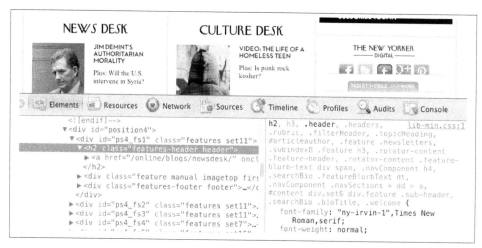

Figure 4-3. Screenshot from newyorker.com showing the NY Irvin font as well the browser console with the CSS referencing that font

At O'Reilly, we take a slightly different approach—we use the same *code* font in the print and digital products. Because O'Reilly publishes books of a technical nature, the code examples are really at the heart of many of our books, so using the same typeface in digital and print captures that "unified design" idea in a subtle way. However, there is one significant difference between the digital and print versions of the font, as Figure 4-4 demonstrates.

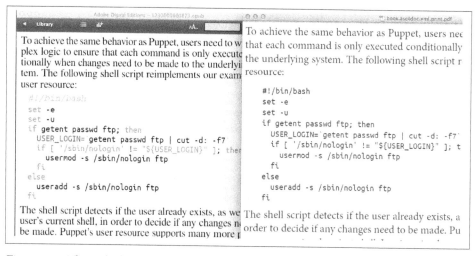

Figure 4-4. The code font that O'Reilly uses is consistent across print and digital, but the digital is in color

The print version of the code is in one color (black, obviously), while we add colored syntax highlighting to digital versions of that same code, which makes the code easier to parse. Figure 4-4 shows the single color and multicolor code blocks side by side,[3] EPUB on the left and print PDF on the right. In this way, we are both embedding and enhancing a typeface.

Embedding for improved glyph coverage

Glyph coverage in most reading system fonts for non-Latin or even Latin-1 Supplement (*http://bit.ly/12nz3Xl*) and Latin Extended (*http://bit.ly/SU3kJh*) is spotty at best. If your EPUB text includes non-Latin or Extended Latin characters, you should consider embedding fonts.

As an example of where font embedding can help with glyph coverage, you can experiment with one of the EPUB 3 sample files that the IDPF provides on a Google project page (*http://bit.ly/11EFl6X*). In the images that follow, I used the EPUB file named *wasteland-otf-20120118.epub* (*http://bit.ly/XXFqBg*), Eliot's *The Waste Land*, which begins with an epigraph taken from *Satyricon* and uses a mix of Latin and Greek characters. The EPUB includes an embedded font named OldStandard, which does a pretty good job of covering Greek characters in the epigraph. Figure 4-5 shows a screenshot in Adobe Digital Editions (ADE), version 2.0.6[4] of the epigraph.

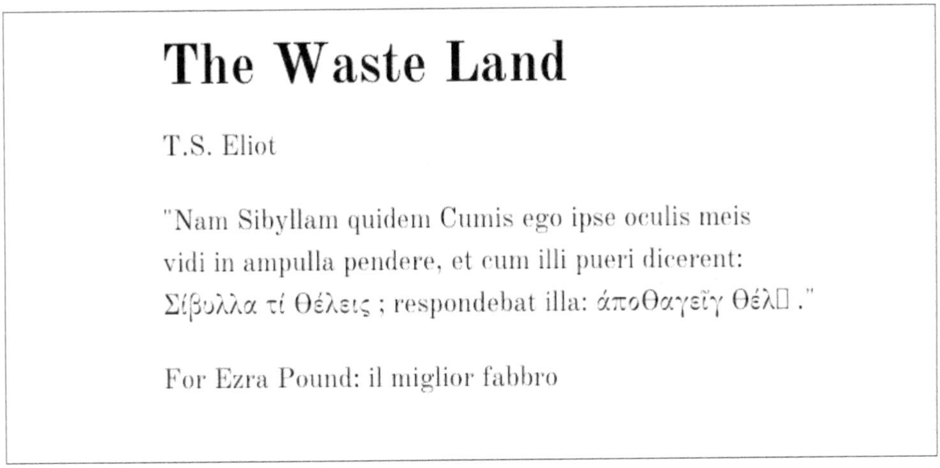

The Waste Land

T.S. Eliot

"Nam Sibyllam quidem Cumis ego ipse oculis meis
vidi in ampulla pendere, et cum illi pueri dicerent:
Σίβυλλα τί Θέλεις ; respondebat illa: άποθαγείγ θέλ☐ ."

For Ezra Pound: il miglior fabbro

Figure 4-5. The epigraph of The Waste Land *includes Latin and Greek characters*

---

3. If you're reading this chapter in print, you'll just have to take my word for it.

4. ADE does not technically support EPUB 3. However, this EPUB provides an NCX fallback for version 2.0.1, so it functions as expected in ADE. Also, the results are similar (although not exactly the same) in reading systems that support EPUB 3, such as Readium and iBooks 3. In other words, ADE's lack of EPUB 3 support is irrelevant in this context.

As you can see in Figure 4-5, one character[5] doesn't render and is replaced with a small rectangle. Not bad, and it could be much worse. Figure 4-6 shows what the same EPUB looks like without an embedded font.

The Waste Land

T.S. Eliot

"Nam Sibyllam quidem Cumis ego ipse oculis meis
vidi in ampulla pendere, et cum illi pueri dicerent:
Σίβυλλα τί ⊠έλεις ; respondebat illa: άπο⊠αγεῖγ ⊠έλ⊠ ."

For Ezra Pound: il miglior fabbro

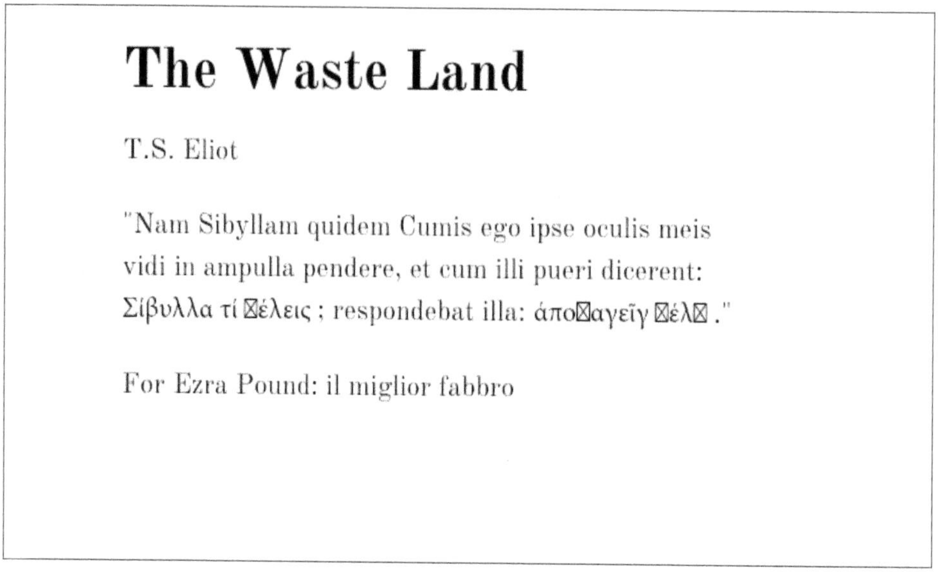

Figure 4-6. The epigraph looks much worse without an embedded font

Experimenting further, you can seek out a font that provides complete coverage for Eliot's epigraph. To test this, I embedded the OTF version of FreeSerif (*http://ftp.gnu.org/gnu/freefont/*) in the EPUB, which created the results that you see in Figure 4-7.

Results will vary across reading systems, of course. If you decide to embed, you should plan to test in the reading systems that you care about. See "Subsetting a Font" (page 137) for some ideas on how you could further optimize font embedding for better glyph coverage.

---

5. It's a COPTIC SMALL LETTER SHEI (*http://bit.ly/Z3bTaL*), for the morbidly curious.

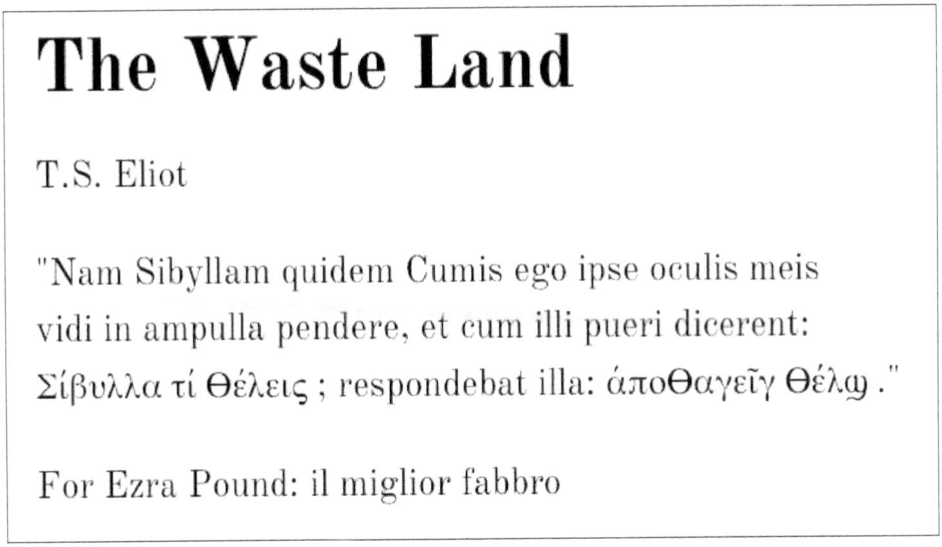

The Waste Land

T.S. Eliot

"Nam Sibyllam quidem Cumis ego ipse oculis meis
vidi in ampulla pendere, et cum illi pueri dicerent:
Σίβυλλα τί Θέλεις ; respondebat illa: ἀποΘαγεῖγ Θέλῳ ."

For Ezra Pound: il miglior fabbro

Figure 4-7. The complete epigraph, courtesy of the rich set of glyphs found in FreeSerif

One thing I would warn against is *assuming* that, because you are using non-Latin characters, you must automatically embed. As Murata Makoto explains in Chapter 8, some reading systems will look for and attempt to honor the `xml:lang` and/or `lang` attribute, as described in detail on the WC3's Internationalization Best Practices (*http://bit.ly/ UnJF2N*) page. Chapter 8 includes examples of how to use each attribute in accordance with the EPUB 3 specification.

Anecdotally, earlier this year, I discovered that the `xml:lang` worked surprisingly well while assembling an EPUB that used simplified Chinese characters for all text that wasn't code (Figure 4-8).

The rendering shown in Figure 4-8 is accomplished with a combination `xml:lang` and UTF-8, and no embedded fonts. The text renders equally well in iBooks, Adobe Digital Editions, and (after conversion via KindleGen) KF8.

 If you're wondering how adding `xml:lang` would affect the Greek examples from *The Waste Land* earlier in this section, the EPUB in fact *includes* the `xml:lang` and `lang` attributes (crack it open and take a look at the file named *wasteland-content.xhtml*), but they seem to have no effect. Such inconsistent behavior across reading systems is why you should assume nothing and always be sure to test and build QA into your process.

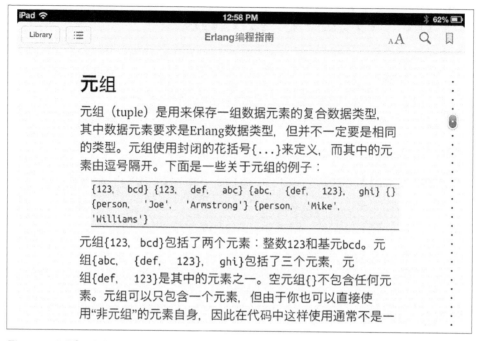

Figure 4-8. This EPUB uses no embedded fonts

This section has only scratched the surface of what you should consider if you're working with non-Latin character sets. See Chapter 8 for coverage of advanced topics such as proper encodings, vertical writing, writing modes, and ruby.

Embedding for specialized or technical reasons

You might consider embedding a font if you publish specialized or highly technical content. For example, if you publish content with complex mathematical equations, most reading systems are not equipped with the fonts needed to display the equations correctly. Now that the EPUB specification has support for MathML, as explained in "MathML" (page 72), the opportunity exists to couple semantically marked-up equations with a robust, math-centric font, such as the STIX Font (*http://www.stix fonts.org/*)—once the reading systems support these features consistently, of course.

As you've seen in previous examples in this chapter, we at O'Reilly routinely embed UbuntuMono (*http://font.ubuntu.com/#charset-mono-regular*) for code listings. Because O'Reilly is a technical publisher, having a good code font is an important part of the reader experience. We choose to embed four variants of this font because most reading systems have a single monospace font, which—if it exists at all—is almost invariably Courier New. UbuntuMono is more condensed, has much better glyph coverage, and creates a uniform design with the print product, as described in "Embedding to create a consistent look and feel across "platforms"" (page 123). Some reading systems (Figure 4-9) do not include a monospace font at all, so embedding one becomes crucial in this case.

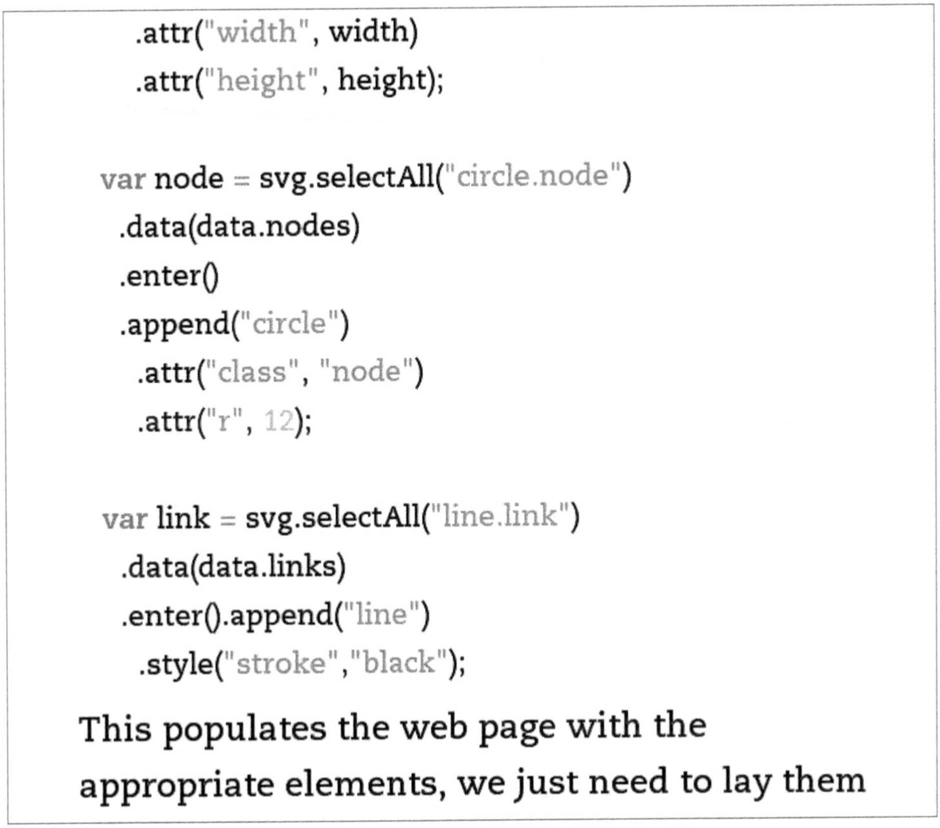

```
    .attr("width", width)
    .attr("height", height);

  var node = svg.selectAll("circle.node")
    .data(data.nodes)
    .enter()
    .append("circle")
     .attr("class", "node")
     .attr("r", 12);

  var link = svg.selectAll("line.link")
    .data(data.links)
    .enter().append("line")
     .style("stroke","black");
```

This populates the web page with the appropriate elements, we just need to lay them

Figure 4-9. While it is not technically an EPUB reader, the Kindle Paperwhite is an example of a recently released reading device with no monospace font—not good if you're a technical publisher

When reading systems don't include the fonts you need to present your technical or specialized content in the expected way, you have almost no choice but to embed a font.

Why not just use an image?

When considering your options on how to address missing or specialized glyphs, you might wonder, "Why not just use an image?" It's true that you can swap in an image of a character instead of embedding a fallback font, but I don't recommend it as the "best practice." Once you set a character as an image, that character is unfindable in search, typographically ugly and uneven, and useless for accessibility (see Chapter 9 for more on accessibility). For these reasons, using an image for an unusual character should be an absolute last resort.

Font Embedding in EPUB 3

Font embedding hasn't changed significantly from 2.0.1 in the EPUB 3 specification, but as described on the IPDF's website (*http://bit.ly/T523Pp*), there are a few notable revisions:

1. EPUB 3 *requires* reading systems to support font embedding for OpenType and WOFF formats (see the sidebar "What's WOFF?" if this format is unfamiliar to you). The fact that support for font embedding is now a requirement marks a shift from the 2.0.1 specification, which states that a reading system "may" support (*http://bit.ly/TepdTg*) font embedding. For publishers and content creators that wish to embed fonts—for any of the reasons described in "Maybe You Should" (page 122) —this change is encouraging because it means that, in order to be fully compliant with EPUB 3, a reading system must support this feature.

2. EPUB 3 formally includes a font obfuscation algorithm. This obfuscation method is not new; it previously existed as an "informational document (*http://idpf.org/epub/20/spec/FontManglingSpec_2.0.1_draft.htm*)." As you'll learn in "Obfuscating Fonts" (page 134), having font obfuscation exist out of the specification was a mistake that contributed to a lot of confusion that persists to this day. By making font obfuscation a formal part of the EPUB specification, the IDPF gave the industry— font foundries, content creators, and reading system vendors alike—a single method for "mangling" fonts.

What's WOFF?

WOFF is a format that is being developed for presenting fonts on the Web, usually in a web browser on a screen. The W3C has a terrific FAQ (*http://www.w3.org/Fonts/WOFF-FAQ*) if you're looking to learn the basics, and WOFF File Format 1.0 (*http://dev.w3.org/webfonts/WOFF/spec/*) has the deep technical details. Adding WOFF support to the EPUB 3 specification is in line with the IDPF's goal of aligning EPUB with other emerging web standards, such as HTML5 and CSS3.

Diving into the EPUB 3 specification further, you'll find a few other tidbits that are worth learning and keeping in mind in the context of font embedding:

EPUB 3 stipulates that reading systems must support @font-face (http://bit.ly/WmXmkP)

The EPUB 2.0.1 specification indicates that the following descriptors must be supported:

```
font-family
font-style
font-variant
font-weight
font-size
src
```

It does not, however, require support for @font-face, which is necessary for font embedding. EPUB 3 fixes that problem while requiring reading system support for the same CSS descriptors with the exception of font-variant, which is removed from the specification as a requirement, and unicode-range, which is added as a requirement.[6]

EPUB 3 stipulates that reading systems are required to provide a fallback for embedded fonts

The EPUB 3 specification identifies embedded fonts as a *Foreign Resource (http://bit.ly/V5AmrT)*, which in turn is defined as "A Publication Resource that is not a Core Media Type." Anything that is designated a Foreign Resource requires at least one fallback. For embedded fonts, providing a fallback means that the reading system must use the W3C rules for matching font styles (*http://bit.ly/R3RKg0*).

EPUB 3 includes a CSS Profile with extensions for font styling

As you can read about in the specification itself (*http://bit.ly/ZgWl39*), EPUB 3 guards against CSS specifications that are in progress and will potentially change by establishing a CSS Profile, which is employed with the -epub- prefix. See CSS Text Level 3 (*http://bit.ly/UAHSrO*) to learn about the -epub- prefixed properties relating to styling text, such as -epub-hyphens* and -epub-line-break.

How to Embed Fonts

The method for embedding a font in an EPUB hasn't changed since 2.0.1 in the EPUB 3 specification. There are three basic steps:

---

6. Just because font-variant has been removed from the list of @font-face descriptors, it doesn't necessarily mean that reading systems won't include support for it, just that support isn't required. So your small caps may be safe.

1. Add the font to your EPUB package.
2. Include the font file in the OPF <manifest>.
3. Use @font-face in the EPUB CSS to reference the font.

Optionally, you can add (and may be required to add, depending on your the license) font obfuscation and use font subsetting. Let's look at the required steps first. Again, I'm going to use an example from the EPUB samples (*http://bit.ly/ZOPWv4*) that the IPDF provides. Specifically, I'll use *wasteland-woff-20120118.epub* (*http://bit.ly/V6K4u7*).

Add the Font to Your EPUB Package

You'll want to use a font in either the OTF or WOFF format. If you have a font in another format (e.g., TTF), consider converting the font to one of the supported formats or check if your font foundry has the font in one of the supported formats.

 You may find during your testing that other font formats, such as TTF or even SVG, seem to work just fine in some reading systems. The EPUB 3 specification, however, now *requires* reading system support for OTF and WOFF, so why take chances on other formats? Your best option is to use OTF or WOFF. In her blog post (*http://bit.ly/ZOUqCa*) on this same topic, Liza Daly suggests using FontForge (*http://fontforge.org/*) (which supports both OTF and WOFF) for conversion. We've used this method at O'Reilly, and it has worked well.

To see an example of a font embedded in an EPUB, change the file extension of the *wasteland-woff-20120118.epub* file to *.zip*, and use your favorite ZIP utility to unzip the file. In this example, the EPUB creator includes three variants of the font face OldStandard.

Include the File in the EPUB Manifest

The manifest exists in the OPF file. Open *wasteland.opf* with any text editor, and you can see the manifest and how each font file is referenced:

```
<manifest>
...
<item id="css-fonts" href="fonts.css" media-type="text/css" />
<item id="css-night" href="wasteland-night.css" media-type="text/css" />
<item id="font.OldStandard.regular" href="OldStandard-Regular.woff"
  media-type="application/font-woff"/>
<item id="font.OldStandard.italic" href="OldStandard-Italic.woff"
  media-type="application/font-woff"/>
```

```
<item id="font.OldStandard.bold" href="OldStandard-Bold.woff"
  media-type="application/font-woff"/>
...
</manifest>
```

The manifest includes references to the fonts themselves as well as to the CSS that declares those fonts (see the next section). The `id` is any unique identifier that you wish to use. Just make sure not to use an identifier that already exists in the manifest. The `href` points to the file itself. In this case, the file is in the top directory, but if you wish, you can just as easily add the files to a folder named "fonts," in which case you'd just need to update the `href` accordingly:

```
href="fonts/OldStandard-Regular.woff"
```

Finally, there is the `media-type`, which is predefined based on the font format. WOFF uses `application/font-woff`, while OTF takes `application/vnd.ms-opentype`.

Reference the Font in the EPUB CSS

Once you've added the font file to the manifest, you need to reference it in the CSS file. Using that same EPUB as an example, open the *fonts.css* file in any text editor. Each font file is declared with the `@font-face` rule. Here's one example:

```
@font-face {
    font-family: 'OldStandard';
    font-weight: normal;
    font-style: normal;
    src:url(OldStandard-Regular.woff) format('woff');
}
```

The name you used for the `font-family` is arbitrary, but it seems wise to use the name of the font. That same `font-family` name can be reused for the different variants. So for the boldface version of font, the EPUB creator adds:

```
@font-face {
    font-family: 'OldStandard';
    font-weight: bold;
    font-style: normal;
    src:url(OldStandard-Bold.woff) format('woff');
}
```

Note that `url` points to the file itself, so if you were to move it to another directory, you'd need to update the `url`, too. For example, if the file resides in a directory named "fonts," you'd update the `url` to the following:

```
src:url(fonts/OldStandard-Regular.woff) format('woff');
```

Now that you've declared the font, you need to tell the reading system *where* to apply it. To see where the font is being applied in the *Wasteland* example, open the file named *wasteland.css*. The font is used for the body of the XHTML file that exists in the EPUB:

```
body {
    margin-left: 6em;
    margin-right: 16em;
    color: black;
    /* use sans-serif as fallback to make the difference obvious */
    font-family: 'OldStandard', sans-serif;
    background-color: rgb(255,255,245);
    line-height: 1.5em;
}
```

As you can see in this example, the EPUB creator uses the sans-serif system font as a fallback, and he has given his reason for doing so in a comment. OldStandard is a serif font, so he's using sans-serif so that he can easily spot instances in which OldStandard is missing a glyph and is falling back to the system font. In "Embedding for improved glyph coverage" (page 125), you saw an example of a glyph that was missing from both OldStandard and the sans-serif system font. I had to embed a different font altogether to get full coverage.

If you're embedding a font *strictly* as a fallback (and not for aesthetic or other reasons), you could reverse the order so that the system font is used by default, but the embedded font in employed as the fallback:

```
font-family: serif, 'DejaVuSerif';
```

DejaVu (*http://dejavu-fonts.org/*) is a good fallback because it has solid glyph coverage for Unicode characters outside the standard Latin blocks, and its license permits embedding.

Obfuscating Fonts

Font obfuscation (sometimes called mangling) is a process for changing a font file so that it cannot be extracted from an EPUB file and reused in other contexts. Technically, this means modifying the first 1,040 bytes of the file. If you want the nitty-gritty technical details, please refer to the relevant section (*http://bit.ly/UduxFD*) of the EPUB 3 specification.

Font obfuscation has been the source of much confusion. If you dig around the Web, you'll find plenty of blog posts (*http://bit.ly/SU9ah6*) and forum chatter (*http://bit.ly/ZPTFbO*) full of confused and frustrated ebook makers trying to make sense of it all. The confusion stems largely from the fact that, until recently, the IDPF and Adobe had competing font obfuscation algorithms, and reading systems supported one or the other. If you used the Adobe obfuscation method, your embedded font would render correctly on maybe the NOOK but not in iBooks, and so on.

Font obfuscation is not DRM

Adding font obfuscation to your file is not the same as adding digital rights management (DRM). An EPUB file can have no DRM—in other words, it can be moved to and read in any reading system that supports EPUB—but still include font obfuscation. Furthermore, an embedded and obfuscated font will render in all reading platforms that support embedded fonts. When you add obfuscation, you make it more difficult for a reader to unzip the EPUB file, extract the font, and install it on another system. When you add DRM, on the other hand, you encrypt the entire contents of the EPUB file, and you lock the reader into a single device or reading platform.

Because reading systems were split on which font obfuscation method they supported, EPUB creators were forced to create two versions of the file, one of each using the two methods. However, as of this writing, the major reading systems are no longer split in this regard and are using the obfuscation recommended by the IDPF. Therefore, preparing two files is no longer necessary. If you come by such advice on the Web, it is based on outdated information. To confirm this, I reviewed the EPUB that I mentioned in "Embedding to create a consistent look and feel across "platforms"" (page 123), *Art Space Tokyo*, which Craig and Ron prepared with embedded fonts that were obfuscated using the IDPF obfuscation method. The fonts render as expected in major reading systems such as NOOK, iBooks, Adobe Digital Editions, and even Amazon's Kindle Fire (after conversion to KF8 via KindleGen).[7]

InDesign started using the IDPF font obfuscation method in version CS6. Previous versions of InDesign used the Adobe obfuscation method.

While that's good news for ebook developers, the confusion around obfuscation will undoubtedly persist because the few tools that exist for obfuscation don't always use the IDPF method. The biggest offender in this regard is any version of Adobe InDesign before CS6, which uses the Adobe obfuscation method. Any EPUB file that is created with an older version of InDesign (up to and including CS5.5) has font embedding that is not compatible with major reading systems such as iBooks. Since InDesign is the tool of choice for many ebook creators who have not yet updated to version CS6, it is little wonder that there is so much confusion.

---

7. The *Art Space Tokyo* is EPUB 2.0.1 and not EPUB 3, but it's not relevant. Even major reading systems that are not yet fully compliant with EPUB 3 (i.e., nearly all of them) are supporting the EPUB 3 obfuscation method now.

How Do I Know Which Obfuscation Method My Software Is Using?

You can easily check which type of obfuscation your software is applying to a font. Once you've added the obfuscation (InDesign adds it automatically), change the file extension from *.epub* to *.zip*, and unzip the file with the zip utility of your choice. Look for a file named *encryption.xml*. Open it and you should see a line that identifies the Encryption Method Algorithm as either http://www.idpf.org/2008/embedding (IDPF) or http://ns.adobe.com/pdf/enc#RC (Adobe). You want the IDPF method, so if you don't have that, you need to use another tool. Simply changing a line in the *encryption.xml* will not work. You need a tool that employs the IDPF algorithm that is supported by the major reading systems. Without it, the reading systems won't be able to decipher and display your embedded font.

Besides InDesign CS6, there are few tools available for adding the IDPF font obfuscation. For EPUBs created without InDesign, you could use a tool called Sigil (*http:// code.google.com/p/sigil/*) to add obfuscation (Figure 4-10).

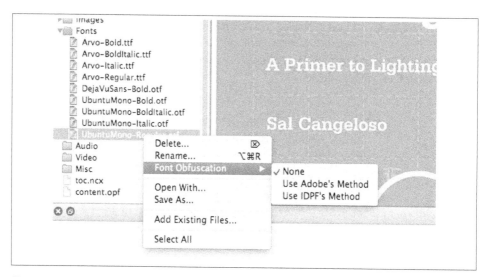

Figure 4-10. Sigil allows you to add the IDPF font obfuscation method

My own tests with Sigil were very encouraging, as it seems to apply the IDPF obfuscation correctly. The fonts that I tested rendered as expected on the major reading platforms. Now that the reading systems are supporting the same obfuscation method, we should see more tools like Sigil emerge, which will make adding font obfuscation easier.

Subsetting a Font

When you embed a font, you can optionally choose to *subset* it. When you subset a font, you include only the glyphs that you need, i.e., the characters that are actually used in the EPUB. For example, suppose your embedded font includes support for small letter alpha (α), but alpha is not used anywhere in your EPUB. If you were to subset the font before embedding it, the character information for the alpha would be thrown out since it is not needed in the context of your EPUB.

The primary advantage of subsetting an embedded font is that doing so reduces the file size, sometimes significantly. To give you an idea of how subsetting can affect file size, let's look at the example in Figure 4-7 again. I prepared another EPUB file of *The Waste Land*, but this time I used DejaVuSerif (*http://dejavu-fonts.org/wiki/Main_Page*), which has support for 2,888 glyphs and a file size of 562 KB. I then prepared yet another version of the EPUB, only this time I subsetted the font so that it included support for the 18 glyphs that I needed for the epigraph. The results were dramatic: the file size dropped from 562 KB to 15 KB, and the characters rendered as expected. With these results in mind, subsetting is an attractive option when you want to embed a font for more robust glyph coverage without introducing "bloat."

Subsetting is not…
Subsetting a font is not the same thing as obfuscating a font. You can subset a font and you can obfuscate a font, or any combination therein. Any given font can be both obfuscated and/or subsetted.

While it makes sense to subset a font when you embed it, there are few tools that make it easy to do so. As with obfuscation, Adobe InDesign CS6 is probably the best commercial tool available for subsetting. When you create an EPUB file with InDesign CS6, it both subsets and obfuscates embedded fonts by default, which is arguably the best possible result since you are effectively addressing licensing requirements and file size concerns simultaneously. The counterargument might be that InDesign is overzealous since there is no way to disable subsetting and obfuscation.

If you're not producing your EPUB files via InDesign CS6, your subsetting options are limited. In *The Waste Land* example above, I used the @font-face Kit Generator (*http://bit.ly/TwKKsf*) found on Font Squirrel. If you choose "Expert" mode, the Kit Generator gives you several options related to subsetting. You can even choose the exact characters that you wish to subset, which is what I did for the epigraph. While this tool is useful, it has several limitations. For example, it won't accept a font with a file size of over 2 MB. Also, it is somewhat slow (my test took several minutes) and can only be used via the Font Squirrel web interface. Before font subsetting can be a viable option in production workflows that are not centered around InDesign, we're going to need more and better tools.

Licensing Fonts for Embedding in EPUB

When you purchase a font, you are obtaining a license to use that font under specific terms as spelled out in the End User License Agreement (EULA). Licenses are typically purchased from a font foundry (such as Monotype Imaging or Adobe) or typeface designers operating independently. Licenses for fonts purchased via traditional means (a website vendor, for example) rarely cover font embedding in the way that we mean in the context of EPUB, and there is potential confusion around the terminology, as described in the sidebar "A Note on the Term "Embedding"" (page 138). As described in this useful FAQ from Monotype (*http://bit.ly/Ubh8mH*), standard font licenses typically allow installation of the font on a number of servers or workstations for use on print products. Additional (and usually separate) licensing is available for embedding a font on a website or an EPUB.

A Note on the Term "Embedding"

In this blog post (*http://adobe.ly/106owg7*) on licensing fonts for the Web, Adobe takes issue with the term "embedding" in the context of the Web as potentially inaccurate and confusing given the fact that font licenses have traditionally used the same term in the context of PDF:

> For many years, Adobe's font EULA has allowed embedding in electronic documents —the most obvious example of which is PDF. But despite the widespread use of the term "embedding" when talking about web fonts, it's best to not consider the use of @font-face "embedding." With something like PDF, font data is actually copied into a document and becomes part of its content—self-contained and portable. Importantly, the font data ceases to be a separate, usable font file, which protects the font from unauthorized use.

This potential source of confusion also applies to "embedding" in EPUB. Be careful to keep this ambiguity in mind when reviewing font licenses for possible embedding in EPUB. An Adobe license, for example, may in fact *permit* the use of embedding, but probably not in the way that we mean in the context of EPUB.

Because font embedding in EPUB is almost never covered under standard font EULAs, you're probably going to need to go through extra steps in order to obtain the proper license. As described in "Maybe You Should" (page 122), there are plenty of good reasons to embed fonts, so the extra work may very well be worthwhile. You have a couple of options, covered in the next sections.

Use an Open Font

If commercial font licensing in EPUB seems intimidating and perhaps just not worth the added overhead, you can still enjoy some of the benefits of embedding by using a font with an open license. Services such Google web fonts (*http://www.google.com/webfonts*) and Font Squirrel (*http://www.fontsquirrel.com/*) offer hundreds fonts that are free for commercial use. Google web fonts has the added bonus of being optimized for the screen, so they should look good in many reading systems. If nothing else, these services provide a fun and free way to experiment without having to worry about a license should you decide to embed the font in your final product.

Be careful when choosing fonts that are "open." Just because a font is free and open does *not* mean that you can use it in a commercial product, i.e., an EPUB that you sell. The two major open font licenses are SIL Open Font License (*http://bit.ly/10PCnfC*), which allow embedding (although the term "bundling" may be more appropriate in this context; see 1.15 of the SIL FAQ (*http://bit.ly/UkZfMR*)) in commercially sold products, and the General Public License (GPL) with the Font Exception clause (*http://bit.ly/YTWFPJ*), which is much less clear. Just to get a sense of the variety of licenses, take a look at the Wikipedia open source Unicode typefaces page (*http://bit.ly/UIOJ5J*). Unless you are using a service like Font Squirrel or Google web fonts, be sure to review the "open" license for your particular font.

Contact the Foundry Directly

If you want to include a commercial font, consider contacting the foundry directly. The types of licenses that are available for font embedding can vary among foundries and the fonts that they offer. Also, keep in mind that EULAs are evolving rapidly along with the maturation of ebook ecosystems, so it may be a good idea to check in every few months with your foundry to learn what new options may be available to you.

In Defense of Font Foundries and Typeface Designers

Given the sometimes limited licensing options, it can be easy to become frustrated with foundries and the typeface designers that they represent. Keep in mind that just as publishers and reading device makers are still figuring out the Wild West that is digital book publishing, foundries are too. When you speak with your foundry to negotiate licensing terms, help them understand the obstacles that you're facing so that they can continue to adjust their terms. For obvious reasons, foundries *want* you to embed commercial fonts. Also, they can offer expertise to content creators on which fonts work best in which reading systems and why. In other words, if you are embedding commercial fonts in EPUB, work with your foundry as a partner, not just a vendor.

The terms for commercial licensing for font embedding is typically tied to volume and/or term length. For example, a foundry may ask you to pay an annual fee based on the number of EPUB files sold in that year. As you might imagine, such an arrangement would be difficult to track and manage and may be untenable for some publishers.[8] A more manageable, if potentially more expensive, arrangement might be based on the number of titles you generally publish each year along with a lifetime license to each embedded font.

A commercial font EULA for embedding is also likely to require some combination of DRM, subsetting, and obfuscation. Remember, as described earlier in the chapter, these types of protection are *not the same thing*. In this respect, the EPUB 3 specification for font obfuscation is terrific news because major font foundries were on the EPUB 3 working group and directly involved in developing and approving the algorithm. The font foundries' acceptance of this obfuscation method coupled with the fact that major reading systems are now supporting it gives content creators a standard they can embrace with confidence. On the other hand, there are few tools for subsetting, and content creators should be (and are) wary of the life cycle of proprietary DRM. If your foundry is insisting on DRM, subsetting, and obfuscation, see if you can renegotiate the terms to include obfuscation only (perhaps reminding them that it is the standard). In any case, adding any one of these three protection options is likely adding an extra step to your production workflow, so plan accordingly.

The worst thing that you can do is to embed a commercial font and ignore the licensing altogether. By doing so, you are putting you or your organization at risk. Weigh the pros and cons, and if a commercial font is needed for your content and your publishing goals, reach out to your font foundry.

---

8. If this is the best your foundry can offer you, walk away, seriously.

CHAPTER 5

Multimedia

One of the primary drivers of the EPUB 3 revision was the publishing community's desire to natively include audio and video content in publications, a key ingredient in breaking EPUB out of the static confines of the printed page. In our ever-growing world of tablet computers, it's simply not feasible or realistic to expect content creators to make do with the artificial print compromise of two-dimensional images where video works better, or to include text transcripts and quotes in place of audio. By adopting HTML5, the uncertainty of plug-in support that has held back multimedia publications is now a thing of the past.

With the requirement to print becoming less of a roadblock for many genres, and going ebook-only is no longer equated with publishing suicide, the growth in fully integrated multimedia books can only continue from here on. Why limit readers to text instructions in science, technology, engineering, and mathematics (STEM) materials when you can also embed a video illustrating exactly how to carry out a procedure or experiment? Why paint in words alone the impact of a powerful piece of music when you can embed a recording for the reader? While the plain-Jane novel will undoubtedly continue on in its current form, publishing can now be much richer and deeper than text-and-headings novels.

In keeping with the nature of this guide, this chapter won't cover the endless ways you might integrate audio and video content into a work. Instead, it will demonstrate the issues of including content as they pertain to EPUB production. You also won't be subjected to a long-winded history of audio and video on the Web, because it's a dry and boring subject. Suffice it to say, all you really need to know is that multimedia was not initially a part of the HTML specification, and that largely accounts for the world of proprietary plug-ins that we've all come to know and loathe over the years.

From the early hypermedia void emerged the various formats, frameworks, and players that enabled the inclusion of audio and video content in browsers, many still with us today (RealMedia, QuickTime, Windows Media, Flash, etc.). The resulting haphazard approach to multimedia has been a bane of interoperability for the Web ever since, as browsers often require multiple players in order to be able to render the variety of media types found out in the wild. And that's the short story of why you're ever and always installing and updating plug-ins for your browser.

If you take this situation and apply it to ebooks, it's not hard to see why multimedia integration has lagged the ebook revolution, aside from just the lack of rendering on eInk devices. In EPUB, interoperability and reliability of rendering are key requirements for technological inclusion in the specification, and expecting readers to find and install plug-ins in an ebook environment is problematic, because even if the reader has an Internet connection and can find the required player, installing it for a browser on the device isn't necessarily the same as installing it for an ebook reading system running on the device (e.g., the reading system might not recognize plug-ins on the system, might ignore the content regardless of what plug-ins are installed, etc.).

But none of this pain is to suggest that adding audio and video was not possible before the new revision. You could technically embed multimedia in any EPUB 2 publication using the object element (with a fallback), but the odds of that content successfully playing weren't great. Support simply wasn't part of the specification, and unless the reading system provided plug-in support (as Adobe Digital Editions did for Flash video) or added support for the new multimedia elements despite the specification (Apple iBooks and Barnes & Noble's NOOK Color) readers would see only the fallback prose or image. EPUB 2s with rich content were not common, as a result.

EPUB 3 changes all that, with one caveat...

The Codec Issue

If this book were only about HTML5, and we were following a typical pedagogical learning curve, this chapter would probably begin by looking at the new audio and video elements and how to use them. And we'll get to that. Unfortunately, much of the discussion in this chapter is going to be colored by a big nuisance in HTML5 (the lack of support for a common video codec), so that's where we'll instead have to start (and learning curves are just a bore, anyway).

 EPUB 3 requires support for both MP3 and AAC-LC (MP4) audio, so the issues with video in this chapter are not cross-cutting.

The problem of a lack of a common video codec gets magnified when ported to EPUB because it breaks one of the core features of the format: the predictability of rendering. EPUBs are not just websites in a box, as you've already seen, even if that's the easy way to think about them. EPUB is more like a subsetting of HTML, because you don't often have the full power of the Web at your fingertips while reading an ebook.

The subsetting can feel like a nuisance if you're used to the freedom of the Web, but it ensures that reading systems are able to render all content without the reader having to install anything, which, as already noted, is often not possible. And that's where the problem of a lack of common video support starts to bring us full circle to the problem of plug-in support. It's not quite as problematic, as you'll see, but it has the potential to make your content just as unrenderable.

But to jump back to the revision, agreement on support for a single video codec was the one fly in the ointment of complete interoperability (dreaming of a DRM-free world, of course). After a number of attempts to find consensus, the end result was a kind of stalemate between support for H.264 and VP8, without consensus on being able to support both (similar to what happened with support on the broader Web, but there initially between H.264 and Ogg Theora and then later WebM). The practical outcome of this stalemate, as with HTML5, is that producers are free to embed *any* video container/codec combination they please, and reading system developers can choose to support *any* combination they please, including none at all.

More practically, the video options are going to be limited. In the interests of interoperability, the IDPF strongly urges developers and content creators to use one or both of the VP8 and H.264 codecs, and those two are the mostly likely ones to find support in reading systems based on the discussions that took place in the working group. In other words, there may be no *de jure* standard, but deviate from the *de facto* one at your own risk.

 One sticking point with H.264, not just in EPUB, is whether it is royalty free or not. Although declared royalty free for free Internet video use by the licensing organization (MPEG-LA) in 2010, that condition wouldn't apply to the sale of retail EPUBs. An excellent discussion of the issues around H.264 is available here (*http://www.engadget.com/ 2010/05/04/know-your-rights-h-264-patent-licensing-and-you/*).

But "limited" options don't rule out the very real problem that you're likely going to have to duplicate all your video content in order to ensure your EPUB will render for all readers, and even then there is no guarantee of playback if a reading system supports only another option like Ogg Theora. That begs the question: what can you do to minimize the impact?

The first piece of advice is to consider the distribution channel you put your EPUBs into, and what format(s) the devices that connect to it are likely to support. If you're publishing to Apple's iBookstore, for example, you're required to use the H.264 codec to encode video in the M4V file format. Since only Apple devices with the ability to decrypt Apple's DRM will be able to access the publication, there'd be no point including alternate formats.

 The BISG EPUB 3 support grid (*http://bit.ly/UACFly*) can help in determining which devices support which formats as more information becomes available.

But you'll only avoid transcoding your videos if you plan to distribute your EPUB through a single vendor, or can find a common format across the ones you use. That's rarely a realistic option. Targeting devices also descends video into the same sphere as DRM and walled gardens, where content can't travel from one device to another. Throw in the browser as cloud reading system, and things get even murkier.

A better alternative is to provide the option to the reading system to pick the format it supports. It doesn't necessarily introduce barriers to distribution, like doubling the size of your EPUB file, but isn't an instant panacea, either.

But it's time to switch gears at this point, and look at the media elements themselves to see how this can be done. We'll pick back up on the problem of video as we encounter potential options exposed through the markup.

 The codec debate in EPUB 3 is not closed, but has been deferred until consensus can be achieved. Any future update of the specification could see support for one or more codecs codified, at which point all discussion in this chapter about content duplication would be happily made moot.

The Media Elements

The new HTML5 `audio` and `video` elements probably won't seem all that awe inspiring as we look them over, at least from a markup perspective, but they really do represent a huge step forward in terms of cross-compatibility of content (the video codec issue aside). Plug-ins were not just a pain because they had to be installed, but also because they run in a distinct space allocated by the reading system. While many people never notice or care about this distinction, users of assistive technologies are only too aware of the black boxes these plug-in spaces represent, as the players running in them offer wildly varied accessibility support and often come with surprise keyboard traps.

HTML5 does away with this problem by bringing the rendering back into the reading system, enabling it to control playback without launching a plug-in application. And that also means that content creators can now control playback, too; it's possible to create your own media players using HTML elements and JavaScript. EPUB 3 even allows you to create script-free players, as you'll see at the end of this chapter. This change also makes it possible for assistive technologies to more reliably interact with media content, as even custom controls can now be made accessible via the document object model (DOM).

Sources

There are two methods to identify the audio or video resource to load. The first is to add a `src` attribute to the appropriate element:

```
<audio src="audio/clip01.mp3"/>
```

```
<video src="video/clip01.webm"/>
```

This attribute either contains a relative reference to an audio or video clip in the EPUB container, as in the preceding example, or it can reference resources outside the container. Yes, you have been hearing right if you've noticed the various hints in this book about audio and video content being located inside *or* outside the container. Unlike EPUB 2, where all your resources had to be bundled into the container file, EPUB 3 makes a special exception for audio and video. The potential size issue in distributing this content, especially when it might have to be duplicated in more than one format, was the primary motivator, as you might imagine. But allowing content outside the container also leads to a host of other issues (pardon the pun), which we'll deal with as we go.

Not surprisingly, then, you can tweak the previous example to indicate that a video resource has to be retrieved from the Web as follows:

```
<video src="http://www.example.com/video/clip01.webm"/>
```

But note when referencing external resources in a content document that you need to identify as much in the package document manifest. This is done by adding the `remote-resources` property to the entry for the containing file. The entry for the content document containing this clip might be marked up like this:

```
<item id="c01"
      src="chapter01.xhtml"
      media-type="application/xhtml+xml"
      properties="remote-resources"/>
```

Also be aware that even though the video resource is not in the EPUB container, you still need to include a manifest entry for it:

```
<item id="vid01"
      src="http://www.example.com/video/clip01.webm"
      media-type="video/webm"/>
```

The manifest lists all content items that are used in the direct rendering of the publication, so even though audio and video may live remotely, entries for them are still required.

Returning to the src attribute, one of its prime limitations is that it can only be used to specify a single audio or video resource. As just discussed about the need to include at least two possible video formats to minimize playback issues, this attribute probably isn't going to be a reliable fit for anything but audio content, or targeted distribution.

So how do you handle video? The HTML5 working group mitigated the problem of variable codec support by allowing one or more source elements as the children of the audio and video elements. Identical to the src attribute just mentioned, each of these source elements includes its own src attribute defining the location of a potential resource.

You could now account for varying reading system support for video by providing both WebM and M4V video options as follows:

```
<video>
   <source src="video/v001.webm"/>
   <source src="video/v001.m4v"/>
</video>
```

The reading system can now step through each of the source elements until it finds a format it can play back for the reader.

The source element is an *alternative* to using the src attribute on the audio or video element; you cannot use the src attribute and the source elements together. Doing so will also cause your EPUB to fail a validation check, because a reading system will ignore the child source elements in such cases, even if it cannot play the resource referenced on the parent element.

Although this tagging represents a working solution for the multiple codec issue, at least in terms of providing potential options, it's still not a very efficient one. When provided only the src attribute, the reading system will have to inspect the resource defined in each source tag to determine if the referenced audio or video can be played.

A src attribute on the audio or video element provides the same limited information, but when there is only one format, either the reading system can play it as it attempts to load it or it can't, so there isn't the same potential for wasted time checking for playback compatibility.

To speed up the identification of supported formats (or rapid elimination of unsupported formats, depending on your world view) you can add the appropriate media type to each source element in a type attribute. If you haven't come across media types before, they are a standardized way of identifying file formats over the Internet, consisting of the general resource family followed by a unique subtype (e.g., *application/javascript*, *audio/mp3, text/css*).

By adding the media type to each source element, the reading system no longer has to inspect the referenced resources as it steps through the list; it can determine playback compatibility by matching the media type against the known types it can play. It may also mean that every person reading your EPUB isn't querying your servers every time a document with multimedia resources in it is loaded, if you remotely host your content.

You can add the media types to each source tag in the previous example as follows:

```
<video>
    <source src="video/v001.webm" type="video/webm"/>
    <source src="video/v001.m4v" type="video/x-m4v"/>
</video>
```

One caveat here is to make sure you don't incorrectly enter the media type when adding this attribute. When you specify the value, the reading system will take your word (the type value) over inspecting the resource. If you enter the wrong media type value, a reading system that could play the clip will assume that it can't and continue checking the other source elements for a format it does support. A validator like epubcheck won't report an issue either, because it has no way of knowing whether the type is invalid or some new format.

In most cases, the src and type attributes are all you need to provide the reading system to minimize any potential playback lag and unnecessary querying, but there is one more bit of information you can add to improve the compatibility discovery process: the codecs used. If you specify only the media type, you're providing information only about the audio or video container, not about how the information contained in it is encoded.

For the benefit of those who aren't familiar with video containers, it wouldn't hurt to stop for a quick bit of background here. You can think of a video container in much the same way as an EPUB container, as packaging the resources needed for proper playback. Containers can include video and/or audio tracks, and sometimes also subtitle tracks. A video isn't just one big data mash-up, in other words, but separate streams of information bundled together.

The flexibility of these containers isn't restricted to just the type and number of streams that can be included, but it also extends to the codecs that can be used to encode the information in those streams. Some containers may strictly regulate the codecs that can be used, but others are general purpose in nature. The more flexible the container format, the less sure the reading system will be that it can play the format based only on the container identified in the media type.

So why does this matter to you? In many cases it doesn't (WebM and M4V are predictable without the extra codec information), but if you want to write code to alter what gets displayed if the video cannot be rendered, for example, you need to be as precise as possible. The more general the information you provide when using general-purpose containers, the more likely the reading system is to say "maybe" when asked if the video will play (the JavaScript `canPlayType` function, which is used to test for compatibility, literally returns "maybe" in response).

For example, instead of just indicating that you're using an MP4 container:

```
<source src="video/v001.mp4" type="video/mp4"/>
```

you could add a list of the specific codecs used for the audio and video tracks by adding the `codecs` parameter to the `type` attribute like this:

```
<source src="video/v001.mp4" type='video/mp4; codecs="avc1.42E01E, mp4a.40.2"'/>
```

The attribute now relays to the reading system that the video is encoded using the H.264 baseline codec and there is also an audio track encoded using AAC-LC (one of the EPUB-supported audio formats).

You'll notice that the quoting on the `type` attribute was flipped in the previous example so that double quotes surround the embedded codecs parameter. Although it doesn't normally matter which characters you use to quote attribute values in HTML, the inner `codecs` parameter must always use double quotes, so this is one case where you can't just use your own preference.

Of course, few people actually memorize these codec strings, so don't worry if they seem impossibly dense or you don't even know how you go about figuring out what to input.

The `source` element definition (*http://dev.w3.org/html5/spec/single-page.html#the-source-element*) in the HTML5 specification lists many of the most common types for easy cut and paste, so you don't have to know what `avc1.42E01E` actually means, as long as you generally know what format you used to encode your audio and video.

 For space-saving reasons, the examples in the rest of this chapter will omit the `codecs` parameter.

Size matters

When looking at the source media content and ways to duplicate it, a closely linked corollary discussion is how to handle the inevitable size issue. If you publish your content through one of the major retailers, you're going to run into caps on the size of the content you can distribute. Apple's iBooks, for example, has a 2 GB limit with a recommendation to strive for much smaller sizes because of space and playback issues (200 MB being noted in their guidelines). Barnes & Noble has a cap at 600 MB (smaller for PubIt! publishers).

As you've already seen, one content strategy the EPUB working group made allowances for in the specification was to enable audio and video resources to live outside the container. If you are targeting a specific distribution channel and brand of reading system, but know that your content could be rendered on others, you could embed the more common video format and remotely host the version that's less likely to be needed by readers:

```
<video>
    <source src="video/v001.webm" type="video/webm" type="video/webm"/>
    <source src="http://www.example.com/video/v001.m4v" type="video/x-m4v"/>
</video>
```

Hosting the resources on a remote server comes with its own unique issues, though. It might get you in the online bookstore, and the reader won't have the initial wait for their download of your EPUB to complete, but inevitably that content has to make it to their system.

Another negative of web hosting is that it may lead to repeated downloads for the same resource by the same reader, depending on how often the local cache on the reading system is cleared or how many devices they read on. You also need to consider the persistence of the links you include in your EPUBs, because once your ebook is released those links will become permanent to the buyer of the ebook. Security of your hosted content is always a consideration, too.

The point here is not to scare you off remote hosting, only to highlight that the decision to go that route needs to be more than just about how to minimize size. Developing a comprehensive content management strategy as part of any decision to remotely host content is highly recommended, because it will get you into thinking about how to mitigate these issues and avoid discovering pitfalls only after you've begun distributing.

Remote hosting isn't the only solution to the size issue, of course. Your choice in audio/ video format and codec use will also affect the size of your final EPUB. Some distribution channels don't offer flexibility, at least for video, but encoding your audio to AAC-LC (MP4) typically results in smaller file sizes than equivalent encoding in MP3, for example. As we're in the business of creating ebooks first and foremost, whether you need to use the highest quality resolutions and bitrates in your audio and video content is another question you need to consider. Is the reader really going to notice or be upset if they don't have perfect audio and video clarity?

Optimizing Playback

The ability of the human ear to distinguish differences in quality diminishes the higher quality the sound becomes. The average listener can easily tell the difference between human narration encoded at 32 kbps and 128 kbps, but not so much between 64 kbps and 128 kbps. Music sounds good at 128kbps to the lay audiophile, but generally only trained ears that know the distortions to listen for can tell the difference when compared to 256 kbps or 320 kbps.

This isn't to suggest that you should strive for the least quality content you can get by with, but when it comes to distribution, sometimes compromises that aren't going to radically alter the reader's enjoyment of the work have to be made. Compromise might even be necessary to effectively deliver the content to the device. Providing the reader with choice of quality is not a bad idea, in other words.

So how can you offer different quality audio and video formats depending on the reader's device and/or connection speed?

The answer, unfortunately, is that there are no native methods available. When a reading system steps through the source elements, it cannot tell what resolution and/or bitrate were used, and even if it could, which one to render is not a decision the reader necessarily wants the device to make for them. As soon as the reading system finds a source that can be played back, it will typically use that source. Since there is no container or codec difference, only you as the content creator know which is "high" quality and which is "low."

You can still offer the reader the option of high- or low-quality audio or video (and levels in between), but it requires scripted solutions. The following example shows a simple set of controls that flip the source depending on what quality the reader has selected:

```
<script>

function switchQuality(q) {

    var src = new Array();
        src.low = 'http://www.example.com/video/clip01-lowres.mp4';
        src.hi = 'http://www.example.com/video/clip01-hires.mp4';

    var vid = document.getElementById('video1');
    var low_btn = document.getElementById('lowres');
    var hi_btn = document.getElementById('hires');

    if (q == 'low') {
        low_btn.setAttribute('hidden', 'hidden');
        hi_btn.removeAttribute('hidden');
        vid.src = src.low;
    }

    else {
        hi_btn.setAttribute('hidden', 'hidden');
        low_btn.removeAttribute('hidden');
        vid.src = src.hi;
    }

    vid.load();
    vid.play();
}
</script>

<video id="video1" src="http://www.example.com/video/clip01-hires.mp4"/>

<p id="video1-lowres" class="small">
  Switch to
  <button id="lowres" onclick="switchQuality('low')">Lower Quality</a>
  <button id="hires" onclick="switchQuality('hi')"
      hidden="hidden">Higher Quality</a>
</p>
```

If the default high-quality video is too slow, or even if the reader just wants to minimize their potential wireless bill, they can switch to the lower quality version before any playback begins. You could make this example more sophisticated, so that if the reader switches mode mid-video they aren't forced back to the beginning, but that's left as another exercise for the reader.

Preloading

One issue that wasn't covered in the discussion of remote hosting of resources was preloading the data for the user. The EPUB 3 package document has mechanisms in place to allow reading systems to determine which media resources are outside the container (the remote-resources property), and potentially download and cache them, but there is an implicit assumption there that all the resources are necessary and will be rendered in full by every reader. The reality is that reading systems don't currently prefetch remote content as soon as a book is opened, and readers run a spectrum from those who won't stop reading to watch or listen to a media resource to those who will watch every second of every clip.

As the content creator, though, you'll often have a reasonable idea of how likely someone is to consume your content. If a video clip is integral to following the narrative, and in the primary narrative flow, chances are good that someone is going to watch it, at least the first time they read through the section. If the resource is part of a sidebar, the number of viewers will drop, as many readers skip supplementary information.

The more likely the reader is to consume the content, the more helpful it is to have that content ready for them as soon as they want to begin playback. Unfortunately, you can't really control what a reading system will do, but HTML5 does allow you to give the reading system a hint as to what you would like it to do through the `preload` attribute.

This attribute takes any of the following values:

none
> Indicates that it is unlikely the reader will consume the content, or you wish to avoid unnecessary server traffic, so wait until the reader initiates playback before fetching any data.

metadata
> Indicates that it is possible the reader will consume the content, but the reading system can download the resource metadata and potentially some content just in case.

auto
> Indicates that the reader is expected to play back the content, or bandwidth is not an issue, so the reading system can start downloading the resource immediately.

Knowing that few people are going to be interested in watching our video of paint swatches drying, for example, you could set the `none` value to request that no data be grabbed in advance:

```
<video prefetch="none">
    <source src="paintDrying.webm" type="video/webm"/>
</video>
```

In keeping with the freedom of the reading system to do what it pleases, there is no default value when the attribute is not specified, and the reading system can ignore whatever you do specify.

Another Option

It's worth noting at this point that even though EPUB has required audio formats, there's nothing preventing you from using specialized formats if they better fit your needs (e.g., better compression/quality). The only requirement is that a fallback in either MP3 or MP4 be provided. For example, you could use multiple source elements to designate a preferred format you've included in the container (Speex), with a fallback (MP3) on a remote server as follows:

```
<audio>
    <source src="audio/clip001.spx" type="audio/x-speex"/>
    <source src="http://www.example.com/audio/clip001.mp3" type="audio/mp3"/>
</audio>
```

This kind of fallback approach would work well in controlled environments where you can predict that the majority, or preferably all, of your readers will be using reading systems that support your nonstandard content. Otherwise, it could backfire on you if all readers request the MP3s on your server.

Control

Having finally exhausted all there is to say about audio and video sources, the next piece of functionality exposed by the audio and video elements is control over playback. Sometimes surprising when first encountering these elements, the reader is not provided any means of controlling playback by default. You, as the content creator, are required to provide playback functionality, whether by skinning your own player or by enabling the default reading system controls.

Fortunately, enabling the native controls is as simple as including a controls attribute on each multimedia element:

```
<audio ... controls="controls"/>
```

```
<video ... controls="controls"/>
```

It's still a bit odd that by default readers are provided no means to control playback, but as the native controls aren't the most glamorous, the HTML5 working group undoubtedly expected more people would skin their own players.

Using video as an example, Figure 5-1 shows the three possible scenarios readers may encounter: video without any controls, video with native controls enabled, and custom controls below the video.

Figure 5-1. A video with no controls, with native controls enabled, and with custom controls

The rendering is similar for audio, but unless you specify the controls attribute on the audio element, or include your own controls, the user won't see anything at the point where the audio is embedded (e.g., background music). If you take away the video display area, you essentially have the default audio controls, as shown in Figure 5-2.

Figure 5-2. The native audio controls exposed by Readium

You should always plan for the least functionality in a reading system and enable the native controls by default. Even if you skin your own player, there is no guarantee that a reading system will support JavaScript, leaving the reader with no way to activate the media (you'll see a feature EPUB 3 introduces to also work around this problem later). The HTML5 specification does state that "if scripting is disabled for the media element, then the user agent should expose a user interface to the user," but no known reading systems do so at this time, and the wording does not make it a requirement for them to do so in the future.

Outside of some really specialized uses of video (such as embedding in canvas), there are few pressing reasons against giving the reader any control; most are just aesthetic. One example might be automatically playing a video as a transition between chapters or parts in a novel and not wanting the video to appear overlaid with controls.

You can initiate the playback part by adding the autoplay attribute:

```
<video ... autoplay="autoplay">
```

When playback is automatically started in this way, the controls, if visible, will immediately fade out from view, so any aesthetic displeasure they cause is fleeting. A better solution than not providing playback control would be to add a few seconds delay at the start of the video so that the controls are gone by the time the actual content begins.

Most readers will hardly notice the presence of the controls, because cognitively it will take a moment to process the new page anyway, and a delayed start will give the reader time to orient themselves to what is about to happen (loading a page and having a video immediately begin is startling even if you know it's coming).

Also remember that EPUB is reflowable content, and you can't control the "page" size, before jumping too quickly on autoplay bandwagon. Audio and video content that is set to autoplay will normally be initiated as soon as the first page of content is rendered, not when the element first becomes visible in the viewport. If you automatically start a clip that ends up even a page or two deep, for example, imagine the confusion when the reader gets startled by a ghostly, detached audio track as the first page loads with no audio or video player on it.

Even the trend to features as seemingly innocuous as background mood music to augment the reading experience are a bad idea without some means of disabling the sound. This kind of background audio can impact on the accessibility of your content, because someone using a reading system's built-in text-to-speech rendering might be forced to struggle through the overlapping audio. Lacking controls, only the reading system volume will be available, and it will move both tracks higher and lower in sync.

But why make any assumptions? Instead of placing readers in a position where they have to work around your design choices, the simpler route is to always enable the controls and then selectively disable them when scripting is available, by none other than scripted methods! If your own scripted controls will work in the reading system, remove the native controls in your code with a few lines of JavaScript (using jQuery to simplify iterating over both audio and video elements):

```
<script>
$(document).ready( function() {
    $('audio, video').each( function() {
            this.removeAttribute("controls");
        });
});
</script>
```

This kind of progressive enhancement of audio and video content will leave all readers happy, regardless of whether the experience is exactly how you wanted it to be or not.

Posters

The poster attribute is used with the video element to control the initial image displayed to the reader before video playback begins. In the past, what would be displayed when video content was initialized was up to the plug-in, but was often either a black screen or the first frame of the video. Rarely the most appealing use of the real estate.

With the `poster` attribute, you get to specify the image you want shown. If we were writing a movie themed book, for example, we could indicate that we want an image of curtains to show by default as follows:

```
<video width="320" height="180" controls="controls" poster="img/curtains.png">
```

When the reader first encounters the video, it will now show the custom image shown in Figure 5-3.

Figure 5-3. Poster image of theatre curtains

Poster images must be included in the EPUB container, even if the associated video resource is remotely hosted (the exception applies only to the audio and video resources themselves). On the bright side, you never have to worry about whether the image will render or not like you do with the video content itself. Even if your content cannot be played back, the poster image will still be rendered. You'll see why this is useful soon.

Dimensions

Always setting the height and width of your video content should be a given. Reading systems will attempt to determine the dimensions from the video metadata, but this circles back to the problem of remotely hosting content and the reader not having an active Internet connection. If you haven't specified any dimensions, and the resource isn't available, the reading system will next check if you've specified a poster image and use its dimensions. As a last resort, it will default to rendering a 300 px by 150 px viewing area.

You can either set the height and width attributes on the element:

```
<video id="vid01" ... width="640" height="360">
```

or via CSS:

```
<style type="text/css">
video#vid01 {
    width: 640px;
    height: 360px;
    max-width: 100%;
}
</style>
```

Setting the max-width property to 100%, as in this example, is also recommended to ensure that your video properly scales down to the available viewing area.

> The audio element does not include these attributes, since audio has no visible size. You cannot change the size and space that the default audio controls occupy.

The Rest

And for completeness, here's a quick recap of the media-specific attributes that aren't critical enough to warrant their own discussion:

crossorigin
Sets the credential flag (anonymous or use-credentials) to use for cross-origin resource sharing (CORS). Setting CORS allows a video clip to be embedded in a canvas without tainting the canvas, for example. It is not necessary to set this attribute just because the audio or video resource is hosted remotely, even though all remote resources are on a different domain from the EPUB. For more information, see the W3C Cross-Origin Resource Sharing (*http://www.w3.org/TR/cors/*) specification.

loop
Indicates that the audio or video clip is to be continuously replayed (e.g., background music).

mediagroup
Allows multiple audio or video clips to be controlled by a common set of controls (e.g., to provide sign-language transcription beside an audio or video clip).

muted
Indicates that audio is muted by default.

Timed Tracks

Built-in playback and playback control are not the end of the advances that the new audio and video elements bring to EPUB 3. Both elements also now allow timed text tracks to be embedded using the HTML5 track element.

If you're wondering what timed text tracks are, you're probably more familiar with their practical names, such as captions, subtitles, and descriptions. A timed track provides instructions on how to synchronize text (or its rendering) with an audio or video resource: to overlay text as a video plays, to include synthesized voice descriptions, to provide signed descriptions, to allow navigation within the resource, etc., as shown in Figure 5-4.

Figure 5-4. Video containing subtitled text at the bottom of the screen

Don't underestimate the usefulness of subtitles and captions; they are not a niche accessibility need. There are many cases where a reader would prefer not to be bothered with the noise while reading, are reading in an environment where it would bother others to enable sound, or are unable to hear clearly or accurately what is going on because of background noise (e.g., on a subway, bus, or airplane). The irritation they will feel at having to return to the video later when they are in a more amenable environment pales next to someone who is not provided any access to that information.

It probably bears repeating at this point, too, that subtitles and captions are not the same thing, and both have important uses that necessitate their inclusion. Subtitles provide the dialogue being spoken, whether in the same language as in the video or translated, and there's typically an assumption the reader is aware which person is speaking. Captions, however, are descriptive and provide ambient and other context useful for someone who can't hear what else might be going on in the video in addition to the dialogue (which typically will shift location on the screen to reflect the person speaking).

There are currently two competing technologies for writing timed tracks: Timed Text Markup Language (TTML) and Web Video Text Tracks (WebVTT). TTML is an XML-based language that provides a greater range of features than WebVTT. WebVTT, on the other hand, is text-based and often simpler to create for the average web content producer:

```
<--! TTML: -->

<tt xml:lang="en" xmlns="http://www.w3.org/ns/ttml">
    <body region="subtitleArea">
        <div>
            <p xml:id="sub001" begin="4.50s" end="11.50s">
```

```
                The EPUB 3 specification is young. It was
                less than 2 months ago now, that the IDPF
            </p>
        </div>
        ...
    </body>
</tt>


<--! WEBVTT: -->

WEBVTT

1
00:04.500 --> 00:11.500
The EPUB 3 specification is young. It was less than 2 months ago now, that the
IDPF


...
```

A typical aside at this point would be to detail how to create these tracks in a little more detail, but plenty of tutorials abound on the Web, in addition to the specifications themselves. Because the technologies are not unique to EPUB, we'll not go down the road of analyzing both formats. Understanding a bit of the technology is not a bad thing, but similar to writing effective descriptions for images, the bigger issue is having the experience and knowledge about the target audience to create meaningful and useful captions and descriptions.

The issues involved in creating effective captions are also beyond what could be reasonably handled in this book. From the fonts you choose, to maintaining contrast, to potentially editing dialogue to deal with the fact that most people can't read as fast as the persons on the screen can talk, there are many issues involved in captioning and not a lot of authoritative references for the lay person. If you don't have the expertise, engage those who do. Transcription costs are probably much lower than you'd expect, especially considering the small amounts of video and audio most ebooks will likely include.

 For a recap of captioning issues, see Olivier Nourry's presentation slides (*http://bit.ly/WMtJYa*) for "Making Videos More Accessible to the Deaf and Hard of Hearing."

Instead, it's time to learn how these tracks can be attached to your audio or video content using the track element. The following example shows a subtitle and caption track being added to a video:

```
<video width="320" height="180" controls="controls">
  <source src="video/v001.webm"/>
  <track
     kind="subtitles"
     src="video/captions/en/v001.vtt"
     srclang="en"
     label="English"/>
  <track
     kind="captions"
     src="video/captions/en/v001.cc.vtt"
     srclang="en"
     label="English"/>
</video>
```

The first three attributes on the `track` element provide information about the relation to the referenced video resource: the `kind` attribute indicates the nature of the timed track you're attaching, the `src` attribute provides the location of the timed track in the EPUB container, and the `srclang` attribute indicates the language of that track.

The `label` attribute is different, because it provides the text to render when presenting the options the reader can select from. The value, as you might expect, is that you aren't limited to a single version of any one type of track so long as each has a unique label. You could expand the previous example to include translated French subtitles as follows:

```
<video width="320" height="180" controls="controls">
  <source src="video/v001.webm" type="video/webm"/>
  <track
     kind="subtitles"
     src="video/captions/en/v001.vtt"
     srclang="en"
     label="English"/>
  <track
     kind="captions"
     src="video/captions/en/v001.cc.vtt"
     srclang="en"
     label="English"/>
  <track
     kind="subtitles"
     src="video/captions/fr/v001.vtt"
     srclang="fr"
     label="Fran&amp;#xE7;ais"/>
</video>
```

This example uses the language name for the label only to highlight one of the prime deficiencies of the `track` element for accessibility purposes. Different disabilities have different needs, and how you caption a video for someone who is deaf is not necessarily how you might caption it for someone with cognitive disabilities, for example.

The weak semantics of the `label` attribute are unfortunately all that is available to convey the target audience. The HTML5 specification, for example, currently includes the following `track` for captions (fixed to be XHTML compliant):

```
<track
  kind="captions"
  src="brave.en.hoh.vtt"
  srclang="en"
  label="English for the Hard of Hearing"/>
```

You can match the kind of track and language to a reader's preferences, but you can't make finer distinctions about who is the intended audience without reading the label. Not only have machines not mastered the art of reading, but native speakers find many ways to say the same thing, scuttling heuristic tests.

The result is that reading systems are going to be limited in terms of being able to automatically enable the appropriate captioning for any given user. In reality, getting one caption track would be a huge step forward compared to the Web, but it takes away a tool from those who do target these reader groups and introduces a frustration for the readers in that they have to turn on the proper captioning for each video.

You've seen the difference between subtitles and captions earlier, but the `kind` attribute can additionally take the following two values of note:

descriptions
> Specifying this value indicates that the track contains a text description of the video. A descriptions track is designed to provide missing information to readers who can hear the audio but not see the video (which includes blind and low-vision readers, but also anyone for whom the video display is obscured or not available). The track is intended to be voiced by a text-to-speech engine.

chapters
> A chapters track includes navigational aid within the resource. If your audio or video is structured in a meaningful way (e.g., scenes), adding a chapters track will enable readers of all abilities to more easily navigate through it.

Being able to add more than one version of the same "kind" of track brings us to a last attribute for the `track` element: `default`. If you were to provide captions for more than one audience, for example, you could specify one to render by default when the reader has no preferences that could match a more precise version. Using the earlier example with multiple subtitles in different languages, you could specify that English should render by default by adding this attribute to the `track` tag:

```
<video width="320" height="180" controls="controls">
  <source src="video/v001.webm" type="video/webm"/>
  <track
    kind="subtitles"
    src="video/captions/en/v001.vtt"
```

```
        srclang="en"
        label="English"
        default="default"/>
    <track
        kind="subtitles"
        src="video/captions/fr/v001.vtt"
        srclang="fr"
        label="Fran&amp;#xE7;ais"/>
</video>
```

But the downside of the `track` element that hasn't yet been mentioned is that it remains unsupported in browser cores at the time of this writing (at least natively), which means EPUB readers also may not support tracks right away. There are some JavaScript libraries that claim to be able to provide support now (colloquially called *polyfills*, as they fill the cracks), but that assumes the reader has a JavaScript-enabled reading system.

 Although support will develop in time, if waiting is not an option, you can write the captions directly into your video (open captioning). Mock closed-captioning can also be provided by including a video with no captions and an equivalent with open captions and providing a scripted button to toggle between the versions.

Fallbacks

The last aspect of the `audio` and `video` elements to discuss is how to provide fallbacks in case of a lack of support. Traditionally, when you think of a fallback, you think of content that will be rendered in place of the element. HTML5 `audio` and `video` are a bit confusing, because their fallbacks are not for reading systems that support HTML5. A reading system is not going to determine whether the supplied audio and video clips can be played and render fallback content if not, only whether it recognizes the `audio` and `video` tags. This is true for all compliant EPUB 3 reading systems.

If a reader were to open your publication in an EPUB 2 reading system, which is only required to support the XHTML 1.1 element set, the new `audio` and `video` tags most likely would not be recognized (with a few exceptions like we noted at the outset of the chapter). In older reading systems, the tags are treated much like generic block or inline elements, depending on the context in which they are used. Without a fallback message, nothing would be presented to the reader.

For compatibility with these legacy reading systems, you can avoid holes in your content by including fallback HTML content inside of the elements to render instead.

You could add a paragraph containing a message about the available video formats as follows:

```
<video width="320" height="180" controls="controls">
  <source src="video/v001.webm" type="video/webm"/>
  <source src="video/v001.m4v" type="video/x-m4v"/>
  <p>Sorry, but your reading system does not support HTML5 video.
    This video is available in
    <a href="video/v001.webm">WebM</a> and
    <a href="video/v001.m4v">M4V</a> formats.
    It can also be
    <a href="http://www.example.com/mybook/videos">viewed online</a>.</p>
</video>
```

A reading system that doesn't support audio or video is probably unlikely to be able to play the supplied formats, but if you can host the media online for viewing it is one way to give readers an equivalent experience.

You aren't limited to text, either. If you want to facilitate playback on EPUB 2 reading systems that supported Flash video, for example, you could embed an object element. The final fallback text would then be moved inside the object for those reading systems that don't support Flash either:

```
<video width="320" height="180" controls="controls">
  <source src="video/v001.webm" type="video/webm"/>
  <source src="video/v001.m4v" type="video/x-m4v"/>
  <object width="400" height="300" data="video/v001.swf">
    <param name="movie" value="video/v001.swf"/>
    <p>Sorry, but your reading system does not appear to
      support the embedded video formats (WebM and M4V)
      or Flash playback.</p>
  </object>
</video>
```

What you absolutely don't want to do is embed transcripts and accessible descriptions or content equivalents inside these elements. As EPUB 3 reading systems must support the elements in order to be compliant with the specification, whether or not they actually render the audio or video content, the reader should never be presented the embedded information, and it will not be available to assistive technologies.

Alternate Content

The obvious problem with eInk devices in an age of multimedia content is that they simply aren't up to the task of rendering sight and sound. It's easy to overstate how much audio and video content will make its way into publications, but what do you do if you are an author and are worried that a segment of your readers won't get the full experience?

Not including the content simply because some devices won't render it may be a safe approach, but it's also not a terribly practical one, especially considering all the devices that now support multimedia experiences. If you can provide the reader a deeper, richer experience through enhanced content, dumbing it down to the least capable device is probably not going to sell you more books in the long run, anyway.

But providing alternative content is not an easy task with audio and video. A proper EPUB 3 eInk reading system should not present fallback content within the elements, as, again, it's only for EPUB 2 reading systems. A compliant reading system should present either your poster image, some other visual image where the content would have been (similar to the disabled display that appears when web-hosted content cannot be reached, for example) or nothing at all. This makes the inclusion of transcripts and alternate content a much bigger concern.

Unfortunately, at this time there isn't a completely reliable way to alternate the content depending on the capabilities of the device. Using script and progressive enhancement techniques to determine whether the audio/video content is renderable, and present an alternate option if not, is not likely to work, because eInk devices are the least likely to provide scripting support.

The epub:switch element might seem like another option to present an alternate layout depending on support, but as of writing there is no mechanism for using it to alternate display based on support in HTML5-compliant devices for audio and video content.

For now, the best option is to ensure maximum accessibility of your content. Although not seamless, this may include adding a link to a document containing the alternate representation you prefer readers to see when the audio/video cannot be rendered, instead of trying to alternate the display based on the capabilities of the device. If you're going to make the effort to provide an alternate layout, giving the reader the choice to pick which they prefer enhances the consumability of your publication overall.

And don't forget that readers have many options these days to read their ebooks. Even if they generally use a dedicated eInk device, they may switch to a cloud reader to take full advantage of your book. The more a device is seen as a limitation to reading, the more readers will move to more capable devices. If you offer no reason for readers to switch, then it stands to reason they never will.

 There remains an open issue in HTML5 to consider a dedicated attribute for linking transcripts. If implemented, this would greatly simplify the process of adding this information, which is typically linked to from somewhere near the resource.

Triggers

The new `epub:trigger` element was added to EPUB 3 to provide a declarative (script-free) means of controlling multimedia elements. It allows you to easily create controls like play, pause, resume, mute and unmute for your audio and video content using standard HTML5 elements, without having to go out and learn JavaScript. If you hate that the native controls are overlaid on your video content, but were afraid to go script your own interface, you're going to love what this element allows you to do.

The first thing to know is that `epub:trigger` is not itself a content element; it's not a button, nor does it add anything to your document. It is more like a watcher element that listens for reader actions and performs them without any coding. You add at least one for each event that the reader triggers by clicking, pressing, or otherwise activating your controls, hence the name `epub:trigger`.

In order to use this element in your XHTML documents, you need to declare both the epub and ev (XML Events) namespaces on the root element as follows:

```
<html xmlns="http://www.w3.org/1999/xhtml"
      xmlns:epub="http://www.idpf.org/2007/ops"
      xmlns:ev="http://www.w3.org/2001/xml-events">
```

To ease into how this element works, we'll look at the markup for the video we're going to control first. The `video` element tagging should be self-explanatory now:

```
<video id="video1" controls="controls">
   <source src="../video/shared-culture.mp4" type="video/mp4"/>
   <source src="../video/shared-culture.webm" type="video/webm"/>
</video>
```

You only need to note here the `id` attribute that has been defined, because its value (`video1`) will be used later to indicate this is the target of the various actions we're going to define. You may have noticed that the default controls have also been enabled, even though reading systems are required to support this functionality without scripting if they support audio and video. We'll come back to why this is still a good practice later.

With the easy part out of the way, let's turn now to the controls the reader will be interacting with. Here is how they typically should be marked up to assure that the triggers will work as expected:

```
<span
      id="resume-button"
      aria-controls="video1"
      role="button"
      tabindex="0">play</span>
```

You're probably wondering why you would use a span when you're just making a button. Good question, but as you'll hopefully remember from Chapter 3, support for form elements is not guaranteed in EPUB 3. Are reading systems going to emerge that don't support form elements? Hard to say, but you can decide if it just makes more sense to use the simpler and more semantically correct button:

```
<button id="resume-button" aria-controls="video1">play</button>
```

When repurposing elements as buttons, do make sure to look over "WAI-ARIA" (page 269) in Chapter 9. Not all elements can be tabbed to, or activated, by readers using their keyboard to access your content, so don't copy this example from the EPUB verbatim:

```
<span id="resume">Play/Resume</span>
```

Some readers will be able to click on the area to activate this control, but only links and form elements are natively keyboard accessible. When you use a span, you also need a tabindex attribute and a role attribute with the value button to indicate to ATs that it can be activated.

Since we're conveniently talking about ARIA and accessibility, note also the aria-controls attribute that keeps reappearing on these examples. This attribute identifies the element that is being controlled, ensuring an assistive technology can determine what element has been manipulated when a control is activated (e.g., to update its current state). Its value is the ID of the video defined earlier (video1); the first instance where you'll make use of that ID, but not the last.

But to return to the button markup, you'll notice that it also has an id attribute, which is required for every element that the reader will use to control your multimedia. Its value will be used later to indicate to the trigger which element it has to watch. Quickly duplicating the previous markup, we can generate a simple set of playback controls as follows:

```
<div class="trigger-ctrl center">
   <span
        id="resume-button"
        aria-controls="video1"
        role="button"
        tabindex="0">play</span>
   <span
        id="pause-button"
        aria-controls="video1"
        role="button"
        tabindex="0">pause</span>
   <span
        id="mute-button"
        aria-controls="video1"
        role="button"
        tabindex="0">mute</span>
```

```
<span
        id="unmute-button"
        aria-controls="video1"
        role="button"
        tabindex="0">unmute</span>
</div>
```

Adding some styling to the buttons, our video and controls might appear as shown in Figure 5-5.

Figure 5-5. Video with stylized play, pause mute and unmute buttons

Your first observation seeing this image might be that it's a bit odd that none of the button pairs (play/pause and mute/unmute) has a disabled initial state. It might further strike you as odd that both the mute and unmute options are visible, because volume is typically toggled in an on/off state. The initial release of the trigger functionality only provides basic playback capabilities, however. We'll look at these limitations more as we go, but future updates to the specification should hopefully see the available functionality expanded if the feature catches on.

Now we need to get a grasp on how the triggers work. In a way, they're not that different from the audio and video elements; they provide a declarative way of saying what it is you want to have happen, without going into the details of how the functionality has to work. In the same way that the reading system takes care of the details of decoding your video and playing it back, it also follows the instructions you put in the triggers and automagically performs the playback actions for you.

The trigger functionality is defined through a set of required attributes that must be added to each epub:trigger element:

ev:observer
> The ID of the element to watch for a user action (the button elements you just defined, for example).

ev:event

The type of event to watch for. The value can be any DOM Level 2 event (*http://www.w3.org/TR/2000/REC-DOM-Level-2-Events-20001113/*), such as click, mousedown, select, focus, blur, etc.

action

The action that we want the reading system to perform. Currently the following actions can be specified:

show

Changes the CSS visibility property of the specified element to visible

hide

Changes the CSS visibility property of the specified element to hidden

play

Activates playback from the beginning of an audio or video clip

pause

Pauses playback of an audio or video clip

resume

Resumes playback of an audio or video clip

mute

Mutes the sound of an audio or video clip

unmute

Unmutes the sound of an audio or video clip

ref

The element that we want the action to be performed on (similar to the aria-controls attribute discussed earlier)

 Although epub:trigger is defined as for use controlling any kind of multimedia content, it is practically limited to audio and video at this time, because all action values except show/hide are restricted for use with audio and video.

From these four attributes, you can build some complex actions without having to know a lick of JavaScript.

First, let's make a trigger to enable playback. Looking back at the controls we defined earlier, you know the ev:observer attribute has to be set to the value resume-button to match the button's ID:

```
<epub:trigger
            ev:observer="resume-button"/>
```

Next, add the device-agnostic event `click` in the `ev:event` attribute (it handles mouse clicks and keyboard and touch activations):

```
<epub:trigger
            ev:observer="resume-button"
            ev:event="click"/>
```

You aren't going to use the `play` action here because you don't want the reader to restart the video from the beginning every time (`play` is the equivalent of a full reset). Instead, you'll use the `resume` action, because `resume` is generic in nature and does not actually require playback of the audio or video clip to have been initiated in order to use (i.e., you can "resume" from the 00:00:00 mark):

```
<epub:trigger
            ev:observer="resume-button"
            ev:event="click"
            action="resume"/>
```

And finally, use the `video` element's ID `video1` in the `ref` attribute to tell the reading system that's the video you want played:

```
<epub:trigger
            ev:observer="resume-button"
            ev:event="click"
            action="resume"
            ref="video1"/>
```

And that's all there is to creating a trigger. Under the hood, when the reading system encounters this trigger while processing the markup, it knows to automatically set up a listener to monitor for clicks on the `span`. When a matching event occurs, it also does the hard work of making the video playback begin.

The process of building triggers never changes from this pattern. For each action you want performed, you define what to watch, what to watch for, what action to trigger, and on what element.

The pause button is virtually identical, with only the element to watch in the `ev:ob server` attribute and action to perform in the `action` attribute changing:

```
<epub:trigger
            ev:observer="pause-button"
            ev:event="click"
            action="pause"
            ref="video1"/>
```

And likewise for the mute and unmute options:

```
<epub:trigger
            ev:observer="mute-button"
```

```
                ev:event="click"
                action="mute"
                ref="video1"/>
    <epub:trigger
                ev:observer="unmute-button"
                ev:event="click"
                action="unmute"
                ref="video1"/>
```

But the fun doesn't stop there. You aren't limited to watch for only a single event, or to perform only a single action when the event fires. For example, you'd probably want to start the reader off with only an option to mute the sound and hide the unmute button. Clicking the mute button you just defined will work great to silence the audio, but now what? If you've hidden the unmute button, it will still be invisible, so the reader has no way to turn the sound back on.

Trigger to the rescue! Simply define a second `trigger` to watch for a click on the mute button and `show` the unmute button, plus a third `trigger` to `hide` the mute button so that the interface is less cluttered:

```
    <epub:trigger
                ev:observer="mute-button"
                ev:event="click"
                action="mute"
                ref="video1"/>
    <epub:trigger
                ev:observer="mute-button"
                ev:event="click"
                action="show"
                ref="unmute-button"/>
    <epub:trigger
                ev:observer="mute-button"
                ev:event="click"
                action="hide"
                ref="mute-button"/>
```

But here's where limitations of the functionality start to come into play. The hiding and showing of content is currently tied only to the CSS `visibility` property. While this property renders an element invisible, it leaves a space in the page where the element will be positioned when it is made visible again (i.e., to collapse the space you have to set the `display` property to `none`).

Figure 5-6 shows how this problem would materialize as you try to alternate showing the mute and unmute buttons. In the image on the left, the buttons appear to be left aligned with the video, but in fact they are centered. You just can't see the unmute option yet. In the image on the right, the unmute option becomes visible after muting, but there is now a space where the mute option used to be.

Figure 5-6. Spacing issues that result from making controls invisible but without collapsing the space they occupied

There are, of course, ways to minimize the obviousness of these gaps, but visual readers will always have to deal with the flip-flopping location.

Another limitation of the `trigger` element is that the specification currently doesn't define a way to control the volume of the video independently of the device volume. You can mute and unmute, but the reader cannot raise or lower the volume. There's also no way to enable forward and reverse movement through a clip's timeline, so the reader would have to start playback over each time they want to review some segment. As we've been hinting at, triggers do not account for the full range of functionality that the native controls provide, which is why you should have those controls enabled, even if it is potentially redundant.

Rather than look at triggers as an all-or-nothing solution at this time, you should consider using them only as complements to the native controls. The muting and unmuting options would be useful on their own for shutting off background music without worrying about script support, for example. Or you might use triggers to start playback from within your content and once the clip is playing let the user interact with the native controls.

Because some EPUB 2 reading systems support the `audio` and `video` elements, but will not support new EPUB 3 features like the `trigger` element, enabling the native controls continues to make the most sense.

To put everything together, though, including the unmute and pause functionality, which follow the patterns just discussed, you get the following set of triggers:

```
<epub:trigger
            ev:observer="resume-button"
            ev:event="click"
            action="resume"
            ref="video1"/>
<epub:trigger
            ev:observer="pause-button"
            ev:event="click"
            action="pause"
            ref="video1"/>
<epub:trigger
            ev:observer="mute-button"
            ev:event="click"
            action="mute"
            ref="video1"/>
<epub:trigger
            ev:observer="mute-button"
            ev:event="click"
            action="show"
            ref="unmute-button"/>
<epub:trigger
            ev:observer="mute-button"
            ev:event="click"
            action="hide"
            ref="mute-button"/>
<epub:trigger
            ev:observer="unmute-button"
            ev:event="click"
            action="unmute"
            ref="video1"/>
<epub:trigger
            ev:observer="unmute-button"
            ev:event="click"
            action="show"
            ref="mute-button"/>
<epub:trigger
            ev:observer="unmute-button"
            ev:event="click"
            action="hide"
            ref="unmute-button"/>
```

It may not yet be a perfect replacement for either the native controls or scripted interfaces, but the potential as the specification evolves is definitely intriguing.

CHAPTER 6

Media Overlays

Having looked at embedding audio content within documents, the natural progression is to look now at how to provide synchronized audio narration, another of the key new additions introduced in EPUB 3. Media overlays, as you're about to see, are the secret behind how this magic works.

When you watch words get highlighted in your reading system as a narrator speaks, the term *media overlay* probably doesn't immediately jump to mind to describe the experience, but what you are in fact witnessing is a media type (audio) being layered on top of your text content. Apple was the first to adopt this technology, adding it to their support of EPUB 2 under the name Read Aloud while the EPUB 3 specification was still being finalized, but other reading systems, like Readium, have since appeared offering beta support. Even Amazon has jumped into the synchronization game, if not with the same media overlays technology.

But the ability to synchronize text and audio in ebooks isn't a new development in the grander scheme of ebook formats. It goes back fifteen years in DAISY digital talking books, and even further in antecedents to that format. The value of text and audio synchronization for learning has an equally long history, which is why the technology is so important across the entire spectrum of readers. Media overlays are more than just an accessibility feature of EPUB 3, in other words.

Overlays enable any reader to quickly and easily switch from one reading modality to the other. For example, you don't have to be interested in reading along with the words to find value. You might switch from visually reading a book while at home to listening aurally while commuting on the train to work. You might want to temporarily switch from visual to audio reading while turbulence is rocking you around on your latest business trip and making you sick to your stomach, and then switch back when it passes.

But overlays run even deeper than the ability to switch from visual to aural for casual reading. Imagine you are working in an environment where you need your hands free, but also need to hear instructions or have a QA checklist read back. If you turn on a media overlay, you can listen while you work. No need for embedded videos. No need to rely on potentially incomprehensible text-to-speech (TTS) rendering.

Foreign language learning is another example of where overlays shine. Without precise audio pronunciations, books that teach second languages are often extremely difficult to follow. Listen to the proper pronunciation while you read and you'll be fluent in no time. There's a lot more to media overlays than just storybook reading for children.

The audiovisual magic that overlays enable in EPUBs is just the tip of the iceberg, too. Overlays represent a bridge between the audio and text worlds, and between mainstream and accessibility needs, which is what really makes this new technology so exciting.

From a mainstream publisher's perspective, overlays provide a bridge between audio-book and ebook production streams. Create a single source using overlays, and you could transform and distribute across the spectrum from audio-only to text-only. If you're going to create an audiobook version of your ebook, it doesn't make sense not to combine production, which is exactly what EPUB 3 allows you to do now. Your source content is more valuable by virtue of its completeness, and you can also choose to target and distribute your ebook with different modalities enabled for different audiences.

From a reader's perspective, media overlays ensure they can purchase a format that provides adaptive modalities to meet their reading needs: they can choose which play-back format they prefer, or purchase a book with multiple modalities and switch between them as the situation warrants—listening while driving and visually reading when back at home, for example.

In other words, media overlays are the answer to a lot of problems on both sides of the accessibility fence.

The EPUB Spectrum

Audio synchronization brings a new dimension to ebooks. The old line that clearly separated ebook functionality from audiobook playback is gone, and in its place is a new spectrum that crosses from one extreme to the other. The new possibilities between the traditional formats can be broadly broken down into three categories:

Full text and audio
> Providing full text and full audio narration can be seen as the center of the spectrum, blending the full power of ebooks with audiobooks.

Mixed text and audio

A step in the text direction is full text with partial audio. Not every producer will want to narrate every section of their book. Back matter (bibliographies, indexes, etc.), for example, is often tedious and expensive to narrate. Media overlays can be provided for the primary narrative, and back matter left to the reading system's text-to-speech functionality to voice.

Structured audio

A step in the direction of audiobooks yields structured audio. Picture being able to quickly and easily move through an audiobook using the power of the EPUB navigation document and you can see the benefit of an audiobook wrapped up as an EPUB.

The most common use for media overlays will undoubtedly be to provide either a full or partial audio track covering the text content of the EPUB. Looking at the DAISY production world, where similar kinds of books have been made for many years now, it's possible to project two models for how these kinds of EPUBs will be recorded.

The first is to load the publication into recording software that allows the narrator to synchronize the text with their narration as they go. The DAISY Tobi tool is one example of software that enables this kind of recording (it is currently being upgraded to support EPUB 3). The other model, which is seeing some traction already, is to record the audio (e.g., using Audacity) and then export synchronization points and merge them with the text, whether manually through another application or automatically.

Which of these models will work for your production process depends on your intended outputs. Recording on top of the text is simple and easy for anyone from a self-publisher to a large publisher to do. The downside is it requires waiting until the very end of the text production process before recording can begin (i.e., after the EPUB output and QA stages, meaning archiving and reusing the audio may require extracting it from the EPUB). Recording the audio separately and then synchronizing has many challenges for books of any size, and is most effective when the process can be automated (e.g., automatically synchronizing the text with the audio using third-party tools that can analyze audio waveforms and return the sync points).

Full audio also does not mean that a human has to narrate the entire text, either. Because support for the new text-to-speech enhancements is going to take time to develop, pre-recording synthetic narration and synchronizing it with an overlay is a possibility. This approach would be useful for recording back matter for distribution, for example.

Using EPUB to create structured audio files is another intriguing possibility, and one that has been largely overlooked so far. Text content is still needed, but in this scenario, the content of your EPUB is simply a document that lists the major headings (i.e., so that you have a text point to synchronize with the audio, but we'll get to those details shortly).

If you start with a full text-and-audio-synchronized EPUB, though, it would be simple to process it down to this type of enhanced audiobook. It will take some XSLT programming talent, but all you'd have to do is strip away everything but the major headings from both your content and overlay documents to get your structured audio EPUB.

Overlays in a Nutshell

Although the only realistic way to work media overlays into your ebook production process is through recording tools and/or applications that can automatically map your audio to your text, this book wouldn't be complete if we left it at that and didn't look under the hood to see exactly how the technology works.

The first thing to understand is that an overlay is just a specialized kind of XML document, one that contains the instructions a reading system uses to synchronize the text display with the audio playback. Overlays are expressed using a subset of SMIL that we'll cover as we move along, combined with the epub:type attribute for adding semantic information.

 SMIL (pronounced "smile") is the shorthand way of referring to the Synchronized Multimedia Integration Language. For more information on this technology, see *http://www.w3.org/TR/SMIL*

Each content document in your publication can have its own overlay document, which may synchronize audio with all or some of the text in it. After the reader initializes playback of the audio, each successive overlay document is loaded in parallel with the loading of the new content document. For example, when the end of Chapter 1 is reached, the reading system automatically loads Chapter 2 and simultaneously looks up its corresponding overlay document to continue playback. This is how the appearance of seamless playback is maintained, much the way the reader never notices the transition from one content document to the next while reading visually.

The order of the instructions in each overlay document is what defines the logical reading order for the ebook when in playback mode. The reading system automatically moves through these instructions one at a time, or a reader can manually navigate forward and backward, including escaping and skipping of unwanted structures (e.g., using the forward and back arrows, similar to how rich markup assists traversing content using an assistive technology). See "Skipping versus Escaping" (page 236) for more.

As a reading system encounters each synchronization point, it determines from the provided information which element has to be shown (by its id) and the corresponding position in the audio track at which to start the narration. The reading system will then load and highlight the word or passage for you at the same time that you hear the audio play. When the audio track reaches the end point you've specified (or the end of the audio file if you haven't specified one), the reading system checks the next synchronization point to see what text and audio to load next.

This process of playback and resynchronization continues over and over until you reach the end of the book, giving the appearance to the reader that their system has come alive and is guiding them through it.

Synchronization Granularity

As you might suspect at this point, the reading system can't synchronize or play content back in any way other than what has been defined. For example, as a reader, you cannot dynamically change from word-to-word to paragraph-by-paragraph synchronization to suit your reading preference. The magic is only as magical as the content creator makes it, at least at this time.

With only a predefined level of playback granularity available, the decision on how fine a playback experience to provide has typically been influenced by the disability you were targeting, going back to the origins of the functionality in accessible talking books. Books for blind and low-vision readers are often only synchronized to the heading level, for example, and omit the text entirely (structured audio). Readers with dyslexia or cognitive issues, however, often benefit more from word-level synchronization, using full-text and full-audio playback to aid in comprehension and following the narrative.

But reader ability is not the only consideration in a mainstream format like EPUB 3. Coarser synchronization (for example, at the phrase or paragraph level) can be useful in cases where the defining characteristics of a particular human narration (flow, intonation, emphasis) add an extra dimension to the prose, such as with spoken poetry or religious verses. Word-level synchronization can add value in educational contexts where a reader may need to step back over words multiple times.

One convenient aspect of media overlays is that even though you can only define a single overlay per content document, it doesn't mean you can't mix granularity levels within one. Consider language learning. You may opt to synchronize to the paragraph level for sections of explanatory prose while providing word-by-word synchronization for practical examples the reader is most likely to want to easily step through. Finer granularity may only add value in certain situations, in other words.

But let's turn to the practical construction of an overlay now to discover why the complexity increases by how granular your synchronization is. Understanding this issue will give better insight into the model you ultimately decide to use.

Constructing an Overlay

Every overlay document begins with a root `smil` element and a body, as exemplified in the following markup:

```
<smil
    xmlns="http://www.w3.org/ns/SMIL"
    xmlns:epub="http://www.idpf.org/2007/ops"
    version="3.0">
    <body>
        ...
    </body>
</smil>
```

There's nothing exciting going on here but a couple of namespace declarations and a `version` attribute on the root. These are static in EPUB 3, so of little interest beyond their existence. There is no required metadata in the overlays themselves, which is why even though a `head` element exists in the specification there is rarely a need to use it (it exists only for custom metadata, so this book doesn't cover it).

Of course, in order to now illustrate how to build up this shell and include it in an EPUB, we're going to need some content. We'll be using the *Moby Dick* ebook that Dave Cramer, a member of the EPUB working group, built as a proof of concept of the specification for the rest of this section. This book is available from the EPUB 3 Sample Content site (*http://code.google.com/p/epub-samples/downloads/list*).

Figure 6-1 shows the first page of Chapter 1, displayed in Readium. We'll be looking at synchronizing this text as we go.

If you look at the content document for Chapter 1 in the source, you'll see that the HTML markup has been structured to showcase different levels of text/audio synchronization. After the chapter heading, for example, the first paragraph has been broken down to achieve fine synchronization granularity (word and sentence level), whereas the following paragraph hasn't been subdivided and represents a very coarse level of synchronization.

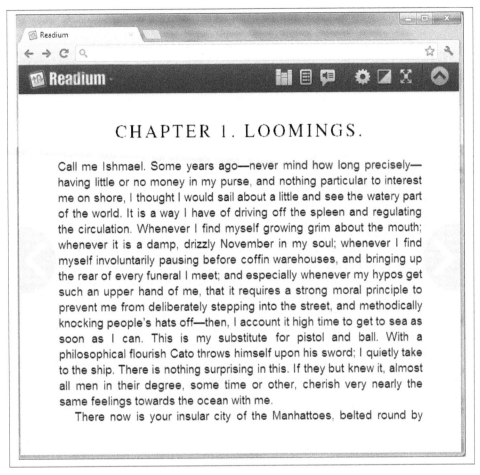

Figure 6-1. Chapter 1 of Moby Dick, displayed in Readium

Compressing the markup in the file to just what we'll be looking at, we have:

```
<section id="c01">
  <h1 id="c01h01">Chapter 1. Loomings.</h1>

  <p>
    <span id="c01w00001">Call</span>
    <span id="c01w00002">me</span>
    <span id="c01w00003">Ishmael.</span>
    <span id="c01s0002">Some years ago...</span> ...
  </p>

  <p id="c01p0002">
```

```
        There now is your insular city of the Manhattoes, belted round by...
      </p>
      ...
    </section>
```

You'll notice that each element containing text content has an id attribute, because that's what you'll reference when you synchronize with the audio track.

 A less intrusive alternative to using elements and IDs is found in "EPUB Canonical Fragment Identifiers" (page 65). Canonical Fragment Identifiers can reference anywhere into the text, but no tools can generate these yet, and no reading systems support them for overlay playback or highlighting.

The markup additionally includes span tags to differentiate words and sentences in the first p tag. The second paragraph only has an id attribute on it, because you're going to omit synchronization on the individual text components it contains to show paragraph-level synchronization.

Sequences

You can now use this information to start building the body of the overlay. Switching back to the empty overlay document, the first element to include in the body is a seq (sequence):

```
<body>
  <seq
      id="id1"
      epub:textref="chapter_001.xhtml#c01"
      epub:type="bodymatter chapter">

  </seq>
</body>
```

The seq element serves the same grouping function the corresponding section element does in the markup, and you'll notice the textref attribute references the section's id. The logical grouping of content inside the seq element likewise enables escaping and skipping of structures during playback, as you'll see with some structural considerations discussed later.

The epub:type attribute has also reappeared. Similar to its use in content documents, it provides structural information about the kind of element the seq represents. Here it conveys that this seq represents a chapter in the body matter. Although the attribute isn't required, there's little benefit in adding seq elements if you omit any semantics, because a reading system will not be able to provide skippability and escapability behaviors unless it can identify the purpose of the structure.

It may seem redundant to have the same semantic information in both the markup and overlay, but remember that each is tailored to different rendering and playback methods. Without this information in the overlay, the reading system would have to inspect the markup file to determine what the synchronization elements represent, and then re-synchronize the overlay using the markup as a guide. Not a simple process. A single channel of information is much more efficient, although it does translate into a bit of redundancy. You also wouldn't typically be crafting these documents by hand, and a recording application could potentially pick up the semantics from the markup and apply them to the overlay for you.

Parallel Playback

You can now start defining synchronization points by adding par (parallel) elements to the seq, which is the only other step in the process of building an overlay document. The par element, as its name suggests, is going to define what has to be synchronized in parallel. It must contain a child text element and may contain a child audio element, which define the fragment of your content and the associated portion of an audio file to render, respectively. (We'll address why the audio element is optional in "Advanced Synchronization" (page 187).)

For example, here's the entry for the primary chapter heading:

```
<par id="heading1">
  <text src="chapter_001.xhtml#c01h01"/>
  <audio
    src="audio/mobydick_001_002_melville.mp4"
    clipBegin="0:00:24.500"
    clipEnd="0:00:29.268"/>
</par>
```

The text element contains a src attribute that identifies the filename of the content document to synchronize with and a fragment identifier (the value after the # character) that indicates the unique ID of a particular element within that content document. In this case, the element indicates that *chapter_001.xhtml* needs to be loaded and the element with the id c01h01 displayed (the h1 in our sample content, as expected).

The audio element likewise identifies the source file containing the audio narration in its src attribute and defines the starting and ending offsets within it using the clipBegin and clipEnd attributes. As indicated by these attributes, the narration of the heading text begins at the mid-24-second mark (to skip past the preliminary announcements) and ends just after the 29-second mark. The milliseconds appended to the start and end values give an idea of the level of precision needed to create overlays and why people typically don't mark them up by hand. If you are only as precise as a second, the reading system may move readers to the new prose at the wrong time or start narration in the middle of a word or at the wrong word.

But those concerns aside, that's all there is to basic text and audio synchronization. So, as you can now see, no reading system witchcraft was required to synchronize the text document with its audio track! Instead, the audio playback is controlled by timestamps that precisely determine how an audio recording is mapped to the text structure. Whether synchronizing down to the word or moving through by paragraph, this process doesn't change.

To synchronize the first three words "Call me Ishmael" in the first paragraph, for example, simply repeat the process of matching element IDs and audio offsets:

```
<par>
    <text src="chapter_001.xhtml#c01w00001"/>
    <audio
        src="audio/mobydick_001_002_melville.mp4"
        clipBegin="0:00:29.269"
        clipEnd="0:00:29.441"/>
</par>
<par>
    <text src="chapter_001.xhtml#c01w00002"/>
    <audio
        src="audio/mobydick_001_002_melville.mp4"
        clipBegin="0:00:29.441"
        clipEnd="0:00:29.640"/>
</par>
<par>
    <text src="chapter_001.xhtml#c01w00003"/>
    <audio
        src="audio/mobydick_001_002_melville.mp4"
        clipBegin="0:00:29.640"
        clipEnd="0:00:30.397"/>
</par>
```

You'll notice each clipEnd matches the next element's clipBegin here because you have a single continuous playback track. Finding each of these synchronization points manually is not so easy, though, as you might imagine.

Synchronizing to the sentence level, however, means only one synchronization point is required for all the words the sentence contains, thereby reducing the time and complexity of the process several magnitudes. The par is otherwise constructed exactly like the previous example:

```
<par>
    <text src="chapter_001.xhtml#c01s0002"/>
    <audio
        src="audio/mobydick_001_002_melville.mp4"
        clipBegin="0:00:30.397"
        clipEnd="0:00:44.783"/>
</par>
```

The process of manually creating overlays is primarily complicated by the total number of time and text synchronizations involved, as is undoubtedly becoming clear. Moving up another level, paragraph-level synchronization reduces the process several more magnitudes, as all the sentences can be skipped. Here's the only entry you'd have to make for the entire 28 second paragraph:

```
<par>
    <text src="chapter_001.xhtml#c01p0002"/>
    <audio
        src="audio/mobydick_001_002_melville.mp4"
        clipBegin="0:01:46.450"
        clipEnd="0:02:14.138"/>
</par>
```

But manually creating these files is rarely a realistic option, except perhaps with very short children's books. Narrating on top of the text makes the process much simpler, but only to a point. Narrating to the heading, paragraph, or even sentence level can be done relatively easily with trained narrators, as each of these structures provides a natural pause point for the person reading, a simplifier not available when performing word-level synchronization.

Using a recording tool to synchronize to the word level is generally too complex to do while narrating, even if the narrator is assisted by someone else controlling the setting of sync points while they talk. Human language is too fast and fluid to keep up with, and a manual process is too prone to errors (e.g., syncing too quickly or too slowly).

Another process that holds promise is to use applications that can take the text and audio and generate the media overlay for you, although none are known to exist at this time specifically for EPUB overlays. As noted at the outset, there are commercial programs that can analyze an audio file and return the start and end point that corresponds to a provided string of text. It's already possible to use these to feed in the text from an EPUB and generate an overlay, but the process requires a developer to glue the pieces together. The costs of software and development will put this process out of reach of any but large-scale producers, at least at this time.

One other consideration to be aware of is that the greater the granularity you choose, the less likelihood there is for playback issues. If you opt to synchronize to the paragraph level, and only part of the paragraph is showing in the viewport, the page won't turn until the entire paragraph is finished being read (i.e., narration will continue onto the hidden part on the next page). The reader will have to manually switch pages, or wait. (This problem gets masked in fixed-layout books by virtue of each page constituting a new document.)

Although the ideal is to provide word-level synchronization, all of the above considerations will play into the kind of synchronized EPUB you can create, which is why there is no simple answer to which you should produce. You're going to have to find a balance between what would provide the best playback experience and what your production processes are capable of handling.

Adding to the Container

Although that wraps up the overlay document itself, you're not completely done yet. There are still a few quick details to run through in order to now include this overlay in our EPUB.

Assuming you save the overlay as *chapter_001_overlay.smil*, the first step is simply to include an entry for it in the manifest:

```
<item
    id="chapter_001_overlay"
    href="chapter_001_overlay.smil"
    media-type="application/smil+xml"/>
```

You then need to include a media-overlay attribute on the manifest entry for the corresponding content document for chapter one:

```
<item
    id="xchapter_001"
    href="chapter_001.xhtml"
    media-type="application/xhtml+xml"
    media-overlay="chapter_001_overlay"/>
```

The value of this attribute is the ID you created for the overlay in the previous step.

Finally, you need to add metadata to the publication file indicating the total length of the audio for each individual overlay and for the publication as a whole. For completeness, you'll also include the name of the narrator:

```
<meta property="media:duration" refines="#chapter_001_overlay">0:14:43</meta>
...
<meta property="media:duration">0:23:46</meta>
<meta property="media:narrator">Stuart Wills</meta>
```

The refines attribute on the first meta element specifies the ID of the manifest item we created for the overlay, because this is how you match the time value up to the content file it belongs to. The lack of a refines attribute on the next duration meta element indicates it contains the total time for the publication (only one can omit the refines attribute).

Styling the Active Element

The last detail to look at is how to control the appearance of the text as it is being narrated. You aren't at the mercy of the reading system, but can tailor the appearance however you want through CSS.

The Media Overlays specification defines a special `media:active-class` metadata property that tells the reading system which CSS class to apply to the active element.

For example, if you defined the following `meta` tag in the package document metadata:

```
<meta property="media:active-class">-epub-media-overlay-active</meta>
```

you could then apply a yellow background to each section of prose as it is read by defining the following CSS class definition:

```
.-epub-media-overlay-active
{
    background-color: rgb(255,255,0)
}
```

Figure 6-2 shows how Readium displays the highlighting when media overlay playback is turned on.

Figure 6-2. Text highlighting in Readium

Be mindful of the reading experience before going too crazy with this functionality. If you set a dark background color, for example, you may obscure the text that is being read. Setting a thick border to surround each word as it is read can also reduce the legibility of your text. Simple yellow backgrounds are traditionally how highlighting is done, as they are not distracting and do not obscure the text.

And do not add this CSS class to any of the elements in your content documents, or they will have a yellow background by default. The reading system will automatically apply the class to each element referenced in a `par`'s `text` child element as it becomes active. You only need to make sure that every content document that has an overlay links to the style sheet that defines this class. If the reading system cannot find it in an attached style sheet, it may use its own default rendering, or it may use nothing at all. Avoid the risk.

Structural Considerations

We briefly touched on the need to escape nested structures, and skip unwanted ones, but let's go back to this functionality as a first best practice, because it is critical to the usability of the overlays feature in exactly the same way markup is to content-level navigation.

If you have the bad idea in your head that only par elements matter for playback, and you can go ahead and make overlays that are nothing more than a continuous sequence of these elements, get that idea back out of your head. It's the equivalent of tagging everything in the body of a content file using div or p tags.

Using seq elements for problematic structures like lists and tables provides the information a reading system needs to escape from them.

For example, here's how to structure a simple list:

```
<seq id="seq002" epub:type="list" epub:textref="chapter_012.xhtml#ol01">
    <par id="list001item001" epub:type="list-item">
       <text src="chapter_012.xhtml#ol01i01"/>
       <audio src="audio/chapter12.mp4" clipBegin="0:26:48" clipEnd="0:27:11"/>
    </par>
    <par id="list001item002" epub:type="list-item">
       <text src="chapter_012.xhtml#ol01i02"/>
       <audio src="audio/chapter12.mp4" clipBegin="0:27:11" clipEnd="0:27:29"/>
    </par>
    ...
</seq>
```

A reading system can now discover from the epub:type attribute the nature of the seq element and of each par it contains. If the reader indicates at any point during the playback of the par element list items that they want to jump to the end, the reading system simply continues playback at the next seq or par element following the parent seq. If the list contained sub-lists, you could similarly wrap each in its own seq element to allow the reader to escape back up through all the levels.

A similar nested seq process is critical for table navigation: a seq to contain the entire table, individual seq elements for each row, and table-cell semantics on the par elements containing the text data.

A simple three-cell table could be marked up using this model as follows:

```
<seq epub:type="table" epub:textref="ch007.xhtml#tbl01">
    <seq epub:type="table-row" epub:textref="ch007.xhtml#tbl01r01">
       <par epub:type="table-cell">...</par>
       <par epub:type="table-cell">...</par>
       <par epub:type="table-cell">...</par>
    </seq>
</seq>
```

You could also use a `seq` for the table cells if they contained complex data:

```
<seq epub:type="table-cell" epub:textref="ch007.xhtml#tbl01r01c01">
  <par>...</par>
  ...
</seq>
```

But attention shouldn't be given only to `seq` elements when it comes to applying semantics. Readers also benefit when `par` elements are identifiable, particularly for skipping:

```
<par id="note21" epub:type="note">
  <text src="notes.xhtml#c02note03"/>
  <audio src="audio/notes.mp4" clipBegin="0:14:23.146" clipEnd="0:15:11.744"/>
</par>
```

If all notes receive the semantic as in the previous example, a reader could disable all note playback, ensuring the logical reading order is maintained. All secondary content that isn't part of the logical reading order should be so identified so that it can be skipped.

This small extra effort to mark up structures and secondary content does a lot to make your content more accessible.

Advanced Synchronization

Synchronizing text and audio is not the only feature media overlays provide. We've already made the case that not all audio may be narrated, but some sections, such as back matter, could be left to the reading system's text-to-speech capabilities. That doesn't mean that you have to omit an overlay for those sections you don't narrate and leave it to the reader to turn on TTS playback.

You might skip human narration for a bibliography, for example, but provide human narration for additional appendices that follow it. In this case, you want to provide a linear progression through the content, and allow the reader to decide when to drop in and out of playback mode. If you omit an overlay for the TTS section, the reader will immediately drop out of playback when it is reached, and have to manually navigate to the next section and then re-enable the new overlay.

To create an overlay that automatically triggers the reading system TTS capabilities, you simply omit an `audio` element from the `par`. To return to the earlier *Moby Dick* example, you could set the first heading to be read by TTS like this:

```
<par id="heading1">
  <text src="chapter_001.xhtml#c01h01"/>
</par>
```

When all of the referenced text content has been rendered by the TTS engine, the reading system will move to the next `par`.

Another application for media overlays is to automatically begin playback of embedded multimedia resources. Overlays wouldn't be nearly so powerful if a reader had to skip all your audio and video clips in order to listen to the playback, or drop out of playback each time one was encountered.

To automatically start playback of an audio or video clip, you simply reference its id in a text element.

For example, if you had the following video element in Chapter 1:

```
<video id="vid01" src="video/v01.mp8" controls="controls"/>
```

you could initiate its playback with the following par:

```
<par id="heading1">
   <text src="chapter_001.xhtml#vid01"/>
</par>
```

When encountering a text element that references an audio or video element, the reading system is expected to play the clip in its entirety before moving on to the next par.

You can also layer audio narration on multimedia clips by including an audio element in the par (e.g., to provide video scene descriptions for blind readers):

```
<par id="heading1">
   <text src="chapter_001.xhtml#vid01"/>
   <audio src="desc/c01.mp4" clipBegin="0:8:30.000" clipEnd="0:17:33.500"/>
</par>
```

When adding an audio track, be aware that the length of the audio clip will constrain how much of the video gets rendered. If your audio track is shorter than the length of the video, for example, playback will end when the audio track runs out.

 This automatic playback functionality is only available for content referenced from the audio and video elements. You cannot use overlays to initiate content in an object, for example.

Audio Considerations

Before moving on, it's worth looking briefly at the audio files containing the narration. Like audio in content documents, the audio narration referenced in overlay documents can also live outside the EPUB container. When hosting remotely, the manifest entry for the overlay must indicate this fact:

```
<item
    id="chapter_001_overlay"
    href="chapter_001_overlay.smil"
    media-type="application/smil+xml"
    properties="remote-resources"/>
```

Remote hosting may cause playback issues for readers, because there will inevitably be a delay the first time that playback is initiated and the reader has to wait for the buffer to fill. Unless the reading system can detect and buffer the next document's audio track before reaching the document, which none are known to do at this time, this lag may occur with each new document in the spine.

The sheer size of the audio narration may require external hosting, but one option to increase performance might be to include the first audio file in the container so that it can begin playing immediately. Assuming that reading systems get more sophisticated in their rendering of overlays, this would potentially allow the reading system to focus its resources on buffering the next remote audio file.

CHAPTER 7

Interactivity

Liza Daly

Vice-President of Engineering, Safari Books Online

Why would you want a book to be interactive?

For many readers, a book's immutability is a feature rather than a bug. A print book does not demand anything from the user but their full attention. It does not entice the reader to click, to comment, to share, or to tweet. It promises total immersion in the text, a direct conduit to the author's thoughts.

Yet there are many cases where the static nature of the traditional book is perhaps an artifact of print technology rather than the canonical best form for the content. Books that aim to teach complex, real-world subjects could benefit from the opportunity for readers to engage with the material. New forms of storytelling can encourage readers to choose new paths, or let the reader dig deeply into the narrative, uncovering hidden motivations through careful discovery. Books packaged with their primary source material could be rich scholarly resources, allowing researchers to independently verify assertions or build follow-on experiments out of raw data. Far from being a de facto distraction, interactive publications have only begun to be explored.

EPUB 3 provides the capability to do all of the above, but author beware: interactivity remains at the vanguard of ebook support. The more the publication deviates from a traditional book, the less likely it is to be fully crossplatform. Many EPUB 3 reading systems will never support interactivity, and the standard is not specific about how conditional or partial support should be best implemented. Careful testing is required.

Support for interactive elements is described in EPUB 3 Content Documents (*http://idpf.org/epub/30/spec/epub30-contentdocs.html*). This document will be referenced throughout this section.

First Principles: Interaction Scope and Design

The EPUB 3 specification defines two *inclusion models* that affect the scope of the document that scripting can potentially modify in response to user input or script action. The larger the scope of the interaction, the less likely it is that the EPUB will be interoperable.

Ebooks present a particular challenge here for two reasons:

- Reading systems use different models of content display. While typically this is a choice between a paginated, print-like view and a scrolling, web-like view, it may also include viewportless readers (audio or Braille), specialized viewport sizes (serial presentation of very short snippets or single lines), or unusual configurations such as two-up or even three- or four-up page layouts. Any of these layouts may cause unexpected behavior when the DOM is modified in place.
- Unlike web browsers, ebook readers have a range of unique affordances to bring up navigation controls, settings, or metadata. A content author cannot know precisely which user events may be hijacked for the reading system's own use, or the specific order in which events may fire.

For both of these reasons, scripts should modify as little of the DOM as possible. The specification even has support for reading systems which *prohibit* global modification of DOM. These systems are said to support only *container-constrained scripting* and should indicate that as part of their `epubReadingSystem` object support. Conversely, potentially modifying any part of the DOM is known as *spine-level scripting*, meaning such scripts are capable of modifying any DOM object that can be discovered via the reading system by traversing documents found in the Publications Metadata spine.

Progressive Enhancement

Progressive enhancement is a design principle in which the goal is to develop the most accessible version of content first, as the primary version, and gradually add layers of enhancement based on the capabilities of the reading system, device, and end user. While the final product of a progressive enhancement workflow can be indistinguishable from one arrived at via a graceful degradation approach, the intent behind progressive enhancement is to view the accessible version of the content as the canonical one, rather than designing a high-resolution, heavily visual, interactive experience as the "real" content and then downgrading that presentation to an accessible version as an afterthought.

Progressive enhancement can be seen as complementary to a "mobile first" design approach. In both cases, the content creator understands that all users—regardless of ability—benefit from fast, concise, flexible access to information. By designing for a mobile and/or accessible audience first, the content creator is able to pare down the enhancements to only those that are most critical to consuming the content, and typically pays dividends in reducing unnecessary costly investment in eye candy that only serves to distract readers.

Because digital books are often specifically meant to educate, creating thoughtful publications that are highly accessible and cross-platform is even more critical than in general web development. All EPUB 3 content authors are strongly encouraged to consider developing interactive publications in a progressive enhancement approach, limiting those scripted qualities to only the most necessary, and ensuring that the nonscripted presentation contains valuable content in its own right.

 The IDPF provides accessibility guidelines in the context of progressive enhancement techniques in its EPUB 3 Accessibility Guidelines: Progressive Enhancement (*http://idpf.org/accessibility/guidelines/content/ script/pe.php*).

Procedural Interaction: JavaScript

Executing embedded source code from a procedural programming language is a prerequisite for most forms of ebook interactivity. While EPUB 3 does allow content creators to embed an arbitrary executable as the object element, in the majority of cases, interactive publications will be created through the use of in-book source code. Because JavaScript is the de facto standard scripting language for SVG and HTML5, EPUB 3 content documents can be assumed to be scriptable only if they contain JavaScript code. The standard does not define which versions of JavaScript (ECMAScript) are required for support; content creators should defer to the most commonly supported features in web browsers for best results.

JavaScript in EPUB 2

Use of scripts in EPUB 2 was discouraged though not explicitly forbidden. iBooks will run JavaScript code in both EPUB 2 and EPUB 3 documents, with specific implementation details as described in Apple's proprietary best practices documentation. Developers should not expect to find widespread support of scripting in EPUB 2–only reading systems and should produce only EPUB 3 publications when scripting is required.

The EPUB 3 epubReadingSystem Object

Reading systems that support scripting are required to provide the navigator.epubRea dingSystem property. This allows developers to query the reading system about its scripting support and the specific scripting properties that it makes available.

A simple way to find out whether a script-aware reading system supports this property is to query the epubReadingSystem object:

```
<script type="text/javascript">
alert("Name: " + navigator.epubReadingSystem.name +
    " / version: " + navigator.epubReadingSystem.version +
    " / layoutStyle " + navigator.epubReadingSystem.layoutStyle);
</script>
```

At this time, `navigator.epubReadingSystem` is supported in both iBooks (Figure 7-1) and Readium (Figure 7-2).

Figure 7-1. Output from the epubReadingSystem object in iBooks

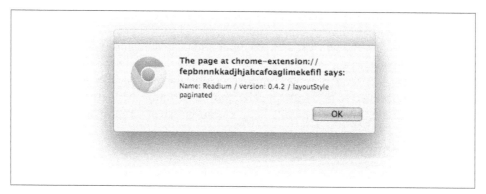

Figure 7-2. Output from the epubReadingSystem object in Readium

Consult the Book Industry Study Group (BISG) EPUB 3 (*http:// www.bisg.org/what-we-do-12-152-epub-30-support-grid.php*) support grid for updated information on support of this and other scripting properties.

Detect features

Through its `hasFeature()` method, `epubReadingSystem` allows content authors to query the exact characteristics of the reading system's scripting support. The following features are required to be reported by any system that implements `epubReadingSystem`:

`dom-manipulation`
  Spine-level scripts are allowed to make structural changes to the DOM.

`layout-changes`
  Spine-level scripts may modify attributes and CSS styles that affect content layout.

`touch-events`
  The device supports touch events and the reading system passes touch events to the content.

`mouse-events`
  The device supports mouse events and the reading system passes mouse events to the content.

`keyboard-events`
  The device supports keyboard events and the reading system passes keyboard events to the content.

`spine-scripting`
  Spine-level scripting is supported.

Each of these will return `true` or `false` depending on the support available.

The important point to note about EPUB 3 event handlers is that the reading system passes the event to the content. Modern screen-based reading systems will naturally support input from a mouse or keyboard, but to provide consistent navigational interfaces, the reading system may choose to not pass those events down into the book's DOM. This could be true even for reading systems implemented in JavaScript: they may deliberately suppress event propagation into the content viewport.

Even if a reading system explicitly does *not* support passing through mouse events, it is safe to assume that it will still allow users to trigger ordinary hyperlink and anchor-based navigation. (If it doesn't, consider reporting a bug!)

In its default implementation, Readium will return "true" for all but touch-events (*http://bit.ly/11EhtQZ*). The absence of touch-events should *not* be taken to mean that the reading system is wholly touch-incompatible: since any web-based reading system could potentially be run on a touch-capable device, consider touch-events to mean events which are specific to *touch only*, such as multitouch or swipe. Since touch events are typically delegated to mouse events in the absence of touch-specific listeners, most publications can safely concern themselves only with mouse-events when considering non-keyboard interaction.

Use preventDefault to avoid reading system default behavior

If a particular area of text has interactivity triggers but is not wrapped in an a element, the reading system may call your custom event and then run its own behavior. If the user touched towards the edge of the margin, for example, the reading system may turn the page before your event has been processed by the reader (who probably didn't want to turn the page after all).

Though not part of the specification, it is likely that most reading systems will honor the preventDefault method called on the event and not propagate the event further. However, it is important to ensure that preventDefault and other event code does not absolutely prevent the user from engaging with the reading system's native controls. For example, don't bind preventDefault to the entire HTML body!

At the time of this writing, Apple specifically endorses the use of preventDefault for scripts running inside of iBooks.

Always query epubReadingSystem!

Very simple scripted applications, especially container-constrained scripts, may not require testing any of the previous features. For example, a script that modifies only a fixed-size canvas without any user input does not necessarily care about the reading system's layout style or what types of events are supported. Nevertheless, when authoring EPUB 3 scripted content you should always check epubReadingSystem before executing any code.

Because most EPUB 3 reading systems are implemented using HTML5-compatible browser rendering engines, they will typically have JavaScript support *by default*. For security reasons, some choose to deliberately disable any in-book scripts, but others may not. Therefore, it is possible for a reading system to implicitly support JavaScript without explicitly supporting *JavaScript in EPUB*. This could result in serious incompatibility between the reading system and the publication.

For maximum compatibility, content authors who want to include scripting should wrap *all* executable code in a check for the existence of epubReadingSystem, to avoid unexpected behavior when a reading system was not intended to be script-compatible. The simplest way to do this is to wrap into an initialization function a check that the property exists:

```
document.onload = function () {

  if (navigator && navigator.hasOwnProperty('epubReadingSystem') {
    runEbookScripts();  // This is the only entry point to script documents
  }
};
```

Inclusion Models

EPUB 3 scripted documents define the range of elements that can be accessed by interactive components using one of two inclusion models: container-constrained or spine-level scripting. The inclusion model describes the extent to which the script can access and manipulate the DOM of the parent, spine-level content document. For many applications, the container-constrained model would result in fairly onerous development, because it requires creation of discrete subdocuments for each interactive component. While most publications are likely to use the spine-level scripting model, understanding the intent of the container-constrained model is useful, because emulating that will provide the best results in cross-platform, accessible EPUBs.

Container-constrained scripts

The container-constrained inclusion model requires that a script be associated only with an embedded subcomponent rather than the main content document. The most likely example would be an iframe with an explicit width and height that contained a smaller content document with its own script. The contained script would interact only with the DOM of its own content document, not the parent.

The potential advantage of this approach is that the scripted area has an explicitly defined bounding box, and thus could be laid out by the reading system without concern for shifts in numbers of pages or other document stability issues.

 At the time of this writing, there are no scripting-enabled reading systems that support *only* the container-constrained model.

The specification requires that reading systems that support scripting *always* support the container-constrained model. It might be natural to assume, then, that a best practice would be to always use container-constrained markup if the use case supports it. But this would be a mistake, because wrapping each interactive component in an `object` or `iframe` is awkward and bears no resemblance to interactive content authoring on the Web. Additionally, iframes in EPUB publications are extremely uncommon (and sometimes explicitly disallowed in legacy EPUB 2 reading systems). It is unlikely that most reading systems have been extensively tested with documents that include `iframe`. At this time, we strongly recommend avoiding creating EPUB 3 documents with the container-constrained inclusion model.

 Container-constrained scripts as defined by the specification are not inherently *safer* from a privacy or security perspective; they are only more likely to be interoperable. A container-constrained script may still have the ability to access user data, such as reading preferences or form input, or even have access outside of the reading system itself. True security is implemented at the level of the reading system or device, not the EPUB 3 specification. See EPUB 3 and Scripted Content Documents (*http://bit.ly/11ELuzY*) by Joseph Pearson for a good analysis of the difference between security considerations and ebook rendering stability.

Spine-level scripting

Spine-level scripts have access to the DOM of the primary EPUB 3 Content Document as referenced by the Publications Metadata. This is the inclusion model employed by all script-aware EPUB 3 readers today and is likely to remain dominant. Content authors are probably safe to expect this inclusion model, but it is always worth checking via the `epubReadingSystem` object.

Even though the specific container-constrained inclusion model is *not* recommended for real-world use, the overall intent of the model is well considered: spine-level publications should seek to minimize the number of changes to document metrics (particularly length but also width or overall document layout).

 One way to minimize negative effects on pagination when employing content transformations via scripting is to pair scripted documents with a fixed-layout rendering mode. Here too, though, content authors must take care not to allow scripts to exceed the defined boundaries of the fixed-layout page, because the reading system will not automatically be able to scroll or repaginate the viewport accordingly. And, of course, fixed-layout documents come with their own downsides and accessibility concerns.

Ebook State and Storage

Scripts can directly modify only the EPUB content document to which they are attached. This is not a limitation for most simple interactivity use cases, where the script drives a quiz or animated example. It does present a challenge when a choice a user makes in one chapter should affect content presentation in another—for example, in a branching story. In nonfiction, the restriction could also be a problem for authors who want to have large interactive publications, such as textbooks, and want to track student performance on in-book quizzes throughout the reading experience.

One solution to this problem of intra-publication communication is to store information in a globally accessible place and have each content document check that area for updated data. HTML5 offers a number of storage options, from traditional web cookies to the localStorage and sessionStorage models, to one of the full-blown HTML5 database APIs such as IndexedDB or the now-deprecated but widely available Web SQL.

The EPUB 3 specification neither requires or prohibits the presence or use of any of the storage mechanisms above. Indeed, like JavaScript itself, many of these will come "for free" with the HTML rendering engine packaged with the ebook reader. However, reading system developers may choose to exclude or block access to any of those APIs. In some cases, they may be unofficially supported in one version and then removed in a later version. Ebook ecosystems which support syncing across devices are not likely to sync ancillary storage or state. Publications that use these features may need to clearly communicate their limitations to readers, and provide adequate fallbacks for reading systems that support scripting but *not* the desired storage mechanism.

Identifying Scripted Content Documents

A content document that includes scripts of either inclusion model *must* be declared as such in the Publication Metadata, as defined in the Publications 3.0 specification (*http://idpf.org/epub/30/spec/epub30-publications.html#scripted*). The property scripted must be included as part of the item definition for that document:

```
<item
      properties="scripted"
      id="c1"
      href="chapter-with-scripting.xhtml"
      media-type="application/xhtml+xml" />
```

Creating fallbacks

If a reading system encounters a scripted publication and does *not* support scripting, it has two options according to the specification:

- Look for manifest-level fallbacks (*http://bit.ly/VwO4Us*) in the Publication Metadata.

- Look for an epub:switch block (*http://bit.ly/W4NlKL*) inside the scripted content document and execute the defined fallback.

At the time of this writing, it is unknown how many reading systems will implement epub:switch. It was a mechanism included in EPUB 2 [as opf:switch (*http://idpf.org/epub/20/spec/OPS_2.0.1_draft.htm#Section2.6.3*)] that did not see wide adoption. Similarly, publication-level fallbacks may also not be widely used or deployed.

A third, and likely best, fallback mechanism is to implement the scripted content as *progressive enhancement* rather than with any explicit declarative fallback mechanism: create the fallback content as the native HTML markup and *replace* that content with the scripted enhancement through JavaScript itself. For example:

```
<div class="quiz">
  <p class="question">How much wood could a woodchuck chuck? </p>
  <ol class="answers">
    <li> <a href="answers.html#correct" role="button">Two</a> </li>
    <li> <a href="answers.html#correct" role="button">Five</a> </li>
    <li> <a href="answers.html#incorrect" role="button">Ten</a></li>
  </ol>
</div>
```

In this example, the EPUB would contain a static page that simply displayed "correct" or "incorrect" based on the quiz and could be traversed as a normal hyperlink in a non-scripted reading environment. But packaged with a script, the script could "hijack" the anchor link, instead display an in-page pop up with the answer, and potentially even tally the number of correct/incorrect results. No explicit fallback required.

Animation and Graphics: Canvas

The HTML5 canvas element allows a publication to contain an almost unlimited variety of widgets. Canvas-based interactivity has a number of attractive qualities for a content author:

- Canvas is widely supported in all modern browser engines, with almost no cross-browser compatibility issues.
- A canvas element is naturally of a fixed height and width, meaning it provides a *container-constrained* space for interactive components, and thus is not subject to layout issues involving pagination.
- A number of popular JavaScript graphics libraries are compatible with canvas, including Processing.js (*http://processingjs.org/*).

A significant downside is that *canvas is not natively accessible*. Content authors should take care to provide thoughtful fallbacks to canvas-based interactivity.

Best Practices in Canvas Usage

It is possible to simply place textual canvas fallbacks inside the `canvas` element itself:

```
<canvas width="200" height="200" id="leaves">
  An interactive animation that, when clicked, presents an image of trees
  changing their leaf color and then shedding their leaves.
</canvas>
```

However, typically, the purpose of a `canvas` element is to convey information that would be difficult to express using textual information itself. (If the canvas is simple enough to describe in words, it probably didn't need to be coded in the first place!) Also, just because a `canvas` element exists doesn't mean that it's impossible to make it accessible. WAI-ARIA roles can instead help to describe the canvas and potentially let a visually impaired user interact with it.

In this case, `role="button"` informs the reading system that the canvas is one that a user can click on to interact:

```
<canvas ... role="button" tabindex="0" aria-label="Tree leaf demo">
  An interactive animation that, when clicked, presents an image of trees
  changing their leaf color and then shedding their leaves.
</canvas>
```

Another option to creating an accessible canvas is to wrap it in elements that are themselves more accessible, such as `figure`:

```
<figure>
  <figcaption>
    <span class="caption">Figure 1 — During certain seasons, trees will drop
    their leaves in preparation for cold weather. The leaves typically change
    color from green to red, orange, or yellow just before falling.</span>
  </figcaption>
  <canvas width="200" height="200" id="leaves" role="button"
          tabindex="0" aria-label="Tree leaf demo">
    An interactive animation that, when clicked, presents an image of trees
    changing their leaf color and then shedding their leaves.
  </canvas>
</figure>
```

This approach is likely to be appropriate for many uses of canvas in EPUB 3, where they are typically playing the role of an illustrative figure.

The most accessible approach is to prepare a complete shadow DOM (*http://msdn.micro soft.com/en-us/library/hh968259(v=vs.85).aspx*) inside the `canvas` element. In this implementation, the script controlling the canvas also manipulates fallback elements. This approach works best when presenting textual data, such as charts or graphs, but can also be used to hook into audio events or to present semantic elements that help explicate the text.

In this final example, the shadow DOM elements can be revealed one after the other, read either by a screenreader or through embedded audio, conveying the progressive nature of tree leaf change even without the benefit of the canvas animation or any kind of visual presentation:

```
<figure>
  <figcaption>
    <span class="caption">Figure 1 – During certain seasons, trees will drop
      their leaves in preparation for cold weather. The leaves typically change
      color from green to red, orange, or yellow just before falling.</span>
  </figcaption>
  <canvas width="200" height="200" id="leaves" role="button"
          tabindex="0" aria-label="Tree leaf demo">
    <header>
      This demonstration describes the stages of leaf change that deciduous
      trees undergo during transition to the cold season.
    </header>
    <ol>
      <li>Trees will respond to decreasing length of daylight with a series of
          chemical changes that reduce the presence of chlorophyll in the
          leaves.</li>
      <li>When chlorophyll disappears from a leaf, previously hidden colors of
          red, orange, and yellow are revealed.</li>
      <li>Gradually the leaves turn from their fall colors
          into dead leaves.</li>
      <li>Eventually the dead leaves fall from the tree due to wind, rain, or
          their own weight.</li>
    </ol>
  </canvas>
</figure>
```

 The IDPF provides updated guidelines on accessible canvas implementations, called EPUB 3 Accessibility Guidelines: Canvas. (*http://idpf.org/accessibility/guidelines/content/script/canvas.php*)

Canvas in a Nonscripted Reading System

A curious consequence of using HTML5-compatible rendering engines as ebook readers is that there may be cases where the reading system does not want to support scripted content, but may not default to rendering an inline canvas fallback.

The HTML5 canvas specification (*http://bit.ly/10ms2Yq*) requires that the absence of JavaScript support be sufficient to trigger the display of canvas fallbacks:

> In non-visual media, and in visual media if scripting is disabled for the canvas element or if support for canvas elements has been disabled, the canvas element represents its fallback content instead.

However, some reading systems may only be post facto disabling JavaScript in contained publications, while retaining JavaScript use for their own purposes (or may be implemented entirely in JavaScript). In this scenario, the reading system cannot rely on the browser's canvas fallback behavior and will have to implement fallback rendering itself.

Since it is unclear whether this will occur in practice, content authors should consider using `canvas` as part of a progressive enhancement approach, injecting the `canvas` element *with JavaScript*, while authoring the document markup using an image or other fallback. For best results, ensure that the block to be replaced has the same dimensions as the `canvas`, to allow the reading system to properly paginate as soon as the DOM is available. If a `canvas` or other element is added by JavaScript after rendering/pagination, unexpected results may occur.

Object

EPUB 3 supports the `object` element for use with arbitrary embedded executables that are not natively supported in EPUB 3 reading systems. A common use case would be to include proprietary applets or Adobe Flash applications.

For the most portable, accessible publication, insert the `object` inside the content of an `epub:switch` element and provide an equivalent fallback. The fallback should itself be highly accessible; don't create a fallback that is simply an image if it would be possible to include descriptive text as well.

Don't use Flash to embed multimedia assets like video or audio if it would be possible to use the native `video` or `audio` elements with a compatible codec.

 While the `embed` element is part of HTML5 and is theoretically included in EPUB 3, content creators are strongly discouraged from using it, because there is no prescribed method for including a fallback. It is extremely unlikely that one will encounter an EPUB 3 reading system which supports `embed` but not `object`.

In general, `object` is likely to be appropriate only for publications that are meant to be used within a well-defined reading ecosystem. Mobile devices are typically limited in their support of third-party binaries, and users can rarely install extensions inside of ebook readers. When possible, prefer components that use native HTML5 APIs (i.e., canvas, video, audio, with or without JavaScript) to provide interactive experiences in EPUB 3.

Other Graphical Interaction Models

Though not specifically designed for scripted interactivity, SVG may be attractive as an alternative to canvas or object for the following reasons:

- SVG is a native content document type in EPUB 3, and its support is required of reading systems.

- SVG *may* be more accessible than canvas due to its declarative nature (but it is not inherently more accessible).

- A number of JavaScript libraries use SVG as their drawing engine as it provides some advantages over canvas, especially in line-drawing applications where a vector library is highly optimized.

Content authors producing for any number of technical fields should specifically consider the D3 visualization library (*http://d3js.org/*), which is seeing wide use on the Web. D3 can produce beautiful, high-performance results and has been adopted by *The New York Times* and others for data-driven interactive graphs, charts, and complex visualizations.

Other graphical libraries, such as three.js (*http://mrdoob.github.com/three.js/*), allow the developer to choose between canvas or svg as the output engine. (three.js also supports WebGL, but EPUB 3 has no requirement that reading systems support WebGL and its presence should not be automatically expected).

Note, however that most visualization libraries do not have accessibility as a primary use case and may need extensive work to provide interactive but accessible implementations. You might need to employ static fallbacks instead.

Accessibility and Scripting Summary

Chapter 9 addresses a number of important considerations when providing script-driven content (especially with an element that is natively not accessible, like canvas). Consult the accessibility guidelines, but the important points can be summarized as such:

- Avoid creating publications that *require* scripting support.
- Test your scripted publications with JavaScript disabled.
- Use WAI-ARIA (*http://www.w3.org/TR/wai-aria/*) attributes to guide screenreaders in rendering rich interactive components.
- Use a progressive enhancement approach to scripting, canvas, and object-based elements.

CHAPTER 8

Global Language Support

Murata Makoto

CTO, Japan Electronic Publishing Association

Although EPUB 2 was widely adopted in North America for ebook production, and to some extent in Europe, it has begun to gain traction worldwide only since the advancements made in EPUB 3 to support a more diverse range of languages, writing modes, and styles. The sudden growth in IDPF membership in new areas, most notably Asia, that has occurred both during and since the release of EPUB 3 reinforces that the format is now truly the global standard for ebooks.

Back when the EPUB 3 revision was first being chartered, the lack of global language support was recognized as one of the key deficiencies that needed to be addressed. It was difficult at that time to use EPUB for books in Arabic, Hebrew, Japanese, Chinese, and Taiwanese (among many others), because it lacked effective mechanisms to handle more than left-to-right, horizontal text flows. To overcome this problem, the IDPF created the Enhanced Global Language Support subgroup to carry out an examination of the issues needed to upgrade support during the EPUB 3 revision. I, Murata Makoto, was the lead of that group, and this chapter will review the mechanisms that we developed to address these issues.

The goal of this chapter is twofold. First, it gives a tutorial of those features of EPUB 3 for global language support. Second, it shows best practices for EPUB authors. Some of the practices outlined are prescriptive, while others are intended to be thought-provoking. It is hoped that these best practices will help such authors to establish dos and don'ts for particular tasks at hand.

Note that this chapter is not dedicated to a particular natural language, but is rather intended to cover the general requirements for producing in many languages. Unfortunately, due to the space constraints of a book, the examples in this chapter cover only a few languages, most notably Japanese. For additional examples, you are encouraged to visit the EPUB 3 Sample Documents Project (*http://code.google.com/p/epub-samples/*), where you will be able to obtain ebooks in a range of languages.

Before we move on to look at the EPUB features for global languages, we must acknowledge the internationalization activities in the Unicode consortium, the W3C, and others. Internationalization of EPUB 3 would not have been possible without their work, because the specification leverages much of what they have done. Similar to how EPUB has aligned itself with existing web and accessibility standards, this close alignment solidifies the future of global language support in the specification.

Characters and Encodings

The first step toward internationalization of information technology is to represent all characters in the world as bit combinations. Fortunately, the advent of Unicode has made this first step significantly easier, and EPUB 3 uses Unicode. Unfortunately, the use of Unicode does not solve all problems around characters. This section presents the use of Unicode in EPUB 3 and considers remaining problems, such as characters in names and private characters.

Unicode

Unicode covers a rich set of characters for virtually all languages, and EPUB 3 allows the use of almost any Unicode character as part of XHTML or SVG content documents. Unicode might not be perfect for every content creator in every case, of course, but it is easily the best there is for document encoding at this time.

Unicode has a dual nature: it defines both a standard set of code points that map character data (e.g., that code point 26093 or U+65ED represents the Unicode Han Character 旭, which is "rising sun; brilliance; radiant") and also how to encode this information (i.e., how to map Unicode character sequences to corresponding byte sequences for storage).

Unicode provides two important encodings that enable this translation: UTF-8 and UTF-16. Both encodings can represent every character in the Unicode character set. UTF-8 is upper-compatible with US-ASCII (i.e., ASCII files are valid UTF-8 files), while UTF-16 represents each character by two bytes (in most cases) or four bytes (in rare cases). You must use either of these two encodings for representing XHTML and SVG content documents in EPUB 3, as well as CSS style sheets, because the specification prohibits the use of other encodings.

UTF-8 has largely become the *de facto* choice for encoding Unicode and is strongly encouraged for all your content (UTF-16 is rarely used). What you must not do is use legacy encodings such as Shift_JIS. Not only is it against the requirements of the specification, but doing so means that your content will likely break on many reading systems, especially if you want to distribute your content on a global scale.

Advocating the use of Unicode for representing characters might sound straightforward, since it is required, but it is nevertheless important. Later in this chapter, you'll see that it has not always been used when it should be.

Declaring Encodings

XML declarations, which are specified at the beginning of XML documents, can be used to declare the encoding of the document. Since XHTML content documents (including navigation documents), SVG content documents, media overlay documents, PLS lexicon files, and NCX files, as well as files under the *META-INF* directory, are all XML documents, they should include an XML declaration that indicates the encoding. To declare that the document is encoded as UTF-8, include the declaration using the `encoding` pseudoattribute like this:

```
<?xml version="1.0" encoding="utf-8"?>
```

Here, for example, is how a typical package document is marked up:

```
<?xml version="1.0" encoding="utf-8"?>
<package xmlns="http://www.idpf.org/2007/opf"
         version="3.0"
         xml:lang="ja" ...>
  ...
</package>
```

Since XHTML content documents are also HTML5, you can also use the `meta` element `charset` attribute to declare the encoding:

```
<meta charset="utf-8" />
```

The `charset` attribute is used only when XHTML content documents are parsed as HTML5 rather than XML (which is not how reading systems are required to behave), but you lose nothing by including this element. It will ensure that your content renders properly if it does get used outside of normal EPUB contexts, for example:

```
<?xml version="1.0" encoding="utf-8"?>
<html xmlns="http://www.w3.org/1999/xhtml" xml:lang="ja"
      xmlns:epub="http://www.idpf.org/2007/ops">
<head>
  <meta charset="utf-8" />
  <title>—</title>
```

```
    ...
</head>
    ...
</html>
```

Finally, CSS style sheets have their own mechanism for declaring encodings: the @char
set rule. It is recommended that all style sheets declare @charset "utf-8"; at the
beginning:

```
@charset "utf-8";

html
{
    -epub-writing-mode: vertical-rl;
    font-family: 'foobar', "HiraMinProN-W3", "@MS 明朝", serif, sans-serif;
    font-size: 14pt;
    margin: auto 1em;
    padding: 1em 0;
    max-height: 28em;
    background-color: #fff4e7;
}
    ...
```

Private Characters

Historically, users of CJK ideographic characters (Japan, Taiwan, Hong Kong, and
mainland China, among others) have complained about the lack of characters in coded
character sets. To work around this problem, they have incorporated private "characters"
at unallocated code points and used such characters in legacy documents. This use of
private characters is not standardized and has varied from producer to producer and
region to region, making the upgrading of legacy content problematic, as well as the
rendering of these characters when fonts are changed.

However, Unicode now contains more than 70,000 CJK ideographic characters, which
is far more than is offered in legacy character sets (e.g., JIS X 0208, which contains only
6,355 CJK ideographic characters). Some CJK Unicode fonts such as IPA 明朝 (IPA
Mincho) and 花園明朝 (Hanazono Mincho) also now support most of the CJK ideographic characters. In other words, the need for private characters is only likely to decrease moving forward.

Furthermore, Unicode has introduced *ideographic variation selectors* (IVS for short) for
indicating glyph variations of ideographic characters. IVS implementations have started
to appear in the market very recently. The introduction of IVS is also likely to decrease
requirements for private characters, because most private characters are actually glyph
variations of existing characters.

You should avoid the use of private characters and instead use allocated code points of Unicode wherever possible. The use of Unicode characters and well-designed fonts provide advantages beyond private characters, such as better rendering, even after magnification, and better accessibility.

 Although the conversion of legacy documents to EPUB 3 is easier if we continue to use private characters, it is better to work to end this reliance on appropriating unused code points for special purposes. It may take more human resources to find appropriate Unicode characters for the private characters in legacy documents, but once your data has been fixed, it will be better for archiving and future reuse.

If you must use private characters in EPUB publications, you have two options:

Embed OpenType, WOFF, or SVG fonts
Represent private characters by using unallocated code points in Unicode and embedding fonts for these code points within the EPUB publication. EPUB reading systems are required to support two types of font formats (OpenType and WOFF) and may also support SVG fonts. This approach allows better font rendering even after magnification. However, there are some drawbacks. First, authors are required to create fonts, which is often beyond their skill set. Second, when reading systems or users prefer to use different fonts, private characters either become invisible or exhibit font differences with neighboring characters. Third, accessibility (such as text to speech) becomes hopeless. See Chapter 4 for font embedding techniques.

Embed images
Embedding images is simpler, because it does not require code points and Unicode. Rather, private characters are represented by images referenced by <img> elements within XHTML content documents. The biggest advantage of this approach is easy migration from legacy documents, which already have such <img> elements. However, there are significant disadvantages. First, text rendering quality is often poor because of image magnification and misalignment of the baseline or center. Second, accessibility typically becomes a lost cause because of all the problems that images of text introduce (covered in more detail in Chapter 9).

Names

EPUB 3 also allows the use of non-ASCII characters in names, such as XHTML anchor names, as well as file and directory names; you can specify these names using any script you prefer. For example, the Kusamakura EPUB available from the EPUB 3 Sample Documents Project (*http://code.google.com/p/epub-samples/*) contains XHTML content documents named as follows:

```
後付.xhtml
目次.xhtml
表紙.xhtml
```

Furthermore, the package document of this EPUB contains several non-ASCII names. The `unique-identifier` attribute of the `package` element specifies a non-ASCII name 青空文庫の番号. The `id` attribute of the `dc:title` is 題名, the `id` attribute of the `meta` element is 著者, and the `id` attribute of the `item` element and the `idref` attribute of the `itemref` element specify 一. Finally, the `media-overlay` attribute of the `item` element is 一_overlay. For example:

```
<?xml version="1.0" encoding="UTF-8"?>
<package xmlns="http://www.idpf.org/2007/opf" version="3.0" xml:lang="ja"
        prefix="foaf: http://xmlns.com/foaf/spec/"
        unique-identifier="青空文庫の番号"> <!--pub-id-->
    ...
    <dc:title id="題名" xml:lang="ja-JP" dir="rtl">草枕</dc:title>
    <meta property="dcterms:creator" id="著者">夏目 漱石</meta>
    <manifest>
        ...
        <item id="一" href="xhtml/一.xhtml" media-type="application/xhtml+xml"
          media-overlay="一_overlay"/>
        ...
    </manifest>
    <spine toc="ncxtoc" page-progression-direction="rtl">
        ...
        <itemref idref="一" linear="yes"/>
        ...
    </spine>
</package>
```

Although some implementations may fail to handle non-ASCII characters (and the space character), there are significant advantages to using scripts that people are comfortable with. If your language can be expressed using the ASCII character set, for example, picture being required to name your files and directories using only characters it doesn't include and you will understand the barrier to adoption this places on many users.

Poor implementations will not be improved if people continue to fall back on ASCII characters just in case non-ASCII characters might not be supported. Older EPUB 2 reading systems are more likely to have issues with non-ASCII characters, but the many other problems that have hindered global use in older reading systems make targeting compatibility with these devices problematic to begin with.

The syntax for file and directory naming in EPUB packages is detailed in section 2.4 of the OCF specification (*http://idpf.org/epub/30/spec/ epub30-ocf.html#sec-container-filenames*). See also "Package Validation" (page 323) in Chapter 11 for information on epubcheck warning messages about non-ASCII characters and the space character.

Specifying the Natural Language

A best practice for all content creators is to declare the natural language of each XML document in the publication, as well as any changes that occur in specific ranges of text. This is particularly important for XHTML and SVG content documents. The EPUB reading system uses the specified language for hyphenation, for example, and it has many benefits for accessible rendering of your content.

With the exception of XHTML content documents, the rule is simple: use the xml:lang attribute and specify a language tag as the attribute value (e.g., en for the English language):

```
<?xml version="1.0" encoding="UTF-8"?>
<svg xmlns="http://www.w3.org/2000/svg" xml:lang="en">

</svg>
```

In the case of XHTML content documents, the rule is not quite so simple. In addition to xml:lang, HTML5 provides the lang attribute. This begs the question: which of these two attributes should you use?

We recommend the xml:lang attribute always be used, because XHTML content documents are of the application/xhtml+xml core media type and are expected to be parsed as XML (EPUB 2 reading systems will only recognize this attribute, as well). However, it is not a bad idea to also specify the lang attribute, as long as both attributes specify the same value. The lang attribute addresses the case that XHTML content documents are parsed as HTML, and some older assistive technologies recognize only this attribute. For example:

```
<?xml version="1.0" encoding="utf-8"?>
<html xmlns="http://www.w3.org/1999/xhtml" xml:lang="ja"
      xmlns:epub="http://www.idpf.org/2007/ops">
  <head>...</head>
  <body>
    <section epub:type="chapter" xml:lang="en">...</section>
    <section epub:type="chapter">...</section>
  </body>
</html>
```

In this example, the natural language for the entire document is Japanese but the natural language for the first chapter is English.

W3C provides Internationalization Best Practices: Specifying Language in XHTML & HTML Content (*http://www.w3.org/TR/i18n-html-tech-lang/*) (W3C Working Group Note 12 April 2007), although HTML5 is not considered.

Vertical Writing

In vertical writing, characters in a line are arranged from top to bottom, lines in a column are arranged from right to left, and columns in a page are arranged from top to bottom, as shown in Figure 8-1.

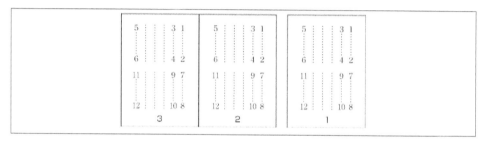

Figure 8-1. Direction of arrangement of characters in vertical writing

Meanwhile, in horizontal writing, characters in a line are arranged from left to right, lines on a column are arranged from top to bottom, and columns in a page are arranged from left to right, as shown in Figure 8-2.

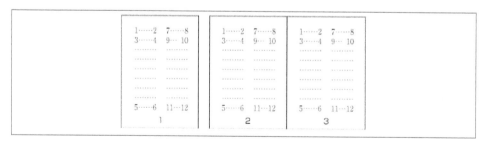

Figure 8-2. Direction of arrangement of characters in horizontal writing

Many Asian countries and regions (notably Japan, Taiwan, and Hong Kong) use both vertical writing and horizontal writing. The Japanese style of vertical writing is extensively discussed in Requirements for Japanese Text Layout (*http://www.w3.org/TR/jlreq/*) (W3C Working Group Note 3 April 2012). This document goes by the name JLREQ for short. (The previous figures are borrowed from JLREQ.)

Mainland China and Korea also used vertical writing, but they do so rarely now. Inner Mongolia uses vertical writing, but theirs is special in that lines on a page are arranged from right to left rather than from left to right.

EPUB 2 did not support vertical writing, because the combination of XHTML 1.1 and CSS 2 did not support it. This omission was considered fatal, especially in Japan and Taiwan. The Enhanced Global Language Support subgroup worked hard to introduce vertical writing to EPUB 3, but it would not have been possible without significant contributions from the W3C CSS WG, because vertical writing of EPUB 3 is inherited from a CSS module called *Writing Modes*.

As of this writing, CSS Writing Modes is still a W3C working draft and is thus unstable, but EPUB 3 incorporates properties for vertical writing from this module. This feat was accomplished by separating the syntax and semantics. EPUB 3 adopts the syntax of a specific working draft of the CSS writing modes and relies on the latest version of CSS writing modes for the semantic definitions. To be precise, EPUB 3 borrowed properties from CSS Writing Modes 2011-04-28 and added the `-epub-` prefix to them.

This approach comes with a number of risks, the biggest of which is that the semantics continue to change, thus causing different results on different reading systems. These differences are then magnified as the initial rudimentary implementations of the properties get evolved to keep pace with the changes.

To control such risks, it is best to avoid complicated combinations of vertical and horizontal writing at this time.

 Combination of vertical and horizontal writing is not unusual, especially for magazines. Even relatively simple books in vertical writing may have tables in horizontal writing.

Writing Modes

The most important CSS property for vertical writing is `-epub-writing-mode`. Vertical writing is enabled by specifying `vertical-rl` as the value of this property, which also indicates a right-to-left block flow direction.

 The Inner Mongolia style of vertical writing is indicated by `vertical-lr`, which indicates left-to-right.

Since it is recommended to avoid combinations of vertical and horizontal writing, this property should be applied to the root `html` element and no other elements. The entire document is then rendered in the vertical writing mode.

The following example of vertical writing (displayed in Readium and shown in Figure 8-3) is a Japanese novel 草枕 (Kusamakura) by 夏目漱石 (Natsume Soseki), and is available from the EPUB 3 Sample Documents Project (*http://code.google.com/p/epub-samples/*):

```
@charset "utf-8";

html
{
    -epub-writing-mode: vertical-rl;
    ...
}
```

一

山路を登りながら、こう考えた。智に働けば角が立つ。情に棹させば流される。意地を通せば窮屈だ。とかくに人の世は住みにくい。

Figure 8-3. A Japanese novel **草枕** *(Kusamakura)*

This example specifies `-epub-writing-mode`, but does not specify the prefix-less `writing-mode` property or proprietary extensions like `-webkit-writing-mode`. Avoid the prefix-less property, because the final recommendation of CSS Writing Modes may change the syntax of this property. Specifying proprietary extensions (such as `-webkit-`) is also not recommended, because support for the properties is growing in reading systems and these extensions should not be necessary.

Immature but Important Properties

CSS Writing Modes includes two other important properties: `text-orientation` and `text-combine-horizontal`. Unfortunately, it is too early to recommend best practices or provide tutorials for them. The `text-orientation` property controls the glyph orientation, and `text-combine-horizontal` combines multiple characters into the space of a single character in vertical writing. See the latest document of CSS Writing Modes for further information.

Page Progression Direction

When you hold a Western book (to be precise, Western codex), the spine is on the left. When reading one, you move from the left page to the right page, and within each page follow the text from the left to the right. Such a book (shown in Figure 8-4) is said to have the *left-to-right* (LTR) page progression direction.

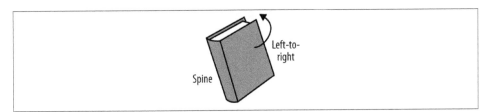

Figure 8-4. Left-to-right page progression direction

But not every area of the world reads from left to right. Many languages read in the opposite direction, from right to left (RTL), where the codex is held with the spine to the right and reading moves from the right-side page to the left, as shown in Figure 8-5.

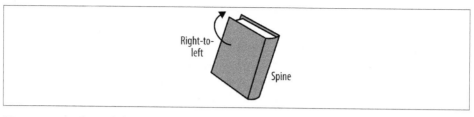

Figure 8-5. Right-to-left page progression direction

The RTL page progression direction is used for Arabic and Hebrew books, where characters in a line are arranged from right to left, and columns in a page are arranged from right to left, as shown in Figure 8-6.

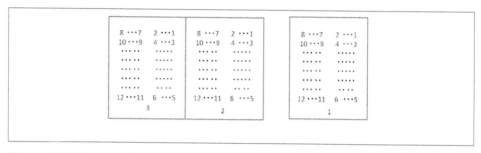

Figure 8-6. Direction of arrangement of characters (Hebrew and Arabic)

Asian books with vertical writing (except the Inner Mongolia style) also have the RTL page progression direction, because you begin with the rightmost line.

EPUB 2 did not support the RTL page progression direction, because EPUB 2 reading systems were often hardwired with right-arrow and left-arrow buttons that represent the next and previous page, respectively.

EPUB 3 now supports RTL direction, however, and recent EPUB reading systems have started to integrate support for right-to-left reading. In other words, when the document direction is RTL, the right-arrow and left-arrow buttons represent the previous and next page, respectively. This added feature contributes to internationalization of EPUB significantly.

The following four examples of the RTL page progression direction are available from the EPUB 3 Sample Documents Project (*http://code.google.com/p/epub-samples/*).

The first example (shown in Figure 8-7) is again the Japanese novel *Kusamakura*, and the second (shown in Figure 8-8) is 阿 Q 正伝 (*The True Story of Ah Q*) by 鲁迅 (Lu Xun) in traditional Chinese. Both examples show two pages in the spread, and you begin with the right page and then read the left page.

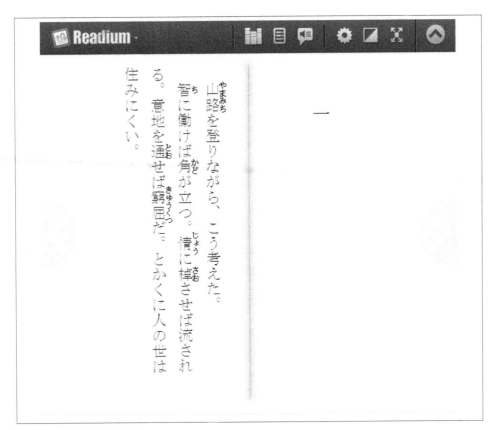

Figure 8-7. A spread in a Japanese novel, 草枕

Figure 8-8. A spread in a Chinese novel, 阿Q正傳

The third and fourth examples are an Arabic book (shown in Figure 8-9) and a Hebrew book (shown in Figure 8-10). Again, you begin with the right page in a spread and then read the left page.

بشريًّا، تتألف كلّ المواد الحيّة على كوكبنا الأرض من خلايا، باستثناء الفيروسات (سنعود إليها لاحقًا). الكائنات الأكثر بساطة، كالبكتيريا مثلًا، ليست مكوّنة سوى من خليّة واحدة وتُدعى «وحيدة الخليّة». معظم الكائنات الحيّة الأخرى، سواء كانت تسمى إلى عالم الحيوانات أو النباتات، هي نتيجة اندماج عدد كبير من الخلايا بطريقة معقدة وشديدة الدقّة.

فالكائن البشري الراشد مؤلَّف من نحو مليون مليار خليّة.

لكن، من أين تأتي هذه الخلايا؟ في الواقع، إنّ وراء نشوء كلّ كائن حيّ ظاهرة تلقيح خليّة ذكريّة (المنى، السداة...) لخليّة أنثويّة (البويضة،

الفصل الثاني
ما هو السرطان؟

من أين تأتي الحياة؟

حسنًا! إن أردنا أن نفهم الآن كيف يمكن للأغذية التي نتناولها أن ترفع أو تخفض احتمالات إصابتنا بالسرطان، علينا أن نفهم كيف «يعمل» السرطان[1].

أوّلًا، لنتخيّل أنّ كلّ أشكال الحياة وكلّ المواد الحيّة مؤلَّفة من قطع صغيرة يمكنها أن تندمج وتتكاثر، وتُدعى الخلايا.

سواء كانت نبته أو حيوانًا أو كائنًا

Figure 8-9. A spread in an Arabic book, Le Vrai Régime anti-cancer

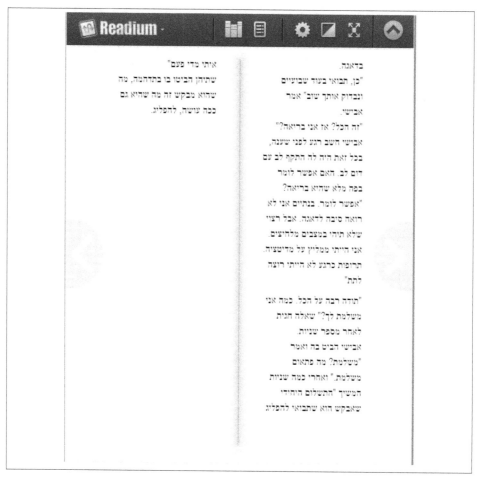

Figure 8-10. A spread in a Hebrew book, מפליגים בישראל

EPUB 3 provides two mechanisms for controlling the page progression direction. One controls the global direction and is specified at the package document, while the other controls the direction of each HTML content document and is specified within a CSS style sheet.

Global Direction

The `spine` element in the publication document has an optional `page-progression-direction` attribute. By specifying `rtl` as the value of this attribute, for example, the author can indicate that the publication has a global right-to-left direction:

```
<?xml version="1.0" encoding="UTF-8"?>
<package xmlns="http://www.idpf.org/2007/opf" version="3.0"...>
  ...
```

```
<spine toc="..." page-progression-direction="rtl">
  <itemref idref="..." linear="yes"/>
  <itemref idref="..." linear="yes"/>
  ...
</spine>
</package>
```

There is no default value when this attribute is omitted; the reading system will render the content in whatever is its default manner.

Content Direction

The page progression of each XHTML content document is automatically computed from the `-epub-writing-mode` property and the `dir` attribute of the root `html` element (see W3C CSS Writing Modes (*http://www.w3.org/TR/css3-writing-modes/*) for details). The `dir` attribute controls the character progression direction within each line (e.g., for enabling right-to-left progression for Hebrew and Arabic text).

You don't need to know the computation procedure in detail, but simply consider two cases of the right-to-left page progression direction. One can safely assume that the left-to-right page progression direction is used otherwise.

Case 1: Hebrew or Arabic

The `dir` attribute on the `html` element specifies `rtl`, but the `-epub-writing-mode` property is not explicitly specified (or the value `horizontal-tb` is specified). In this case, the right-to-left direction is used:

```
<?xml version="1.0" encoding="utf-8"?>
<html dir="rtl"
      xmlns="http://www.w3.org/1999/xhtml"
      xmlns:epub="http://www.idpf.org/2007/ops">
...
</html>
```

Case 2: Vertical writing (but not in the Inner Mongolia style)

The value `vertical-rl` of the `-epub-writing-mode` property is applied to the HTML element, but the `dir` property is not explicitly specified (or the value `ltr` is specified). In this case, the right-to-left direction is used.

The EPUB 3 specification allows both LTR and RTL page progressions to coexist within a single EPUB publication. What is more, some physical books have both directions. One such book in Japan has a prose-only part and a math-and-prose part. The prose-only part uses vertical writing and thus the page progression direction is RTL. Meanwhile, the math-and-prose part uses horizontal writing, and thus the page progression direction is LTR.

It is recommended, however, that you use only a single direction as the global direction and the direction of each XHTML content document. If an EPUB publication contains both directions, it becomes difficult for the reading system to provide an intuitive user interface.

That said, the direction of an XHTML content document does not matter if this content document is guaranteed to be a single page (e.g., a fixed layout page). It is quite reasonable to construct an EPUB publication from a sequence of such single-page XHTML content documents and specify the RTL global direction at the EPUB package document while implicitly specifying the LTR direction in each XHTML content document.

 Although CSS 2.1 allows the `direction` and `unicode-bidi` properties, EPUB 3 does not allow them. Use the `dir` attribute, instead.

Ruby and Emphasis Dots

Another important requirement, particularly for Asian languages, is to provide pronunciation information with character data. Because these languages contain many unique characters, readers are often not familiar with the more obscure ideograms and require pronunciation guides. Including the correct pronunciation is also vital in learning and instructional materials.

In addition to pronunciation, readers need to know the correct stressing of words, which is not done using italics as in Western languages. This section looks at the mechanisms EPUB 3 includes to address these needs.

Ruby

In Japan, Taiwan, Hong Kong, and mainland China, ruby is often used as annotations to CJK ideographic characters. JLREQ defines ruby as follows:

> Ruby is a small-sized, supplementary text attached to a character or a group of characters in the main text. A run of ruby text, usually attached to the right of the characters in vertical writing mode or immediately above them in horizontal writing mode, indicates the reading or the meaning of those characters.

Although JLREQ is dedicated to Japanese text, this definition applies to ruby in Taiwan, Hong Kong, and mainland China as well.

In Japan, ruby text typically consists of Hiragana or Katakana characters (Japanese phonetic characters), rather than CJK ideographic characters. In Taiwanese bopomofo ruby, ruby text consists of simple characters and tone marks for representing phonetics. In Hong Kong and mainland China, ruby text is pinyin, which is transcription into Latin script.

Figure 8-11 shows an example of ruby in the novel 草枕 (Kusamakura), as rendered in Readium.

Figure 8-11. Japanese ruby

EPUB uses HTML5 `ruby` elements, which contain text chunk and `rt` elements. The text chunk is ruby base, to which ruby is attached. The content of an `rt` element is ruby text.

The HTML markup for the above ruby looks like this:

```
<ruby>両隣<rt>りょうどな</rt></ruby>
```

No CSS properties are required for rendering this XHTML fragment, but the CSS style sheet for Kusamakura includes the following rule for the `rt` element to control the size of ruby text:

```
rt {
    font-size: 50%;
}
```

JLREQ states that the size of ruby text should be about a half of the base text size, which this rule ensures.

When including ruby, you need to make sure that there is enough space between lines to fully render it. Set the line height by specifying the `line-height` property. For example, the following CSS sets the `line-height` property to 175%:

```
p {
    line-height: 1.75;
}
```

If the value of `line-height` is less than the sum of the font sizes of the base text and the ruby text, the ruby text might overlap with the base text of the adjacent line. Because the previous example sets the line height larger than the sum of the font sizes of the base text and the ruby text (i.e., 150%), you can expect sufficient rendering room.

In the previous example, the ruby base is a sequence of two characters (両隣), and the ruby text is a sequence of five characters (りょうどな). Such ruby is called *group-ruby*. Line breaks within group-ruby are not recommended. For example, suppose that the HTML fragment is changed:

```
<ruby>両<rt>りょう</rt></ruby><ruby>隣<rt>どな</rt></ruby>
```

Now, there are two ruby elements in this fragment. The ruby base of the first ruby is a single character (両), and the ruby base of the second is also a single character (隣). This ruby is called *mono-ruby*. The expected layout is slightly different from the group-ruby example. First, line breaking between the first and second characters is allowed. Second, ruby text for the first character should not be above the second character, and the ruby text for the second character should not be above the first character.

 Another type of ruby, called *jukugo-ruby*, is beyond the scope of this book. Details of mono-ruby, group-ruby, and jukugo-ruby are found in 3.3 Ruby and Emphasis Dots in JLREQ (*http://www.w3.org/TR/jlreq/ #ruby_and_emphasis_dots*).

In order to increase the legibility of the ruby text (which is roughly 50% of the character size of the body text), Japanese publishers often substitute small kana characters (e.g., や and ッ) with large kana characters (e.g., や and ツ), which are different Unicode characters, in their EPUBs. This begs the question, should we use large kana characters for ruby text from the beginning?

Such in-advance substitutions are not recommended, however, because it makes natural language processing, such as text-to-speech, more difficult. Automatic translation from small kana characters to large ones should preferably be done by the EPUB reading system, through CSS. Here is a CSS fragment for enabling such conversions:

```
rt {
    ...
    text-transform: -epub-fullsize-kana;
}
```

Emphasis Dots

In Japan, Taiwan, Hong Kong, and mainland China, characters are emphasized by attaching emphasis dots rather than italicizing them. *Emphasis dots* are symbols placed alongside a run of ideographic or hiragana/katakana characters. Figure 8-12 shows an example of emphasis dots, as rendered by Readium.

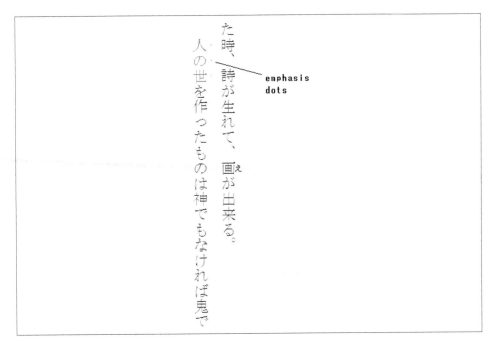

Figure 8-12. Emphasis dots

EPUB 3 has two properties for emphasis dots: `-epub-text-emphasis-style` and `-epub-text-emphasis-color`. The former controls the shape of emphasis dots, while the latter controls the color.

EPUB 3 also has `-epub-text-emphasis`, which is a shorthand property for setting both `-epub-text-emphasis-style` and `-epub-text-emphasis-color` in one declaration.

These properties were originally borrowed from CSS Text 2011-04-12 (*http://bit.ly/10lCu2w*), but they are now moved to a derived specification called CSS Text Decoration (*http://bit.ly/105Cbnz*).

The HTML fragment for the first chunk of emphasis dots looks like this:

```
<span id="fmse_0001"><strong class="sesame_dot">人の世</strong>を作ったもの
は...</span>
```

And here's the CSS for `strong.sesame_dot`:

```
strong.sesame_dot
{
    font-weight: normal;
    -epub-text-emphasis-style: sesame;
    color: #0000FF;
    -epub-text-emphasis-color: #FF0000;
}
```

The position of emphasis dots depends on the writing mode and natural language in effect. In the case of vertical writing, emphasis dots appear at the right of characters. In the case of vertical writing, emphasis dots for Japanese appear at the top of characters, while those for Chinese appear at the bottom of characters. For more information, see 3.4. Emphasis Mark Position (*http://www.w3.org/TR/css-text-decor-3/#text-emphasis-position-property*) in W3C CSS Text Decoration Module Level 3.

Line Breaks, Word Breaks, and Hyphenation

The EPUB 3 revision also introduced CSS properties for controlling hyphenation, line breaks, and word breaks. These properties were borrowed from CSS Text module, but again, because the module was not a final recommendation at the time, you must use the -epub- prefix with them. The -epub-hyphens property controls hyphenation. The value none disables hyphenation. The value manual allows hyphenation only if characters (e.g., U+00AD "soft hyphen" and U+2010 "hyphen") explicitly define hyphenation opportunities. The value auto further allows hyphenation as determined automatically by a language-appropriate hyphenation program. However, for auto to work correctly, it is important to specify the xml:lang attribute appropriately. For example, if xml:lang="en" is specified, auto provides hyphenation for the English language. The -epub-line-break property controls line breaking for CJK languages, where the space character is not used as a separator between words. There are four permissible values (strict, normal, loose, and auto), which define strictness of line-breaking rules. Setting the value auto allows the reading system to determine the rules to apply, which may result in more or less restrictive rules being applied depending on the length of lines. The names of the other three values imply the type of line breaking that results from their use.

The -epub-word-break property controls word breaking. There are three permissible values, namely break-all, keep-all, and normal. The value break-all is for CJK text containing non-CJK experts, and the value keep-all is for non-CJK text containing CJK experts. The value normal indicates normal rules for word breaking.

Itemized Lists

To improve list rendering, EPUB 3 also retains numbering options for itemized lists that were dropped from CSS 2.1. EPUB 3 inherits the `list-style-type` property from CSS 2.1, which controls numbering of itemized lists, and retains the `cjk-ideographic`, `hebrew`, `hiragana`, `hiragana-iroha`, `katakana`, and `katakana-iroha` values from CSS 2. These values were considered essential for list numbering in CJK and Hebrew texts.

These values were dropped from CSS 2.1 because they were not implemented when the scope of CSS 2.1 was finalized, but they have since been implemented, so there is no danger in their use.

CHAPTER 9
Accessibility

In EPUB 3 we have an ebook format that embraces that there is no single universal way to access information. *Any* reader may switch between reading modalities at *any* time. Sighted readers, for example, will switch and listen to books be read in many situations not amenable to visual reading, and will often read captions instead of listening to a video. Nonvisual readers may switch between tactile and audio for many of the same reasons.

Although we're only just beginning to understand what the shift to ebooks entails, for both production and the reading experience, much has been learned about the creation of accessible digital content. We may not know yet which new EPUB 3 features are going to take off with the reading public, or in what ways, but the ability to make those features more universally accessible has evolved dramatically, to the point where we can anticipate needs better and meet them up front instead of after the fact.

In the last decade, in particular, the W3C's Web Accessibility Initiative (WAI) has made significant progress toward making HTML-based content more accessible. A common pitfall of inaccessible formats has been to ignore existing accessibility work, or fork off from it, but EPUB 3 has instead been woven into current best practices. By adopting HTML5 as one of the two primary means of representing content, not only does it immediately make a lot of people knowledgeable about web accessibility knowledgeable about ebook accessibility (even if they don't yet realize it), but it also keeps focus on moving forward collaboratively instead of striking out on a parallel or competing path.

But the accessibility of EPUBs represents more than just a *de facto* inheritance of HTML features. The presence of the ebook accessibility community in the standards process allowed for the identification and inclusion of many additional features to enhance multimodality reading experiences, from text-to-speech enhancement mechanisms to text/audio playback synchronization to improved semantics and missing description mechanisms, all of which will be covered in this and the next chapter.

The real consequence of this change is that you need to prepare content to be accessed by readers in a variety of different ways, not just visually, and that is what this chapter is all about. If we're actually going to take advantage of the opportunity that EPUB 3 affords, a larger audience needs to understand how readers will interact with your books (whether listening to text-to-speech playback, reading along with a soundtrack, plugging in a refreshable braille display, zooming your content, enabling captions to watch a video, or otherwise) and how those interactions is tied to good data practices.

But try and turn your brain off to the word *accessibility* as you read and focus instead on the need to create rich, flexible, and versatile content that can make the reading experience better for everyone. That's the inclusive publishing model we're finally evolving toward, after all.

Accessibility and Usability

Before diving into the best practices themselves, we must clarify the distinction made between *accessibility* and *usability* in this chapter. These two terms are often used in overlapping fashion and can mean different things to different people. For the sake of this chapter, we'll use the following definitions:

Accessibility
> The intrinsic capabilities present in the EPUB 3 content: the quality of the data and meaning that can be extracted from it, the built-in navigational capabilities, and additional functionality, such as text and audio synchronization (media overlays) and synthetic speech enhancements. The publisher of an EPUB has control over the accessibility of their publication, whether directly through the tools they use to generate the source or in post-production workflows.

Usability
> The ability of a reader to access the content on any given reading system in her preferred modality. A publisher may make an EPUB 3 publication rich with accessibility features, but if a reader does not have the right device or assistive technology to access those features, the publication itself is not at fault. Other necessary features simply cannot be embedded in markup, such as the ability to easily zoom and pan content.

Accessibility of content is obviously the focus of this chapter, since making devices usable is a topic unto itself and outside the realm of content production. But that's not to say that usability won't pop up from time to time. The EPUB specification bakes in some requirements on the reading system side to improve usability, and awareness of usability issues does influence the need for rich content.

It is important to note here, too, that you should not let current usability influence your decision making about accessibility. A typical practice is to target the industry-leading platform and build around its capabilities (and deficiencies), but what value does this bring you in the long term? Think of the cost that resulted from making Internet Explorer–only websites when it held over 90% of the market as an example of where following the leader can take you. Your books will hopefully sell well for years to come, but unless you enjoy reformatting from scratch each time you look to upgrade or enhance, it pays to put the effort into making them right the first time.

The interdependence of accessibility and usability does complicate the notion of universal accessibility of content and often frightens people trying to get a grasp on what they need to do for production. Our hopefully not-too-heretical advice is not to get bogged down at that level of technical detail if you're just getting started. Strive to make content as widely accessible as possible by making it as rich as possible. Even small efforts to improve the reading experience will be appreciated, but if you never try, you'll just be perpetuating the self-fulfilling myth that accessible content is too difficult or too expensive to make.

And never forget that the work you do matters, even if accessible content often goes unheralded. There are a lot more readers than you might think who are going to appreciate the efforts you put into being more inclusive, even if you don't come out of the gates meeting every single criteria. It's not just print disabled who benefit from accessible digital content, after all. With EPUB 3 opening the door to new rich multimedia experiences, you need to think beyond traditional print disabilities and recognize that ebooks have the potential to exclude a greater segment of the population if not done with care:

- The inability to hear embedded audio and video is a concern for persons who are deaf or hard of hearing.
- Interactivity and animations that rely on color recognition have the potential to exclude those who are color blind or have difficulty distinguishing blended contrasts.
- The new trend toward voice-activated devices has the potential to make reading for people with speech impairments difficult.

But this is still framing the issue as one of disability, when in fact what we want to talk about is choice in reading methods. Anyone can be affected by a *situational disability* in which he cannot interact with the content in his preferred modality. For example:

- Someone trying to read on a cell phone will gain an appreciation for the difficulty of reading small sections of prose at a time, just as someone with low vision experiences when reading using zooming software.

- Someone attempting to read on her deck on a bright summer day, angling and holding her tablet close to her face to follow the prose, will understand the difficulty experienced by someone with age-related sight loss and/or who has trouble with contrasts.

- Someone sitting on the subway who has to turn on subtitles in an embedded video to read the dialogue will experience one way a person who is deaf interacts with the video.

- Someone trying to learn a new language will understand the value of proper text-to-speech voicing and/or human narration for comprehension.

It's time to toss aside the ability/disability labels and embrace choice and difference. Accessibility is critical for some and universally beneficial for all.

Fundamentals of Accessibility

This section deals with the core text and image basics. Although some of the points will sound familiar, and probably seem like a return to the early days of the Web for some, useful markup for nonvisual reading is still not being produced. The Web 20 years on is still not the most accessible place, after all.

Much of this problem remains educational. If you don't understand why tagging matters, you're not going to know what you could be doing better and won't know what to verify before the data goes out the door. Tool support still needs to mature, of course, but blaming tools for the inaccessibility of content is overlooking the responsibility of the producer.

So even if you consider yourself a markup pro and are ready to jump further into the chapter, note that these sections don't just introduce elements and attributes but also explain why they matter for reading. The more you understand the process of how content gets consumed by assistive technologies, the better decisions you'll be able to make about how to tag any structure. And the more you understand, the better ebooks you'll create.

When reading this chapter, note that many of the practices outlined parallel those defined in the Web Content Accessibility Guidelines (WCAG) 2.0 (*http://www.w3.org/TR/WCAG/*). Although EPUB 3 has its own requirements and peculiarities, the WCAG guidelines are the standard for creating accessible HTML-based content. This section draws on only the most common practices for ebook production, but that does not imply that guidelines not covered here (whether WCAG or otherwise) are less valuable or can be ignored. The IDPF is also developing an accessibility section on its website, which includes the EPUB 3 Accessibility Guidelines (*http://www.idpf.org/accessibility/guide lines*). That site includes a customizable quality assurance checklist together with explanatory guidelines for verifying your content.

Structure and Semantics

The best way to begin a discussion on accessible data is by looking at the role that structure and semantics play in making content comprehensible and navigable by readers. Although the terms are fairly ubiquitous when it comes to discussing markup languages and data modeling generally (because they are so important to the quality of your data and your ability to do fantastic-seeming things with it), they are often bandied about in ways that make them sound geeky and inaccessible to all but data architects.

You're probably used to hearing the terms defined along these lines, for example: *structure* is the elements you use to craft your EPUB content, and *semantics* is the additional meaning you can layer on top of those structures to better indicate what they represent.

But that's undoubtedly a bit esoteric if you don't go mucking around in your markup on a regular basis, so let's take a more descriptive approach to their meaning. Another way to think about their importance and relationship is via a little reformulation of Plato's "Allegory of the cave." In this dialogue, if you've (intentionally) forgotten your undergrad Greek philosophy, Socrates describes how the prisoners in the cave can see only shadows of the true forms of things on the walls as they pass in front of a fire, and only the philosopher kings will eventually break free of the chains that bind them in ignorance and come to see the reality of those forms.

As we reformulate Plato, the concept of generalized and specific forms is all that you need to take away from the original allegory, as getting from generalized to specific is the key to semantic markup. In our new content world view, the elements we use to mark up a document represent the generalized reflection of the reality we are trying to express. At the shadow level, so to speak, a chapter and a part and an introduction and an epilogue and many other structures in a book all function in the same way, like encapsulated containers of structurally significant content.

These general forms allow for the creation of markup grammars, such as HTML5, without element counts in the thousands to address every possible need. In other words, a generalized element retains the form of greatest applicability at the expense of specifics. The HTML5 grammar, for example, solved the problem of a multitude of structural containers with only slightly differing purposes by introducing the `section` element.

But what help is generalized markup to a person, let alone a reading system, let alone to an assistive technology trying to use the markup to facilitate reading? Not much, of course. Try making sense of a markup file by reading just the element names and see how far you get; a reading system isn't going to fare any better despite a developer's best efforts. HTML5 may now allow you to group related content in a section element, but without reading the prose for clues, all you know is that you've encountered a seemingly random group of content called "section." This is structure without semantics.

You might try to determine the importance of the content by sneaking a peek ahead at the section's heading (assuming it has one), but unless the heading contains some keyword like "part" or "chapter," you still won't know why the section was added or how the content is important to the ebook as a whole. And cheating really isn't fair, as making applications perform heuristic tests like looking at content can be no small challenge. This is both the power and failing of trying to process generalized markup languages and do meaningful things with what you find: you don't have to account for a lot, but you also don't often get a lot to work with.

Getting back to our analogy, though, it's fair to say we're all philosopher kings when it comes to the true nature of books; we aren't typically interested in, and don't typically notice, generalized forms when reading. But, whether we realize it or not, we rely on our reading systems being able to make sense of these structures to facilitate our reading, and much more so when deprived of sensory interactions with the device and content. When ebooks contain only generalized structures, reading systems are limited to presenting only the basic visual form of the book. Dumb data makes for dumb reading experiences, because reading systems cannot play the necessary role of facilitator when given little to nothing to work with. And that's why not everyone can read all digital content.

It's not always obvious to sighted readers at this point why semantics are important for them, though, as they just expect to see the visual presentation the forms provide and to navigate around with fingers and eyes. But that's also because no one yet expects more from their digital reading experience than what they were accustomed to in print. One practical example of taking advantage of EPUB 3's new rich data is footnotes in Apple's iBooks. As mentioned in Chapter 3, the iBooks application uses the semantic information that identifies notes and their referents to automatically provide pop-up functionality. If you don't enrich your data, your footnotes are rendered as plain text.

Rich data has many other uses. Knowing whether a section is a chapter or a part as you skip forward through your ebook can keep you from having to open the table of contents. Knowing where the body matter section begins can allow a reading system to jump you immediately to the beginning of the story instead of the first page of front matter. Knowing where the body ends and back matter begins could allow the reading system to provide the option to close the ebook and go back to your bookshelf; it might also allow links to related titles you might be interested in reading next to be displayed.

Without semantically rich data, only the most rudimentary actions are possible. With it, the possibilities for all readers are endless.

But to wrap up the analogy, while some of us can read in the shadow world of generalized markup, all we get when we aim that low is an experience that pales to what it could be, and one that needlessly introduces barriers to access. If these terms now make sense, you can hopefully now appreciate better why semantics and structure have to be applied in harmony to get the most value from your data. The accessibility of your ebook is very much a reflection of the effort you put into it. The reading system may be where the magic unfolds for the reader, but all data magic starts with the quality of the source.

With that bit of high-level knowledge under your belt, it's time to see how the two work together in practice in EPUB 3 to make content richer and more accessible.

Data Integrity

The most important rule to remember when structuring your content is to use the right element for the right job. It seems like an obvious statement, but too often people settle for the quick solution without thinking about its impact (look no further than the Web for examples of markup run amok). Print-to-digital exports are also notorious for taking the path of least complexity (creating a p-soup of output that wraps most everything in paragraph tags). In fairness, though, print layout programs typically lack the information necessary for the export to be anything more than rudimentary; it's under-utilization of the features they offer that leads to simplistic markup. One might be tempted to argue here that we need new tools that insert semantic structures instead of text boxes with styles, but that's a story for another day.

When good semantic markup has been used, reading systems and assistive technologies can take advantage of specialized tags to do the right thing for you, but there's little they can do if you don't give them any sense of what they're encountering. When it comes to EPUB 3, make sure you know the new HTML5 element definitions. Chapter 3 covers many of the new additions, but reading the specification definitions is the best way to orient yourself to the full range of uses.

And remember that structure is not about what you want an element to mean. The changes to the HTML5 element definitions may not always make the most sense, but twisting definitions and uses to fit your own desires isn't going to make you a friend of accessibility, either. Reading systems and assistive technologies are developed around common conventions.

And whatever you do, don't perpetuate the sin of wrapping div and span tags around any content you don't know how to handle. In a nod to good data, although somewhat unenforceable, it's actually a violation (*http://bit.ly/WMv0yj*) of the EPUB 3 specification to create content that uses generic elements in place of more specific ones, and it doesn't take long to check if there really is no other alternative first.

When you make up your own structures using generic tags, you push the logical navigation and comprehension of those custom structures onto the reader and potentially mess up the HTML5 document outline used for navigation. Sighted readers may not notice anything, but when reading flows through the markup, convoluted structures can frustrate the reader and interfere with her ability to effectively follow the narrative flow.

If you don't discover an existing element that fits your need, the process of checking will typically reveal that you're not alone in your problem, and that community-driven solutions have been developed. Standards and conventions are the friend of accessibility. And if you really don't know and can't find an answer, ask. The IDPF maintains an accessibility forum (*http://idpf.org/forums/epub-accessibility*) where you can seek assistance.

There are, of course, going to be many times when you have no choice but to use a generic tag, but when you do, always try to attach an `epub:type` attribute with a specific semantic. The more information you can provide, the more useful your data will be.

Take the converse situation into consideration when creating your content, too. You aren't doing readers a service by finding more, and ever complex, ways to nest simple structures. The more layers you add the harder it can be to navigate, as I already mentioned. Over-analyzing your data can be as detrimental to navigation as under-analyzing.

For people who cannot visually navigate your ebook, this basic effort to properly tag your data reduces many of the obstacles of the digital medium. The ability to skip structures and escape from them starts with meaningfully tagged data. The ability to move through a document without going to a table of contents starts with meaningfully tagged data.

Skipping versus Escaping

Skipping and escaping are terms that are going to come up again repeatedly.

Skipping, as you might expect, is the ability to ignore elements completely, to skip by them. Accessible reading systems typically provide the ability for the reader to specify the constructs they want to ignore, such as sidebars, figures, notes, and page numbers.

Escapable content typically consists of deep-nested or repetitive structures (such as those found in tables and lists) that a user may want to leave and continue reading at the next available item following the escaped content (a reading system's user interface would normally provide quick access to the "escape" command, so that the operation can easily be called repetitively, if needed).

The integrity of your data is also a basic value proposition. Do you expect to throw away your content and start over every time you need to rerelease, or do you want to retain it and be able to easily upgrade it over time? Structurally meaningful data is critical to the long-term archivability of your ebooks, the ability to easily enhance and release new versions as technology progresses, as well as your ability to interchange your data and use it to create other outputs. If you start making bad data now, expect to pay for your mistakes later.

Separation of Style

Some old lessons have to be continuously relearned and reinforced, and not mixing content and style is a familiar friend to revisit whenever talking about accessible data.

To be clear, separating style does not mean avoiding the `style` attribute and putting all your CSS in a separate file, even if that is another good practice we'll get back to later in the chapter. Rather, separation of style refers to not expecting the visual appearance of your content alone to convey meaning to readers. Style is just a layer between your markup and the device that renders it, not an intrinsic quality you can rely on to say anything about your content.

Typographic conventions had to convey meaning in print because that was all that was available. When a visual reader sees bold or italicized text in an increased font size, they understand it represents a new heading, for example. Use CSS to draw the text of a p or div in larger font and there is nothing in the markup to alert nonvisual readers that there is anything special about that paragraph or div. Here are some examples of using appropriate markup over styling, many of which will be covered in more detail throughout the remainder of this section:

```
<!-- Bad: --> <div class="heading">A Long Time Coming</div>
<!-- Good: --> <h1>A Long Time Coming</h1>

<!-- Bad: (breaks the first word when using text-to-speech) -->
<p><img src="bigO.png" alt="O"/>nce upon a time</p>

<!-- Good: -->
<p class="first">Once upon a time ...</p>

<style type="text/css">
   p.first:first-letter {
      font-size: 200%;
      margin: 0em 0.2em 0em 0em;
      float: left;
   }
</style>

<!-- Bad: -->
<div class="list">
   <span class="block-item">1. Apples</span>
   <span class="block-item">2. Oranges</span>
   ...
```

```
</div>

<!-- Good: -->
<ol>
    <li>Apples</li>
    <li>Oranges</li>
    ...
</ol>

<!-- Bad: -->
<div class="box">
    <p class="heading">Black Holes</p>
    ...
</div>

<!-- Good: -->
<aside>
    <h2>Black Holes</h2>
    ...
</aside>
```

Typographic conventions are still useful for conveying semantic information to sighted readers, of course, but visual reading is just one modality. It should not be given paramount importance at the expense of others, especially since there is nothing about making rich data that doesn't mean you can't still make visually rich renderings. Leave style in that in-between layer where it targets visual readers, and keep your focus on the quality of your markup so that everyone wins.

The most basic rule of thumb to remember is that if you remove the CSS from your ebook, you should still be able to extract the same meaning from it as though nothing had changed, which is what the preceding examples were designed to show. Your markup is what should ultimately be conveying your meaning. If you rely solely on position or color or whatever other stylistic flair you might devise, you're taking away the ability of a segment of your readers to understand the content.

Semantic Inflection

Chapter 3 already covered the epub:type attribute in "epub:type and Structural Semantics" (page 68), but we must re-address its value for accessibility. In case it needs repeating, semantics are not just an exercise in labeling elements; these semantics are what enable intelligent reading experiences.

If you have 25 definition lists in an ebook, each with a particular use, there's no way for a reading system to determine which one represents the glossary if you don't have a semantic applied:

```
<dl id="glossary" epub:type="glossary">
    ...
</dl>
```

Adding semantics to each `section` also enables a reading system to inform the reader where they are in the content, especially when no heading is present:

```
<section epub:type="epigraph">
  <blockquote>
    <p>for hate's sake I spit my last breath at thee</p>
  </blockquote>
</section>
```

Readers familiar with *Moby Dick* will know that this is a quote, but anyone using audio playback who wasn't aware of the origin wouldn't necessarily know why the words are suddenly announced to them, especially if the epigraph followed a table of contents, for example. A reading system could provide the reader the option to announce the current section, in which case it could be made perfectly clear that the reader is listening to the epigraph.

Language

As mentioned in Chapter 8 in "Specifying the Natural Language" (page 211), setting the language of your content documents is critically important to their accessibility. In an age of cloud readers, assistive technologies might not have access to the default language if you don't (unless they rewrite your content file to include the information in the package document, which is a bad assumption to make).

If you don't set the default language, you can impact on the ability of the assistive technology to properly render text-to-speech playback and on how refreshable Braille displays render characters.

Logical Reading Order

Although you'll hear that all EPUB 3s have a default, or linear, reading order, it's not necessarily the same thing as the logical reading order, or primary narrative. The EPUB 3 `spine` element in the publication manifest defines the order in which a reading system should render content files as you move through the publication. This default order enables a seamless reading experience, even though the publication may be made up of many individual content files (e.g., one per chapter).

Though the main purpose of the `spine` is to identify the sequence in which documents are rendered, you can use it to distinguish primary from auxiliary content. You can attach the `linear` attribute to the child `itemref` elements to indicate whether the referenced content file contains primary reading content or not.

For example, textbooks commonly place the answer key for questions at the end of chapter into a separate file, with a link to the key in the content. In this case, the key could be read linearly after the end of the chapter, but it doesn't make a lot of sense, so you mark them as nonlinear:

```
<spine>
   ...
   <itemref idref="chapter1"/>
   <itemref idref="chapter1-key" linear="no"/>
   <itemref idref="chapter2"/>
   <itemref idref="chapter2-key" linear="no"/>
   ...
</spine>
```

A reader could now ignore these sections and continue following the primary narrative uninterrupted. But this capability is only a simple measure for distinguishing content that is primary at the macro level; it's not effective in terms of distinguishing the primary narrative flow of the content within any document. (Although in the case of simple works of fiction that contain only a single unbroken narrative, it might be.)

Sighted readers don't typically think about the logical reading order within the chapters and sections of a book, but that's because they can visually identify the secondary content and read around it as desired. A reading system, on the other hand, doesn't have this information to use for the same effect unless you add it (those semantics, again).

Keeping style separate from content, you can, for example, give a sidebar a nice colorful border and offset it from the narrative visually using a div and CSS, but you've limited the information you're providing to only a select group when all you use is style:

```
<style type="text/css">
   div.fake-sidebar {
      border: 1px solid rgb(0,0,0);
      background-color: rgb(230,230,230);
   }
</style>

<div class="fake-sidebar">
   ...
</div>
```

Using a div means a reading system will not know by default that it can skip the sidebar if the reader has chosen to only follow the primary narrative, since there is no telling one div from another by class attributes alone. Someone listening to the book using a text-to-speech engine will have the narrative interrupted at the point of insertion when you incorrectly tag content in this way.

The only solution at the reader's disposal might be to slowly move forward until she finds the next paragraph that sounds like a continuation of what she was just listening to (unidentified div elements aren't typically escapable). Picture trying to read and keep a thought with the constant interruptions that can result from sidebars, notes, warnings, and all the various other peripheral text material a book might contain.

For this reason, you need to make sure to properly identify content that is not part of the primary narrative as such, as reviewed in Chapter 3 regarding the new HTML5 additions in content documents. The `aside` element is particularly useful when it comes to marking text that is not of primary importance:

```
<aside epub:type="sidebar">
   ...
</aside>
```

Now, a reading system can detect from the tagging that the content is supplemental, allowing it to be skipped. Even seemingly small steps, like marking all secondary images and figures in `figure` tags, allows the reader to decide what additional information they want presented.

Sections and Headings

As mentioned in the introduction to this section, always group related content that is structurally significant in `section` elements to facilitate navigation, and always indicate why you've created the grouping using the `epub:type` attribute:

```
<section epub:type="epilogue">
   ...
</section>
```

The entries in the table of contents in your navigation document are all going to be structurally significant, which can be a helpful guide when it comes to thinking about how to properly apply the `section` element. Some additional ideas on structural significance can be gleaned from the terms in the EPUB 3 Structural Semantics Vocabulary (*http://idpf.org/epub/vocab/structure/*). For example, a non-exhaustive list of semantics for sectioning content includes:

- Foreword
- Prologue
- Preface
- Part
- Chapter
- Epilogue
- Bibliography
- Glossary
- Index

Semantics are especially helpful when a section does not have a heading. Sighted readers are used to the visual conventions that distinguish dedications, epigraphs, and other front matter that may be only of slight interest, for example, and can skip past them. Someone who can't see your content has to listen to it if you don't provide any additional information to assist them.

Headingless, unidentified content also means the person will have to listen to it long enough to figure out why it's even there. Have you just added an epigraph to the start of your book, and skipping the containing section will take them to the first chapter, or are they listening to an epigraph that starts the first chapter and skipping the sec tion will take them to chapter two? These are the impediments you shift onto your reader when you don't take care of your data.

When the section does contain a heading, there are two options for tagging: numbered headings that reflect the current level or h1 headings for every section. At this point in time, using numbered headings is recommended, as support for navigation via the structure of the document is still developing:

```
<section epub:type="part">
   <h1>Part I</h1>

   <section epub:type="chapter">
      <h2>Chapter 1</h2>
      ...
   </section>
</section>
```

Numbered headings will also work better for forward-compatibility with older EPUB reading systems.

Using an h1 heading regardless of the nesting level of the section will undoubtedly gain traction moving forward, though. In this case, the h1 becomes more of a generic heading, as traversal of the document will occur via the document outline and not by heading tags (the construction of this outline (*http://bit.ly/WmVojM*) is defined in HTML5).

And remember that titles are an integral unit of information. If you want to break a title across multiple lines, change font sizes, or do other stylistic trickery, use spans and CSS and keep the display in the style layer. *Never* add multiple heading elements for each segment. Use span elements if you need to visually change the look and appearance of headings:

```
<!-- Bad: -->
<h1>Chapter</h1>
<h3>One</h3>
<h1>Loomings</h1>


<!-- Good: -->
<h1>Chapter <span class="chapNum">One</span> Loomings.</h1>
```

You could use the following CSS class to change the font size of the span to treat it as a block element (i.e., place the text on a separate line):

```
span.chapNum {
    display: block;
    margin: 0.5em 0em;
    font-size: 80%
}
```

If you fragment your data, you fragment the reading experience and cause confusion for someone trying to piece back together what heading(s) they've actually run into. Beware heading markup like this that looks compliant:

```
<section>
    <h1>Chapter title</h1>
    <h2>Subtitle</h2>
    <h3>Additional subtitle</h3>
    ...
</section>
```

The HTML5 outlining algorithm treats this markup as three separate sections, or the equivalent of:

```
<section>
    <h1>Chapter title</h1>
    <section>
        <h2>Subtitle</h2>
        <section>
            <h3>Additional subtitle</h3>
            ...
        </section>
    </section>
</section>
```

A new section is implied for each new heading you add after the initial heading for the section, which can cause problems for someone trying to navigate by the document outline (e.g., using hotkeys to jump from section to section).

HTML5 does not include a reliable mechanism to hide subheadings that use the h# elements. The hgroup element was a part of the specification for masking additional heading elements:

```
<section>
    <hgroup>
        <h1>Chapter title</h1>
        <h2>Subtitle</h2>
        <h3>Additional subtitle</h3>
    </hgroup>
</section>
```

Here, the highest numbered heading in the hgroup is treated as the section heading and the others are effectively masked from the outlining algorithm. But this markup looks in peril of being removed as of this writing. It now appears that hgroup will be split out from the main HTML5 specification, so whether it persists in its current form in a sub-specification, gets rolled back in later, is replaced by an alternative solution for masking the outline, or more than one option is adopted is anyone's guess.

So, for now, you have to assume that headings floating around in your body indicate new sections.

Context Changes

A nasty side-effect of current print-based export processes is that changes in context are visually styled using CSS and/or with images. When you use the CSS margin-top property to add spacing, you're taking away from anyone who can't see the display that a change in context has occurred. Graphics to add whitespace are no better, because they don't typically specify an alt value and are ignored by assistive technologies. Graphics that include asterisms or similar as the alt text are slightly better, but are still a sub-optimal approach in that they don't convey any meaning except through the reading of the alt value.

Some people would argue that context breaks represent the borders between untitled subsections within sections, but from a structural and navigational perspective, it's typically not true, or wanted, so don't be too tempted to add section elements.

HTML5 has, in fact, addressed this need for a transitioning element by changing the semantics of the hr element for this purpose.

You can now cleanly identify transition points as follows:

```
<p>... the world swam and disappeared into darkness.</p>

<hr class="transition"/>

<p class="nonindent">When next we met ...</p>
```

By default, this tag would include a horizontal rule, but you can use CSS to turn off the effect and leave a more traditional space for visual viewing:

```
hr.transition {
    width: 0em;
    margin: 0.5em 0em;
}
```

or you could add a fleuron or other ornament:

```
hr.transition {
    background: url('img/fleuron.gif') no-repeat 50% 50%;
    height: 1em;
    margin: 0.5em 0em;
}
```

Styling the hr element ensures that the context change isn't lost in the rush to be visually appealing.

Having an element dedicated for this purpose also means that you can do without a class attribute on the p tag following the hr, if you want to ensure that all paragraphs are visually styled as non-indented for visual readers. As shown earlier in the section on separating style, you could use CSS selectors to find the first paragraph following the transition:

```
hr + p {
    text-indent: 0em;
}
```

Lists

You typically wouldn't expect to need advice that you should use lists for sets of related items, but if you rely too heavily on print tools to create your content, the result will be paragraphs made to look like list items, or single paragraphs that merge all the items together using only br or span tags to separate them:

```
<!-- Bad: -->

<p>Hydrogen<br/>Helium<br/>Lithium<br/>Beryllium ...</p>

<p>Hydrogen</p>
<p>Helium</p>
<p>Lithium</p>
<p>Beryllium</p>
...

<div class="list">
    <span class="list-item">Hydrogen</span>
    <span class="list-item">Helium</span>
    <span class="list-item">Lithium</span>
    <span class="list-item">Beryllium</span>
    ...
</div>
```

If you don't use proper list structures, readers can get stuck having to traverse the entire set of items before they can continue with the narrative flow (in the case of one paragraph per item) or having to listen to every item in full to hear the list (when br or span tags are used).

A list element, on the other hand, provides the ability both to move quickly from item to item and to escape the list entirely. It also allows a reading system to inform a reader how many items are in the list and which one they are at for referencing. Picture a list with tens or hundreds of items, such as the periodic table, and you'll get a sense for why this functionality is so useful:

```
<ol>
    <li>Hydrogen</li>
    <li>Helium</li>
    <li>Lithium</li>
    <li>Beryllium</li>
    ...
</ol>
```

Using paragraphs for lists also leads people to resort to visual trickery with margins to emulate the deeper indentation that a nested list would have. These kinds of illusions take away from all but sighted readers that there exists a hierarchical relationship. The correct tagging allows readers to navigate the various levels with ease.

As a final note, always use the right kind of list:

ol

> Used when the order of the items is important

ul

> Used when there is no significance or weak significance to the items (e.g., just because you arrange items alphabetically does not impart meaning to the order)

dl

> Used to define terms, mark up glossaries, etc.

Lists have these semantics for good purpose, so don't use CSS to play visual games with them.

Tables

The reflowable, paginated nature of ebook reading has fortunately kept tables from being used for presentational purposes in ebooks. In theory, this should have been a good thing. The complex nature of tables relative to limited rendering area of typical reading systems has led to the worse practice of excluding the data in favor of images of the table, however. How helpful is a picture of data to someone who cannot see it?

The motivating hope behind this practice seems to be that images will take away rendering issues on small screens, but don't fall into this trap. Not only are you taking the content away from readers who can't see the table, but even if you can see the images they often get scaled down to illegibility and/or burst out the side of the reading area on the devices that this technique is presumably meant to enhance the tables on (notably eInk readers that have no zooming functionality).

Consider also what you're doing when you add a picture: you're trying to address a situational disability (the inability to view an entire table at once) by creating another disability (only limited visual access to the content). If you properly mark up your data, readers can find ways to navigate it, whether via synthetic speech or other accessible navigation mechanisms. Obsessing about appearance is natural, but ask yourself how realistic a concern it should be when people read on cellphone screens? Give your readers credit to understand the limitations their devices impose, and give them the flexibility to find other ways to read.

When it comes to marking up tables, the fundamental advice for making them accessible from web iterations past remains true:

- Always use th elements for header cells.
- Wrap your header in a thead, in particular when including multirow headings.
- Use the th scope attribute to give the applicability of the heading (e.g., whether to the row or column). This attribute is not necessary for simple tables where the first row of th elements, or a th cell at the start of each row, defines the header(s).
- If the header for a cell cannot be easily determined by its context, and especially when multiple cells in a multirow header apply, add the headers attribute and point to the appropriate th element(s).

These heading requirements allow anyone navigating your table to quickly determine what they're reading at any given point in it, which is the biggest challenge that tables pose outside of perhaps escaping from them. It's easy to get lost in a sea of numbers, otherwise.

The following example shows how these practices could be applied to a table of baseball statistics:

```
<table>
    <caption>1927 New York Yankees</caption>
    <thead>
        <tr>
            <th rowspan="2">Player</th>
            <th id="reg-hd" colspan="3">Regular Season</th>
            <th id="post-hd" colspan="3">Post Season</th>
        </tr>
        <tr>
            <th id="reg-ab">At Bats</th>
            <th id="reg-hits">Hits</th>
            <th id="reg-avg">Average</th>
            <th id="post-ab">At Bats</th>
            <th id="post-hits">Hits</th>
            <th id="post-avg">Average</th>
        </tr>
    </thead>
    <tbody>
        <tr>
            <td>Lou Gehrig</td>
            <td headers="reg-hd reg-ab">584</td>
            <td headers="reg-hd reg-hits">218</td>
```

```
          <td headers="reg-hd reg-avg">.373</td>
          <td headers="post-hd post-ab">13</td>
          <td headers="post-hd post-hits">4</td>
          <td headers="post-hd post-avg">.308</td>
      </tr>
   </tbody>
</table>
```

The headers attribute on the td cells identifies both whether the cell contains a "Regular Season" or "Post Season" statistic, as well as the particular kind of stat from the second header row. The value of this tagging is that a reading system or assistive technology can now announce to the reader that they are looking at "regular season hits" when presented the data for the third column, for example.

There's also no reason why this functionality can't be equally useful to sighted readers, except that it's rarely made available. You've already seen the problem of visually rendering table data on small screens, and there's an obvious solution here to the problem a sighted reader will have of seeing perhaps only a few cells at a time and not having the visual context of what they're looking at. But whether mainstream devices begin taking advantage of this information to solve these problems remains to be seen.

It's also good practice to provide a summary of complex tables to orient readers to their structure and purpose in advance, but the summary attribute has been dropped from HTML5. This loss is slightly less objectionable than the longdesc attribute removal you'll learn about when we get to images, because prose attributes have many limitations, from expressivity to international language support.

The problem is that HTML5 doesn't replace these removals with any mechanism to allow the discovery of the same information, instead deferring to the aria-describedby attribute to point to the information (see "WAI-ARIA" (page 269) later in this chapter for more information). This attribute, however, may make the information even less generally discoverable to the broader accessibility community, as only persons using assistive technologies will easily find it.

The proposed HTML5 solutions for adding summaries (such as using the caption element) also don't take into account the need to predictably find this information before presenting the table. The information can't be in any of a number of different places with the onus on the person reading the content to find it.

The details element could work as a nonintrusive mechanism for including descriptions, at least until a better solution comes along. This element functions like a declarative show/hide box. Unfortunately, it suffers from a lack of semantic information that the epub:type attribute cannot currently remedy (i.e., there are no terms available for identifying whether the element contains a summary or description or something else). You instead must use a child summary element to carry a prose title, as in the following example:

```
<details>
    <summary>Summary</summary>
    <p>...</p>
</details>
```

 The value of the summary element represents the clickable text used to
expand/close the field and can be whatever you choose.

If you then take a small liberty with the meaning of the aria-describedby attribute to
also include summary descriptions, you could reformulate the HTML5 specification
example to include an explicit pointer to the details element:

```
<table aria-describedby="tbl01-summary">
    <caption>
        Characteristics with positive and negative sides.
        <details id="tbl01-summary">
            <summary>Summary</summary>
            <p>Characteristics are given in the second column...</p>
        </details>
    </caption>
    ...
</table>
```

In this markup, a nonvisual reader can now find the summary when encountering the
table, while a sighted reader will only be presented the option of whether to expand the
details element. It may not prove a great solution in the long run, but until the landscape settles it's the best on offer.

 Because the details element is a dynamic forms element, documents
that make use of it must be marked as scripted in the package document manifest. It also means there is some potential that the element
won't be supported by all reading systems.

Figures

If a book contains illustrative information, such as images or charts or code examples
that are not in the primary narrative flow (i.e., whose positioning is not critical to its
placement in the markup), this content should be wrapped in figure tags:

```
<figure>
    <img src="images/blob.jpeg" alt="the blob"/>
</figure>
```

Because figures typically include a caption providing a numeric identifier and/or brief description for inclusion, the HTML5 specification has also defined a special figcaption element:

```
<figure>
  <img src="images/blob.jpeg" alt="the blob"/>
  <figcaption>
    Figure 3.7 &amp;#x2014; The blob is digesting Steve McQueen in this
    unreleased ending to the classic movie.
  </figcaption>
</figure>
```

Grouping content using figure tags makes it simpler for a reader to navigate and understand your content, as it's another impediment to the logical reading order removed. They can opt to skip all secondary figures and escape from them when the correct markup is used.

Unfortunately, there is little support for these two new elements by assistive technologies as of this writing, so they get treated as no better than div elements. That said, it's still preferable to future-proof your data and do the right thing, as support will catch up, especially since the only other alternative is semantically meaningless div elements.

 Although a comprehensive chart of accessibility support for reading systems does not exist as of writing, the EPUB test suite project should help close this information hole in time. The HTML5 Accessibility (*http://html5accessibility.com/*) website is also an excellent reference for the current state of the art in browser technology. Although reporting browser support, it can provide insights into where reading system support is as the underlying engines are typically the same.

Images

Images present a challenge for a variety of disabilities, and the means of handling them are not new, but HTML5 has added a new barrier in taking away the longdesc attribute for out-of-band descriptions. As mentioned in the discussion of tables, you're now left to find ways to incorporate your accessible descriptions in the content of your document or link to them externally.

 At the time of this writing, the longdesc attribute is expected to be moved into a sub-specification track at the W3C. This may mean it will be available in EPUB 3 at a future date as an add-on to HTML5, but cannot be counted on.

To keep consistent with the earlier suggestion for tables, wrapping the img element in a figure and using a details element as a child of the figcaption may suit your needs, as shown in the following example:

```
<figure aria-describedby="fig01-desc">
   <img src="images/blob.jpeg" alt="the blob"/>
   <figcaption>
      Figure 3.7 — The blob is digesting Steve McQueen in
      this unreleased ending to the classic movie.
      <details id="fig01-desc">
         <summary>Description</summary>
         <p>
            In the photo, Steve McQueen can be seen floating within the
            gelatinous body of the blob as it moves down the main
            street ...
         </p>
      </details>
   </figcaption>
</figure>
```

But this option is viable only when the image is not in the logical reading order and can be wrapped in a figure. If the image must be accessible at the point where it is inserted in order for the narrative to make sense, other means will be needed.

One option would be to include a hyperlinked text label pointing to your long description:

```
<p>
   <img src="images/blob.jpeg" alt="the blob"/>
   <br/><a href="blob-desc.xhtml">Description</a>
</p>
```

This would allow the accessible description to live external to the content. Notice that this example doesn't include an aria-describedby attribute, because only the text of the associated element gets rendered to a reader using an assistive technology. In this case, the word "Description" would be announced; the reader would not be presented with the option to link to the description.

It is also possible to hide the content and embed it in the content document:

```
<p>
   <img src="images/blob.jpeg"
   alt="the blob" aria-describedby="fig01-desc"/>
</p>
<p id="fig01-desc" style="display: none; visibility: hidden;">
   In the photo, Steve McQueen can be seen floating within the
   gelatinous body of the blob as it moves down the main
   street ...
</p>
```

Content that is styled *invisible* is normally not rendered by assistive technologies, but WAI-ARIA allows hidden content to be referenced from the `aria-describedby` and `aria-labelledby` attributes. In this case, the assistive technology is expected to announce the text content of the referenced hidden element.

 WAI-ARIA does not yet standardize this method for use with the `hidden` attribute (it has not yet been updated to HTML5), but this will likely change moving forward.

But that muckiness aside, it's much more pleasant to note that the `alt` attribute has not changed, even if confusion around its use still abounds. The `alt` attribute is not a short description; it's intended to provide a text equivalent that can replace the image for people for whom the image is not accessible/available.

Best practices for writing the alternative text extend beyond the scope of this book. For more information, see the W3C document *HTML5: Techniques for providing useful text alternatives* (*http://www.w3.org/TR/html-alt-techniques/*) and the guidelines written by Jukka Korpela. (*http://www.cs.tut.fi/~jkorpela/html/alt.html*)

Of particular note for accessible practices, however, is that even though the `alt` attribute always has to be present on images, it does not always have to contain a text alternative:

```
<img src="rounded-corner.jpg" alt=""/>
```

This little fact often gets overlooked. If you add text to an `alt` attribute, you're indicating that the image is meaningful to the content and requesting that the reader pay attention to it. Images that only exist to make content look pretty should include empty `alt` attributes, as that allows reading systems and assistive technologies to skip readers past them without interrupting their reading experience.

 The HTML5 specification does allow an `img` element to omit an `alt` attribute if information about the image is not known and it is contained in a `figure` element with only a `figcaption` (one example given is photo upload sites where a user does not provide a text description). As the possible scenarios for omitting are not very applicable to EPUB production, and the `alt` value is typically expected to be filled in later, your images should never omit the attribute.

SVG

Rounding out the tour of image functionality is SVG. Just how accessible SVG really is comes up for debate every so often, and while you can argue that it can be more accessible than non-XML formats like JPEG and PNG, no one can apply any blanket statement, like "SVG is completely accessible." Like all content, an SVG is only as accessible as you make it, and when you start scripting one, for example, you can fall into all the typical inaccessibility traps.

The advantages of SVG for accessibility are noteworthy, though. You can scale SVG images without the need for specialized zoom software (and without the typical pixelation effect that occurs when zooming raster formats), the images are assistive technology–friendly when it comes to scripting and can be augmented by WAI-ARIA, and you can add a title and a description directly to the markup without resorting to the messy techniques the img element requires:

```
<svg:svg xmlns:svg="http://www.w3.org/2000/svg">
   <svg:title>Figure 1.1, The Hydrologic Cycle</svg:title>
   <svg:desc>
      The diagram shows the processes of evaporation, condensation,
      evapotranspiration, water storage in ice and snow, and
      precipitation. ...
   </svg:desc>
   ...
</svg:svg>
```

 The SVG working group provides the guide *Accessibility Features of SVG* (*http://www.w3.org/TR/SVG-access/*), which covers accessible SVG content production.

The accessibility hooks are also why SVG has been promoted up to a first-class content format (i.e., your ebook can contain only SVG images; they don't have to be embedded in XHTML files). But if you are going to go with an image-only ebook, the quality of your descriptions is going to be paramount, as they will have to tell the story that is lost in your visual imagery. And to be frank, sometimes descriptions will simply fail to capture the richness and complexity of your content, in which case you should consider fallback text serializations.

MathML

Why is MathML important for accessibility? Consider the following simple description of an equation: the square root of a over b. If you hastily added this description to an image of the corresponding equation, what would you expect a reader who couldn't see your image to make of it? Did you mean they should take the square root of a and divide that by b, or did you mean them to take the square root of the result of dividing a by b?

The lack of MathML support until now has resulted in these kinds of ambiguities arising in the natural language descriptions that accompanied math images. Ideally, your author would describe all their formulas, but the ability to write an equation doesn't always translate into the ability to effectively describe it for someone who can't see it. And sometimes you have to make do with the resources you have available at hand at the time you generate the ebook, and lacking both academic and description expertise is a recipe for disaster.

MathML takes the ambiguity out of the equation, as assistive technologies have come a long way in terms of being able to voice math equations now. Some Word plug-ins can even enable authors to visually create equations for you without having to know MathML, and other tools can convert LaTeX to MathML. The resources are out there to support MathML workflows, in other words.

Although EPUB 3 now provides native support for MathML, it is still a good practice to include an alternate text fallback using the `alttext` attribute, because not all reading systems will support voicing of the markup:

```
<m:math
   xmlns:m="http://www.w3.org/1998/Math/MathML"
   alttext="Frac Root a EndRoot Over b EndFrac">
   <m:mfrac>
      <m:msqrt>
         <m:mtext>a</m:mtext>
      </m:msqrt>
      <m:mi>b</m:mi>
   </m:mfrac>
</m:math>
```

 The preceding description was written in MathSpeak. For more information, see the MathSpeak™ Initiative homepage (*http://www.gh-mathspeak.com/*).

If the equation cannot be described within an attribute (e.g., it would surpass the 255 character limit, or requires markup elements, like ruby, to fully describe), the description should be written in XHTML and embedded in an `annotation-xml` element as follows:

```
<m:math xmlns:m="http://www.w3.org/1998/Math/MathML">
  <m:semantics>
    <m:mfrac>
      ...
    </m:mfrac>
    <m:annotation-xml
        encoding="application/xhtml+xml"
        name="alternate-representation">
      <span xmlns="http://www.w3.org/1999/xhtml">
        Frac Root a EndRoot Over b EndFrac
      </span>
    </m:annotation-xml>
  </m:semantics>
</m:math>
```

Note that a `semantics` element now surrounds the entire equation. This element is required in order for the addition of the `annotation-xml` element to be valid.

There is much more to making MathML equations accessible than just adding descriptions, from accounting for implied operators to invisible separators to the best way to tag the parts of equations. For an excellent guide to markup best practices for equations, see the MathML in DAISY Structure Guidelines (*http://www.daisy.org/z3986/structure/ SG-DAISY3/part2-math.html*). These guidelines will likely be ported to reflect EPUB markup in the near future, but the best practices outlined in the document are relevant regardless of the underlying grammar the MathML is embedded in.

Footnotes

Footnotes present another challenge to reading enjoyment. Prior to EPUB 3, note references could not be easily distinguished from regular hyperlinks, and the notes themselves were typically marked up using paragraphs and divs, which impeded the ability to skip through them or past them entirely.

Picture yourself in a position where you might have to skip a note or two before you can continue reading after every paragraph, or manually listen to each new paragraph to determine if it's a note or a continuation of the text. The practice of grouping all notes at the end of a section is slightly more helpful, but it still interferes with the content flow however you read.

The `epub:type` attribute helps solve both these problems when used with the new HTML `aside` element, as in the following example:

```
<p>...<a epub:type="noteref" href="#n1">1</a> ...</p>

<aside epub:type="footnote" id="n1">
  ...
</aside>
```

The `noteref` term in the `epub:type` attribute identifies that the link points to a note, which allows a reading system to alert the reader they've encountered a footnote reference. It also provides the reader the ability to tell the reading system to ignore all such links if she wants to read the text through uninterrupted. Don't underestimate the irritation factor of constant note links being announced!

Likewise, the `aside` element has also been identified as a footnote, permitting the reading system to skip it if the reader has chosen to turn off footnote playback. Putting the note in an `aside` also indicates that the content is not part of the main document flow.

But footnotes are often a nuisance for all readers; sighted readers typically care just as little to encounter them in the text. Identifying all your notes could also allow the reading system to automatically hide them from sighted readers, saving sometimes limited screen space for the narrative prose. The iBooks rendering mentioned at the outset is a practical example of developers taking full advantage of the semantics to enable specialized pop-out rendering of notes. You should still lay out the notes for visual reading (e.g., at the end of each chapter in a `footer` element), because not every reading system will provide specialized handling.

Page Numbering

It might seem odd to talk about page numbering in a digital format guide, but ebooks have been used by students the world over for more than a decade to facilitate their learning in a world only just weaning itself off print. Picture yourself using an ebook in a classroom where print books are still used. When the professor instructs everyone to open their book to a specific page, your ebook will be most unhelpful if you can't find the same location. Or think about trying to quote a passage from a novel in your final paper and not being able to indicate where in the print source it came from. Page numbers are not an antiquated concept quite yet.

One practice, which was never conformant to the EPUB specification, was to include page numbers using anchor tags, as in the following example:

```
<a name="page361"/>
```

Although this provides an accurate jump location for the print pages, unless a reading system does a heuristic inspection of the `name` attribute's value to determine the page number, there's not a lot of value to this kind of tagging. These kinds of anchor points did give a location for navigating from the NCX page list, and it did keep the number from being rendered, but it's also lost data. It also remains invalid to add anchors like this in HTML5, because the name attribute is not included for use on the `a` element.

EPUB 3 once again calls on the `epub:type` attribute to include better semantics:

```
<span xml:id="page361" epub:type="pagebreak">361</span>
```

What the span contains is now clearly stated, and the page number no longer has to be extracted from an attribute and separated from a prefix that could be "p" or "pg" or "page". It's now up to the reader and the reading system to determine when and how to render this information, if at all. Make sure if you use this method that you don't also include a default style sheet rule like the following to hide the page number from visual readers:

```
span[epub|type='pagebreak'] {
    display: none;
}
```

Setting the `display` property to `none` will remove the element from rendering, which will also make it impossible for the reading system to jump readers to the page location.

If ensuring that page numbers are never visible is a priority, you could use another method of paginating with empty `span` and/or `div` elements:

```
<span xml:id="page361" epub:type="pagebreak" title="361"/>
```

This ensures that the page number won't be visible, but it also means that reading systems would have to account for two methods of determining the page number to announce: the value of the element or the value of the `title` attribute attached to it.

When you do include page numbering, remember that you should also include the ISBN of the source it came from in the package metadata:

```
<dc:source>urn:isbn:9780375704024</dc:source>
```

Inclusion of the ISBN is recommended, because it can be used to distinguish between hardcover and softcover versions (and between different editions) of the source book. All of these typically would have different pagination, which would affect the ability of the reader to accurately synchronize with the print source in use.

This will ensure that students, teachers, professors, and other interested parties can verify whether the digital edition matches the course criteria. Of course, the eventual ideal will come when everyone is using digital editions, sharing bookmarks, and maybe even auto-synchronizing with the professor's edition.

But there are also other settings beyond educational where page numbers can be useful, too. Reading is also a social activity, and being able to reference by page numbers in leisure books allows for easier participation in reading groups, for example.

The world isn't completely digital yet, so don't dismiss out of hand the need for print-digital referencing when you're producing both formats for a book.

Styling

Best practices for using CSS for styling are complicated, both because support in reading systems can be inconsistent and because accessibility can, and cannot, be tailored through the reading system itself.

Providing advice like not using small font sizes when virtually every reading system provides the ability to manually tailor the display size may seem moot, for example, but you still force your readers to have to bump their displays up and down each time you assume your tiny text will be readable. Likewise, suggestions that readers can modify the default foreground and background color schemes to better fit their needs assumes that such functionality is available. Dropping in a new style sheet and/or customizing CSS is not often as possible in ebooks as it is in browsers.

The range of issues that can arise from bad styling of content are equally as diverse as those that can arise from inaccessible markup and need to be avoided as much as possible at the creation stage, so that the burden is not shifted to the reader to make the content work. Much of this chapter deals with the issues nonvisual readers face, but bad styling can impact across the spectrum of visual readers, which is typically the bulk of the market for your ebooks.

Avoiding Conflicts

There is something to be said for cleanly separating content from style at the file level. The cascading nature of styles means that the declaration closest to the element to be rendered wins. If you plaster `style` attributes all over your content, you can interfere with the ability of a reader to apply an alternate style sheet to improve the contrast or to change the color scheme, because the local definition may override the problem the reader is attempting to fix. Consequently, suggesting that you avoid the `style` attribute like the plague is actually not an overstatement.

More realistically, though, you should be able to use CSS classes for all your needs. If, for some reason, you do have to add a `style` attribute, avoid using it to apply general stylistic formatting. Keeping your style definitions in a separate file simplifies their maintenance and facilitates their reuse on the production side anyway, and this simple standard practice nets you an accessibility benefit.

Color

The choices you make in color play an important role in the ability of readers to perceive and read your content. Colors are not just an aesthetic consideration, because statistics show that around 8% of the male population suffers from some form of color blindness, for example. The choices you make can impede the ability of visual readers to fully perceive your content and/or follow your intent and meaning.

The following subsections look at some of the pitfalls that can be avoided by carefully considering the choices you make. Also note that these issues are not just limited to the CSS styling of content, but are also applicable to any image-based content, whether graphics, canvas, video, or other.

Deficiencies

Color blindness rarely ever manifests as a complete lack of color perception but is typically a deficiency in processing one of the red, green, or blue light spectrums by the cones of the eye. Someone with color blindness sees colors that normally include their deficiency shifted, causing the resulting color to appear differently from someone without the deficiency. For example, someone with red color blindness might not be able to detect red hyperlinks from regular black text without another visual cue.

When making choices in foreground and background colors, you should always be aware that certain combinations can cause problems for color-blind readers. Combinations to avoid include:

- Red and green
- Dark red and black
- Blue and yellow

Never relying on color alone to indicate important information is a key way to avoid problems in your content. When creating charts or graphs, for example, include labels and/or patterns to clearly distinguish the regions and relationships. For links, as noted previously, include additional indicators, whether bolding or underlines, to disambiguate them.

Contrast

Ensuring that sufficient contrast is maintained between foreground and background colors to ease reading is key to the perceivability of your content. A good place to start is to ensure a minimum 4.5:1 contrast ratio as required for AA rating by WCAG 2.0. Because the contrast can be calculated from the colors used, there are many free tools available that can analyze your XHTML content and determine if you're in compliance.

Note, too, that although black on white provides the highest contrast, it can also be problematic for many readers, causing headaches with prolonged reading. Using off-white backgrounds can help reduce eye strain, but there's no simple answer to what foreground and background color combination is best, and no consensus. This is one case where reading system flexibility is key, because different readers have different preferences.

Additionally, try to avoid placing text on top of richly textured backgrounds, as are often found in pictures. The more visual noise there is behind the text the more difficult it can be to differentiate for all readers. Also avoid layering different shades of the same color on top of each other, because this also makes reading harder for everyone.

Luminosity

Using two equally light or dark colors in combinations can also make reading difficult, because it becomes hard to discern one from the other. If a reader is able to change the foreground or background color independently of the other, this may not pose a problem. For images, however, changing the luminosity (e.g., to grayscale) will not make the content any more perceptible, because both colors will shift in parallel.

Using two bright colors together (such as red/green, blue/orange, and blue/green) can also cause an effect called *visual vibrations* in scrolled environments, where the image appears to flicker as it moves. More information on this effect can be found on the Vibrating Color Combinations (*http://accessibility.psu.edu/brightcolors*) page on the Penn State AccessAbility site.

Hiding Content

To meet accessibility requirements on the Web, it's a common practice to hide the content that should be rendered only to readers using assistive technologies like screen readers. In many cases, these practices don't work as expected in browsers, and less so in reading systems.

Some tricks include hiding the content using CSS, positioning the content off screen, and clipping regions to have no height or width. Some of these simply don't work: hidden content is not announced, for example. Some are unreliable or won't work across reading systems, such as clipping content (which isn't supported outside of fixed layouts) and positioning content off screen (which few reading systems allow).

The only time an assistive technology will announce text hidden using the CSS `display: none` or `visibility: hidden` is when the hidden element is referenced by a `aria-describedby` or `aria-labelledby` attribute (and only the text of the element is voiced; all markup it contains is ignored).

Emphasis

The use of stylized `span` elements to add emphasis is another problematic feature of programs that export EPUB content. This section could have been placed in the markup practices section, because markup is usually what's wanted in many cases, but the CSS styling of emphasis is most problematic, because it conveys no meaning except to visual readers.

Assistive technologies do not add voice emphasis when CSS italics and bolding are used. They do not pick up on these attributes at all, because CSS is not the semantically correct way to convey this information. Four elements should be used in preference to CSS styling:

em
> For vocal stress

strong
> To convey importance

i
> To indicate an alternate voice or mood, as well as for semantic uses (e.g., identifying names)

b
> For keywords and other semantic uses, but conveys no voice or mood change

And bear in mind that these elements do not need to be presented as bold or italics based on the default styling of them. If voice emphasis is done with bolding, use em tags but style them as bolded.

CSS should be used only when the styling is purely presentational, because there is no way to automate the correct semantics back into a document that simply identifies instances of italics and bolding, as there isn't a simple 1:1 mapping. As just noted, the presentation doesn't necessarily match the tagging.

Fixed Layouts

Making fixed-layout documents accessible is complicated by their variable nature. A fixed-layout document may be composed entirely of images (comics, manga) or a mixture of text on image (children's books, magazine articles), and pure-text layouts are not out of the question, either. The less you rely on images, the easier it is to make the content accessible, but there will always be issues when content cannot fit the available space. From zooming to being able to move around the image, fixed layouts introduce usability issues.

It also may be the case that reader configuration options are disabled in reading systems that support fixed layouts, further impacting on the usability. To keep the precise layout of the page, reading systems may prevent the reader from altering any of the styling, from not being able to change font family or size to preventing any alteration of the CSS, including to improve contrast. There is no prose in the Fixed Layout specification that encourages an over-adherence to the desires of the content producer, for example, but to ensure rendering integrity it is expected that reading systems will strictly adhere to the layout defined.

Because this practice runs counter to everything discovered about web usability and its early attempts to erect barriers to user configuration, there is hope that such draconian measures won't materialize. But, when considering the use of fixed layouts, you should be aware that you're making a decision that accessibility is secondary to appearance.

The issues for accessibility with fixed layouts are potentially more numerous, too: a lack of text equivalents, problems of making text equivalents that can convey the interactivity and richness of the pages, unordered content at markup level that distorts the reading order, and at a basic level that reading systems may not support this metadata and all the positioning work will be lost and the resultant reflowed publication will be unusable by all readers.

In reading this section, also bear in mind that it is not isolated from the practices discussed throughout the rest of this chapter. Fixed layouts are just another way of presenting content, so every good practice still applies, even if they won't all be repeated. The following two points are particularly important:

- Take extra care with choices in color and preserving foreground/background contrast, because text and image content gets overlapped in fixed layouts.
- The markup must still present a logical reading order. Because content can be placed anywhere on the page through CSS does not excuse jumbling the content at the markup level.

The following sections present some additional options to mitigate the problems that can arise in the production of specific forms of fixed layout.

Image Layouts

The first type of fixed layout to discuss are those that set the page size for rendering of bitmap image content. This method of fixed layout is used to stop the reading system from scaling the image to fit the available screen dimensions, which can cause the image to become pixelated, distorted, or simply hard to make out. Comic books and manga are the prime examples, but cover pages and full-page plates in a book are other potential uses.

A distinction can be drawn between images that are the content of the publication versus those that supplement it (e.g., a page of a comic versus a center plate). Why this matters relates to the effectiveness of any of the fallbacks you'll have to provide. Handling a fixed page that contains an image that is supplementary to the primary narrative is really no different than handling the same image had it been embedded in the reflowing content, the methods for which were covered in the previous section.

The only difference is that the image is typically fully sized to the available area, meaning that there often won't be room for a caption and/or description. This information can, and should, still be included in the markup. Earlier sections discussed the problems inherent in hiding content generally, but since fixed layout images will completely cover the viewing area, you can use absolute positioning together with the CSS z-index property to layer the image over the text content (a higher z-value on the image means the rest of the content will be layered underneath). For example, given the following simplified fixed-layout document body for a single image and description:

```
<body>
    <figure>
        <img id="img01" src="img01.jpg" alt="..."/>
        <figcaption id="desc01">...</figcaption>
    </figure>
</body>
```

you could apply the following CSS to layer the image over the description:

```
<style>
#img01, #desc {
    position: absolute;
    top: 0px;
    left: 0px;
    width: 700px;
}

#img01 {
    height: 500px;
    z-index: 2;
}

#desc {
    background-color: rgb(255,255,255)
    z-index: 1;
}
</style>
```

This will effectively bury the description under the image on reading systems that support fixed layouts, while presenting a standard figure on those that don't. In either case, nonvisual readers will be able to access the description inline with your content, because it won't be hidden from assistive technologies (i.e., it isn't truly hidden from rendering, as happens when using the hidden attribute and CSS display and visibility properties).

Using z-index does still leave a problem for visual readers who would benefit from the description, because the text is now hidden from them. To get around the discovery issue, you could wrap the image in an a tag that exposes the description when clicked:

```
<a href="#full" onclick="showDescription()" title="Click for description"><img
id="img01" src="img01.jpg" alt="..."/></a>
```

When the reader activates the link by clicking on the image, you simply switch the z-index of the underlying description element to a higher value, thus moving it to the front. When they click again, reverse and push back behind.

To handle reading systems without scripting, you could also use the CSS `:target` selector to catch a click on the image and change the CSS, but support for this selector cannot be guaranteed in reading systems.

To see a working example of this kind of technique, have a look at *The Voyage of Life* in the EPUB 3 samples project. This publication goes even fancier, using an embedded figure with thumbnail. When clicked, `z-index` and opacity are used to create an appealing visual thumbnail overlay, as shown in Figure 9-1.

Figure 9-1. Pop-over image description

Although providing descriptions is feasible for standalone images, the problem becomes more complex the more the primary narrative is dependent upon being able to see the image. When images carry the narrative, such as in comics and manga, providing a simple description that will suffice as equivalent content rarely works. More typically, you need to provide a text serialization.

One idea currently in the works is to provide alternate rendition mapping between image-based and fixed layout publications and their text equivalents (the Advanced Hybrid Fixed Layout Working Group). Not only would this allow the reader to select the more appropriate content form, but it might also allow readers to switch between renditions while maintaining their location. Because work is only in the early discovery phase, no suggestions can be given as to how this will manifest in an actual publication.

Before moving on, one additional consideration with fixed layout images is to avoid using the CSS `background-image` property to set them. By using CSS, not only do you take away the ability to provide a description, but nonvisual readers will lose any indication that the page contains anything at all. They will encounter silence if trying to use TTS playback and no text content on a refreshable braille display. At a very minimum, if you always use `img` tags and `z-index`, you can provide a basic `alt` text description so that the reader has some context that content is there.

Mixed Layouts

Moving slightly further along the spectrum of fixed layouts, mixed layouts are predominantly image based but position text on top of an image or stylized background.

In the best-case scenario, the background image is purely decorative and does not add to the primary narrative. If the text fully conveys all necessary information, the background that it is overlaid on can be treated like any other presentational image and a description excluded.

The more difficult case, again, is when the image moves the narrative along, whether directly or indirectly. A simple example might be a children's book in which the imagery is followed at the bottom of the page by text, or text is interspersed throughout the page, weaving around the image content. Although sometimes the imagery is just illustrative of the text, more often the two are tied together to set the scene.

Even more complex is when the text content is directly tied to the image content. Similar to comics, dialogue spoken by an illustrated character in the scene could be embedded as a dialogue bubble instead of written into the image, for example.

You can take steps to help facilitate readers with these kinds of mixed layouts. Key among these is to ensure that the image and text content is logically ordered in the markup. If you can read the story clearly from the markup, someone using an assistive technology should also be able to follow along.

If you are going to use images of characters but layer their dialogue as text content, maintain image/dialogue sequences in the markup, even if this is not how the content appears visually. Illustrated characters that speak to each other often face each other on the page, and their dialogue bubbles fall between them (i.e., image/dialogue, dialogue/ image). For example, the following markup could be easily styled to reverse the position of Alice's dialogue for visual rendering, but the narrative makes better sense when the image is presented first in the markup:

```
<img id="caterpillar" src="caterpillar.jpg" alt="The Caterpillar sitting on his
mushroom takes the hookah out of his mouth"/>
<p class="c-dlg">And who are <em>YOU</em>?</p>
<img id="alice" src="alice.jpg" alt="Alice looking down shyly at her feet"/>
<p class="a-dlg">I, I hardly know, sir. I know who I <em>WAS</em> when I got up
this morning.</p>
```

And don't be afraid to think outside the box a bit. The previous example shows a clear case where you would have two distinct images, but even if your image appears contiguous there is nothing to stop you from breaking it up into smaller pieces if different regions need different explanations and/or a single explanation would impede the ability to tie a description of an area to the relevant text. You have full control over the positioning of elements in fixed layout pages, so, like a jigsaw puzzle, you can position multiple pieces into a single seamless-looking whole.

Another option is to consider the new page templating functionality defined in the Advanced Adaptive Layout information document (*http://idpf.org/epub/pgt/ csspgt-20120808.html*) to avoid fixed layouts altogether. This specification was only finalized in September 2012, so as of this writing there isn't widespread support for production or rendering, but as it gains traction it will provide a way to define the flow of text content through regions on a page, removing one need for fixed layouts (e.g., simplifying magazine article layouts).

Text Layouts

Fixed text layouts should be the easiest to make accessible, because you might not need any additional information to supplement the text. But don't assume that because the text is present you don't even need to consider a description. Fixed-position text is typically done for some specific effect, so finding a way to impart that information to the reader would be considerate.

Also be mindful of where and how you position the text, because the dimensions of the page may limit what is viewable by readers. If you position a small bit of text on the far right edge of the page (in a left-to-right language), a low vision reader may not be aware that it is even there.

Interactive Layouts

Finally, and perhaps the most complex, are interactive fixed layouts. A children's books might mix three different dimensions in order to create a page: text, background, and dynamic (animated) objects. The logical reading order in this case is only one part of the story, because the child's curiosity and imagination are also triggered to provide an opportunity to interact with the characters or scene.

When making interactive content accessible, keep in mind that the goal is not to rip all the fun out of the feature and leave a segment of readers with dull, rote text explanations. Strive to keep the fun and enjoyment in the work by making the dynamic content accessible.

But interactive layouts are also the perfect segue into the final section of the chapter on scripted interactivity. Now that you've learned the range of content forms a fixed layout can take, the challenge is to apply what you'll learn in the next section to animate them.

Scripted Interactivity

Whether you're a fan of scripted ebooks or not, EPUB 3 has opened the door to their creation, so we'll finish this chapter by looking at some of the potential accessibility pitfalls and how to avoid them.

Progressive Enhancement

One of the key new terms you'll hear in relation to the use of scripting in EPUB 3 is *progressive enhancement*. The concept of progressive enhancement is not original to EPUB, nor is it limited to scripting. This chapter has actually made a case for many of its other core tenets, such as separation of content and style, content conveying meaning, etc. Applied in this context, however, it means that scripting must only enhance your core content.

You've already learned why structure and semantics should carry all the information necessary to understand your content, but that presupposes that it is all available. The ability for scripts to remove access to content from anyone without a JavaScript-enabled reading system is a major concern not just for persons using accessible devices, but for all readers.

And that's why scripting content comes with conditions in EPUB 3 (*http://idpf.org/epub/ 30/spec/epub30-contentdocs.html#confreq-cd-scripted-spine*). You must not block access to content by hiding it behind script; enhancements to the text must be layered progressively so that publications remain consumable regardless of what functionality is enabled on the reading system.

If you try to circumvent the specification requirement and treat progressive enhancement as just an "accessibility thing," you're underestimating the readers that are going to rely on your content rendering properly without scripting. Picture buying a book that has pages glued together and you'll get an idea of how excited your readers will be that you thought no one would notice. You can also expect JavaScript support in EPUB 3 reading systems, so even a segment of your readership you might not be thinking will see the unscripted version will be affected by the decisions you make.

Meeting the general requirement to keep your text accessible is really not asking a lot, though. As soon as you turn to JavaScript to alter (or enable) access to prose, you should realize you're on the wrong path. To this end:

- Don't include content that can only be accessed (made visible) through scripted interaction.

- Don't script-enable content based on a reader's preferences, location, language, or any other setting.

- Don't require scripting in order for the reader to continue moving through the content (e.g., choose your own adventure books).

Whether or not your prose can be accessed is not hard to test, even if it can't be done reliably by validators like epubcheck (*http://code.google.com/p/epubcheck/*). Turn off JavaScript and see if you can navigate your document from beginning to end. You may not get all the bells and whistles when scripting is turned off, but you should be able to get through with no loss of information. If you can't, you need to review why prose is not available or has disappeared, why navigation gets blocked, etc., and find another way to do what you were attempting.

Don't worry that this requirement means all the potential scripting fun is being taken out of ebooks, though. Content can be enhanced in every imaginable way by manipulating the DOM properly. Games, puzzles, animations, quizzes, and any other content you can think of that requires scripting are also all fair game for inclusion. But when it comes to including these, there are two considerations to make (similar to choosing when to describe images):

- Does the scripted content you're embedding include information that will be useful to the reader's comprehension (demos, etc.), or is it included purely for pleasure (games)?

- Can the content be made accessible in a usable way and can you provide a fallback alternative that provides the same or similar experience?

The answer to the first question will have some influence over how you tackle the second. If the scripted content provides information that the reader would otherwise not be able to obtain from the prose, you should consider other alternative forms for making that information available, for example:

- If you script an interactive demo using the `canvas` element, consider also providing a transcript of the information for readers who may not be able to interact with it.

- If you're including an interactive form that automatically evaluates the reader's responses, also include access to an answer key.

- If you're adding a problem or puzzle to solve, also provide the solution so the reader can still learn the steps to its completion.

None of these suggestions are intended to remove the responsibility to try and make the content accessible in the first place, though. Scripting of accessible forms, for example, should be a trivial task for developers familiar with WAI-ARIA (you'll see some practices in the coming section). But trivial or not, because scripting will not necessarily be available, it's imperative that you provide other means for readers to obtain the full experience.

If the scripted content is purely for entertainment purposes, create a fallback commensurate with the value of that content to the overall ebook (if it absolutely cannot be made accessible natively). As with decorative images, a reader unable to interact with nonessential content is not going to be hugely interested in reading a five-page dissertation on each level of your game. A simple idea of what it does will usually suffice.

WAI-ARIA

Although fallbacks are useful when scripting is not available, you should still aim to make your scripted content accessible to all readers. Enter the W3C Web Accessibility Initiative's (WAI) Accessible Rich Internet Application (ARIA) specification (*http://www.w3.org/TR/wai-aria/*).

The technology defined in this specification can be used in many situations to improve content accessibility. For example, you've already encountered the `aria-describedby` attribute when learning how to add descriptions and summaries.

The following three common cases for scripting will illustrate how ARIA can enhance the accessibility of EPUBs: custom controls, forms, and live regions.

Custom controls

Just to be clear, custom controls are not standard form elements that you stylize to suit your needs. Those are the good kinds of custom controls (if you want to call them custom), because they retain their inherent accessibility traits whatever you style them to look like. Readers will not have problems interacting with these controls as they natively map to the underlying accessibility APIs, so they will work regardless of the scripting capabilities any reading system has built in.

A *custom control* is the product of enhancing an HTML element with a script to emulate a standard control, or building up a number of elements for the same purpose. Using images to simulate buttons is one of the more common examples, and custom toolbars are often created in this way. There is typically no native way for a reader using an accessible device to interact with these kinds of custom controls, however, because they are presented to them as whatever HTML element was used in their creation (e.g., just another `img` element in the case of image buttons).

It would be ideal if no one used custom controls, and you should try to avoid them unless you have no other choice, but the existence of ARIA reflects the reality that these controls are also ubiquitous. The increase in native control types in HTML5 holds out hope for a reduction in their use, but it would be neglectful not to cover some of the basics of their accessible creation. Before launching out on your own, it's good to know what you're getting into.

 Widely available toolkits, such as jQuery (*http://jquery.com/*), bake ARIA accessibility into many of the custom widgets they allow you to create. You should consider using these if you don't have a background in creating accessible controls.

If you aren't familiar with ARIA, it provides a map between the new control and the standard behaviors of the one being emulated (e.g., allowing your otherwise-inaccessible image to function identically to the button element as far as the reader is concerned). This mapping is critical, because it allows the reader to interact with your controls through the underlying accessibility API. (The ARIA specification includes a graphical depiction (*http://www.w3.org/TR/wai-aria/introduction#contractmodel*) that can help visualize this process.)

Or, put differently, ARIA is what allows the HTML element you use as a control to be identified as what it represents (button) instead of what it is (image). It also provides a set of attributes that can be set and controlled by script to make interaction with the control accessible to all. As the reader manipulates your now-identifiable control, the changes you make to these attributes in response get passed back to the underlying accessibility API. That in turn allows the reading system or assistive technology to relay the new state on to the reader, completing the cycle of interaction.

But to get more specific, the role an element plays is defined by attaching the ARIA role element to it. The following is a small selection of the available role values (*http://www.w3.org/TR/wai-aria/roles#widget_roles*) you can use in this attribute:

- alert
- button
- checkbox
- dialog
- menuitem
- progressbar
- radio
- scrollbar
- tab

- tree

Here's how you could now use this attribute to define an image as an audio clip start button:

```
<img src="controls/start.png"
     id="audio-start"
     role="button"
     tabindex="0"
     alt="Start"/>
```

Identifying the role is the easy part, though. Just as standard form controls have states and properties that are controlled by the reading system, so too must you add and maintain these on any custom controls you create.

A *state*, to clarify, tells you something about the nature of the control at a given point in time: if an element represents a checkable item, for example, its current state will either be checked or unchecked; if it can be hidden, its state may be either hidden or visible; if it's collapsible, it could be expanded or collapsed; and so on.

Properties, on the other hand, typically provide meta information about the control: how to find its label, how to find a description for it, its position in a set, etc.

States and properties are both expressed in ARIA using attributes. For example, the list of available states currently includes all of the following:

- aria-busy
- aria-checked
- aria-disabled
- aria-expanded
- aria-grabbed
- aria-hidden
- aria-invalid
- aria-pressed
- aria-selected

The list of available properties is much larger, but a small sampling includes:

- aria-activedescendant
- aria-controls
- aria-describedby
- aria-dropeffect

- `aria-flowto`
- `aria-labelledby`
- `aria-live`
- `aria-posinset`
- `aria-required`

 See section 6.6 (*http://www.w3.org/TR/wai-aria/states_and_proper ties#state_prop_def*) of the ARIA specification for a complete list of all states and properties, including definitions.

EPUB 3 content documents support all of these state and property attributes, and their proper application and updating as your controls are interacted with is how the needed information gets relayed back to the reader.

 You only have to maintain their values; you don't have to worry about the underlying process that identifies the change and passes it on.

The natural question at this point is which states and properties do you have to set when creating a custom control? It would be great if there were a simple chart that could be followed, but unfortunately, what you apply is very much dependent on the type of control you're creating and what you're using it to do. To be fully accessible, you need to consider all the ways in which a reader will be interacting with your control, and how the states and properties need to be modified to reflect the reality of the control as each action is performed. There is no one-size-fits-all solution, in other words.

 To see which properties and states are supported by the type of control you're creating, refer to the role definitions (*http://www.w3.org/TR/wai-aria/roles#role_definitions*) in the specification. Knowing what you can apply is helpful in narrowing down what you need to apply.

If you don't set the states and properties, or set them incorrectly, it follows that you'll impair the ability of the reader to access your content. And implementing them badly can be just as frustrating for a reader as not implementing them at all. You could, for example, leave the reader unable to start your audio clip, unable to stop it, stuck with volume controls that only go louder or softer, etc. Her only recourse will be shutting down the ebook and starting over.

You need to be aware of some accessibility pitfalls when you roll your own solutions. Some will be obvious, like a button failing to initiate playback, but others will be more subtle and not caught without extensive testing, which is also why you should engage the accessibility community in checking your content.

But let's take a look at some of the possible issues involved in maintaining states. Have a look at the following much-reduced example of list items used to control volume:

```
<ul>
    <li role="button"
        tabindex="0"
        onclick="increaseVolume('audio01')">Louder</li>

    <li role="button"
        tabindex="0"
        onclick="decreaseVolume('audio01')">Softer</li>
</ul>
```

This setup looks simple, because it omits any states or properties at the outset, but now consider it in the context of a real-world usage scenario. As the reader increases the volume, you'll naturally be checking whether the peak has been reached in order to disable the control. With a standard button, when the reader reached the maximum volume, you'd just set the button to be disabled with a line of JavaScript; the button gets grayed out for readers and is marked as disabled for the accessibility API. Nice and simple.

List items can't be natively disabled, however (it just doesn't make any sense, because they aren't expected to be active in the first place). You instead have to set the aria-disabled attribute on the list item to identify the change to the accessibility API, remove the event that calls the JavaScript (as anyone could still activate and fire the referenced code if you don't), and give sighted readers a visual effect to indicate that the button is no longer active.

Likewise, when the reader decreases the volume from the max setting, you need to re-enable the control, re-add the onclick event, and re-style the option as active. The same scenario plays out when the reader hits the bottom of the range for the volume decrease button.

In other words, instead of having to focus only on the logic of your application, you now also have to focus on all the interactions with your custom controls. This extra programming burden is why you should avoid rolling your own. This is a simple example, too. The more controls you add, the more complex the process becomes and the more potential side-effects you have to consider and account for.

If you still want to pursue your own controls, though, or just want to learn more, the Illinois Center for Information Technology and Web Accessibility (*http://test.cita.uiuc.edu/aria/*) maintains a comprehensive set of examples, with working code, that is worth the time to review. You'll discover much more from their many examples than this chapter could reproduce. The ARIA authoring practices guide also walks through the process of creating an accessible control (*http://www.w3.org/TR/wai-aria-practices/#accessiblewidget*).

A quick note on `tabindex` is also in order, because you no doubt noticed it on the preceding examples. Although this is actually an HTML attribute, it goes hand in hand with ARIA and custom controls because it allows you to specify additional elements that can receive keyboard focus, as well as the order in which all elements are traversed (i.e., it improves keyboard accessibility). It is critical that you add the attribute to your custom controls; otherwise, readers won't be able to navigate to them.

 The elements a reader can access by the keyboard by default is reading system–dependent, but typically, only links, form elements, and multimedia and other interactive elements receive focus by default. Keep this in mind when you roll your own controls, otherwise readers may not have access to them.

Here's another look at our earlier image button again:

```
<img src="controls/start.png"
     id="audio-start"
     alt="Start"
     role="button"
     tabindex="0"/>
```

By adding the attribute with the value 0, you've enabled direct keyboard access to this `img` element. The 0 value indicates that you aren't giving this control any special significance within the document, which is the default for all elements that can be natively tabbed to. To create a tab order, you could assign incrementing positive integers to the controls, but be aware that this can affect the navigation of your document, because all elements with a positive `tabindex` value are traversed before those set to 0 or not specified at all (in other words, don't add the value 1 because to you it's the first element in your control set).

In many situations, too, a single control would not be made directly accessible. The element that contains all the controls would be the accessible element, as in the following example:

```
<div role="group" tabindex="0">
    <img role="button" ... />
    <img role="button" ... />
</div>
```

Access to the individual controls inside the grouping div would be script-enabled. This would allow the reader to quickly skip past the control set if he isn't interested in what it does (otherwise, he would have to tab through every control inside it).

 See the HTML5 specification for more information on how this attribute works (*http://dev.w3.org/html5/spec/Overview.html#attr-tabindex*).

A last note for this section concerns event handlers. *Events* are what are used to trigger script actions (onclick, onblur, etc.). How you wire up your events can impact on the ability of the reader to access your controls, and can lead to keyboard traps (i.e., the inability to leave the control), so you need to pay attention to how you add them.

You could add an onclick event to our image button to start playback as follows:

```
<img src="controls/start.png"
     id="audio-start"
     alt="Start"
     role="button"
     tabindex="0"
     onclick="startPlayback('audio01')"/>
```

But, if you accidentally forget the tabindex attribute, a reader navigating by keyboard would not be able to find or access this control. Even though onclick is considered a device-independent event, if the reader cannot reach the element, she cannot use the Enter key to activate it, effectively hiding the functionality from them.

You should always ensure that actions can be triggered in a device-independent manner, even if that means repeating your script call in more than one event type. Don't rely on any of your readers using a mouse, for example.

But again, it pays to engage people who can test your content in real-world scenarios to help discover these issues than to hope you've thought of everything.

Forms

Forms are another common problem area ARIA helps address. To repeat, though, the first best practice when creating forms is to always use the native form elements that HTML5 provides. See the previous section again for why rolling your own is not a good idea.

When it comes to implementing forms, the logical ordering of elements is one key to simplifying access and comprehension. The use of tabindex can help to correct navigation, as just covered, but it's better to ensure your form is logically navigable in the first place. Group form fields and their labels together when you can, or place them immediately next to each other so that one always follows the other in the reading order.

And always clearly identify the purpose of form fields using the `label` element. You should also always add the new HTML5 `for` attribute so that the labels can be located regardless of how the reader enters the field or where they are located in the document markup. This attribute identifies the `id` of the form element the `label` element labels:

```
<label id="fname-label" for="fname">First name:</label>

<input type="text"
       id="fname"
       name="first-name"
       aria-labelledby="fname-label" />
```

This example also adds the `aria-labelledby` attribute to the `input` element, to ensure maximum compatibility across systems, but its use is critical if your form field is not identified by a `label` element (only `label` takes the `for` attribute). Because the `label` element can be used in just about every element that can carry a label, there's little good reason to omit using it.

For example, if you have to use a table to lay out your form, don't be lazy and use table cells alone to convey meaning:

```
<table>
   <tr>
      <td>
         <label id="fname-label" for="fname">First name:</label>
      </td>
      <td>
         <input type="text"
                id="fname"
                name="first-name"
                aria-labelledby="fname-label" />
      </td>
   </tr>
   ...
<table>
```

 You also should include the `for` attribute regardless of whether the label precedes, follows, or includes the form field.

Another pain point comes when a reader fills in a form only to discover after the fact that you had special instructions he was supposed to follow. When specifying entry requirements for completing the field, include them within the `label` or attach an `aria-describedby` attribute so that the reader is informed right away:

```
<label for="username-label">User name:</label>

<input type="text"
```

```
        id="uname"
        name="username"
        aria-labelledby="username-label"
        aria-describedby="username-req" />
```

```
<span id="username-req">User names must be between 8 and 16 characters in
length and contain only alphanumeric characters.</span>
```

The new HTML5 `pattern` attribute can also be used to improve field completion. If your field accepts regular expression–validatable data, you can add this attribute to automatically check the input. When using this attribute, the HTML5 specification recommends the restriction be added to the `title` attribute.

You could reformulate the previous example now as follows:

```
<input type="text"
        id="uname"
        name="username"
        aria-labelledby="username-label"
        pattern="[A-Za-z0-9]{8,16}"
        title="Enter a user name between 8 and 16 characters in length
and containing only alphanumeric characters" />
```

Another common nuisance in web forms of old has been the use of asterisks and similar text markers and visual cues to indicate when a field was required, as there was no native way to indicate the requirement to complete. These markers were not always identifiable by persons using assistive technologies. But HTML5 now includes the `required` attribute to cover this need. ARIA also includes a required attribute of its own. Similar to labeling, it's a good practice at this time to add both to ensure maximum compatibility:

```
<input type="text"
        id="uname"
        name="username"
        aria-labelledby="username-label"
        pattern="[A-Za-z0-9]{8,16}"
        title="Enter a user name between 8 and 16 characters in length
and containing only alphanumeric characters"
        required="required"
        aria-required="true" />
```

An accessible reading system could now announce to the reader that the field is required when the reader enters it. Adding a clear prose indication that the field is required to the `label` is still good practice, too, because colors and symbols are never a reliable or accessible means of conveying information:

```
<label for="uname">User name: (required)</label>
```

ARIA also includes a property for setting the validity of an entry field. If the reader enters invalid data, you can set the `aria-invalid` property in your code so that the reading system can easily identify and move the reader to the incorrect field. For example, your scripted validation might include the following line to set this state when the input doesn't pass your tests:

```
document.getElementById('address').setAttribute('aria-invalid', true);
```

 You must not set this state by default; no data entered does not indicate either validity or invalidity.

In addition to labeling individual form fields, you should also group and identify any regions within your form (a common example on the Web is forms with separate fields for billing and shipping information). The traditional HTML `fieldset` element and its child `legend` element cover this need without special attributes.

So, to try and sum up, the best advice with forms is to strive to make them as accessible as you can natively (good markup and logical order), but not to forget that WAI-ARIA exists and has a number of useful properties and states that can enhance your forms to make them more accessible.

Live regions

Although making the primary narrative in your ebook dependent on script must be avoided, that doesn't mean you can't dynamically insert or modify any text. Automatically displaying the result of a quiz or displaying the result of a calculation are just a couple of examples of cases where dynamic prose updates would legitimately be useful for readers. You may also want to provide informative updates, such as the number of characters remaining in an entry field.

The problem with these kinds of dynamic updates is how they're made available to readers using assistive technologies. When you update the main document by rewriting the inner text or HTML of an element, how that change gets reported to the assistive technology, if at all, is out of your control in plain old HTML.

The update could force the reader to lose their place and listen to the changed region every time, or it could be ignored entirely. ARIA has solved this problem with the introduction of live regions, however.

If you're going to use an element to insert dynamic text, you mark this purpose by attaching an `aria-live` attribute to it. The value of this attribute also tells an assistive technology how to present the update to the reader. If you set the value `polite`, for example, the assistive technology will wait until an idle period before announcing the change (e.g., after the user is done typing for character counts). If you set it to `asser tive`, the reading system will announce the change immediately (e.g., for results that the reader is waiting on).

You could set up a simple element to write results to with no more code than this:

```
<div id="result" aria-live="assertive"/>
```

When you write the result to this `div`, the new text will be read out immediately. Be careful when using the `assertive` setting, however. You can annoy your readers if their system blurts out every inconsequential change you might happen to write as it happens.

If you write out results a bit at a time, or need to update different elements within the region, the `aria-busy` attribute should be set to `true` before the first write to indicate to the reading system that the update is in progress. If you don't, the reading system will announce the changes as you write them. As long as the state is marked as busy (`true`), the reading system will wait for the state to be changed backed to `false` before making any announcement.

You should also take care about how much information you inform the reader of. If you're updating only small bits of text, the reading system might only announce the new text, leaving the reader confused about what is going on. Conversely, you might add a new node to a long list, but the reader might be forced to listen to all the entries that came before it again, depending on how you have coded your application.

The `aria-atomic` attribute gives you control over the amount of text that gets announced. If you set it to `true` for a region, all the content will be read whenever you make a change inside it. For example, if you set a paragraph as live and add this attribute, then change the text in a `span` inside it, the entire paragraph will be read. In this example, writing the reader's body mass index value to the embedded `span` will cause the whole text to be read:

```
<p aria-live="true" aria-atomic="true">
    Your current BMI is: <span id="result"/>
</p>
```

If you set the attribute to `false` (or omit it), only the prose in the element containing the text change gets announced. Using our last example, only the body mass index value in isolation would be announced.

You can further control this behavior by also attaching the `aria-relevant` attribute. This attribute allows you to specify, for example, that all node changes in the region should be announced, only new node additions, or only deletions (e.g., for including data feeds). It can also be set to only identify text changes. You can even combine values (the default is `additions text`).

You could use these attributes to set up a fictional author update box using an ordered list as follows:

```
<p id="feed-label">What's the Author Saying...</p>
<ol id="feed"
    aria-live="polite"
    aria-atomic="true"
    aria-relevant="additions"
    aria-labelledby="feed-label">
    ...
</ol>
<a href="http://www.example.com/authorsonline">Go online to view</a>
```

Now, only the new list items added for each incoming message will be read. The old messages you pull out will disappear silently. (And this example also adds a traditional link out for anyone who doesn't have scripting enabled!)

There are also special roles that automatically identify a region as live. Instead of using the aria-live attribute to indicate our results field, you could have instead set up an alert region as follows:

```
<div role="alert" id="results"/>
```

The following roles are also treated as indicating live regions: marquee, log, status, and timer.

And that's a quick run-through of how to ensure that all readers get alerted of changes you make to the content. It's not a complicated process, but you need to remember to ensure that you set these regions otherwise a segment of your readers will not get your updates.

 These sections have attempted to provide an easy introduction to ARIA and the features it provides to make EPUB content accessible.

For additional information, some good starting points include: the coverage given in *Universal Design for Web Applications* (*http://shop.oreilly.com/product/9780596518745.do*) by Wendy Chisholm and Matt May (also an excellent guide to accessible web content development); Gez Lemon's introduction to creating rich applications (*http://bit.ly/VbKIZF*); and, of course, the authoring practices guide (*http://bit.ly/W4TkPM*) that accompanies the ARIA specification.

Canvas

Another anticipated use for scripting is to automate the new HTML5 canvas element. This element provides an automatable surface for drawing on, whether it's done by the content creator (games, animations, etc.) or the reader (drawing or writing surface), which is why it wasn't covered with the rest of the semantics and structure elements.

Although a potentially interesting element to use in ebooks, at this time, the canvas element remains largely a black hole to assistive technologies. A summary of the discussions (*http://bit.ly/VbbgX6*) that have been taking place to fix the accessibility problems as of this writing is available on the Paciello Group website. Fixes for these accessibility issues will undoubtedly come in time, perhaps directly for the element or perhaps through WAI-ARIA, but it's too soon to say.

So, is the answer to avoid the element completely until the problems are solved? It would be nice if you could, but wouldn't be realistic to expect of everyone. Using it judiciously would be a better course to steer.

For now, including accessible alternatives is about all you can do. If you're using the element to draw graphs and charts, you could add a description with the data using the aria-describedby attribute and the techniques we outlined while dealing with images. If you're using the element for games and the like, consider the issues we detailed at the outset of the section in determining how much information to give.

With canvas, we really have to wait and see, unfortunately.

Metadata

Bringing up the topic of metadata usually triggers thoughts about the need to include title and author information in an ebook. While certainly a necessity, this kind of traditional metadata is not what we're going to delve into now.

One of the big issues facing people with disabilities as they try to enter the ebook market is how to discover the quality of the ebooks they want to buy. One ebook is not the same as another, as you've seen, and readers need to know what they're getting when they pay for your product. And you should be rewarded for your commitment to accessibility by having your ebooks stand out from the crowd.

Unfortunately, in the past, once you pushed your ebook into a distribution channel, whatever good work you had done to make your content accessible would become indistinguishable from all the inaccessible content out there to the person on the purchasing end. At about the same time that EPUB 3 was being finalized, however, the people at EDItEUR introduced a new set of accessibility metadata for use in ONIX records. This metadata plugs the information gap.

 This guide can't possibly explain all of ONIX, nor would it be the appropriate place to do so. If you are not familiar with the standard, please visit the EDItEUR website (*http://www.editeur.org*) for more information.

An ONIX record, if you're not familiar, is an industry-standard message (XML record) that accompanies your publication, providing distributors with both content and distribution metadata. This information is typically used to market and sell your ebook, and these new properties now allow you to enhance that information with the accessible features your ebook includes. Retailers can then make this information available in the product description, for example, so readers can determine whether the ebook will adequately meet their needs. It's also not a stretch to imagine this information being integrated into bookstore search engines to allow readers to narrow their results based on their needs.

To include accessibility metadata in your ONIX record, you use the `ProductFormFea` `ture` element, which is described in the standard as a composite container for product information (e.g., it is also used to provide product safety information). To identify that the element contains accessibility information, it must include a `ProductFormFeature` `Type` child element with the value 09, as in the following example:

```
<ProductFormFeature>
   <ProductFormFeatureType>09</ProductFormFeatureType>
   ...
</ProductFormFeature>
```

When this value is encountered, it indicates that the value of the sibling `ProductForm` `FeatureValue` element is drawn from ONIX for Books codelist 196 (*http://bit.ly/ 10mATt9*), which defines the new accessible properties and the values to use in identifying them. As of this writing, this codelist includes the following properties:

- No reading system accessibility options disabled (10)
- Table of contents navigation (11)
- Index navigation (12)
- Reading order (13)
- Short alternative descriptions (14)
- Full alternative descriptions (15)
- Visualised data also available as non-graphical data (16)
- Accessible math content (17)
- Accessible chem content (18)
- Print-equivalent page numbering (19)
- Synchronised pre-recorded audio (20)

So, for example, if your EPUB contains accessible math formulas (using MathML), you would indicate it as follows:

```
<ProductFormFeature>
    <ProductFormFeatureType>09</ProductFormFeatureType>
    <ProductFormFeatureValue>17</ProductFormFeatureValue>
</ProductFormFeature>
```

Likewise, to indicate accessible chemistry content (using ChemML), use the value 18:

```
<ProductFormFeature>
    <ProductFormFeatureType>09</ProductFormFeatureType>
    <ProductFormFeatureValue>18</ProductFormFeatureValue>
</ProductFormFeature>
```

You must repeat the `ProductFormFeature` element for each accessibility requirement your EPUB meets; it is *not valid* to combine all your features into a single element.

You must also ensure that you make yourself familiar with the requirements for compliance before adding any accessibility properties; each of the properties defined in codelist 196 includes conformance criteria. EPUB requires table of contents navigation, for example, but the addition of the required navigation document does not automatically indicate compliance. You need to include full navigation, plus navigation to any tables and figures, before you comply with the table of contents navigation requirement. Likewise, all EPUBs have a reading order defined by the spine element in the package document, but that does not mean you comply to including a reading order. You need to ensure that sidebars and footnotes and similar information has been properly marked up so as not to interfere with the narrative flow, as discussed in the section on the logical reading order.

It is additionally worth noting that these three properties aren't directly related to the content of your EPUB:

- Compatibility tested (97)
- Trusted intermediary contact (98)
- Publisher contact for further accessibility information (99)

Each of these properties requires the addition of a child `ProductFormFeatureDescription` element to describe compliance:

```
<ProductFormFeature>
    <ProductFormFeatureType>09</ProductFormFeatureType>
    <ProductFormFeatureValue>97</ProductFormFeatureValue>
    <ProductFormFeatureDescription>
        Content has been tested to work on iBooks, Sony Reader and Adobe Digital
        Editions in both scripting enabled and disabled modes.
    </ProductFormFeatureDescription>
</ProductFormFeature>
```

Whatever compatibility testing you've performed should be listed using code 97, so that readers can better determine the suitability of your ebook for their purposes. Not all reading systems and assistive technologies work alike, or interact well together, and real-world testing is the only way to tell what does and does not work.

There are organizations who specialize in testing across a broad spectrum of devices who can help you evaluate your content, because this kind of evaluation can be no small undertaking. A good practice to develop, for example, might be to periodically have typical examples of content coming out of your production stream tested for compatibility issues. The resulting statement could then be reused across much of your content, as long as the features and markup used remain consistent.

Once you start getting creative with your content (e.g., using extensive scripted interactivity), you should engage experts as early on in the process as you can to ensure any statement you make remains true.

The other two codes provide contact information for the people in your organization, or at a trusted intermediary, who can provide additional accessibility information:

```
<ProductFormFeature>
  <ProductFormFeatureType>09</ProductFormFeatureType>
  <ProductFormFeatureValue>99</ProductFormFeatureValue>
  <ProductFormFeatureDescription>
     accessibility-officer@example.com
  </ProductFormFeatureDescription>
</ProductFormFeature>
```

If you're providing educational materials, for example, you'll want to provide educators a way to be able to contact you to determine whether your content will be accessible by students with various needs that may not be specifically addressed in your compatibility testing statement or in the available metadata properties.

Text-to-Speech (TTS)

An alternative (and complement) to human narration, and the associated costs of creating and distributing it, is speech synthesis—when done right, that is. The mere thought of synthesized speech is enough to make some people cringe, though, because it's still typically equated with the likes of poor old much-maligned Microsoft Sam and his tinny, often-incomprehensible renderings. Modern high-end voices are getting harder and harder to distinguish as synthesized, however, and the voices on most reading systems and computers are getting progressively more natural sounding and pleasant to the ears for extended listening.

But whatever you think of the voices, the need to be able to synthesize the text of your ebook is always going to be vital to a segment of your readers, especially when human narration is not available. It's also generally useful to the broader reading demographic, as you'll see later in this chapter.

And the voice issues are a bit of a red herring. The real issue here is not how the voices sound but the mispronunciations the rendering engines make and the frequency with which they often make them. The constant mispronunciation of words disrupts comprehension and ruins reading enjoyment, because it breaks the narrative flow and leaves the reader to guess what the engine was actually trying to speak. It doesn't have to be this way, though; the errors occur because the mechanisms to enhance default synthetic renderings haven't been made available in ebooks, not because there aren't any.

But to step back slightly, synthetic speech engines aren't inherently riddled with errors; they just fail because word pronunciation can be an incredibly complex task, one that requires more than just the simple recognition of character data. Picture yourself learning a new language and struggling to understand why some vowels are silent in some situations and not in others, or why their pronunciation changes in seemingly haphazard ways, not to mention trying to grasp where phonetic boundaries are and so on. A rendering engine faces the same issues with less intelligence and no ability to learn on its own or from past mistakes.

The issue is sometimes as simple as not being able to parse parts of speech. For example, consider the following sentence:

> An official group *record* of past achievements was never kept.

A speech engine may or may not say "record" properly, because record used as noun is not pronounced the same way as when used as a verb.

The result is that most reading systems with built-in synthetic speech capabilities will do a decent job with the most common words in any language but can trip over themselves when trying to pronounce complex compound words, technical terms, proper names, abbreviations, numbers, and the like. Heteronyms (words that are spelled the same way but have different pronunciations and meanings) also offer a challenge, because you can't always be sure which pronunciation will come out. The word *bass* in English, for example, is pronounced one way to indicate a fish (bass) and another to indicate an instrument (base).

When you add up the various problem areas, it's no surprise there's a high frequency of errors. These failings are especially problematic in educational, science, medical, legal, tax, and similar technical publishing fields, as you might expect, where the proper pronunciation of terms is critical to comprehension and being able to communicate with peers.

The ability to correctly voice individual words is a huge benefit to all readers, which is why you should care about the synthetic rendering quality of your ebooks. Even if all your readers aren't going to read your whole book via synthetic speech, everyone comes across words they aren't sure how to pronounce, weird-looking character names, etc. In the print world, they'd just have to guess at the pronunciation and live with the nuisance of wondering for the rest of the book whether they have it right in their head or not (barring the rare pronunciation guide in the back, of course).

The embedded dictionaries and pronunciations that reading systems offer are a step up from print, but typically are of little to no help in many of these cases, because specialized terms and names don't appear in general dictionaries. Enhancing your ebooks even just to cover the most complicated names and terms goes a long way to making the entire experience better for all. Enhanced synthetic speech capabilities are a great value-add to set you apart from the crowd, especially if you're targeting broad audience groups.

Synthetic speech can also reduce the cost to produce audio-enhanced ebooks. Human narration is costly and typically only practical for novels, general nonfiction, and the like. But even in those kinds of books, are you going to have a person narrate the bibliographies and indexes and other complex structures in the back matter, or would it make more sense to leave them to the reader's device to voice? Having the pronunciation of words consistent across the human-machine divide takes on a little more importance in this light, unless you want to irk your readers with rotten-sounding back matter (or worse, omitted material).

As mentioned when discussing media overlays in Chapter 6, some reading systems already give word-level text-audio synchronization in synthetic speech playback mode, surpassing what most people would attempt with an overlay and human narration. As each word is fed for rendering it gets highlighted on the screen automatically; there's nothing special you have to do.

The cost and effort to improve synthetic speech is also one that has the potential to decrease over time as you build reusable lexicons and processes to enhance your books.

But enough selling of benefits. You undoubtedly want to know how EPUB 3 helps you, so let's get on with the task.

The new specification adds three mechanisms specifically aimed at synthetic speech production: PLS lexicon files, SSML markup, and CSS3 Speech style sheets. This chapter explores each of these in turn and shows how you can now combine them to optimize the quality of your ebooks.

PLS Lexicons

PLS files are XML lexicon files that conform to the W3C Pronunciation Lexicon Specification (*http://www.w3.org/TR/pronunciation-lexicon/*). The entries in these files identify the word(s) to apply each pronunciation rule to. The entries also include the correct phonetic spelling, which provides the text-to-speech engine with the proper pronunciation to render.

Perhaps a simpler way of understanding PLS files, though, is to think of them as containing globally applicable pronunciation rules: the entries you define in these files will be used for all matching cases in your content. Instead of having to add the pronunciation over and over every time the word is encountered in your markup, as SSML requires, these lexicons are used as global lookups.

Consequently, PLS files are the ideal place to define all the proper names and technical terms and other complex words that do not change based on the context in which they are used. Even in the case of heteronyms, it's good to define the pronunciation you deem the most commonly used in your PLS file, as it may be the only case in your ebook. It also ensures that you know how the heteronym will always be pronounced by default, to remove the element of chance.

The PLS specification does define a role attribute to enable context-dependent pronunciations (e.g., to differentiate the pronunciation of a word when used as a verb or noun), but support for it is not widespread and no vocabulary is defined for standard use. For the purposes of this chapter, we'll defer context-dependent differentiation to SSML, as a result, even though a measure is technically possible in PLS files.

But let's take a look at a minimal example of a complete PLS file to see how they work in practice. The following example defines a single entry for *acetaminophen* to cure our pronunciation headaches:

```
<lexicon
    version="1.0"
    alphabet="x-sampa"
    xml:lang="en"
    xmlns="http://www.w3.org/2005/01/pronunciation-lexicon">
    <lexeme>
        <grapheme>acetaminophen</grapheme>
        <phoneme>@"sit@'mIn@f@n</phoneme>
    </lexeme>
</lexicon>
```

To start breaking this markup down, the `alphabet` attribute on the root `lexicon` element defines the phonetic alphabet we're going to use to write our pronunciations. In this case, the example indicates using X-SAMPA.

X-SAMPA is the Extended Speech Assessment Methods Phonetic Alphabet. Being an ASCII-based phonetic alphabet, it's used in this example only because it is easier to write (by mere mortals like this author) than the International Phonetic Alphabet (IPA). It is not clear at this time which alphabet(s) will be supported by reading systems, because none are known to implement this technology.

The `version` and `xmlns` namespace declaration attributes are static values, so nothing exciting to see there, as usual. The `xml:lang` attribute is required and must reflect the language of the entries contained in the lexicon. This example declares that all the entries are in English.

The root would normally contain many more `lexeme` elements than in this example, because each defines the word(s) the rule applies to in the child `grapheme` element(s). (Graphemes, of course, don't have to take the form of words, but for simplicity of explanation, we'll stick to the general concept.) When the string is matched, the pronunciation in the `phoneme` element gets rendered in place of the default rendering the engine would have performed.

Or, if it helps you conceptualize, when the word *acetaminophen* is encountered in the prose, before passing the word to the rendering engine to voice, an internal lookup of the defined graphemes occurs. Because you've defined a match, the phoneme and the alphabet it adheres to are swapped in instead for voicing.

That you can include multiple graphemes may not seem immediately useful, but it enables you to create a single entry for regional variations in spelling, for example. British and American variants of *defense* could be defined in a single rule:

```
<lexeme>
    <grapheme>defense</grapheme>
    <grapheme>defence</grapheme>
    <phoneme>dI'fEns</phoneme>
</lexeme>
```

It is similarly possible to define more than one pronunciation by adding multiple pho neme elements. You could add the IPA spelling to the last example as follows, in case reading systems end up supporting only one or the other alphabet:

```
<lexeme>
    <grapheme>defense</grapheme>
    <grapheme>defence</grapheme>
    <phoneme>dI'fEns</phoneme>
    <phoneme alphabet="ipa">dɪˈfɛns</phoneme>
</lexeme>
```

The alphabet attribute on the new phoneme element is required, because its spelling doesn't conform to the default defined on the root. If the rendering engine doesn't support X-SAMPA, it could now possibly make use of this embedded IPA version instead. It is possible to translate to and from IPA from X-SAMPA, so if you write in one language, you could automatically generate the other. Including variants is one advantage that PLS lexicons have over SSML, where you can use only the spelling defined by the alphabet attribute.

The phoneme doesn't have to be in another alphabet, either; you could add a regional dialect as a secondary pronunciation, for example. Unfortunately, the specification doesn't provide any mechanisms to indicate why you've included such additional pronunciations in the file, or when they should be used, so there's not much value in doing so at this time.

There's much more to creating PLS files than can be covered here, of course, but you're now versed in the basics and ready to start compiling your own lexicons. You only need to attach your PLS file to your publication to complete the process of enhancing your ebook.

The first step is to include an entry for the PLS file in the EPUB manifest:

```
<item href="EPUB/lexicon.pls" id="pls" media-type="application/pls+xml"/>
```

The `href` attribute defines the location of the file relative to the EPUB container root and the `media-type` attribute value `application/pls+xml` identifies to a reading system that we've attached a PLS file.

Including one or more PLS files does not mean they apply by default to all your content; in fact, they apply to none of it by default. You next have to explicitly tie each PLS lexicon to each XHTML content document it is to be used with by adding a `link` element to the document's header:

```
<html ...>
   <head>
      ...
      <link
            rel="pronunciation"
            href="lexicon.pls"
            type="application/pls+xml"
            hreflang="en" />
      ...
   </head>
   ...
</html>
```

There are a number of differences between the declaration for the PLS file in this publication manifest and in the content file. The first is the use of the `rel` attribute to state the relationship, that the referenced file represents pronunciation information. The specific type of pronunciation file, in this case a PLS lexicon, is then specified in the `type` attribute.

You may have also noticed that the location of the PLS file appears to have changed. The EPUB subdirectory has been dropped from the path in the `href` attribute, because reading systems process the EPUB package document differently than they do content files. Resources listed in the manifest are referenced by their location from the container root. Content documents, on the other hand, reference resources relative to their own location in the container. Since we'll store both our content document and lexicon file in the EPUB subdirectory, the `href` attribute contains only the filename of the PLS lexicon.

The HTML `link` element also includes an additional piece of information to allow selective targeting of lexicons: the `hreflang` attribute. This attribute specifies the language to which the included pronunciations apply. For example, if you have an English document (as defined in the `xml:lang` attribute on the root `html` element) that embeds French prose, you could include two lexicon files:

```
<link
      rel="pronunciation"
      href="lexicon-en.pls"
      type="application/pls+xml"
      hreflang="en" />
```

```
<link
    rel="pronunciation"
    href="lexicon-fr.pls"
    type="application/pls+xml"
    hreflang="fr" />
```

Assuming all your French passages have xml:lang attributes on them, the reading system can selectively apply the lexicons to prevent any possible pronunciation confusion:

```
<p>It's the Hunchback of <i xml:lang="fr">Notre Dame</i> not of Notre Dame.</p>
```

A unilingual person reading this prose probably would not understand the distinction being made here: that the French pronunciation is not the same as the Americanization. Including separate lexicons by language, however, would ensure that readers would hear the Indiana university name differently than the French cathedral if they turn on TTS:

```
<lexicon
    version="1.0"
    alphabet="x-sampa"
    xml:lang="en"
    xmlns="http://www.w3.org/2005/01/pronunciation-lexicon">
    <lexeme>
        <grapheme>Notre Dame</grapheme>
        <phoneme>noUt@r 'deIm</phoneme>
    </lexeme>
</lexicon>

<lexicon
    version="1.0"
    alphabet="x-sampa"
    xml:lang="fr"
    xmlns="http://www.w3.org/2005/01/pronunciation-lexicon">
    <lexeme>
        <grapheme>Notre Dame</grapheme>
        <phoneme>n%oUtr@ d"Am</phoneme>
    </lexeme>
</lexicon>
```

When the contents of the i tag are encountered and identified as French, the pronunciation from the corresponding lexicon gets applied instead of the one from the default English lexicon.

Although including regional dialects as entries within the PLS lexicon is problematic, it is possible to create lexicons for regional dialects. Chinese is a prime example, where there are two notable dialects, Mandarin and Cantonese, and many other regional ones. But even English has its peculiarities as spoken by Brits, Americans, Canadians, Australians, Indians, and others.

To account for this variation, you can add the dialect to the hreflang attribute:

```
<link
    rel="pronunciation"
    href="lex/zh/guoyu.pls"
    type="application/pls+xml"
    hreflang="zh-guoyu" />

<link
    rel="pronunciation"
    href="lex/zh/yue.pls"
    type="application/pls+xml"
    hreflang="zh-yue" />
```

The reading system should be able to select the correct dialect to use based on the reader's preferences, but this behavior cannot be guaranteed, because only the primary language may be recognized. For languages like English, where only certain words might be pronounced differently, a simpler approach would be to define the primary dialect the book is written in a default lexicon for the language, and only include regional dialects as separate lexicons. A book by an American author could add British pronunciations like this:

```
<link
    rel="pronunciation"
    href="lex/en/en.pls"
    type="application/pls+xml"
    hreflang="en" />

<link
    rel="pronunciation"
    href="lex/en/br.pls"
    type="application/pls+xml"
    hreflang="en-br" />
```

If the reading system ignores the regional dialect file, the reader will still hear the pronunciation in the language default, which should still be an improvement over the default TTS engine rendering.

Now that you know how to globally define pronunciation rules, it's time to override and/or define behavior at the markup level.

SSML

Although PLS files are a great way to globally set the pronunciation of words, their primary failing is that they aren't a lot of help where context matters in determining the correct pronunciation. Leave the pronunciation of heteronyms to chance, for example, and you're invariably going to be disappointed by the result; the cases where context might not significantly influence comprehension (e.g., an English heteronym like "mobile"), are going to be dwarfed by the ones where it does.

By way of example, remember the example of how context influences pronunciation in the case of bass (the instrument) and bass (the fish) from the previous section. Let's take a look at this problem in practice now:

```
<p>The guitarist was playing a bass that was shaped like a bass.</p>
```

Human readers won't have much of a struggle with this sentence, despite the contrived oddity of it. A guitarist is not going to be playing a fish shaped like a guitar, and it would be strange to note that the bass guitar is shaped like a bass guitar. From context you're able to determine without much pause that we're talking about someone playing a guitar shaped like a fish.

All good and simple. Now consider your reaction if, when listening to a synthetic speech engine pronounce the sentence, you heard both words pronounced the same way, which is the typical result. The process to correct the mistake takes you out of the flow of the narrative. You're going to wonder why the guitar is shaped like a guitar, admit it.

Synthetic narration doesn't afford you the same ease to move forward and back through the prose that visual reading does, as words are only announced as they're voiced. The engine may be applying heuristic tests to attempt to better interpret the text for you behind the scenes, but you're at its mercy. You can back up and listen to the word again to verify whether the engine said what you thought it did, but it's an intrusive process that requires you to interact with the reading system. If you still can't make sense of the word, you can have the reading system spell it out as a last resort, but now you're train of thought is completely on understanding the word.

And this is an easy example. A blind reader used to synthetic speech engines would probably just keep listening past this sentence having made a quick assumption that the engine should have said something else, for example, but that's not a justification for neglect. The problems only get more complex and less avoidable, no matter your familiarity. And the fact that you're asking your readers to compensate is a major red flag that you're not being accessible, because mispronunciations are not always easily overcome, depending on the reader's disability. It also doesn't reflect well on your ebooks if readers turn to synthetic speech engines to help with pronunciation and find gibberish, as mentioned in the previous section.

And the problems are rarely one-time occurrences. When the reader figures out what the engine was trying to say, she will, in all likelihood, have to make a mental note on how to translate the synthetic gunk each time it is encountered again to avoid repeatedly going through the same process. If you don't think that makes reading comprehension a headache, try it sometime.

But this is where the Synthetic Speech Markup Language (SSML) comes in, allowing you to define individual pronunciations at the markup level. EPUB 3 adds the `ssml:al phabet` and `ssml:ph` attributes, which allow you to specify the alphabet you're using and phonemic pronunciation of the containing element's content, respectively. These attributes work in much the same way as the PLS entries reviewed in the previous section, as you might already suspect.

For example, you could revise the earlier example as follows to ensure the proper pronunciation for each use of bass:

```
<p>
    The guitarist was playing a
    <span ssml:alphabet="x-sampa" ssml:ph="beIs">bass</span> that was shaped
    like a <span ssml:alphabet="x-sampa" ssml:ph="b&amp;s">bass</span>.
</p>
```

The `ssml:alphabet` attribute on each span element identifies that the pronunciation carried in the `ssml:ph` attribute is written in X-SAMPA, identical to the PLS `alpha bet` attribute. You don't need a grapheme to match against, because you're telling the synthetic speech engine to replace the content of the `span` element. The engine will now voice the provided pronunciations instead of applying its own rules. In other words, no more ambiguity and no more rendering problem; it really is that simple.

The second `ssml:ph` attribute includes an ampersand entity (`&amp;`), as the actual X-SAMPA spelling is b&s. Ampersands are special characters in XHTML that denote the start of a character entity, so they must be converted to entities themselves in order for your document to be valid. When passed to the synthetic speech engine, the entity will be converted back to the ampersand character. (In other words, the extra characters to encode the character will not affect the rendering.)

Single and double quote characters in X-SAMPA representations similarly need to be escaped, depending on the characters you use to enclose the attribute value.

It bears a quick note that the pronunciation in the `ssml:ph` attribute has to match the prose contained in the element it is attached to. By wrapping `span` elements around each individual word in this example, the translation of text phonetic code is limited to just the problematic words you want to fix. If you put the attribute on the parent `p` element, you'd have to transcode the entire sentence.

The upside of the granularity SSML markup provides should be clear now, though: you can overcome any problem, no matter how small (or big), with greater precision than PLS files offer. The downside, of course, is having to work at the markup level to correct each instance that has to be overridden.

To hark back to the discussion of PLS files for a moment, though, you could further simplify the correction process by moving the more common pronunciation to our PLS lexicon and only fix the differing heteronym:

```
<lexicon
    version="1.0"
    alphabet="x-sampa"
    xml:lang="en"
    xmlns="http://www.w3.org/2005/01/pronunciation-lexicon">
    <lexeme>
        <grapheme>bass</grapheme>
        <phoneme>beIs</phoneme>
    </lexeme>
</lexicon>

<p>
    The guitarist was playing a bass that was shaped like a
    <span ssml:alphabet="x-sampa" ssml:ph="b&amp;s">bass</span>.
</p>
```

It's also unnecessary to define the `ssml:alphabet` attribute every time. If you were using only a single alphabet throughout the document, which would be typical of most ebooks, you could instead define the alphabet once on the root `html` element:

```
<html ... ssml:alphabet="x-sampa">
```

As long as the alphabet is defined on an ancestor of the element carrying the `ssml:ph` attribute, a rendering engine will interpret it correctly (and your document will be valid).

The root element is the ancestor of all the elements in the document, which is why these kinds of declarations are invariably found on it, in case you've ever wondered but were afraid to ask.

Your markup can now be reduced to the much more legible and easily maintained:

```
<p>
    The guitarist was playing a bass that was shaped like a
    <span ssml:ph="b&amp;s">bass</span>.
</p>
```

If you're planning to share content across ebooks or across content files within one, it's better to keep the attributes paired, to eliminate confusion about which alphabet was used to define the pronunciation. It's not a common requirement, however.

But heteronyms are far from the only case for SSML. Any language construct that can be voiced differently, depending on the context in which it is used is a candidate for SSML. Numbers are always problematic, as are weights and measures:

```
<p>
  There are <span
  ssml:ph="w&quot;Vn T&quot;aUz@n t_hw&quot;En4i f&quot;O:r"
  >1024</span>
  bits in a byte, not
  <span ssml:ph="t_h&quot;En t_hw&quot;En4i f&quot;O:r">1024</span>,
  as the year is pronounced.
</p>
```

```
<p>
  It reached a high of <span
  ssml:ph="'T3rti s&quot;Ev@n 'sEntI&quot;greId">37C</span> in the sun
  as I stood outside <span ssml:ph="'T3rti s&quot;Ev@n si">37C</span>
  waiting for someone to answer my knocks and let me in.
</p>
```

```
<p>
  You'll be an <span ssml:ph="Ekstr@ lArdZ">XL</span> by the end of Super Bowl
  <span ssml:ph="'fOrti">XL</span> at the rate you're eating.
</p>
```

Unfortunately, there's no simple guideline to give in terms of finding issues. It takes an eye for detail and an ear for possible different aural renderings. Editors and indexers are good starting resources for the process, because they should be able to quickly flag problem words during production to keep them from needing to be rooted out after the fact. Programs that can analyze books and report on potentially problematic words, although not generally available, are not just a fantasy. Their prevalence will hopefully grow now that EPUB 3 incorporates more facilities to enhance default renderings, because they can greatly reduce the human burden.

The only other requirement when using the SSML attributes that haven't been covered here is that you always have to declare the SSML namespace. The previous examples have omitted the declaration for clarity, and because the namespace is typically specified only once on the root html element as follows:

```
<html ... xmlns:ssml="http://www.w3.org/2001/10/synthesis">
```

Similar to the alphabet attribute, you could have equally well attached the namespace declaration to each instance where you used the attributes:

```
<span
  xmlns:ssml="http://www.w3.org/2001/10/synthesis"
  ssml:ph="x-sampa"
  ...>
```

But that's a verbose approach to markup and generally makes sense only when content is encapsulated and shared across documents, as just noted, or expected to be extracted into foreign playback environments where the full document context is unavailable.

The question you may still be wondering at this point is what happens if a PLS file contains a pronunciation rule that matches a word that is also defined by an SSML pronunciation? How can you be sure which one wins? You don't have to worry, however, because the EPUB 3 specification defines a precedence rule that states that the SSML pronunciation must be honored. There'd be no way to override the global PLS definitions, otherwise, which would make SSML largely useless in resolving conflicts.

But to wrap up, there is no reason why you couldn't make all your improvements in SSML. It's not the ideal way to tackle the problem, because of the text-level recognition and tagging it requires, at least in this author's opinion, but it may make more sense to internal production to only use a single technology and/or support for PLS may not prove universal (it's too early to know yet).

CSS3 Speech

You might be thinking the global definition power of PLS lexicons combined with the granular override abilities of SSML might be sufficient to cover all cases, so why a third technology? But you'd be only partly right.

The CSS3 Speech module is not about word pronunciation. It includes no phonetic capabilities but defines how you can use CSS style sheet technology to control such aspects of synthetic speech rendering as the gender of voice to use, the amount of time to pause before and after elements, when to insert aural cues, etc.

The CSS3 Speech module also provides a simpler entry point for some basic voicing enhancements. The ability to write X-SAMPA or IPA pronunciations requires specialized knowledge, but the `speak-as` property masks the complexity for some common use cases.

You could use this property to mark all acronyms that you intend to be spelled out letter-by-letter, for example. If you add a class called `spell` to the `abbr` elements you want spelled, as in the following example:

```
<abbr class="spell">IBM</abbr>
```

you could then define a CSS class to indicate that each letter should be voiced individually using the `spell-out` value:

```
.spell {
    -epub-speak-as: spell-out
}
```

Now, you're no longer leaving it to the rendering engine to determine whether the acronym is "wordy" enough to attempt to voice as a word now.

Note that the properties are all prefixed with `-epub-`, because the Speech module was not a recommendation at the time that EPUB 3 was finalized. You must use this prefix until the Speech module is finalized and reading systems begin supporting the unprefixed versions.

The `speak-as` property provides the same functionality for numbers, ensuring they get spoken one digit at a time instead of as a single number, something engines will not typically do by default:

```
.digits {
    -epub-speak-as: digits
}
```

Adding this class to the following number would ensure that readers understand you're referring to the North American emergency line when listening to TTS playback:

```
<span class="digits">911</span>
```

The property also allows you to control whether or not to read out punctuation. Only some punctuation ever gets announced in normal playback, because it's generally used for pause effects, but you could require all punctuation to be voiced using the `literal-punctuation` value:

```
.punctuate {
    -epub-speak-as: literal-punctuation
}
```

This setting would be vital for grammar books, for example, where you would want the entire punctuation for each example to be read out to the student. Conversely, to turn punctuation off, you'd use the `no-punctuation` value.

The `speak-as` property isn't a complex control mechanism, but it definitely serves a useful role. Even if you are fluent with phonetic alphabets, there's a point where it doesn't make sense to have to define or write out every letter or number to ensure the engine doesn't do the wrong thing, and this is where the Speech module helps.

Where the module excels, however, is in providing playback control. But this is also an area where you may want to think twice before adding your own custom style sheet rules. Most reading systems typically have their own internal rules for playback so that the synthetic speech rendering doesn't come out as one long uninterrupted stream of monotone narration. When you add your own rules, you have the potential to interfere with the reader's default settings. But in the interests of thoroughness, we'll take a quick tour.

The first stop is the ability to insert pauses. Pauses are an integral part of the synthetic speech reading process, because they provide a nonverbal indication of change. Without them, it wouldn't always be clear if a new sentence were beginning or a new paragraph, or when one section ends and another begins.

The CSS3 Speech module includes a `pause` property that allows you to control the duration to pause before and after any element. For example, you could define a half-second pause before headings followed by a quarter-second pause after by including the following rule:

```
h1 {
    -epub-pause: 50ms 25ms
}
```

Aural cues are equally helpful when it comes to identifying new headings, since the pause alone may not be interpreted by the listener as you expect. The Speech module includes a `cue` property for exactly this purpose:

```
h1 {
    -epub-pause: 50ms 25ms;
    -epub-cue: url('audio/ping.mp3') none
}
```

 Note the addition of the none value after the audio file location. If omitted, the cue would also sound after the heading was finished.

And finally, the `rest` property provides fine-grained control when using cues. Cues occur after any initial pause before the element (as defined by the `pause` property) and before any pause after. But you may still want to control the pause that occurs between the cue sounding and the text being read and between the end of the text being read and the trailing cue sounding (i.e., so that the sound and the text aren't run together). The `rest` property is how you control the duration of these pauses.

You could update our previous example to add a 10 millisecond rest after the cue is sounded to prevent run-ins as follows:

```
h1 {
    -epub-pause: 50ms 25ms;
    -epub-cue: url('audio/ping.mp3') none;
    -epub-rest: 10ms 0ms
}
```

But again, if the case hasn't been made forcefully enough earlier, it's best not to tweak these properties unless you're targeting a specific user group, know their needs, and know that their players will not provide sufficient quality "out of the box." Tread lightly, in other words.

A final property, that is slightly more of an aside, is voice-family. Although not specifically accessibility related, it can provide a more flavorful synthesis experience for your readers.

If your ebook contains dialogue, or the gender of the narrator is important, you can use this property to specify the appropriate gender voice. We could set a female narrator as follows:

```
body {
    -epub-voice-family: female
}
```

and a male class to use as needed for male characters:

```
.male {
    -epub-voice-family: male
}
```

If you added these rules to a copy of *Alice's Adventures in Wonderland*, you could now differentiate the Cheshire Cat using the male voice as follows:

```
<p>
    Alice: But I don't want to go among mad people.
</p>

<p class="male">
    The Cat: Oh, you can't help that.
    We're all mad here. I'm mad. You're mad.
</p>
```

You can also specify different voices within the specified gender. For example, if a reading system had two male voices available, you could add some variety to the characters as follows by indicating the number of the voice to use:

```
.first-male {
    -epub-voice-family: male 1
}

.second-male {
    -epub-voice-family: male 2
}
```

At worst, the reading system will ignore your instruction and present whatever voice it has available, but this property gives you the ability to be more creative with your text-to-speech renderings for those systems that do provide better support.

The CSS3 Speech module contains more properties than covered here, but reading systems are required to implement only the limited set of features described in this section. You may use the additional properties the module makes available (e.g., pitch and loudness control), but if you do, your content may not render uniformly across platforms. Carefully consider using innovative or disruptive features in your content, because this may hinder interoperability across reading systems.

Whatever properties you decide to add, it is always good practice to separate them into their own style sheet. You should also define them as applicable only for synthetic speech playback using a media at-rule as follows:

```
@media speech {

    .spell {
        -epub-speak-as: spell-out
    }

}
```

As noted earlier, reading systems will typically have their own defaults, and separating your aural instructions will allow them to be ignored and/or turned off on systems where they're unwanted.

For completeness, you should also indicate the correct media type for the style sheet when linking from your content document:

```
<link rel="stylesheet" type="text/css" href="synth.css" media="speech" />
```

And that covers the full range of synthetic speech enhancements. You now have a whole arsenal at your disposal to create high-quality synthetic speech.

Validation

To paraphrase a common expression, there are three things you need to know about a finished EPUB 3 file: it must adhere to rules, rules, and damned rules.

Which is only to say that there is nothing unique about EPUB 3 as a document publishing format. The rules are there to ensure that your content can be opened and rendered by any reading system. They can't tell you how your content will look on any given reading system, but they can alert you to bugs that are the result of bad markup. If you skip the validation stage and assume that just because it seemed to be fine testing in a reading system, or a program exported it so it must be valid, you run the risk of a lot of wasted time and effort later.

Some vendors will prevent your file from being distributed if it doesn't validate (which is a good thing), in which case you'll be forced back to this step right away should you try to avoid it. Others may not, or you might distribute the file yourself, in which case it might only be as you get flooded with angry emails from customers that you'll learn all the things you did wrong. Once your reputation is tarnished, even if just in a comments section on a product page, it can be hard to get back. No one appreciates someone who hasn't bothered to do basic validation to ensure their content renders, after all.

This chapter is last in the book not only because it wouldn't make sense to talk about validation before understanding EPUB content, but also because it diverges slightly from the best practices pattern. The best practice is simply to validate your content. Instead, this chapter looks at how to get up and running with the epubcheck validation tool and then spends some time looking at some of the most common error messages you're likely to encounter, including breaking down where they come from in the validation process.

epubcheck

The epubcheck tool is the gold standard as far as EPUB 3 validation goes. The tool has been around since the early EPUB 2 days. It was originally developed by Adobe but is now maintained as an open source tool by the IDPF. It's free to use and modify as you need.

It has also improved significantly both in terms of the scope of what it checks for and the comprehensibility of the error messages it returns, part of a major upgrading it has undergone in conjunction with the release of EPUB 3. There's still work to be done to add CSS and scripting support, but it's come a long way from where it was.

Installing

Before downloading epubcheck, you will need to verify that you have Java installed on your computer. Any version of the Java Runtime Environment will do, which is the version that gets installed when you install Java for your browser (available from the Java website (*http://www.java.com*)).

 To simplify calling Java from the command line, you will need to add the path to the Java executable to the PATH environment variable. On Windows machines, for example, this path is typically `c:\program files\java\jre7`. Instructions on how to add this variable are operating system dependent, but plenty of resources exist on the Web. You can omit this step, but it means manually entering the full path to Java every time you want to run epubcheck.

epubcheck is currently hosted on a Google projects site (*http://code.google.com/p/epub check/*) under the same name. The latest stable build is typically linked to from the main page, but can also be found by clicking on the Downloads tab.

epubcheck does not have an installer, but instead comes as a ZIP file containing the necessary libraries to run. After downloading, simply unzip the contents to a directory in your operating system. The folder will contain the epubcheck *.jar* file and a directory called *lib*, which contains additional libraries that epubcheck depends on to run, as shown in Figure 11-1.

That's it. You now have epubcheck installed on your computer.

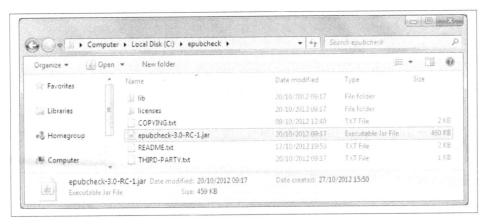

Figure 11-1. epubcheck distribution files

Running

epubcheck is a command-line tool, meaning that you're going to have to become familiar with your operating system's command shell. If you're already familiar with the command line and how to run Java, you can skim this section to get the command line call. If not, the first task is bringing up the command shell:

- Windows users, click the Start menu button and type cmd in the Run box (XP users) or the new search box at the bottom of the Start menu (Vista and Windows 7).
- Mac users need to go to the *Applications/Utilities* directory and double-click on Terminal.
- Linux users may find the shell in a number of different places, and under a number of different names, depending on the flavor and version of Linux they are running.

One of the nuisances of a command-line tool like epubcheck is entering all the necessary paths in order to get it to run. Adding the java executable location to the PATH variable allows you to call it without having to type the full directory path, but what directory you invoke epubcheck from will affect the other paths you have to specify.

If you try to run epubcheck from the default directory your command shell opens in, you'll need to add the full path to both the epubcheck *.jar* file and your EPUB:

```
$ java -jar c:\epubcheck\epubcheck.jar c:\books\mybook\xyz.epub
```

If you change directories in the command shell to the epubcheck directory, you can avoid having to specify the full path to the *.jar* file:

```
$ java -jar epubcheck.jar c:/books/mybook/xyz.epub
```

Conversely, if you navigate to your book directory, you just have to specify the path to the *.jar* file.

The actual epubcheck *.jar* file typically has a build number appended to the end of it (e.g., *epubcheck-3.0-RC-1.jar*). This build number will be omitted from the examples in this chapter, because it is subject to change.

Either way is a nuisance, but you can use a couple tricks to speed things up. The simplest is to use the autocomplete feature that most command shells provide. If you start typing the name of a file or directory, you can press the Tab key to fill the name in automatically. For example, to quickly insert the epubcheck *.jar* file, you could start by typing this:

```
$ java -jar c:\ep
```

Pressing the Tab key should expand the directory to *epubcheck* (if you had another directory in your root drive starting with *ep*, simply press the Tab key again to rotate through the possible options). You can then repeat this shortcut to add the *.jar* file. Because there is only one file starting with the letter *e* in the epubcheck folder, again you could type the one letter e:

```
$ java -jar c:\epubcheck\e
```

Then press the Tab key to expand to the full *.jar* file name.

If you don't like typing at all, another option is to open both the epubcheck and book directories first (e.g., in a My Computer or Windows Explorer window on Windows, or a Finder window on Macs). You can then drag and drop the files into the command shell. For example, first type the Java commands:

```
$ java -jar
```

Then drag the epubcheck *.jar* file onto the Terminal window and drop it. The full path to the file will be automatically inserted:

```
$ java -jar C:\epubcheck\epubcheck.jar
```

You could then do the same to add the EPUB file to validate.

A final option is to create a script to automatically run epubcheck for you. On Windows, create a new text file containing the following command:

```
$ java -jar c:\epubcheck\epubcheck.jar %*
```

Save this file as *epubcheck.bat* in the epubcheck directory. On Linux and Macs, an equivalent shell script might be:

```
#!/bin/sh
java -jar ~/epubcheck/epubcheck.jar $@
```

Save this file as *epubcheck.sh*.

You can now add the epubcheck folder to the PATH environment variable, as you did earlier for the Java executable. If you close and re-open your terminal window after making this change, you can now invoke epubcheck from any directory simply by typing the name of the file you just created, as shown in Figure 11-2.

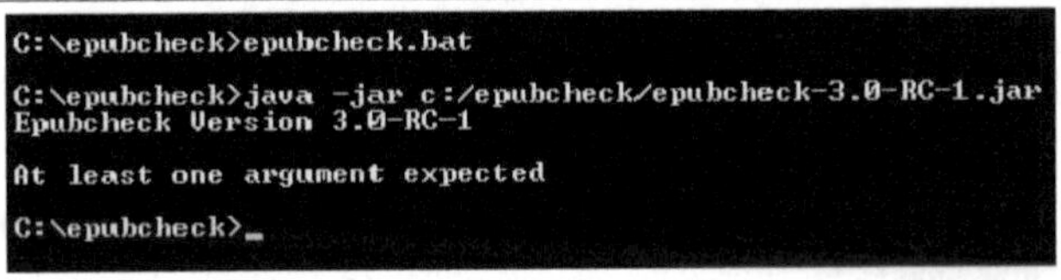

Figure 11-2. Invoking the batch file on Windows

To validate a file, all you need to do now is specify its path after the script filename, regardless of what directory your terminal window initializes in:

```
$ epubcheck.bat c:/books/mybook.epub
```

Again, you could drag and drop the EPUB file if that's simpler.

Working in the Command Shell

For those not intimately familiar with command shells, a couple of commands come in extremely handy when validating:

cls | clear
> Typing this command clears the screen. When running epubcheck for the first time, it's common to get a lengthy report of issues. As you fix them, you'll want to rerun the program, but finding where one report ends and another begins can be extremely difficult. Clearing the screen between runs ensures that all the messages displayed are relevant. The Windows command shell uses cls, while Linux and Macs use clear.

up arrow
> You don't have to retype the command to invoke epubcheck every time you want to run a validation report. Pressing the up arrow will cycle through the commands you've already run. If you clear the screen between runs, for example, you just need to press the up arrow twice to get back to the epubcheck command.

One last trick you can use to improve the command-line experience is to pipe the output to a file for easier reading. Command shells are awfully little windows to try to read error messages in, and flipping between the window and your content to find and understand the problems quickly becomes a headache. Depending on how the command shell is configured, and how many errors and warnings your book has, you may not even be able to scroll back to the beginning of the report, meaning the most critical error might no longer be discoverable.

You aren't restricted to working in the command shell, though. To pipe errors to a file, you add the number 2 followed by a right angle bracket (>) to the end of the command that invokes epubcheck, and then include the path and name of the file to write to.

For example, to pipe errors to the file c:/books/error.txt, invoke epubcheck like this:

```
$ java -jar epubcheck.jar c:/books/mybook.epub 2> c:/books/error.txt
```

As long as you are working with a text editor that automatically updates open files, you should be able to run the command over and over and immediately see the new results. The command shell window in Figure 11-3 shows only the information written to standard output. Errors are listed in the specified text file.

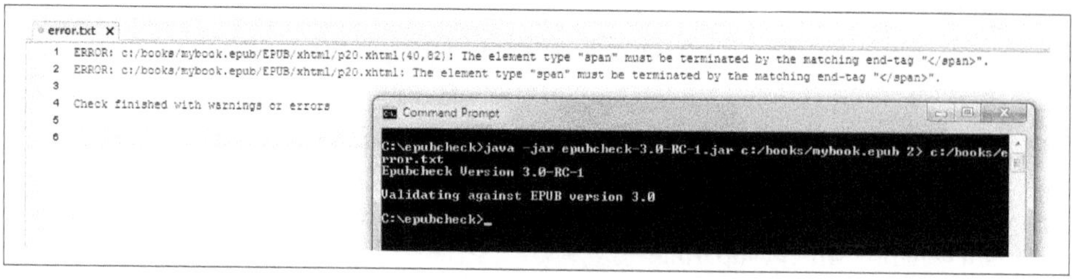

Figure 11-3. Redirecting epubcheck errors to a text file

Options

This section quickly reviews the different ways you can call epubcheck to validate EPUBs.

Validating EPUB archives

The typical use for epubcheck is to validate a completed EPUB archive. To do so, simply include the path to your EPUB after invoking the epubcheck *.jar* file:

```
$ java -jar epubcheck.jar c:/books/mybook.epub
```

Make sure there are no spaces in the directory path to your EPUB or in the filename itself. If there are, you must enclose the entire path in quotes:

```
$ java -jar epubcheck.jar "c:/Users/matt/My Documents/EPUBs/My Book.epub"
```

or URI-escape the spaces as %20:

```
$ java -jar epubcheck.jar c:/Users/matt/My%20Documents/EPUBs/My%20Book.epub
```

If you forget to do this, the following cryptic error is generated:

```
$ java.lang.RuntimeException: For files other than epubs, mode must be
specified!
```

epubcheck will interpret the path as three separate arguments because of the spaces: `c:/Users/matt/My"`, `"Documents/EPUBs/My` and `Book.epub`. Because the first part of the path does not appear to be an EPUB, since it has no extension, epubcheck will report that error and stop processing. The next couple of sections demonstrate what the `mode` argument does.

Validating unpacked EPUBs

Although most people reach the validation stage only at the very end of a project, when they have an archive file for distribution, it's not the only workflow that epubcheck can handle. Being able to work on the unzipped files is extremely helpful, and if you have a folder containing the full structure of your EPUB (*mimetype* file, *META-INF* directory and content), you can run epubcheck on it using the `mode` argument as follows:

```
$ java -jar epubcheck.jar c:/path/to/book -mode exp
```

The `exp` value is short for *expanded*, which doesn't mean that epubcheck will run more tests, just that the input is an unpacked EPUB. This feature saves you from having to zip up your content each time you fix an error in order to see whether your publication will successfully validate.

A related, and largely unknown but extremely useful, feature of epubcheck is the ability to generate an EPUB archive after successful validation of an unpacked directory. If epubcheck returns a successful report (no errors, only warnings), you can request that it also zip up the directory contents by adding a `save` argument to the command:

```
$ java -jar epubcheck.jar c:/path/to/book -mode exp -save
```

If all goes well, you'll find a finished *.epub* file in the directory where you ran the command. epubcheck will use the folder name containing your publication for the finished file.

Note that if you get the following error message, it means that you're working in a directory where you can't write the finished archive file:

```
java.lang.NullPointerException
    at com.adobe.epubcheck.util.Archive.createArchive(Archive.java:102)
    at com.adobe.epubcheck.tool.Checker.run(Checker.java:188)
    at com.adobe.epubcheck.tool.Checker.main(Checker.java:177)
```

The windows command shell initializes by default in the write-protected *Windows\system32* folder, for example. If you change the current directory to one where you have write permissions, the process will run smoothly. Linux and Macs typically start in the user's home directory, so this error should be less common, but if you can't find the file after epubcheck builds it, always check from the directory in which you ran the command.

Validating EPUB component files

You also have the option to validate individual component files using epubcheck (e.g., to validate content before going through the process of zipping your content up into a distribution archive).

To invoke epubcheck on individual files, you need to add the following two arguments to the command line:

mode

The type of file that is being validated. The value must be one of the following:

mo
    Media overlays

nav
    Navigation document

opf
    Package document

svg
    SVG content document

xhtml
    XHTML content document

version

The version of EPUB that the file conforms to. The value can be either 2.0 or 3.0.

To validate a navigation document, for example, you'd invoke the following command:

```
$ java -jar epubcheck.jar nav.xhtml -mode nav -version 3.0
```

Although you can use any mode for EPUB 3 validation, only opf, svg and xhtml can be used to validate EPUB 2 content.

Assessment reports

A new experimental option has been included in the latest version of epubcheck: the ability to generate an assessment report. These reports are XML files that not only contain the errors and warnings generated by epubcheck, but also provide various metadata about the EPUB, such as the Dublin Core metadata properties that have been set, the language of the publication, and what properties are known about its content (e.g., that it contains audio, video, MathML, script, etc.).

To generate a report, you must use the -out argument followed by the file to write the assessment to:

```
$ java -jar epubcheck.jar c:/path/to/book -mode exp -out c:/reports/book.xml
```

At the time of this writing, the report format was not documented on the epubcheck site, but it is described as an extension of the documentMD format (*http://www.fcla.edu/ dls/md/docmd.xsd*). Each report contains a root doc element, which always contains a child document element. This element lists the extracted information:

- The documentInformation element lists the filename (fileName) of the EPUB followed by all Dublin Core properties found (each listed in an element corresponding to its local name).

- The formatDesignation element lists the EPUB mime type and version number (formatName and formatVersion, respectively).

- The assessmentInformation element indicates whether the validation run was successful or not (outcome). If warnings or errors are reported, each message will be included in an outcomeDetailNote element (the type of message is not identified in the markup, but can be determined by the presence of WARNING or ERROR at the start of the element).

- The characterCount element provides the total character count of all text data.

- The Language element provides the language of the publication as set in the package document.

- Zero or more Font elements list all embedded fonts.

- Zero or more Reference elements list all the external links and references.

- Zero or more Features elements list all the unique properties of the content, as defined in the properties attributes on manifest entries.

Here's an example of a condensed assessment report:

```
<doc>
 <document creationDateTime="2012-03-01T20:55:42-05:00">
  <documentInformation>
   <fileName>accessible_epub_3-20121006.epub</fileName>
   <identifier>urn:isbn:9781449328030</identifier>
   <title>Accessible EPUB 3</title>
   <creator>Matt Garrish</creator>
  </documentInformation>
  <formatDesignation>
   <formatName>application/epub+zip</formatName>
   <formatVersion>3.0</formatVersion>
  </formatDesignation>
  <assessmentInformation agentName="epubcheck" agentVersion="3.0-RC-1">
   <outcome>Not valid</outcome>
   <outcomeDetailNote>ERROR: FreeSerif.otf: resource missing</outcomeDetailNote>
  </assessmentInformation>
  <CharacterCount>208463</CharacterCount>
  <Language>en</Language>
  <Font FontName="Free Serif" isEmbeded="true" />
```

```
    <Reference>http://shop.oreilly.com/product/0636920025283.do</Reference>
    <Features>hasScript</Features>
  </document>
</doc>
```

Although these reports are primarily designed for automated workflows, they provide an interesting peek into your EPUBs.

That's as deep as we'll go into this feature, though, because it's still an early experiment and may have changed by the time you read this book. The epubcheck site should be updated to include more information as the report format is formalized, so you can check there for changes.

Help

If you're ever in doubt about how to call epubcheck or want to verify whether features are still supported or new ones have been added, you can request a help listing from the program. Simply add the help argument after calling the *.jar* file:

```
$ java -jar epubcheck.jar -help
```

You should get information about the program and a listing of options similar to the following:

```
Epubcheck Version 3.0-RC-1

When running this tool, the first argument should be the name (with the path) of
the file to check.

If checking a non-epub file, the epub version of the file must be specified
using -v and the type of the file using -mode.

The default version is: 3.0.

Modes and versions supported:
-mode opf   -v 2.0
-mode opf   -v 3.0
-mode xhtml -v 2.0
-mode xhtml -v 3.0
-mode svg   -v 2.0
-mode svg   -v 3.0
-mode nav   -v 3.0
-mode mo    -v 3.0 // For Media Overlays validation
-mode exp          // For expanded EPUB archives

This tool also accepts the following flags:
-save        = saves the epub created from the expanded epub
-out <file>  = ouput an assessment XML document in file (experimental)
-? or -help  = displays this help message
```

Reading Errors

Now that you have a grasp on how to invoke epubcheck to run a validation report, the next challenge is reading the error reports that come back from it. Later sections of the chapter will get into much more detail about what the errors themselves indicate, but this section looks at how to make sense of all the information that gets reported to simplify tracking down and correcting errors.

A typical message from epubcheck follows this basic pattern:

```
[ERROR|WARNING]: [file](line,offset): Message
```

The following is a sample error message that results if a closing quote character is omitted from a `class` attribute, for example:

```
ERROR: c:/epub/accessible_epub_3.epub/EPUB/ch01.xhtml(10,44): The value of
attribute "class" associated with an element type "section" must not contain
the '<' character.
```

Here you can see that this is an error (must be fixed to pass validation), that it is in the file *EPUB/ch01.xhtml* inside the EPUB archive *c:/epub/accessible_epub_3.epub*, and that the error has been found 44 characters into line 10. Even if you don't have an XML-aware editor, jumping to the exact line and character offset should be easy to do in any text editor.

You may not always get file, line, and offset information, depending on the problem. When epubcheck verifies that all items listed in the manifest are in the archive, it does not maintain information about the original package document XML. Consequently, if you have an entry for a nonexistent file, you'll get an error like this:

```
ERROR: c:/epub/accessible_epub_3.epub: OPS/XHTML file EPUB/pr01a.xhtml is miss-
ing
```

This is when being able to interpret where errors are coming from and what they mean is going to be critical. You need to know that all your files are listed in the package document manifest to even begin figuring this kind of message out.

You may also find that the line and character offsets seem misleading. If you were to forget a closing `aside` tag early on in your file, it may not get reported as an error until the containing `section` gets closed:

```
<section>
  ...
  <aside>
    <p>...</p>
    <-- forgot a closing tag here on line 22
  <p>...</p>
  ...
  <p>...</p>
</section> <-- but error reported here on line 196
```

The error message resulting from this tagging might be as follows:

```
ERROR: c:/epub/accessible_epub_3.epub/EPUB/ch01.xhtml(196,3): The element type
"aside" must be terminated by the matching end-tag "</aside>".
```

People new to validation typically want to know why the error location isn't reported on the opening tag to simplify fixing the problem, but you have to bear in mind that there is no problem with the opening tag. The problem is with the closing tag, or lack of one before the section closes, and that doesn't occur until line 196 in this case. The validator does not backtrack to the opening tag to report where the aside opened, because validators simply report what is wrong. For all the validator knows, you simply forgot the end tag at that point.

Part of validating is doing the sleuthing to find where these kinds of problems originate. Just hope that there aren't a lot of asides in your file, because you'll have to check each one in turn to find the broken one! An aside can contain another aside, like a div can contain a div, so the error could take a bit of time to track down.

Beyond the Command Line

Running epubcheck from the command line is not the only option available. Integrating the library more seamlessly into internal workflows is an option, of course, but requires developer help. For those who don't have those kinds of resources available, this section reviews a few other options that can simplify the validation process.

Web Validation

The IDPF currently maintains a web-based version of epubcheck at *http://valida tor.idpf.org/*. To run the validator, you simply select your EPUB file and click the Validate button on the page, as shown in Figure 11-4.

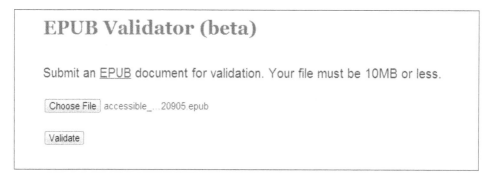

Figure 11-4. IDPF EPUB Validator service

The current version of epubcheck also powers this web service, but instead of command shell error output, you receive messages in the more human-readable table format shown in Figure 11-5.

EPUB Validator (beta)

Results

Detected version: EPUB 3.0

Results: The following problems were found in *accessible_epub_3-20120905.epub*:

Type	File	Line	Position	Message
ERROR EPUB/ch01.xhtml 17			7	element "p" not allowed here; expected the element end-tag, text or element "a", "abbr", "area", "audio", "b", "bdi", "bdo", "br", "button", "canvas", "cite", "code", "command", "datalist", "del", "dfn", "em", "embed", "epub:switch", "i", "iframe", "img", "input", "ins", "kbd", "keygen", "label", "map", "mark", "meter", "ns1:math", "ns2:svg", "object", "output", "progress", "q", "ruby", "s", "samp", "script", "select", "small", "span", "strong", "sub", "sup", "textarea", "time", "u", "var", "video" or "wbr" (with xmlns:ns1="http://www.w3.org/1998/Math/MathML" xmlns:ns2="http://www.w3.org/2000/svg")

Figure 11-5. Web validation results

The web results make it simpler to identify the error type, file, line, and character offset of the reported problem, but this information is the same as is provided in the command shell results shown previously.

Unfortunately, the web interface is not for use by anyone doing commercial validation, and it also has some limitations that work against it even for users who meet the use criteria. For one, you are capped to a maximum file size of 10 MB. While this is not going to be problematic for simple text works, any publication with images, audio and video content, or embedded fonts will quickly go over the cap. It can also be a nuisance, and waste of bandwidth, to continuously upload your EPUB over and over to the IDPF server in order to have it validated. It's not the fastest or most effective use of time depending on how big your EPUB is. Learning to use epubcheck from the command line is a better long-term strategy.

The source for the web service is also not available for general download as of this writing, but it could be made available at a later date once the validator moves out of its beta phase. Installing the service locally, whether on an individual PC running a web server or in a corporate environment, would greatly simplify the validation process for anyone wanting to avoid command line and/or commercial options.

It is possible to use the *.jar* file to create your own web service, but you would have to add a layer to it to parse and format the results in order to provide equivalent table markup.

Graphical Interface

A much-desired feature for epubcheck has been to add a graphical interface to simplify the whole process we've just gone through of configuring programs and paths and selecting files. Unfortunately, at this time, it remains a much-desired feature. The developers are aware of the need, so stay tuned.

Commercial Options

Although the process to manually call epubcheck can seem tedious, especially if you aren't a developer who is regularly in the command shell, there are programs that natively integrate epubcheck and/or can be configured to run external tools like epubcheck from within them.

Prime among these is oXygen Editor (shown in Figure 11-6), which has native support for EPUB 2 and 3 markup editing. oXygen allows you to drag and drop your EPUB archive directly into the program, enabling editing of the content files without having to unzip. It also includes built-in support for the latest epubcheck validator, so all you have to do is click a button to validate your archive. It is also nondestructive, in that it will not modify your source markup when saving and validating.

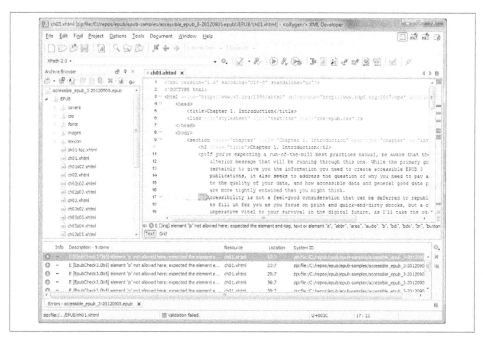

Figure 11-6. oXygen editing interface

Perhaps the most useful feature that oXygen provides is the ability to jump directly to the listed error. By double-clicking on an error in the result pane at the bottom of the program, the file will be automatically loaded (if not already open) and jumped to the corresponding line. oXygen also shows validation errors in red on the side of the text editor, enabling quick location and correction.

Understanding Errors

It's somewhat disheartening to discover that the program you used to author your EPUB has generated invalid content, but it's not atypical. There often aren't straight 1:1 mappings when dealing with export routines that go from an internal layout format to a distribution like EPUB. Adding to that, developers often try to help these processes through heuristic and natural language parsing tricks. The resulting content may appear to be okay in a reading system, but tag soup is not just invalid to the theoretical purity of specifications but causes real-world problems for anyone using the markup to navigate.

This chapter can't possibly be a reference to every single error that you might encounter in every technology that EPUB incorporates, but this section will walk through the main validation stages and look at what can go wrong. Hopefully, with a sense of what epubcheck is doing, even if you can't find your particular problem here, you'll find some hints to where you should be looking.

The other consideration is that error messages change over time, with the hope of making them easier to understand. The obvious result is that the error messages you find in the following sections may not exactly match what epubcheck reports depending on the version you're using.

If there is one best practice to give when it comes to understanding errors (one learned from many years validating markup data), it's to *always* start with the first error reported. Validators don't generally stop at the first problem they find, and the result can be many, many erroneous errors that are simply related to the first problem (e.g., forgetting to include a closing tag can cause every following element to be reported as invalid).

A second, closely related tip, is to validate often. The way that errors cascade can result in some odd issues appearing in your report, so never assume you can always pick out which ones are related to an earlier problem and which ones are unique. That's how you spend time searching for improbable solutions to problems that didn't actually exist. Running validation reports is quick and free, so when in doubt, run the report again.

And finally, note that validators are not infallible. You might find errors being reported that shouldn't be, but there's a difference between an incorrect check of a specification requirement and not being sure what an error means. If you are unsure whether it is the validator that is wrong or your understanding of the message, seek assistance. The IDPF forums (*http://www.idpf.org/forums/*) are a friendly venue where you can ask for help deciphering error reports.

Common XML Errors

As EPUB is a predominantly XML-based format, there are a number of common errors that get reported across document types. If a document is not well formed, or does not meet schema requirements, the error message does not change, only the element and attribute names. Rather than list the same issues over and over, this section will tackle these problems once.

Document errors

Each XML file must have a single root element (e.g., for XHTML documents, this is the html element). epubcheck will generate the following errors if it finds XML files that aren't conformant to this requirement:

Content is not allowed in prolog
> This error occurs when you have text content before the root element. Only the XML declaration, processing instructions, and doctype declarations can precede the root element. It may also be a sign that you've accidentally specified a text file with an XML media type in the manifest.

Content is not allowed in trailing section
> This is the opposite error, where you have text or markup content after the closing root tag.

Element errors

If your markup is not conformant to the schema for a given document type, you'll receive the following errors:

Element X not allowed here; expected the element end-tag, text or element A,B,C
> This is probably the most common element error you'll encounter, and A,B,C usually ends up being a wildly long list of alternative elements. This error can occur either when you've used an element where it's not allowed (e.g., putting a div inside of a p in a content document), or have accidentally forgotten to close an element (e.g., omit a closing </p> tag and every following sibling block element will register as an error).

This error can also indicate that you've inserted an element out of order. The `fig caption` must be the first or last element in a `figure`, for example. If you place it anywhere else, you'll get this error on the elements that follow it. The same applies to table markup. The order of the major divisions in the package document is also enforced (`metadata`, `manifest`, `spine`, `guide`, `bindings`).

This error can also occur if you forget a namespace. MathML and SVG in HTML5 do not require namespaces, for example, so if you forget to declare one, or copy an HTML5 example from the Web, the element might be reported as invalid.

And finally, make sure that you're using lowercase element names. XHTML is case sensitive, so you cannot use element names like `H1` and `SECTION`. If you do, you will also receive this error that they are not allowed. All elements names in the package document are also lowercase. It would be nicer if a distinction could be made between elements that aren't defined and elements that aren't allowed, as used to be the case, but that's a limitation of the RelaxNG schemas you just have to work around.

`Element X incomplete; expected A,B,C`

This error often occurs in the package metadata if you omit one of the three required Dublin Core elements. XHTML content documents don't have a lot of requirements, but they do exist (e.g., the `ruby` element requires at least one child `rt`). You're more likely to encounter this error when you add MathML or SVG to your content documents, as there tend to be more dependencies.

`The prefix X for element Y is not bound`

You've used a prefix on an element without declaring it (e.g., `dc:` on the package metadata elements without declaring `xmlns:dc="http://purl.org/dc/terms/"`). XML declarations are often included on the root element but can be scoped to the most relevant element (e.g., the Dublin Core namespace is typically declared on the `metadata` element, not the root `package` element, because Dublin Core elements are not used outside of the metadata section). This error also occurs in content documents when MathML and SVG embedded without a namespace declared.

`Element X missing required attribute Y`

The specified attribute cannot be omitted. An example is the `unique-identifier` attribute on the `package` document. In content documents, forgetting `href` and `src` attributes is often the cause of this error.

`Element type X must be followed by either attribute specifications, ">"`
`or "/>"`

This error occurs either when you've omitted a closing quote character on an attribute or have forgotten the closing angle bracket on the element.

Attribute errors

Likewise, if you use attributes improperly, schema validation will return the following errors:

`Attribute X not allowed here; expected attribute A,B,C`
> One error type that attributes share with elements is being used in the wrong place. It's not valid to use a `name` attribute on a elements anymore in HTML5, for example. Attributes are also case sensitive, which can cause this error.

`The prefix X for attribute Y associated with an element type Z is not bound`
> Forgetting to declare namespaces is another shared issue. If you receive this message, you don't have an in-scope namespace declaration. This problem typically occurs when using the `epub:type` attribute without declaring the namespace on the root `html` element, for example.

`Duplicate ID X`
> In this case, you have two or more `id` attributes in the same file with the same value. You will need to manually inspect the attributes to determine which one needs to be changed.

`Value of attribute "id" is invalid; must be an XML name without colons`
> This error most often occurs when an `id` attribute value is numeric (e.g., `id="1"`), begins with a number, or contains invalid characters. Although HTML5 has relaxed the restriction that all `ids` start with an alphabetic character, other XML formats allowed in EPUB 3 must still conform to this naming.

`The value of attribute X associated with an element type Y must not contain the '<' character`
> This error may indicate that you've included a left angle bracket character in an attribute, but more often is an indication that you missed a closing quote character on an attribute (i.e., the validator sees the next tag as part of the attribute value).

Character encoding

All XML formats defined by the EPUB specification, including XHTML content documents, must be encoded as UTF-8 or UTF-16. The following errors may occur if your documents do not conform:

`Only UTF-8 and UTF-16 encodings are allowed, detected X`
> Verify that the file is actually encoded as UTF-8 or UTF-16 (don't trust the XML declaration).

`Malformed byte sequence: X. Check encoding`
> This error typically arises when content in one encoding is pasted into a document encoded in another, but can also occur if you transcode your content from one

character set to another. It indicates that there is a sequence of bytes that don't conform to the Unicode specification, so they cannot be resolved to a character. When you view the file, you may not see anything at the location, as the malformed byte may not show as character data. epubcheck does not provide more detailed information, so to find the exact location, you'll typically need to open the invalid file in an XML editor that can report the exact location.

`Any Publication Resource that is an XML-Based Media Type must be a conformant XML 1.0 Document. XML Version retrieved: #`
    You cannot use XML version 1.1 for XML content. If you've included an XML declaration at the top of your file, make sure that the version pseudoattribute is set to 1.0 (`<?xml version="1.0"?>`)

Note that CSS style sheets must also be encoded as UTF-8 or UTF-16. If you create your CSS files as plain ASCII text files, you should not receive an error. The ASCII character set maps to the same range of characters in UTF-8, so all ASCII text files are valid UTF-8 files.

Linking errors

One of the handier features of epubcheck is that it will verify all internal links to see if they can be resolved, and report problems if not:

`'X': referenced resource missing in the package`
    You've attempted to link to the file X, but a matching resource could not be found in the container. Check that the resource exists and that there is an entry for it in the package document manifest.

`'X': fragment identifier is not defined in 'Y'`
    The file Y could be located, but there isn't an element inside it with the id X. Typos and renamed IDs are the most common cause.

Container Errors

Container errors can be some of the most perplexing to solve, because they often arise as a result of the way the content has been zipped up. In order to ensure that your EPUB can be opened and the content discovered, you need to ensure that there are no problems with the packaging. To that end, epubcheck verifies that your EPUB meets all the following conditions:

`File name contains characters disallowed in OCF file names: X`
    See section 2.4 of the OCF specification (*http://idpf.org/epub/30/spec/epub30-ocf.html#sec-container-filenames*) for a list of characters that must not be used in your EPUB filename or any files in it.

Filename contains spaces. Consider changing filename such that URI
escaping is not necessary
> This message is actually just a warning. It is generated because it's possible that a poorly designed reading system might break if there are spaces in your file names (e.g., failing to encode the spaces properly as %20), not because problems are expected.

File name contains non-ascii characters: X. Consider changing filename
> This message is also a warning, similar to the preceding one. Although modern operating systems have no issue with non-ASCII characters in filenames, processing tools sometimes do. If you are targeting older EPUB 2 reading systems, this may be a concern, but it should not affect your decision to use these characters in EPUB 3.

Filename is not allowed to end with '.'
> Ending filenames with a dot is a little more serious, so this is an error. Some operating systems do not handle filenames so named, which can break rendering.

Corrupted ZIP header
> Occurs if the container does not begin with the string PK (i.e., it is not a valid ZIP file).

Cannot read header
> Some form of file corruption has occurred that is preventing the ZIP file from being read.

Length of first filename in archive must be 8, but was #
> If the first filename found in the archive is not eight characters, it cannot be the required *mimetype* file. If you manually zip your archive, you must add the mimetype before you add any other files.

Mimetype entry missing or not the first in archive
> This error is rare but can occur if the first file is eight characters long (to get past the previous check) but is not the *mimetype* file. Again, check how the archive has been zipped.

Extra field length for first filename must be 0, but was #
> Indicates that there is character data between the *mimetype* filename and its content (the extra fields are being used). This error can occur if the program you've used to zip the container adds additional metadata.

Mimetype contains wrong type (application/epub+zip) expected
> Ensure that the media type has been typed correctly.

Mimetype file should contain only the string "application/epub+zip"
> Ensure that there are no extra spaces or linebreaks in the file.

---

epubcheck will also verify that the package document can be located by a reading system. The following errors indicate problems with this discovery process:

Required META-INF/container.xml resource is missing
> Somewhat self explanatory. The *container.xml* file is a required file in the *META-INF* directory, because it identifies the path to the package file.

No rootfiles with media type 'application/oebps-package+xml'
> The *container.xml* file was found, but it does not contain an entry for the package file (check the mediaType attribute value correctly matches the one in the error).

Entry X not found in zip file
> The package document could not be found at the location specified by the root file element.

Package Validation

If you think of validation as a progression through Dante's rings of hell, if your content is packaged properly, the next ring you'll find yourself in is whether your package document has been properly constructed.

The following metadata problems will be reported:

unique-identifier attribute in package element must reference an existing identifier element id
> The unique-identifier attribute does not point to the id value of a dc:identifier element in the metadata section.

character content of element "X" invalid; must be a string with length at least 1
> All metadata must be at least one character in length (whitespace does not count). This error indicates that an empty value was found.

Package dcterms:modified meta element must occur exactly once
> The dcterms:modified property indicates the last modification date of the EPUB, and is used to create the publication identifier, so only one can be included in the metadata.

dcterms:modified illegal syntax (expecting: 'CCYY-MM-DDThh:mm:ssZ')
> Check the time and date specified in the dcterms:modified property matches the specified format. You cannot use abbreviated dates or omit the timestamp.

@refines missing target id: 'X'
> If the refines attribute begins with a hash (#), it must reference the ID of an item in the manifest. This error occurs when a match cannot be found.

epubcheck will also check for problems with resources that should, or shouldn't, be listed in the manifest:

`X file Y is missing`
> You have a reference to a missing resource. *X* identifies the type of file, but is not the media type (*OPS/XHTML* is used for XHTML content documents, *image* is used for any image type, etc.)

`item (X) exists in the zip file, but is not declared in the manifest file`
> Warning that you have a file in the container that is not listed in the manifest.

`'http://X/Y/Z': remote resource reference not allowed; resource must be placed in the OCF`
> This error indicates that you've invalidly referenced a resource outside the container (e.g., a file on the Web from an `object` tag). In older versions of epubcheck, this error was also emitted when remote audio/video clips were not listed in the manifest.

epubcheck will also emit the following errors if resources don't match the information supplied about them:

`Item property: X is not defined for: Y`
> You've attached a `properties` attribute value to a file type to which it doesn't belong (e.g., `mathml` on a JPEG)

`This file should declare in opf the property: X`
> This message occurs when a content document contains a feature that hasn't been declared in the `properties` attribute (e.g., scripting).

`This file should not declare in opf the properties: X`
> The listed properties cannot be verified and should be removed from the `proper ties` attribute for the item.

`Exactly one manifest item must declare the 'nav' property (number of 'nav' items: #).`
> You didn't specify the navigation document or specified more than one.

`Multiple occurrences of the 'cover-image' property (number of 'cover-image' items: #).`
> Similarly for the cover image.

`Object type and the item media-type declared in manifest, do not match`
> The media type declared in the `media-type` attribute on the manifest entry does not match the `type` attribute specified on the `object` tag in the content file.

epubcheck will also alert you if you haven't provided a core media type fallback for a foreign resource:

`Manifest item element fallback attribute must resolve to another manifest item (given reference was 'X')`
> The ID referenced in the `fallback` attribute does not point to another `item`. Check for a typo and that the fallback hasn't been removed.

`Spine item with non-standard media-type 'X' with no fallback`
> You've referenced a file that is not an XHTML or SVG content document from the spine without providing a fallback to one of those two.

`Spine item with non-standard media-type 'X' with fallback to non-spine-allowed media-type`
> Again, you've referenced a foreign resource from the spine, but this time the only fallback found is to another foreign resource.

`Circular reference in fallback chain`
> Each fallback in a fallback chain must be to a unique resource. If one resource in the chain references another earlier in the chain, you end up in an endless loop of incompatible formats.

When adding media overlays, the required metadata is also verified:

`Media overlay items must be of the 'application/smil+xml' type (given type was 'X')`
> Media overlays are SMIL files, so you must make sure the correct media type has been given (i.e., not `application/xml`).

`Item media:duration meta element not set (expecting: meta property= 'media:duration' refines='#X')`
> When attaching a media overlay to a content document, you must add a `meta` element indicating the total audio duration for that document. This error indicates that this property is missing.

`Global media:duration meta element not set`
> You must include a `meta` element with no `refines` attribute containing the cumulative time of all the individual overlays.

And finally, there are a couple of possible errors tested for if you include an NCX for rendering in EPUB 2 reading systems:

`spine element toc attribute must reference the NCX manifest item (referenced media type was 'X')`
> The value of the `toc` attribute on the spine must be the same as the `id` attribute on the manifest entry for the NCX file.

`spine element toc attribute must be set when an NCX is included in the publication`
    If you include an NCX, you must add a `toc` attribute to the spine.

Content Validation

Now, moving to the stage of validating content, providing lists of checks and error messages becomes more difficult. Although the EPUB 3 specification imposes some requirements and restrictions, error messages are more likely to come from the underlying technologies it employs.

Fortunately, many of the issues you'll run into at the content level are similar in nature. In XHTML and SVG content documents, most errors are related to the invalid use of markup we covered in the generic XML errors section.

The following XHTML-specific errors may be reported by epubcheck.

General document and header errors:

`The lang and xml:lang attributes must have the same value`
    When using both language attributes on the same element, their values must match.

`There must not be more than one meta element with a charset attribute per document`
    A document only has one character encoding, so specifying the value twice is redundant and will possibly conflict.

`The sizes attribute must not be specified on link elements that do not have a rel attribute that specifies the icon keyword`
    The `sizes` attribute is only allowed to be used to specify the dimensions of an icon referenced by the `link` element.

`For each Document, there must be no more than one time element with a pubdate attribute that does not have an ancestor article element`
    A document can only have a single publication date. If other `time` elements contain publication dates, they must each be inside a unique `article`.

`For each article element, there must be no more than one time element child with a pubdate attribute`
    Another duplication error. Each `article` can only have a single publication date.

Map element errors:

`Duplicate map name 'X'`
    Two or more `map` elements have the same `name` attribute value, but each must be unique.

The `id` attribute on the `map` element must have the same value as the `name` attribute

Just one of those quirky things that must be true.

Form element errors:

A `select` element whose `multiple` attribute is not specified must not have more than one descendant `option` element with its `selected` attribute set

If you can pick only one option, it doesn't make sense to specify that two or more are set by default.

Audio/video errors:

The `track` element `label` attribute value must not be the empty string

The `label` is used to announce the track type to the readers, so it cannot be empty.

There must not be more than one `track` child of a media element with the `default` attribute specified

As its name suggests, the `default` attribute is used to indicate which track to use when no reader preference is available. Specifying more than one default defeats the purpose of the attribute.

Referencing errors:

The X attribute must refer to an element in the same document (the ID 'Y' does not exist)

Some elements must reference other elements in the document. The `for` attribute on a `label` element, for example, must reference the `id` of the form element it labels.

The X attribute must refer to elements in the same document (target ID missing)

This error is the same as the last, but occurs when an attribute can reference more than one other element. There are a number of ARIA attributes that can reference multiple elements (`aria-describedby`, `aria-labelledby`, `aria-controls`, etc.). Check that each reference can be resolved.

The X attribute does not refer to an allowed target element (expecting: Y)

The attribute references another element, but it is the wrong kind of element. To use `label` again, it would be incorrect for it to point to anything but a form element.

The following errors impose additional restrictions on element and attribute usage that could not be enforced through the structural schema validation stage:

The X element must have a Y attribute

This error occurs if the `bdo` element does not include a `dir` attribute.

The X element must not appear inside Y elements
This error occurs if you attempt to embed one element inside another where it would make no sense or would cause rendering issues, such as an audio/video tag inside another audio or video, an address inside an address, etc.

The X element must have an ancestor Y element
This error occurs when an element is found outside of its expected ancestor. This error specifically occurs when an area tag is found outside of a map and when an image map is not wrapped inside of an a tag.

epub:type property errors:

Undefined property: X
If a property in the epub:type does not have a prefix, it must be defined in the EPUB Structural Semantics vocabulary.

Undeclared prefix: X
You have used a prefix that has not been declared in the prefix attribute on the root html element.

SSML errors:

The ssml:ph attribute must not be specified on a descendant of an element that also carries this attribute
When you use the ssml:ph attribute, the pronunciation is used in place of the text content of the element it is attached to. If you include an ssml:ph on a descendant element, it will never be announced.

CSS errors:

The scoped style element must occur before any other flow content other than other style elements and inter-element whitespace
When adding CSS style definitions scoped to the current element, the style element must be the first child. This can be problematic when scoping styles for figures, as it is invalid to include the style element before a figcaption at the start of the figure.

Alt style sheet errors:

Conflicting attributes found: X
You've specified both horizontal and vertical or night and day.

Entity errors

The following errors occur when you include malformed entities:

The entity &xyz; was referenced, but not declared
You need to change the referenced named entity to a numeric one.

The entity name must immediately follow the '&' in the entity reference
You have an & in your document that needs to be changed to & to be valid.

The reference to entity X must end with the ';' delimiter
You're missing a semicolon at the end of an entity.

Note that the following error is not related to the use of entities in your content:

```
External entities are not allowed in XML. External entity declaration found:
%OEBEntities
```

If you receive this error, you need to remove an XHTML 1.1 DOCTYPE declaration from the invalid file. The current version of epubcheck now handles this issue with a more meaningful message:

```
Obsolete or irregular DOCTYPE statement. External DTD entities are not allowed.
Use '<!DOCTYPE html>' instead.
```

Style

Although epubcheck does include some minimal CSS verification checks, it does not perform true CSS validation. It will not tell you if you've entered property names or values incorrectly or even if you have malformed syntax (incorrect shorthands, missing brackets on definitions, semicolon delimiters at the end of properties, etc.).

Integration of a CSS3-compliant validator is in the future for the program, but is not possible as of this writing. At this time, all you'll be notified of is the presence of properties that are not recommended by the specification (e.g., using position: fixed).

Scripting

A structural validator like epubcheck cannot assist you in finding errors in your code, because it does attempt to interpret any JavaScript you've included. To verify that your code will work as expected, you need to test it in reading systems. Debugging code within reading systems will present its own challenges, unless error reporting materializes with scripting functionality.

It may be possible to validate the code used in individual content files by opening them in a browser, but if your code depends on any EPUB extensions (such as the epubRea dingSystem object), you won't get a useful result. Restrictions on access to the DOM, to the Internet, etc., are only going to be verifiable within reading systems, but at least with these you can sprinkle your code with debugging alerts to verify what is happening under the hood.

Accessibility

Although verifying the structural integrity of your publication is a great first step in ensuring its ability to be read, it is only a small part of what is required to verify that a publication is accessible. A validator can typically only tell you if the markup you've used is valid. What it can't do is tell you if you could have done things better.

epubcheck is no different. It cannot determine for you if content should be part of the logical reading order or not, for example, because that distinction can only be verified by humans. Whether or not elements have been appropriately used is likewise not something epubcheck is good at determining. The list goes on. Chapter 9 covers a number of issues, but there is more to making accessible content than can be covered in a chapter.

To help assist in understanding the issues and verifying that you have met key accessibility criteria, the IDPF is developing reference accessibility guidelines (*http://www.idpf.org/accessibility/guidelines/*) that can be used in conjunction with this book, with the goal of providing broader coverage of the many issues involved. The site also provides a quality assurance checklist, including the ability to dynamically generate a checklist (*http://bit.ly/U6f7pH*) depending on the features your EPUB contains.

The idea of creating an interactive validator for EPUB 3 content has been bandied about since the EPUB 3 specification was finalized, but as of this writing, work on one has not begun. The DAISY Consortium is currently investigating how to improve epubcheck to report accessibility issues and/or create this new tool, and seeking funding for the work, so there are positive signs that accessibility checking will improve in the near future.

About the Authors

Matt Garrish lives and works in Toronto where he does what he can to help bridge the print divide that sadly still keeps much of the world's literature and information from being available to everyone. He's worked closely with CNIB and the DAISY Consortium in their efforts to make the world a more accessible place—including editing the Z39.86 Authoring and Interchange specification—and drew on his years of experience ripping the guts out of EPUBs to make braille when invited to work as the editor of the EPUB 3 revision. He is the author of "What is EPUB 3?."

Markus Gylling has worked in the field of information accessibility since the late nineties. As CTO of the DAISY Consortium, he has been engaged in the development of specifications, tools, and educational efforts for inclusive publishing on a global scale. Markus is the chair of the EPUB 3 Working Group, and during 2011 he lead the development of the EPUB 3 specification. Since October 2011, he serves as CTO of the IDPF alongside his job with the DAISY Consortium. Markus lives and works in Stockholm, Sweden.

Colophon

The animal on the cover of *EPUB 3 Best Practices* is a common goat (*Capra aegagrus hircus*).

The cover image is from *Shaw's Zoology*. The cover font is Adobe ITC Garamond. The text font is Adobe Minion Pro; the heading font is Adobe Myriad Condensed; and the code font is Dalton Maag's Ubuntu Mono.

Index

A

a link, 32
AAC-LC (MP4), 54, 142
absolute IRI, 21
absolute path references, 65
accessibility
  about, xiii, 229
  canvas, 280
  changes in context, 244
  data integrity and, 235
  default language settings, 239
  figures, 249
  fixed layouts, 261–267
  footnotes, 255
  image layouts, 262–265
  images, 250
  lists, 245
  logical reading order, 239
  MathML, 254
  metadata for, 281–284
  object element, 203
  page numbering, 256
  progressive enhancement, 267
  sections and headings, 241
  semantic inflection, 238
  separating style from content, 237
  structure and semantics, 233–235
  styling content for, 258–261
  summary, 204
  SVG, 253
  tables, 246–249
  usability and, 230
  WAI-ARIA, 269–280
Accessible EPUB 3, 85
address element, 61
Adobe, 138
Adobe Digital Editions, 50, 109, 125
Adobe font obfuscation method, 134, 135
Adobe Reader, 25
Advanced Adaptive Layout, 266
alphabet attribute, 288, 289
alt attribute, 252
Alt style sheet validation errors, 328
alt style tags, xii, 99–102
Alt Style Tags specification, 99, 100
alternate-script, 6
altimg attribute, 74
alttext attribute, 254
Amazon Kindle, 122
Amazon MOBI format, 26
ampersands, 55, 294
anchor names, 209
animation and graphics, 200
annotation-xml element, 76, 254
annotations, 58
Apple iBooks, 80, 118, 119, 134, 135, 149, 194, 196, 234, 256

We'd like to hear your suggestions for improving our indexes. Send email to index@oreilly.com.

ARIA role values and attributes, 270
aria-atomic attribute, 279
aria-busy attribute, 279
aria-controls attribute, 166
aria-describedby attribute, 248, 260, 281
aria-disabled attribute, 273
aria-invalid property, 278
aria-labelledby attribute, 260
aria-live attribute, 279
aria-relevant attribute, 279
article tag, 57
aside element, 57, 255
attribute names, 55
attribute validation errors, 320
Audacity, 175
audio element, xii, 60, 142, 144, 154, 188
audio files, 54
audio validation errors, 327
automatic playback functionality, 188
autoplay attribute, 154
auxiliary content, 17, 18

B

b element, 60
background-image property, 79, 265
backmatter property, 72
Barnes & Noble, 149
bdo element, 60
bibliography property, 43
big element, 61
bindings element, 8, 20, 21, 112–115
biographical records, for publications, 21
bitmap image content, 262
bodymatter property, 72
Book Industry Study Group (BISG) EPUB 3
    support grid, 144, 195
button markup, 166

C

Canonical Fragment Identifiers (epubcfis), 65,
    180
canvas element, xiii, 106, 200–203, 280
captions, 158
centering property, 83
chapters value, 161
character encoding validation errors, 320
characters, private, 208
charset attribute, 207

ChemML, 107
cite element, 61
CJK ideographic characters, 208
CJK Unicode fonts, 208
class attribute tags, 100
clipBegin/clipEnd attributes, 181
codecs, xii, 142
codecs parameter, 149
collection (title type), 14
color, 258
color blindness, 259
column properties, 94
column-count property, 93
column-width property, 93
comics, 262, 264
commercial fonts, 139
compatibility testing, 283
compatibility testing statements, 284
container
    adding media overlays to, 184
    validation errors in, 321
    zip file, xxi, 22
container-constrained scripts, 192, 197
container.xml file, xx, 23
content chunking, 67
content documents
    about, xii, xx, 53
    covers, 85–87
    fallbacks, 102–107
    fixed layout publications, 80–84
    MathML, 72–77
    page progression direction, 220
    scripted, 199
    structural semantics, 68–72
    styling, 87–102
    SVG, 78–79, 83
    terminology for, 53
    validation errors in, 326–329
    XHTML, 55–68, 83
content fallbacks, 105
Content MathML, 72
content, hiding, 39–41, 260
contrast, 259
contributed volumes, 19
controls attribute, 153
core media type fallbacks, 54
core media types, 16, 54
Courier New, 129
cover-image property, 17, 85

covers, 85–87
Cross-Origin Resource Sharing, 157
crossorigin attribute, 157
CSS 2.1, xxi, 88
CSS classes, 258
CSS Fonts Level 3, 92
CSS Multicolumn Layout Module, 93
CSS @namespace declarations, 76
CSS Profile, 88, 131
CSS resets, 102
CSS Text Decoration, 225
CSS validation errors, 328
CSS visibility property, 170
CSS3
   about, xxi, xxii
   emphasis elements, 260
   encoding declarations, 207
   fonts, 92
   media queries, 91
   multicolumn layouts, 93
   namespaces, 92
   reading systems and, 62
   referencing fonts in, 133
   Speech module, xiii, xxi, 95, 95, 297–301
   Text module, 95
   validation errors, 329
   Writing Modes module, 94, 213
cue property, 299
custom controls, 269
custom prefix, 4

D

D3 visualization library, 204
DAISY Consortium, 330
DAISY digital talking books, 25, 173
DAISY Structure Guidelines, 255
Daisy Tobi tool software, 175
data chunking, 67
data integrity, 235
dateTime form, 11
dc:contributor element, 10
dc:creator element, 10
dc:date element, 10
dc:identifier element, 9, 12
dc:language element, 9
dc:source element, 10
dc:title element, 9
dc:type element, 10
dcterms vocabulary, 4

dcterms:modified property, 11
default language settings, 239
default reading order, 18
default vocabulary, 2, 3, 15
DejaVu font, 134
DejaVuSerif font, 137
descriptions value, 161
details element, 54, 63, 248
detect features, 195
digital object identifier (DOI), 12
dimensions, 156
dir attribute, 8, 9, 221
direction property, 89, 222
disabled attribute, 34
display attribute, 74, 97
display-seq property, 6, 15
div element, 56, 97, 240
DocBook files, 54
doctype statements, 63
document metadata, 19
document validation errors, 318
DOI (digital object identifier), 12
DOM (Document Object Module), 62, 192, 201
dom-manipulation, 195
DRM (Digital Rights Management), 23, 135, 140
DTBook, 54, 55
DTDs, 63
Dublin Core Metadata Element Set (DCMES),
   2, 9, 10
Dublin core namespace declaration, 9
dynamic updates, 278

E

ECMAScript, 193
EDItEUR, 21, 281
edition (title type), 15
eInk devices, 88, 164
electronic books (ebooks), xix
element names, 55
element validation errors, 318
em element, 60
embed element, 61, 79, 203
embedded fonts
   about, xii, 117
   complexity, 120
   CSS reference to, 133
   defined, 138
   effects on file size, 121
   EPUB 3 specification, 130

fallbacks for, 131
for future compatibility, 122
glyphs, 125
obfuscating, 134–136
procedures for, 131–137
reasons against, 118–121
reasons for, 122–129
subsetting, 137
technical or specialized content, 128
unified design across digital and print products, 123
embedded table of contents, 27
emphasis dots, 224–226
emphasis elements, 260
empty tags, 55
encoding declarations, 207
EncryptedData, 23
EncryptedKey, 23
encryption.xml file, 23, 136
end tags, 55
Enhanced Global Language Support sub-group, 205, 213
entity validation errors, 328
EPUB 2 compatibility
    ASCII characters, 210
    covers, 87
    epub:switch element, 109
    JavaScript, 193
    multimedia, 162
    native audio and video controls, 171
    NCX and, 18, 26
    numbered headings, 242
    page progression direction, 216
    vertical writing, 213
    xml:lang attribute, 211
EPUB 2 reading systems, 48
EPUB 3 Accessibility Guidelines, 233
    Canvas, 202
    Progressive Enhancement, 193
EPUB 3 and Scripted Content Documents (Pearson), 198
EPUB 3 Content Documents, 191
EPUB 3 navigation document (see navigation document)
EPUB 3 Sample Documents Project, 36, 125, 132, 178, 206, 209, 214, 216, 264
EPUB 3 specifications
    about, xxii
    alt style tags, 99, 100

content creation, 235
content documents vs. publication resources, 54
Core Media Types, 16
cross-origin resource sharing, 157
CSS Profile, 131
doctype, 63
encodings, 206
external identifiers, 64
fallbacks for embedded fonts, 131
fixed layouts, 261
font embedding, 117, 130
font obfuscation, 134
headers and footers, 97
HTML markup, 77
inclusion models, 192
MathML, 128
MathML native support, 254
media overlays, 185
MP3 and MP4, 142
navigation document presentation, 28
navigation list types, 29
object element, 203
OpenType and WOFF fonts, 118, 130
page progression direction, 220, 221
Publications 3.0, 199
reading systems usability, 231
role definitions, 272
RTL page progression direction, 216
scripted content documents, 54
scripting content, 267
SSML pronunciation, 297
standardized obfuscation algorithm, 120, 130
storage mechanisms, 199
support for @font-face, 131
SVG, 78
text-to-speech, 287
top level documents, 54
use of tags, 61
WebGL, 204
XHTML5, 55
EPUB 3 Structural Semantics vocabulary, 43, 70, 241
EPUB 3 vocabularies, 2–7
EPUB 3 Working Group, 13, 14, 62
EPUB canonical fragment identifiers, 65, 180
EPUB Content Documents 3.0, xxiii
.epub extension, 22

EPUB Media Overlays 3.0, xxiii
EPUB namespace, 30
EPUB Open Container Format (OCF) 3.0, xxiii, 23
EPUB Publications 3.0, xxii
EPUB Reading System Conformance Test Suite, 88
-epub-hyphens property, 226
-epub-line-break property, 226
-epub-ruby-position, 96
-epub-speak-as, 297
-epub-text-emphasis, 225
-epub-word-break property, 226
-epub-writing-mode property, 213, 221
epub:prefix attribute, 70
epub:switch element, 20, 107–112, 164, 200
epub:trigger element, xii, 165–172
epub:type attribute, xii, 30, 31, 37, 57, 68–72, 92, 180
epubcheck validation tool, 304
   (see also validation)
   about, 304
   archive validation, 308
   build number, 306
   component file validation, 310
   download file, 304
   file directory listing, 304
   generating assessment reports, 310–312
   help listing, 312
   installing, 304
   running, 305–308
   table of validation results, 315
   understanding error reports, 313
   web-based version, 314–315
   zipped file validation, 309
epubReadingSystem, xiii, 192, 193–197
escapable content, 236
EULA (End User License Agreement), 138, 140
event handlers, 275
extended (title type), 15
Extended Latin characters, 125
extensibility, 45
Extensible Metadata Platform, 4, 21
Extension identifiers for EPUB switch, 111

F

fallback attribute, 16, 103
fallback mechanisms
   about, xii, 102

audio and video, 153, 162
canvas, 200, 202
embedded fonts, 131
epub:switch element, 107–112
fallback chains, 103
foreign resources, 16, 21, 54, 112–115
images, 262
intrinsic, 105
manifest, 103–105, 199
MathML, 254
progressive enhancement, 200
scripted content, 199, 268
SVG, 54, 79
XHTML, 54
Field Guide to Fixed Layouts, 84
figcaption element, 60, 250
figure element, 59, 249
file size, 121, 149
file-as property, 6, 10, 15
Firefox, 74, 100
fixed layout publications
   about, 261–262
   content documents, 80–84
   EPUB 3 specification for, 261
   image layouts, 262–265
   interactive layouts, 266
   metadata for, 22
   mixed layouts, 265
   text layouts, 266
fixed property, 89
fixed-layout rendering mode, 198
Flash, 203
@font-face, 92
font foundries, 138, 139
font obfuscation algorithms, 134
font obfuscation tools, 136
Font Squirrel, 137, 139
font-variant, 131
FontForge, 132
fonts, 117
   (see also embedded fonts)
   as fallbacks, 134
   licensing, 138–140
   MathML, 75
   monospace, 129
   referencing in EPUB CSS, 133
   using images for, 128
footer element, 59
footnotes, 58, 70, 255

foreign language learning, 174
foreign resources, 16, 21, 54
forms, 275
FreeSerif font, 126
frontmatter property, 72

G

Gecko-based reading systems, 73
global language support
  about, xiii, 205
  characters and encodings, 206–211
  emphasis dots, 224–226
  itemized lists, 227
  line breaks, word breaks, hyphenation, 226
  natural language declaration, 211
  page progression direction, 215–222
  ruby annotations, 222–224
  vertical writing, 212–215
global page direction progression, 220
glossary property, 44
glyphs, 125
Google Play, 80, 119
Google project site (see EPUB 3 Sample Documents Project)
Google web fonts, 139
GPL (General Public License), 139
graceful degradation approach, 192
grapheme element, 288
graphics, 244
group-position, 6
guide element, 8, 42

H

H.264 codec, 143
Hanazono Mincho, 208
header element, 59
headers and footers, 97
heteronyms, 286
hgroup element, 61
hidden attribute, 28, 39, 48, 252, 260
hr element, 60, 244
href attribute, 16, 21, 34
hreflang attribute, 290
HTML named entities, 64
HTML.next, 110
HTML5
  canvas specification, 202
  EPUB 3 support, 62

forms elements, 54, 62
img element and alt attribute, 252
native APIs, 203
outlining algorithm, 243
phrasing content, 34
structural elements, 56–62
hyphenation, 226

I

i element, 60
id attribute, 6, 16, 19
identifier-type, 6
identifiers, 6, 11–13
ideographic variation selectors (IVS), 208
IDPF (International Digital Publishing Forum), xxi
IDPF EPUB Validator service, 314
IDPF font obfuscation method, 134, 135
idref attribute, 17, 18
iframe, 54, 79, 197
image fallbacks, 109
image layouts, 262–265
images, 128, 209, 250
img element, 79, 252
@import rule, 91
inactive links, 33
inclusion models, 197
InDesign, 135, 137
input types, 60
interactive layouts, 266
interactivity, 193
  (see also JavaScript)
  about, xiii, 191
  canvas for animation and graphics, 200
  progressive enhancement, 192
  scripted, 267–281
International Phonetic Alphabet (IPA), 288
Internationalization Best Practices (W3C), 127
internationalized resource identifier (IRI), 16
intrinsic fallback mechanisms, 105
IPA Mincho, 208
IPDF accessibility forum, 236
ISBN, 12, 257
ISSN, 12
ISTC, 12
item element, 3, 16
itemized lists, 227
itemref element, 3, 18, 22

J

Java Runtime Environment, 304
JavaScript, 193–200
    about, xxi
    checking content without, 268
    container-constrained scripts, 197
    EPUB 2, 193
    epubReadingSystem object, 193
    inclusion models, 197
    reading systems and, 62
    scripted content documents, 54, 199
    spine-level scripting, 198
    storage mechanisms, 199
    support for preventDefault, 196
    validation errors, 329
JavaScript canPlayType function, 148
JLREQ (Requirements for Japanese Text Layout), 212, 222
JPEG, 83, 253
jQuery, 270

K

keyboard-events, 195
kind attribute, 161
Kindle, 122
Kindle Paperwhite, 129
Kit Generator, 137

L

label attribute, 160
label element, 276
landmarks navigation list, 29, 41–44
landscape value, 82
lang attribute, 127
layout-changes, 195
left-to-right (LTR) page progression direction, 215
lexeme element, 288
lexicon element, 288
licensing fonts, xii, 138–140
line breaks, 226
linear attribute, 18
link element, 3, 11, 20
linking, 64
linking validation errors, 321
list elements, 245
list numbering, 49

list-style-property, 227
list-style-type properties, 89
lists
    hiding, 48
    styling, 49
literal-punctuation value, 298
live regions, 278–280
logical reading order, 239
loi property, 43
longdesc attribute, 250
loop attribute, 157
lot property, 43
luminosity, 260

M

M4V, 146
Mac scripts, 24
main (title type), 14
manga, 262, 264
mangling fonts, 134
manifest (see package document-manifest)
manifest element, 8, 15
manifest fallbacks, 103–105
manifest property values, 17
manifest.xml file, 23, 23
MARC records, 3
marc vocabulary, 4
marc21xml-record value, 21
mark element, 60
math property, 77
math tags, 73
MathJax, 73
MathML, xxi, 72–77, 128, 254
mathml property, 17
max-height property, 86
max-width property, 86
@media rule, 91, 91
media elements, 144
    (see also multimedia)
    about, xii, 144
    alternate content, 163
    controlling playback of, 153
    dimensions, 156
    fallbacks, 162
    file size and remote hosting, 149
    media-specific attributes, 157
    poster images, 155
    preloading, 151
    sources of, 145

specialized formats, 153
timed tracks, 157
triggers, 165–172
Media Overlay Document, 17
media overlays
about, xiii, 173
audio narration, 188
constructing, 178–187
container, 184
explained, 176
full text and audio, 174
mixed text and audio, 175
parallel playback, 181–184
playback granularity, 177
reading systems and, 62
sequences in, 180
specification, 185
structural considerations, 186
structured audio, 175
styling, 185
synchronization, 181, 187
media vocabulary, 4
media-overlay attribute, 17, 184
media-specific attributes, 157
media-type attribute, 16, 21
mediagroup attribute, 157
meta element, xii, 3, 5–7, 12, 19
meta-auth, 6
META-INF directory, xx, 22, 24
metadata
accessibility, 281–284
content information, 1
document, 19
fixed layout publications, 22
navigation aids as, 25
publication, 7
vocabularies for, 2–7
metadata chains, 7
metadata element, 5, 8, 9
Metadata Object Description Schema (MODS),
21
metadata.xml file, 23
microdata, 69
Microsoft Word, 25
MIME media type, 16
mimetype file, 24
mispronunciations, 285
mixed layouts, 265
MOBI format, 26

mobile first design approach, 193
MobileRead forum, 121
Mod, Craig, 123
Modernizr, 96
modification date, 11
MODS (Metadata Object Description Schema),
21
mods-record value, 21
monospace fonts, 129
Monotype Imaging, 138
mouse-events, 195
MP3, 54
MP4, 54
multicolumn layouts, 93
multimedia, 144
(see also media elements)
about, xii, 141
codecs, 142
optimizing playback, 150
muted attribute, 157

N
@namespace rule, 92
namespaces, 8, 30, 55, 76, 92
native audio controls, 154
natural language, 211
nav element, 17, 18, 31, 58
nav lists, 31
navigation aids, 25
navigation document
about, xii, 25
adding, 46–47
building, 29–34
embedding as content, 47
hiding lists, 48
landmarks list, 41–44
NCX and EPUB 2 compatibility, 50
page list, 44
repeated patterns in, 31–35
styling lists, 49
tables of contents, 35–41
vs. spine, 18
navigation labels, 34–35
navigator.epubReadingSystem object, 194
NCX (Navigation Control file for XML applications), 18, 26, 50
New York Times, 204
no-punctuation value, 298
non-ASCII characters, 209

non-Gecko-based reading systems, 74
non-Latin characters, 125
non-visual readers, 258
numbered headings, 242
NY Irvin font, 123

O

obfuscating fonts, 134–136
object element, 79, 203
OCF specification, 210
oeb-page-head/oeb-page-foot values, 97
Ogg Theora, 143
Ogg Vorbis, 54
OldStandard font, 125
onclick event, 34
ONIX
    accessibility metadata, 281
    codelist 15, 6
    codelist 196, 282, 283
    codelist 5, 12
    codelist 97, 284
    supply chain metadata, 3, 21
    title types, 14
onix prefix, 4
onix-record value, 21
Open Container Format (OCF) 3.0, 22
open fonts, 139
Open Package Format (.opf file), 2
OpenType fonts, 118, 130, 132, 209
.opf file, 2, 23, 132
OPF2 specification, 11
ordered list (ol), 31
orientation property values, 82
oXygen Editor, 316
O'Reilly Media, 123, 124

P

package document
    about, xii, xx, 1
    adding fonts to, 132
    container file, 22
    fallbacks in, 16
    fixed layout documents, 22, 80
    identifiers, 11–13
    links and bindings, 20
    manifest, xx, 15–17, 103–105, 132, 146
    metadata, 19–22
    metadata element, 9

page progression direction, 220
    spine, xx, 15, 17
    structure of, 8
    titles, 14
    validation errors in, 323–326
    vocabularies for, 2–7
package element, 4, 5, 8
Package ID, 13
page list, 29, 44
page numbering, 256
page progression direction, xiii, 215–222
page-progression-direction attribute, 220
page-spread-left property, 22, 82
page-spread-right property, 22, 82
par element, 181
parallel playback, 181–184
pattern attribute, 277
pause property, 299
PDFs, 54
persistent style sheets, 99
phoneme element, 288
platforming books, 123
playback control, 298
PLS lexicon files, xiii, xxi, 287–292
plug-ins, 61, 144
PNG, 83, 253
polyfills, 162
portrait value, 82
poster attribute, 155
poster images, 155
pre-paginated value, 81
preface property, 43
preferred style sheets, 100
prefix attribute, 4, 20
preload attribute , 152
preloading media content, 151
Presentational MathML, 72
preventDefault, 196
primary content, 17, 18
primary expression, 5, 14
PRISM, 14, 20
prism prefix, 4
private characters, 208
Processing.js, 200
ProductFormFeature element, 282
ProductFormFeatureDescription element, 283
progressive enhancement, 155, 192, 203, 267
Pronunciation Lexicon Specification (W3C),
    287

properties attribute, 47
property attribute, 5, 17, 18, 19
property definitions, 70
proprietary identifiers, 12
publication identifier, 13
publication metadata, xii, xx, 7–11, 199
publication resources, 54
Publications 3.0 specification, 199

R

raster images, 78
RDF vocabularies, xxi
RDFa, 69
Read Aloud (Apple), 173
reading systems
    alternate style sheets, 102
    audio and video fallbacks, 162
    backward compatibility, 27
    captioning, 161
    content display, 192
    content documents, 54
    content fallbacks, 106
    content hiding, 260
    contrast settings, 101
    CSS, 88
    dialects, 292
    EPUB 2, 48, 55
    epub:switch, 200
    epubcfis, 65
    event handlers, 195
    feature support, 62, 230, 301
    fixed layouts, 80
    font obfuscation methods, 136
    font support, 132
    footnotes, 256
    foreign resources, 21, 112
    Gecko- and non-Gecko based, 73
    headers and footers, 97
    images, 86, 252, 263
    landmarks navigation list, 42
    manifest fallbacks, 103–105
    MathML, 72
    media resources, 146, 152
    multi-column layouts, 93
    navigation document, 31
    page numbering, 257
    playback synchronization, 177
    private characters, 209
    progressive enhancement techniques, 96

publication information, 1
    rich data, 68
    semantics, 71
    SVG, 79
    system fonts, 119
    table of contents, 27
    text-to-speech, 187, 285
    validating, 329
    video codecs, 143
Readium, 173, 196
referencing, 64
refines attribute, 5, 7, 19
reflowable value, 81
regional dialects, 291
rel attribute, 21
relative IRI, 21
relative path references, 64
relative URI, 20
remote hosting, 149, 189
remote-resources property, 17, 145, 152
rendition mapping, 84
rendition prefix, 22
rendition:layout property, 22, 81
rendition:orientation property, 22, 81
rendition:page-spread-center property, 22, 82
rendition:spread property, 22, 82
repeated patterns, 31–34
required attribute, 277
required-namespace attribute, 111
Requirements for Japanese Text Layout
    (JLREQ), 212
reserved vocabularies, 2, 3
reset style sheet, 102
resource names, 16
rest property, 299
RFC5646 "Tags for Identifying Languages", 9
rich data, 68, 234
rich typography, xii
right-to-left (RTL) page progression direction,
    215
rights.xml file, 23
role attribute, 6, 10, 166, 272, 288
rp element, 61
rt annotations, 97
rt element, 60
ruby annotations, xiii, xxi, 35, 60, 96, 222–224

S

scheme attribute, 6, 7

scripted content documents, 54
scripted interactivity, 267–281
scripted property , 17
section element, 56, 241
semantic enrichment, 69
semantic inflection, xii, 68, 238
semantics, 70–72, 233–235
semantics element, 255
seq element, 180, 186
sequences (in media overlays), 180
series title, 14
shadow DOM, 201
Shift-JIS, 207
short (title type), 14
Sigil tool, 136
signatures.xml file, 23
SIL Open Font License, 139
situational disability, 231
skipping, 236
small element, 61
SMIL (Synchronized Multimedia Integration
    Language), xxi, 176
source element, 146
source element definition page (W3C), 149
span element, 19, 33
speak-as property, 297
specialized table of contents view, 27
Speex, 54
spine element, 8, 15
spine-level scripting, 192, 195, 198
src attribute, 145, 160
srclang attribute, 160
SSML, xiii, xxi, 292–297, 328
ssml:alphabet attribute, 294
ssml:ph attribute, 294
STIX font, 128
storage mechanisms, 199
strong element, 60
structural semantics, 68–72
structure (for media overlays), 186
style sheets, xii
styles and styling
    accessible, 258–261
    alt style tags, 99–102
    CSS 2.1, 88
    CSS reset style sheets, 102
    CSS3, 91–96
    EPUB CSS profile, 88
    headers and footers, 97

lists in navigation documents, 49
    media overlays, 185
    ruby annotations, 96
    separating content from, 258
subexpression, 5
subsetting fonts, 137
subtitle (title type), 14
subtitles, 158
summary element, 248
SVG, xxi, 78–79, 204, 253
SVG fonts, 209
svg property, 17
SVG working group, 253
svg:foreignObject element, 78
svg:title element, 78
switch property, 17
synchronization
    about, xiii
    advanced, 187
    audio narration, 173
    parallel playback, 181–184
    playback granularity, 177
synthesized speech (see text-to-speech (TTS))
Synthetic Speech Markup Language (SSML) (see
    SSML)

T

tabindex attribute, 166, 274
tables, 246–249
tables of contents, 27, 29, 35–41, 58
Tags for Identifying Languages (RFC5646), 9
text element, 188
text layouts, 266
text-combine-horizontal property, 215
text-orientation property, 215
text-to-speech (TTS)
    about, xiii, 285–287
    advanced synchronization, 187
    audio content rendering, 35
    CSS3 Speech, 297–301
    PLS lexicons, 287–292
    reading systems and, 62
    SSML, 292–297
three.js, 204
thumbnails, 264
time element, 60
Timed Text Markup Language (TTML), 158
timed tracks, xii, 157
TimeInc prefixes, 20

timestamp, 11, 13
title attribute, 277
title-type property, 6, 14, 20
toc attribute, 18
toc nav, 35
touch-events, 195, 196
track element, 157, 159, 160
track element:default, 161
transcripts, 164
triggers, 165
TrueType fonts, xxi
TTF format, 132
type ID, 20
typeface designers, 139
typographical conventions, xiv

U

UbuntuMono, 129
Unicode characters, 77, 206
unicode-bidi property, 89, 222
unicode-range attribute, 131
unified design, 123
unique identifiers, 11
unique-identifier attribute, 9, 12
Universal Design for Web Applications (Chisholm), 280
URI (Uniform Resource Identifier), 4
usability, 230
UTF-16, 206
UTF-8, 127, 206

V

validation, 303
    (see also epubcheck validation tool)
    about, xiii, 303
    accessibility testing, 330
    container errors, 321
    content document errors, 326–329
    CSS errors, 329
    package document errors, 323–326
    package errors, 24
    scripted content, 268
    scripting errors, 329
    understanding errors, 317
    XML errors, 318–321
vertical writing, xiii, 212–215
vertical-lr, 213
Vibrating Color Combinations webpage, 260

video codecs, 143
video containers, 147
video element, xii, 60, 142, 144, 153, 188
video validation errors, 327
viewBox attribute, 83
visual vibrations, 260
vocabularies, 2–5
voice-family property, 300
VP8 codec, 143

W

W3C, 62
W3C dateTime form, 11
WAI-ARIA (Accessible Rich Internet Application), xiii, 166, 201, 204, 269–280
wbr element, 60
WCAG (Web Content Accessibility Guidelines 2.0), xiii, 233
Web Accessibility Initiative (WAI), 229
Web Video Text Tracks (WebVTT), 158
WebGL, 204
WebM, 146
whitespace, 244
WOFF fonts, xxi, 118, 130, 132, 209
word breaks, 226

X

X-SAMPA (Extended Speech Assessment Methods Phonetic Alphabet), 288
XHTML anchor names, 209
XHTML5
    about, xii, xxi, 55
    content chunking, 67
    DTDs, 63
    HTML5, 56–62
    linking and referencing, 64–67
XML
    about, xxi
    Encryption Syntax and Processing Version 1.1 specification, 23
    naming conventions, 56
    Signature specification, 21
    validation errors, 318–321
xml-signature value, 21
xml:lang attribute, 8, 9, 127, 211, 288
xmlns pseudo-attribute, 75
xmlns:epub prefix, 69
xmp prefix, 4

xmp-record value, 21
xsd prefix, 4

Z

z-index property, 263

Have it your way.

Get even more for your money.

Join the O'Reilly Community, and register the O'Reilly books you own. It's free, and you'll get:

- $4.99 ebook upgrade offer
- 40% upgrade offer on O'Reilly print books
- Membership discounts on books and events
- Free lifetime updates to ebooks and videos
- Multiple ebook formats, DRM FREE
- Participation in the O'Reilly community
- Newsletters
- Account management
- 100% Satisfaction Guarantee

Signing up is easy:

1. **Go to: oreilly.com/go/register**
2. **Create an O'Reilly login.**
3. **Provide your address.**
4. **Register your books.**

Note: English-language books only

To order books online:
oreilly.com/store

For questions about products or an order:
orders@oreilly.com

To sign up to get topic-specific email announcements and/or news about upcoming books, conferences, special offers, and new technologies:
elists@oreilly.com

For technical questions about book content:
booktech@oreilly.com

To submit new book proposals to our editors:
proposals@oreilly.com

O'Reilly books are available in multiple DRM-free ebook formats. For more information:
oreilly.com/ebooks

O'REILLY®

Spreading the knowledge of innovators   oreilly.com

Lightning Source UK Ltd.
Milton Keynes UK
UKHW021356090822
407015UK00003B/6